New York
Real Estate

for

BROKERS

Third Edition

ERROL BReth
516 778 773 3

Marcia Darvin Spada

THOMSON
SOUTH-WESTERN

Australia · Canada · Mexico · Singapore · Spain · United Kingdom · United States

SOUTH-

New York Real Estate for Salespersons, Third Edition
Marcia Darvin Spada

VP/Editorial Director:
Jack Calhoun

VP/Editor-in-Chief:
Dave Shaut

Sr. Acquisitions Editor:
Scott Person

Developmental Editor:
Sara Froelicher

Marketing Manager:
Mark Linton

Production Editor:
Todd McCoy

Production Manager:
Patricia Matthews Boies

Manufacturing Coordinator:
Charlene Taylor

Printer:
West Group
Eagan, Minnesota

Cover Designer:
Tippy McIntosh

For permission to use material
from this text or product, contact
us by
Tel (800) 730-2214
Fax (800) 730-2215
http://www.thomsonrights.com

For more information, contact
South-Western
5191 Natorp Boulevard
Mason, Ohio 45040

Or you can visit our Internet site at:
http://www.swlearning.com

Brief Contents

For a complete table of contents, see page iv.

iii

Contents

CHAPTER 2

REAL ESTATE AGENCY DISCLOSURE   58

CHAPTER 5

GENERAL BUSINESS LAW   156

CHAPTER 6　CONSTRUCTION AND DEVELOPMENT　190

SECTION 1　CONSTRUCTION　191

CHAPTER 7

CONVEYANCE OF REAL PROPERTY AND TITLE CLOSING   240

SECTION 1   CONVEYANCE OF REAL PROPERTY   241

CHAPTER 9   TAXES AND ASSESSMENTS   306

CHAPTER **10**   **REAL ESTATE MATH   322**

Preface

It is a well-known fact that people learn best by participating in the learning experience. Every chapter in this textbook provides a variety of activities so that this type of learning takes place. Learning activities include:

- *Putting It to Work* features that give students the opportunity to handle typical problems faced by real estate agents, including:
  - Answering questions typically asked by clients and customers
  - Working with various real estate-related documents such as completing a comparative market analysis, lease, and contract of sale, or identifying parts of a deed
  - Role playing different scenarios to provide a forum for students to work together and generate ideas
- *Chapter Reviews* that put it all together, giving students a chance to practice what they have just learned in each chapter, using *How Would You Respond?* questions along with key term and multiple choice questions

Other features that will assist the student in absorbing the material presented include:

- *Key Terms* lists that open each chapter and help students identify important terminology
- *Learning Objectives* that outline the Department of State's priorities for the material presented in each chapter
- *You Should Know* boxed text that highlights important laws, regulations, and concepts
- *Case Studies* that exemplify the Department of State's stance on a variety of issues
- *Important Points* that synopsize each chapter so that students can easily review the material
- A comprehensive *Sample Broker Exam* that concludes the book, ideal for use as a diagnostic tool to assist students in pinpointing areas needing further study
- A detailed *Glossary* of all key terms presented in the book and related real estate terminology

Each chapter's activities are specifically relevant to the material within the chapter. They are enjoyable for both student and instructor as they provide for lively class discussions and an opportunity for the instructor to interact with students. Answers to all the chapter learning activities and chapter review questions are conveniently located at the end of each chapter.

This accurate and well-researched textbook completely covers the New York–mandated syllabus. In addition to providing an excellent source of information required for the New York real estate licensee, it will prepare students for the state licensing exam using an interactive learning experience that promotes retention and understanding and gives practice in applying the concepts.

SUPPLEMENTS

This new edition includes classroom and distance learning support!

- **Cram for the Exam: Your Guide to Passing the New York State Broker Exam.** Students excel at exam time with the aid of this handy study guide.
- **Student Smartlink™ Tutorial.** This computerized study guide and practice question tool makes learning off campus a snap.
- **Audio CD-ROM.** This content review reinforces learning while learners commute or stay at home.
- **Instructor's Manual.** A complete set of support materials for guiding learning in the classroom and from a distance.
- **Computerized Test.** This easy-to-use computerized test generator saves you time and ensures a confidential testing environment.
- **Cram-for-Exam.com.** This website offers review exams written by that author that similar to the New York exam for both the salespersons and brokers.

Contact your Thomson Learning Representative for more details.

ABOUT THE AUTHOR

Marcia Darvin Spada is the former owner and founder of the Albany Center for Real Estate Education, a New York-licensed proprietary school. A professional educator, Marcia teaches real estate and has developed curricula for numerous real estate courses widely used in colleges, real estate-related organizations, and proprietary schools throughout New York. She has also developed and produced distance learning courses for salespersons, brokers, and appraisers. In addition to *New York Real Estate for Brokers,* she is author of *New York Real Estate for Salespersons, Cram for the Exam: Your Guide to Passing the New York Real Estate Salesperson Exam, Cram for the Exam: Your Guide to Passing the New York Real Estate Broker Exam,* and *Environmental Issues and the Real Estate Professional,* and *The Home Inspection Book: A Guide for Professionals.*

Marcia holds a B.A. and M.A. in English from the State University of New York at Albany and a B.S. in Real Estate Studies from Empire State College. She continues to update the material in this textbook and welcomes all comments. Her email address is marleedare@aol.com.

Acknowledgments

It would have been impossible to cover the breadth of material in this book without the assistance and support of many capable and knowledgeable people. First, I would like to thank my daughter-in-law, Kimberly Spada, coordinator of the Albany Center for

Real Estate Education, and staff members Vanessa Gonzalez and Mary Sofia. Thanks to Noreen Baker for her overall assistance and for her review of the math chapter; to Mary Jo Cosco, John DiIanni, Hal Zucker, Jay Percent, Pat Binzer, and Tony Spada, all of whom reviewed portions of the book, and to Claudia Zucker, who furnished information. A very special thank you to Rita Scharg, who contributed to the writing of Chapter 2. I also thank Seymour J. Baskin, owner of Goodman Realty in Rochester, New York; Tom Cusack, president of Cusack Sales Training Center; and Milton Pachter, Esq., and Arthur Elfenbein, Esq., of NYU Real Estate Institute.

For assistance with the legal aspects of this book, my heartfelt appreciation to the attorneys in my family: my husband, Eugene R. Spada; my sister, Iris M. Darvin; my father, Leonard Darvin; my daughter, Justine L. Spada, and Martin Lazarow. Thanks also to Karen Gneuch, Karen Sideri, and April Pruiksma.

Professionals from a number of New York State and other government agencies supplied information for this book. The following people provided their expertise: James D. Decker, Charles M. Hudson, James R. Covey, Gregory Smead, Kevin Scheuer, Desmond C. Gordon, Stephen Lukowski, Lee C. Kiernan, Richard M. Cowan, Barry A. Bechtel, Charles Lockrow, Peter Shugert, and Richard Tyksinsky. Thanks also to Eileen Taus of the Westchester Board of REALTORS®, who was instrumental in coordinating the New York syllabus on which this book is based.

For their help on current lending policies, thanks to John Biszick, Timothy T. Sherwin, and Tom Tokas and for assistance with tax issues, thanks to accountant Steven J. Lubbe. I also appreciate the assistance of Anne Groski, Rita Merith, Kevin LaPointe, Patrick Reilly, and Priscilla S. Toth, all of the New York State Association of REALTORS®.

I am indebted to the following individuals, organizations, and publishers who allowed me to reprint information or use their forms and illustrations: *Houses, the Illustrated Guide to Construction, Design & Systems*, by Henry S. Harrison, 3rd edition; James A. Ader, Administrator, and Huguette Bushey of the Greater Capital Association of REALTORS®; James A. Ader and the *Albany Times Union* for permission to reprint portions of Mr. Ader's column, "Real Estate Spotlight," in some of the question and answer portions of the book; the Greater Capital Association of REALTORS®; Lynnore Letyko and the Greater Syracuse Association of REALTORS®; Marlene A. Sayers and the Greater Rochester Association of REALTORS®; Michele B. Stoeger and the Otsego-Delaware County Board of REALTORS®, as well as BloombergExcelsior, Inc. and Tuttle Law Print, Publishers, that furnished the real estate forms that appear in the textbook.

I am especially grateful to reviewer Sheila Margolis, owner of Margolis Appraisal Service, Inc., who spent a great deal of time with the manuscript, and to Alexander Frame of the New York Real Estate Institute and Arthur Elfenbein, Esq., of NYU Real Estate Institute. I am extremely indebted to Linda J. Fields, director and owner of the Professional Institute for Real Estate Training in Watertown, New York, not only for her excellent work as a reviewer but for her patient and capable assistance as a consultant.

Lastly, I would like to express my appreciation to Elizabeth Sugg and Gay Pauley. A very special thank you for the guidance and support of editors Scott Person and Sara Froelicher, and editorial assistants Allison Abbott and Jennifer Warner, all of Thomson Learning.

—Marcia Darvin Spada

To the Student

In each chapter, a variety of features and activities help you understand and learn the material. As you come to these in your reading, refer to these instructions.

KEY TERMS

To prepare for the information in the chapter, first look over the list of key terms at the beginning of each chapter. This will help focus your attention on important terminology throughout the chapter.

PUTTING IT TO WORK

In most of the chapters, you will be presented with questions and activities to stimulate your understanding and retention of the material. Some are practice problems involving filling out or identifying the sections of a sample real estate document; others are role-playing activities that involve answering a buyer or seller question. Complete instructions for each activity are given within the chapter, and the *Answer Key* at the end of the chapter contains possible responses.

YOU SHOULD KNOW

In most of the chapters, you will see small sections of boxed text. These boxes highlight either important key terms, laws, or concepts. The topics for this feature are chosen because of their importance to your real estate career and for the probability of these topics appearing on your exams. When studying for exams, review this feature.

CASE STUDIES

Discussion of certain administrative hearings of the New York State Department of State, Division of Licensing Services, regarding alleged violations of license law, codified rules and regulations, or legal precedent are found in several chapters. The events and determinations of these cases will help you understand how alleged violations can occur. You will see how the Department of State, Division of Licensing Services (DOS), interprets certain behaviors on the part of licensees.

The facts described in each case study are from actual administrative hearings within DOS. The accused party is the respondent. DOS, as the party bringing forth the action, is the complainant. The complete text of the hearing is the decision. The decision of the hearing is divided into four sections:

1. The first section of the case deals with the allegations or complaint. These allegations are the reason the hearing was initiated. They deal with what the complainant (in these cases DOS) states the respondent might have done.

2. This second section deals with the findings of fact. This is a recital of what the court believes to have happened.

3. The third section contains the conclusions of law. This section explains what violations were committed by the respondent and also includes the supporting case law to back up the determination.

4. The last section of the case is the determination of the court. This includes the penalty, if any, that is imposed upon the respondent for unlawful behavior.

IMPORTANT POINTS

Each chapter contains a list of points covered in the chapter. Review this list carefully and use it to help you determine what you need to study further.

CHAPTER REVIEW

Each chapter contains a self-test to give you an opportunity to review the material you have learned. The answers appear at the end of each chapter. *Chapter Reviews* contain the following types of questions:

HOW WOULD YOU RESPOND?

These questions are based on situations you may encounter in your real estate career and are designed to stimulate thinking and discussion. Although we provide possible responses, no single response is the only "correct" answer. As you will see in your real estate career, each particular situation can give rise to several responses.

KEY TERMS AND MULTIPLE CHOICE ITEMS

These questions test your understanding of the information that you have studied, your retention of important points, and your ability to interpret the meaning of key terms. After studying the chapter and completing all of the other learning activities, answer the questions. The *Answer Key* at the end of each chapter has answers to these questions as well as to the activities throughout the chapter. Your completed review will serve as a useful study guide and help you prepare for your course exam and New York licensing exam.

REAL ESTATE MATH

When necessary, your instructor may direct you to some of the practice questions in Chapter 10, the math chapter, which contains explanations for computing problems with regard to commissions, area and square footage, finance, closing costs, and ad valorem taxes.

SAMPLE NEW YORK STATE LICENSING EXAM

After completing the text, you are now ready to prepare for your class and state exams. This sample exam is diagnostic, meaning it will help pinpoint areas in which you need further study. It is divided into subject sections so that you can see where you need more review. While taking the exam, know the meaning of each answer choice, even if it is not the correct answer. This alternate choice may pop up on one of your exams!

A FINAL WORD

All of the activities are structured to help you learn and to self-test your understanding of the material. Don't feel uncomfortable if at first you are not doing as well as you think you should. For most students, this is new material, and it will take time to absorb it. Depending on the wishes of the class and instructor, these activities can be done individually, in groups, or with the whole class participating. Don't hesitate to do the activities more than once if you feel you need the practice. You will be gratified to see your proficiency level increase as you progress through the course!

Introduction

KEY TERMS

Code of Ethics and Standards
  of Practice
listing contract
National Association of REALTORS®
  (NAR)

New York State Association of
  REALTORS® (NYSAR)
REALTOR®

Your Career in
Real Estate

IN THIS CHAPTER   If you are reading this textbook, it probably means that you have decided to become a licensed New York State real estate broker or associate broker. If you are not yet a salesperson and do not have two years experience in real estate, you should obtain the textbook, *New York Real Estate for Salespersons* by Marcia Darvin Spada. In New York, you are eligible for a broker license once you have completed the following:

- one year of experience as a salesperson, two or more years of equivalent experience in the real estate business, or a combination of both
- 90 hours of qualifying course education or its equivalent as approved by the New York State Department of State
- passage of the New York broker licensing exam
- payment of the appropriate fees and application approval by the Department of State

BECOMING A REAL ESTATE BROKER

In Chapter 1, you will read the specifics of attaining broker licensure in New York. Individuals applying for broker licensure do not have to prove that they have attained a certain dollar amount of sales or that they have done every imaginable type of real estate activity. The method of verifying experience toward broker licensure is based on a point system (fully explained and illustrated in Chapter 1). As long as you attain the required number of points, your experience can be limited to one area, such as leasing, or to diverse activities.

The following questions answer some common concerns regarding broker licensure. Further information may be obtained from the Department of State, the New York State Association of REALTORS®, local boards of REALTORS®, and the institution where you take your 45-hour qualifying course.

What are some of the real estate activities covered under broker licensure?

For other people, you may:

- list and sell
- rent and manage
- exchange
- auction
- relocate

Other related challenges are available. You can move up to a management position or own your own real estate brokerage firm. You can teach and train others. You can become active in your local and state boards, where political action, education, and community service opportunities, to name a few, exist. The reason why a real estate career is so enticing to people of diverse backgrounds is because it encompasses many different skills, talents, and interests.

What are the other related career opportunities in the real estate profession?

In addition to residential, commercial, industrial, and farm brokerage, real estate-related activities include property management, real estate appraisal, government service, land development, urban planning, mortgage financing, real estate syndication, and real estate counseling. Also, many other types of businesses are based on real estate, including title search and abstract companies, construction, insurance, renovating, and remodeling firms.

What is the difference between a salesperson and broker?

A salesperson may work only under the sponsorship and supervision of a licensed broker. Brokers may operate their own company or opt to work under the supervision of another broker, as do salespeople. These individuals are called associate brokers.

What are the advantages of attaining broker licensure?

Some choose to become brokers because they want to become an owner, partner, or shareholder in a real estate brokerage company. According to New York law, salespersons and associate brokers may not do this. In addition, a broker license indicates to the public that you have attained a degree of experience beyond that of a beginning salesperson. Also, individuals who have been continuously licensed for 15 years and are brokers at the time of renewal (even if part of those years were spent as a salesperson) are exempt from continuing education requirements.

If I have real estate experience, can I become a broker without first becoming a salesperson?

Yes. If you have two years' experience as either an investor, a developer, a property manager, or a salesperson for less than one year together with other real estate experience, or a combination of experience, you may apply for the broker license without first becoming a salesperson. It is up to the Department of State, the regulatory agency in New York that oversees the licensure process, to evaluate your experience and determine its acceptability for broker licensure.

Does my experience as a salesperson, or its equivalent, count if it was not obtained in New York?

Your real estate experience counts whether or not it was obtained in New York. Your experience can also extend as far back as necessary to fulfill application requirements.

Do I need a separate license for residential and commercial sales?

Your New York license will apply to selling both residential and commercial properties.

Can I hold dual licensure?

Yes. You can hold a license as a real estate broker as principal in your own company and work as an associate broker for another company at the same time. You must obtain permission from the broker you are associating with to do this.

Can I change my license from a real estate broker to an associate broker and vice versa?

Yes. On the application that you will now submit, you must choose the license you wish to hold. If, at some time in, you want to switch from an associate broker to a licensed broker in your own name, you will have to reapply and pay the appropriate fee for the new license. A broker or an associate broker license costs $150 for a two-year term.

If I am applying for a broker license based on equivalent experience, do I need to complete the 45-hour salesperson qualifying course?

Most definitely. Unless you feel you have equivalent coursework that you attained in another state or in New York, you must *first* successfully complete the salesperson qualifying course before taking the broker course. Both courses together will give you the required 90 hours of education. If you wish to apply for equivalent course credit for one or both of these courses, you must submit transcripts to the New York State Division of Licensing Services, Bureau of Educational Standards. This address is found in Chapter 1.

Do I have to pass an exam?

You will need to pass two exams to obtain a real estate broker license. First, all 45-hour qualifying courses include an exam. New York also requires you to pass a multiple-choice state licensing exam. Your 45-hour qualifying course will prepare you for both of these exams. The learning activities in this textbook offer you practice in handling exam questions.

If you apply for a broker license based on equivalent experience, you need not pass the salesperson state exam. You need take only the broker state licensing exam. You may not have taken the salesperson qualifying course recently. To help you assess your knowledge of material covered in the salesperson course, complete the diagnostic exam following this introduction. It contains questions from all topics in the salesperson course. Since this test is divided into topics, you can easily assess those areas where you need further study. If you do not do well on this exam, don't despair! Much of the material will be covered in the broker course, although the material is geared to the more experienced real estate practitioner. In addition, you should read the license law pamphlet furnished by the Department of State. (They will send you a copy upon request.)

If you still feel you need further salesperson study, you can purchase the companion textbook to this one, *New York Real Estate for Salespersons.* This book contains all material covered in the salesperson course as well as interactive learning activities. Also available is a student SmartLink™ tutorial, "Preparing for the Real Estate Salesperson Examination." This interactive software package is a quick, enjoyable, and proven method of reviewing relevant material and giving you practice in answering exam questions. To order these items, either ask your course coordinator or call Thomson Learning at 1-800-423-0563.

REAL ESTATE ORGANIZATIONS

National Association of REALTORS®

The largest association is the **National Association of REALTORS® (NAR),** first organized in 1908. NAR does not require a real estate license to be a member. The license requirement is an option for each local board to implement. The local board qualifies for membership at the local level. Membership in NAR is based on three levels: the local board or association; the state association, which in New York is the **New York State Association of REALTORS®**; and the national association. Affiliate membership in NAR is available to those interested in the goals and objectives of the REALTOR® organization but who do not qualify for REALTOR® membership in the local or state associations. Affiliate members do not qualify as REALTORS®, nor may they use the registered mark of the National Association of REALTORS®.

A **REALTOR®** is a professional in real estate who subscribes to a strict code of ethics known as the **Code of Ethics and Standards of Practice,** which is available through NAR. The NAR has developed special institutes that provide designations and certifications in specialized areas of real estate. Some of the institutes and designations are listed in Figure I.1.

Association of Real Estate License Law Officials

Another organization that impacts the real estate business is the Association of Real Estate License Law Officials (ARELLO). This organization was established in 1929 by license law officials on the state commissions to assist one another in creating, administering, and enforcing license laws.

NATIONAL ASSOCIATION OF REALTORS®

REALTOR® Institute
- —Graduate, REALTOR® Institute (GRI)
- —Certified International Property Specialist (CIPS)

American Society of Real Estate Counselors (ASREC)
- —Counselor of Real Estate (CRE®)

Commercial-Investment Real Estate Institute (CIREI)
- —Certified Commercial-Investment Member (CCIM)

Institute of Real Estate Management (IREM)
- —Accredited Management Organization® (AMO®)
- —Accredited Residential Manager® (ARM®)
- —Certified Property Manager® (CPM®)

REALTORS® Land Institute (RLI)
- —Accredited Land Consultant (ALC®)

REALTORS® NATIONAL MARKETING INSTITUTE (RNMI®)
- —Real Estate Brokerage Council: Certified Real Estate Brokerage Manager (CRB®)
- —Residential Sales Council: Certified Residential Specialist (CRS®)

Society of Industrial and Office REALTORS® (SIOR®)
- —Professional Real Estate Executive (P.R.E.)

Women's Council of REALTORS® (WCR)
- —Leadership Training Graduate (LTG)

New York Association of REALTORS®

NATIONAL ASSOCIATION OF RESIDENTIAL PROPERTY MANAGERS

Residential Management Professional (RMP)

Master Property Managers (MPM)

Certified Residential Management Company (CRMC)

NEW YORK ASSOCIATION OF REALTY MANAGERS

Offers the New York Accredited Realty Manager (NYARM) designation recognized and approved by New York State Division of Housing and Community Renewal (DHCR) and the New York City Department of Housing Preservation and Development (HPD)

ASSOCIATED BUILDERS AND OWNERS OF GREATER NEW YORK (ABO)

Offers HUD-certified courses leading to the Registered in Apartment Management (RAM)

BOMI INSTITUTE

Offers education for professional property managers, facility managers, and building engineers

APPRAISAL INSTITUTE

MAI —Appraisers experienced in commercial and industrial properties

SRA —Appraisers experienced in residential income properties

SRPA —Appraisers experienced in valuation of commercial, industrial, residential, and other property

RM —Appraisers experienced in single-family dwellings and two-, three-, and four-unit residential properties (recognized but no longer given)

SREA —Appraisers experienced in real estate valuation and analysis (recognized but no longer given)

FIGURE I.1

Some of the many real estate institutes, societies, and councils, together with their related designations.

DIAGNOSTIC EXAM

Complete this exam to test your knowledge of the salesperson qualifying course curriculum. Select the letter that *best* answers the question. Upon completion, check your responses with the Answer Key at the end of the chapter.

I. License Law and Regulations

1. A salesperson associated with Metro Realty, Inc., obtained an offer for a property listed by Preferred Real Estate Company, which she gave to Sam, the listing agent with Preferred, for presentation to the property owner. Realizing that the offer probably would not be accepted, Sam increased the amount by $3,000 prior to presentation. Which of the following statements correctly characterizes Sam's action?

   A. to make the change a proper and appropriate act, Sam should have obtained the approval of Metro Realty before changing the offer

   B. Sam's action was in violation of his fiduciary obligations and was completely improper

   C. Sam's action would have been appropriate with the seller's consent

   D. Metro Realty, Inc., will be entitled to the entire commission because of Sam's actions

2. A real estate salesperson earned $48,000 in commissions in one year. If she received 60 percent of the 6 percent her broker received, what was her average monthly sales volume?

   A. $66,666
   B. $80,000
   C. $111,111
   D. $133,333

3. If an attorney decides to open a brokerage firm and hire salespersons to work for her, she need NOT do which of the following?

   A. pay license fees to the Department of State

   B. obtain a license from the Department of State

   C. complete 90 hours of qualifying course education

   D. put a visible sign outside the office indicating that she is a real estate broker

II. Law of Agency

4. Which of the following regarding the special agency created by the listing agreement is FALSE? The agent:

   A. has limited authority

   B. may bind the principal to any type of contract

   C. has authority to market the property

   D. has a fiduciary relationship with the principal

5. Which of the following is NOT an obligation of a principal in an agency relationship?

   A. compensation

   B. cooperation

   C. disclosure of material defects to a property

   D. right to terminate at will without legal liability

6. Which of the following applies to subagency?

   A. subagents must be authorized by principals to work for them

   B. subagents are not fiduciaries

   C. subagents need only to belong to MLS to work on behalf of principals

   D. the listing broker only decides who may participate in a subagency relationship

III. Estates and Interests

7. The purchaser of a condominium unit receives title to the land and common areas in which the condominium is situated as a:

   A. tenant by entirety
   B. tenant in common
   C. joint tenant
   D. tenant in severalty

8. Title transferred to another for their lifetime is known as a(n):

   A. fee simple absolute estate
   B. life estate
   C. leasehold estate
   D. estate pur autre vie

48 K of commission

6% of (sole price)

$$\frac{48\,000}{(.06)\ast}$$

$48,000 = X \cdot (06) \ast (60)$

Brokoge

9. When title to real property is held in the name of only one person or entity, it is known as:
    A. ownership in severalty
    B. estate pur autre vie
    C. fee defeasible
    D. single tenancy

10. The most complete form of ownership of real property is:
    A. a freehold estate
    B. fee simple absolute
    C. fee simple on condition
    D. fee simple defeasible

IV. Liens and Easements

11. Which of the following does NOT terminate an easement?
    A. merger
    B. death
    C. grant or deed of release
    D. abandonment

12. Which of the following is NOT a type of easement?
    A. defeasible easement
    B. easement in gross
    C. easement by necessity
    D. easement by prescription

13. Liens, easements, encroachments, and restrictive covenants are all examples of:
    A. emblements
    B. estovers
    C. estates
    D. encumbrances

14. Which of the following is NOT an example of a specific lien?
    A. mortgage
    B. mechanic's lien
    C. income tax lien
    D. real property tax lien

V. Deeds

15. In New York, which one of the following may not convey title to real property through a deed? A(n):
    A. corporation
    B. partnership
    C. developer
    D. individual under the age of 18

16. A deed in which the wording in the granting clause contains "remise and release" is which of the following?
    A. quitclaim deed
    B. special warranty
    C. grant deed
    D. bargain and sale deed

17. Which of the following is NOT an essential element of a valid deed?
    A. acknowledgment
    B. writing
    C. competent grantee
    D. execution by grantor

VI. Contracts

18. The transfer of contract rights is called a(n):
    A. conveyance
    B. contract for deed
    C. counteroffer
    D. assignment

19. An offer to purchase contract is a(n):
    A. unilateral contract
    B. implied contract
    C. express bilateral contract
    D. implied unilateral contract

20. When a purchaser and seller have a valid contract for the sale of real property, the purchaser has:
    A. legal title
    B. no title
    C. equitable title
    D. constructive title

21. When a party purchases an option, the optionee is purchasing which of the following?
    A. contract liability
    B. time
    C. land
    D. exercise

VII. Leases

22. A rental estate created by a lease or rental agreement is called:
    A. freehold
    B. nonhomogeneity
    C. life estate
    D. leasehold estate

23. Which of the following regarding an estate for years is FALSE? It:
    A. exists for only a fixed period of time
    B. can be as short as one day
    C. terminates automatically without either party giving notice
    D. is a lease of uncertain duration

24. An estate at sufferance is characterized by which of the following? A(n):
    A. tenant suffering from lack of heat or other amenity
    B. apartment that has stayed empty for at least one year
    C. tenant who is no longer in lawful possession of the premises
    D. month to month tenancy

25. A situation in which a tenant rents out his apartment to another party but is still responsible to the landlord for the rent is known as a:
    A. triple net lease
    B. landlease
    C. consensual lease
    D. sublease

VIII. Title Closing and Costs

26. If the closing date is November 10 and the seller had paid the real property taxes of $2,880 for the current tax year of January 1 through December 31, which of the following is the correct closing statement entry for taxes?
    A. seller debit of $2,480
    B. seller credit of $400
    C. buyer credit of $400
    D. buyer debit of $2,480

27. RESPA requires lending institutions to provide borrowers with which of the following at the time of or within three days after application for a mortgage loan?
    A. good faith estimate
    B. HUD Form No. 1
    C. disclosure statement
    D. nonrecourse note

IX. Real Estate Finance (Mortgage)

28. Which of the following is NOT a method for a seller to help finance the sale of his property?
    A. second mortgage
    B. contract for deed
    C. FHA-insured mortgage
    D. purchase money first mortgage

29. Which of the following is limited to purchasing FHA-insured and VA-guaranteed mortgages?
    A. Fannie Mae
    B. Freddie Mac
    C. Maggie Mae
    D. Ginnie Mae

30. Which of the following is both a contract of sale and a financing instrument?
    A. installment land contract
    B. sale and leaseback
    C. lease with option to purchase
    D. executed contract

31. A mortgage that provides for installment payments that do not pay off the principal and interest over the mortgage term so that a final large payment is due at the end is known as a(n):
    A. amortized mortgage
    B. balloon mortgage
    C. wraparound mortgage
    D. junior mortgagee

X. Land Use Regulations

32. Deed restrictions that provide for a reversion of title are called:
    A. third party interests
    B. variances
    C. conditions
    D. clauses

33. The zoning board of appeals:
    A. makes policy decisions as to planning
    B. is an interpreter of the zoning ordinance
    C. is the final reviewing body for the decisions it renders
    D. decides the location of various zones in the community

34. Restrictive covenants may NOT be terminated by which of the following?
    A. expiration
    B. transfer of title
    C. failure to enforce on a timely basis
    D. abandonment

35. A developer who files a plat of subdivision that donates land to the municipality for public use has filed a(n):
    A. statutory dedication
    B. common-law dedication
    C. land patent
    D. eminent domain proceeding

XI. Introduction to Construction

36. Before construction or improvements can begin on a property, which of the following must be obtained? A:
    A. certificate of occupancy
    B. building permit
    C. variance
    D. completion bond

37. Plans for on-site wastewater treatment systems must be approved by which of the following New York State agencies or their local offices?
    A. Department of Environmental Conservation
    B. Department of Health
    C. Department of State
    D. these systems do not require approval

38. The part of the site plan that indicates the boundaries and the physical features of the property is the:
    A. topography
    B. infrastructure
    C. portfolio
    D. abstract of title

39. Wooden reinforcements for the openings in the wall where the doors and windows are placed are known as:
    A. rafters
    B. girders
    C. sill plates
    D. headers

XII. Valuation Process

40. Comparative market analyses are based on the supposition that:
    A. many properties are exactly alike
    B. no two properties are exactly alike
    C. many properties are similar in quality, location, and utility
    D. all properties will sell eventually if they stay on the market long enough

41. The assessed value of a property:
    A. is normally a percentage of market value
    B. has nothing to do with market value
    C. is always determined by an appraiser
    D. is set by the federal government

42. The more favorable the terms of a sale are to a buyer:
    A. does not impact the sale of a property
    B. the more quickly the property will sell
    C. always adversely affects the seller
    D. usually causes a lower commission to the salesperson

XIII. Human Rights and Fair Housing

43. The sales associates of Executive Realty, Ltd., obtained several listings in Exclusive Estates by advising homeowners that a number of Asian families were moving into Exclusive Estates and therefore their property values would be substantially depressed. This activity is most accurately described as:

    A. steering

    B. blockbusting

    C. soliciting

    D. redlining

44. When listing a duplex for sale, the broker advises the seller that because the seller lives in the other section of the duplex, the listing is exempt from prohibitions of the New York Human Rights Law. Which of the following statements about the broker's advice is true? The:

    A. broker is acting correctly in advising the seller about the exemption

    B. broker always should give good legal advice to sellers and buyers

    C. broker is in error because the exemption is from the Civil Rights Act of 1866

    D. broker is acting incorrectly in that the property is not exempt because the seller is using a broker

45. An order by the Department of State prohibiting licensees from attempting to obtain listings in specified areas of the state is called a(n):

    A. injunction

    B. executive order

    C. nonsolicitation order

    D. Article 78 proceeding

46. A lender's refusal to make loans for the purchase or repair of dwellings in a certain area based upon some characteristic of property owners in the area is known as:

    A. redlining

    B. blockbusting

    C. filtering

    D. conversion

XIV. Environmental Issues

47. A toxic fibrous substance found in many building materials is known as:

    A. lead

    B. radon

    C. CFCs

    D. asbestos

48. Which of the following does NOT apply under the State Environmental Quality Review Act?

    A. all levels of government must assess the environmental significance of actions that they have discretion to review, approve, fund, or undertake

    B. the environmental assessment process under SEQRA applies to residential structures only

    C. the agency that oversees the assessment process is called the lead agency

    D. if a property is simply transferred from owner to owner and the use is not changed, then the SEQRA process does not apply

49. The Residential Leadbased Paint Hazard Reduction Act applies to:

    A. all residential properties

    B. residential and commercial properties

    C. properties built before 1978

    D. properties built before World War II

XV. Real Estate Salesperson: Independent Contractor or Employee?

50. To qualify as an independent contractor according to the IRS code, real estate agents must comply with which of the following?

    A. hold a valid real estate license

    B. enter into a written contract with the real estate broker stating that the licensee will not be treated as an employee for federal tax purposes

    C. both A and B

    D. A only

DIAGNOSTIC EXAM ANSWER KEY

I. License Law and Regulations
1. B
2. C
3. C

II. Law of Agency
4. B
5. D
6. A

III. Estates and Interests
7. B
8. B
9. A
10. B

IV. Liens and Easements
11. B
12. A
13. D
14. C

V. Deeds
15. D
16. A
17. C

VI. Contracts
18. D
19. C
20. C
21. B

VII. Leases
22. D
23. D
24. C
25. D

VIII. Title Closing and Costs
26. B
27. A

IX. Real Estate Finance (Mortgages)
28. C
29. D
30. A
31. B

X. Land Use Regulations
32. C
33. B
34. B
35. A

XI. Introduction to Construction
36. B
37. B
38. A
39. D

XII. Valuation Process
40. C
41. A
42. B

XIII. Human Rights and Fair Housing
43. B
44. D
45. C
46. A

XIV. Environmental Issues
47. D
48. B
49. C

XV. Real Estate Salesperson: Independent Contractor or Employee?
50. C

Chapter 1

KEY TERMS

administrative discipline

apartment information vendor

apartment sharing agent

Article 12-A

Article 78 proceeding

associate real estate broker

blind ad

breach of contract

commingling

consent decree

escrow account

Federal Trade Commission (FTC)

group boycott

independent contractor

kickback

market allocation agreement

misdemeanor

mortgage banker

mortgage broker

multiple listing service

net listing

price fixing

real estate broker

real estate salesperson

reciprocity

Sherman and Clayton Antitrust Acts

sponsor

tie-in arrangements

trade name

Uniform Irrevocable Consent and Designation Form

LEARNING OBJECTIVES   *Classroom hours: 10*

1. Discuss all occupations that require a broker license in New York.
2. Identify additional licensing and registration requirements for mortgage brokers and bankers.
3. List individuals who are exempt from the requirements of licensure.
4. Identify the steps that must be taken to obtain a real estate broker's license.
5. Describe the basic responsibilities of maintaining a broker's license in New York.
6. Discuss the regulations that are promulgated by the Department of State under Article 12-A.
7. Recognize the liabilities and penalties that exist in connection with potential violations of the regulations.

The Broker's Office: Operation, Management, and Supervision

8. Explain the basic formats of establishing a business entity and the advantages and disadvantages of each.

9. List the basic reasons for antitrust legislation and the liabilities under the law.

10. Discuss the basic independent contractor laws in New York and how they relate to real estate brokers and salespersons.

11. List the needs and the responsibilities of interaction with other brokerage firms.

12. Discuss the causes and decisions of rulings concerning broker's responsibilities to manage and supervise in compliance with license laws.

IN THIS CHAPTER   As a broker, you have a duty to manage and supervise the activities of salespersons in your employ. This chapter discusses obtaining and maintaining licensure, licensure regulations and penalties for noncompliance, antitrust laws and the real estate industry, and the nature of the salesperson/broker independent contractor relationship.

LICENSURE REGULATION

The New York *Department of State (DOS), Division of Licensing Services* is the regulatory agency that oversees and administers the licensure process. *Most of the law pertaining to salespersons and brokers is contained in Article 12-A of the Real Property Law.* Other New York laws, codified rules and regulations, as well as legal precedent also define the licensure process. New York's authority to require licensure falls under its *police power* to protect the health, safety, welfare, and property of its citizens. Part of the purpose of the license law is to protect the public from dishonest dealings by brokers and salespersons and incompetency on the part of real estate licensees.

CATEGORIES AND RESPONSIBILITIES OF LICENSURE

In New York, three categories of licensure exist: real estate broker, associate broker, and salesperson. In most cases, individuals first receive their licensure as salespersons. If they have experience in real estate prior to licensure, they can obtain a broker or associate broker license without first becoming a salesperson. A license is generally required to transact real estate for another individual and for a fee, although certain exemptions are allowed.

A **real estate broker** is *any person, partnership, association, or corporation, who, for another, and for compensation, negotiates any form of real estate transaction.* Real estate brokers supervise and are responsible for the activities of associate brokers and salespersons in their employ. A broker's responsibility is to serve the public with honesty and competency.

An **associate real estate broker** is *a licensed real estate broker who performs the acts described for a broker, but chooses to work under the name and supervision of a licensed broker, who is his* **sponsor.** The licensed broker may be an individual, a corporation, partnership, or trade-name organization. The license allows individuals to retain broker status while functioning as salespeople. Associate brokers follow the same guidelines applicable to salespersons except that, as an identifying term, the words "Broker Associate" must be used.

A **real estate salesperson** is *a person who performs any of the acts set forth in the definition of a real estate broker for compensation but does so only while associated with and supervised by a licensed broker.* These definitions illustrate that a salesperson can engage in the real estate business only when associated with and supervised by a broker. Therefore, a *salesperson or an associate broker cannot operate independently.*

DUTIES THAT REQUIRE LICENSURE

Types of real estate transactions for others and for compensation of any kind covered under real estate licensure include the following:

1. Listing or offering to list real estate for sale
2. Selling or offering to sell real estate
3. Purchasing or offering to purchase real estate
4. Negotiating the exchange of real estate
5. Leasing, renting, or offering to rent real estate. Property managers and leasing agents who are employed by more than one owner or company must be licensed
6. Negotiating or attempting to negotiate a commercial loan. To negotiate a residential mortgage loan, a person or entity must be licensed by the New York Banking Department as a mortgage broker in accordance with Article 12-D, Section 590, of the Banking Law
7. Selling or purchasing real estate at an auction
8. Arranging and coordinating for a fee the relocation of commercial or residential tenants from buildings or structures that are to be demolished, rehabilitated, remodeled, or somehow structurally altered (done by a tenant relocator)
9. Performance of any of the above functions with regard to the *sale* of condominium or cooperative property. Licensed real estate brokers and salespersons who are not acting as *dealers* are not required to register with the Department of Law with respect to the sales of securities that constitute real estate cooperatives, condominiums, and interests in homeowners' associations. A dealer may be *a person, association, or corporation* who is the original owner for the first time sale of these security interests to the public
10. Negotiating the sale or exchange of lots or parcels of land
11. Negotiating the sale of a business for which the value of the real estate transferred is not merely incidental to the transaction but is a significant part of it. If the transaction involves the sale of securities, state or federal laws governing the sale of securities must be adhered to

Property owners are free to engage in real estate transactions on their own behalf without a license.

OTHER REAL ESTATE LICENSES OR REGISTRATION

The following summarizes other types of licenses. None of them requires either a salesperson or broker license. However, individuals applying for a mortgage broker license may use their license as a real estate broker as qualifying experience. Licensed salespersons and brokers may hold these licenses in addition to their real estate license. Care must be taken, however, to *not* engage in activities that pose a conflict of interest between the duties inherent in each of the licenses.

- An **apartment information vendor** is *an individual who, for a fee, engages in the business of furnishing information concerning the location and availability of residential real property, including apartment housing.* The housing may be rented, shared, or subleased. The license fee is $400 for a one-year term (branch office fee: $250), and the apartment information vendor must maintain a trust account in the amount of $5,000 plus $2,500 for each additional office.

- An **apartment sharing agent** is *an individual who, for a fee, arranges and coordinates meetings between the current owners of real property, including apartment housing, who wish to share their housing with others.* The license fee is also $400 per year for a one-year term (branch office fee: $250), and the apartment sharing agent must maintain a trust account in the amount of $2,500 plus a fee of $1,250 for each additional office. Like salesperson and broker licenses, the apartment information vendor and the apartment sharing agents are licensed by DOS, Division of Licensing Services.

- **Appraisal Licensure and Certification.** An appraiser estimates the value of real property. Individuals who appraise properties related in any way to federal transactions in which the transaction value is $250,000 or more must have an *appraisal license* or *certification*. All levels of licensure require a $300 fee for a two-year term. Appraisal licensure/certification is discussed further in Chapter 10.

- A **mortgage banker** is *an individual or an entity licensed by the New York Banking Department to engage in the business of making residential mortgage loans.* Federal and state licensed banks that make mortgage loans are exempt from having to obtain a mortgage banker license. Other individuals or entities who make more than four mortgage loans per year must obtain a mortgage banker license. Mortgage bankers, who are also called mortgage companies, make mortgage loans for the construction of housing and purchase of existing housing. They often specialize in FHA-insured loans and VA-guaranteed loans. A mortgage banker can act as a mortgage broker.

  The requirements for a mortgage banker license are as follows: a net worth of at least $250,000; an existing line of credit of at least $1 million provided by a banking institution, insurance company, or similar credit facility approved by the superintendent of banking; the filing of a surety bond in the amount of $50,000 or the execution of a deposit agreement coupled with a pledged deposit of securities or other assets in the amount of $50,000; five years' experience making residential mortgage loans or conducting similar transactions; demonstration of good character; a background report, provided by a selection of agencies chosen by the banking department; a set of fingerprints; a $74 fingerprint fee; and a $1,000 investigation fee. The license is for a one-year term and costs $1,000. A surety bond or deposit agreement are monies held by a third party who promises to be liable for the payment of another person's debt. The surety bond or deposit agreement, in this case, is used by the Banking Department to reimburse improperly charged consumer fees or to cover banking department fees in the event of liquidation by the licensee.

- A **mortgage broker** is *an individual or an entity registered by the New York Banking Department to engage in the business of soliciting, processing, placing, or negotiating residential mortgage loans.* A mortgage banker and a mortgage broker are quite different. A mortgage banker makes and services mortgage loans. A mortgage broker brings together a lender and a borrower for a fee paid by the lending institution, just as a real estate broker brings together, for a fee, a buyer and seller of real property. To apply for a mortgage broker registration, an applicant must have good standing in the community and two years of credit analysis and underwriting experience, or other relevant experience or education. Licensed New York real estate brokers and attorneys do not have to demonstrate their experience. Licensed salespersons must have participated actively in the residential mortgage business for two years. The application also requires a credit report provided by a selection of agencies chosen by the Banking Department, a set of fingerprints, a $74 fingerprint fee, and a $500 investigation fee. The license is for a one-year term and the registration fee is $500 per term. Individuals employed by either licensed mortgage bankers or mortgage brokers are not required to have a license themselves. For further information and an application for either of the above, contact the Banking Department, State of New York, 2 Rector Street, New York, NY 10006-1894; (212) 709-5574; or access an application online: *http://www.banking .state.ny.us.* (See Table 1.1 that illustrates other licenses related to real estate.)

Exemptions to Licensure

Certain individuals, acting on behalf of various governmental agencies or in a private capacity, may perform those acts permitted to salespersons and brokers without obtaining a real estate license:

1. Attorneys admitted to practice in the New York courts are *exempt* from licensure. Attorneys may act as brokers without obtaining a broker license and may collect commissions. However, they must obtain a license *if they employ salespersons to work under their supervision.* Attorneys may not represent individuals both as their attorney and broker in the same transaction as this would present a conflict of interest.

2. *Public officers* are also exempt while performing official duties (example: a condemnation proceeding in which New York acquires land employing a state agency to undertake the proceeding).

3. *Persons acting in any capacity under the judgment or order of a court* do not need a real estate license. These persons might include trustees in a bankruptcy, guardians, administrators, or executors. (Example: an executor may be empowered through a decedent's will to sell property included in the estate.) Trustees in a bankruptcy also may have the legal right to sell real property included in the bankruptcy.

4. *Tenants' associations and nonprofit corporations* are exempt from licensure. These agencies may be either residential neighborhood or rural preservation companies that are authorized in writing by the commissioner of the New York Department of Housing and Community Renewal or by the New York City Housing Authority to manage residential property owned by the state or the city. The agencies also may be appointed by a court to manage residential property.

5. *Building superintendents* or *maintenance workers* who perform tasks for one owner, such as rent collection, do not require licensure. Similarly, a person employed and empowered by one owner to act on the owner's behalf with regard

TABLE 1.1 Other licenses related to real estate.	LICENSE	NYS REGULATORY AGENCY	TERM	FEE
	Apartment information vendor	Department of State	1 year	$ 400
	Apartment sharing agent	Department of State	1 year	$ 400
	Appraiser licensure/certification	Department of State	2 years	$ 300
	Mortgage banker	Banking Department	1 year	$1,000
	Mortgage broker	Banking Department	1 year	$ 500

to various real estate transactions does not require licensure. Individuals who sell businesses, as business brokers, in which no sale of real property occurs, or when the transfer of real property is incidental to the transaction, do not require licensure. If the transaction includes only an assignment of a lease to the new owner, a real estate license is not necessary.

Unlicensed Assistants

Many real estate businesses utilize unlicensed employees or personal assistants to help with routine tasks. Legally the assistants may engage in any office activities that are not specified in Section 440 of Article 12-A. Some office activities that may be performed by a person who does not hold a license include the following: answering the phone, taking messages, arranging appointments, writing ad copy, typing contract forms for broker approval, and gathering information for a comparative market analysis. This list of duties is not inclusive. The broker is responsible for the supervision and control of an assistant's activities, however, unlicensed assistants' duties are mostly clerical in nature. They should not show apartments, houses, or other real property or discuss the real estate in question either with clients or customers. Unlicensed assistants may be paid directly by either the licensed broker or salesperson. The method of reimbursement for unlicensed activities is best handled on an hourly, per activity, or salaried basis. If compensated on a completed transaction basis, the assistant must be licensed as a real estate salesperson and must receive compensation directly from the licensed broker. Complete guidelines for allowable activities for unlicensed assistants are available from DOS.

REQUIREMENTS FOR OBTAINING LICENSURE

The New York Department of State, Division of Licensing Services, governs the licensure process and has the power to approve all real estate licenses. DOS is also empowered to deny, fine, suspend, or revoke a salesperson or broker license if the licensee violates any license laws. The salesperson and broker applications may be obtained from DOS by phone request, in writing, or online: *http://www.dos.state.ny.us*. The applications may also be available from entities that are approved by DOS to give the 45-hour qualifying courses. Completed applications must be sent to the following address: New York Department of State, Division of Licensing Services, 84 Holland Avenue, Albany, NY 12208-3490. The automated telephone voice response system of DOS that provides general and licensing exam information by category, may be reached by calling (518) 474-4429. DOS representatives are available to answer individual questions. Figure 1.1 lists DOS offices that have information and applications available to the public.

General Requirements

English Language Requirement

Article 12-A specifically states that *applicants must demonstrate a fair knowledge of the English language*. Dictionaries and other language aids are not available during the licensing exam. However, arrangements can be made to assist individuals who have hearing or visual impairments. DOS must be notified in advance to make such arrangements.

Citizenship Requirement

Applicants for the broker license must be U.S. citizens or lawfully admitted permanent residents. A permanent resident is one who has the status of having been lawfully accorded the privilege of residing permanently in the United States as a noncitizen in

FIGURE 1.1

Department of State's Division of Licensing Services office locations.

84 Holland Avenue
Albany, NY 12208-3490

Veterans Memorial Highway
Hauppauge, NY 11788-5501

164 Hawley Street
Binghamton, NY 13901-4053

123 Williams Street
New York, NY 10038-3813

65 Court Street
Buffalo, NY 14202-3471

333 East Washington Street
Syracuse, NY 13202-1428

accordance with immigration laws. Salesperson applicants may fall into one of four categories: citizenship status; permanent residency; a work authorization card obtained from the Immigration and Naturalization Service; or a work permit, which may be obtained by individuals who are sponsored by their employers. New York State residency is not required.

Certificate of Relief from Disabilities

Individuals who have been convicted of a felony either in New York or elsewhere must show evidence of an Executive Pardon, a Certificate of Good Conduct, or Certificate of Relief from Disabilities in order to be eligible for licensure. A *felony* is any serious crime above a misdemeanor and is generally punishable by imprisonment. This certificate is an order from a court to release a convicted felon from certain prohibitions imposed because of a past crime.

Age Requirement

A broker applicant must be at least 19 years old; a salesperson applicant must be at least 18 years old.

Education and Experience Requirements

To obtain a salesperson license, one must successfully complete a New York State-approved 45-hour qualifying course, pass the New York licensing exam, and obtain broker sponsorship. Broker licensure involves the successful completion of 90 hours of approved qualifying education (including the salesperson qualifying course), passage of the New York broker exam, and demonstration of either one year's experience as a salesperson, two years' equivalent real estate experience, or a combination of the two. An associate broker applicant must obtain broker sponsorship. All broker applicants must complete the New York State-approved 45-hour broker qualifying course prior to licensure *and must have first completed the 45-hour salesperson qualifying course.* A high school diploma is not required for licensure. However, applicants who became salespersons prior to November 1, 1979, may use 45 hours of continuing education instead of the salesperson qualifying course together with the broker qualifying course to fulfill requirements for broker licensure.

45-Hour Qualifying Courses

The topics and duration of time devoted to each subject within the 45-hour qualifying courses are mandated by DOS and are uniform throughout the state. Each qualifying course includes an exam.

Topics included in the salesperson qualifying course are License Law and Regulations (3 hours), Law of Agency (8 hours), Real Estate Instruments and Estates and Interests (10 hours), Real Estate Finance (Mortgages) (5 hours), Land Use Regulations (2 hours), Introduction to Construction (3 hours), Valuation Process (3 hours),

Human Rights and Fair Housing (4 hours), Environmental Issues (3 hours), Real Estate Mathematics (3 hours), and Real Estate Salesperson–Independent Contractor/Employee (1 hour).

Topics included in the broker qualifying course are The Broker's Office—Operation, Management, and Supervision (10 hours), Real Estate Agency Disclosure (Review) (4 hours), Real Estate Finance II (5 hours), Real Estate Investments (5 hours), General Business Law (5 hours), Construction and Development (4 hours), Conveyance of Real Property and Title Closing and Costs (Review) (3 hours), Real Estate Property Management (5 hours), Taxes and Assessments (2 hours), and Local Concerns (2 hours).

The Bureau of Educational Standards within the New York Division of Licensing Services oversees the approval of all qualifying and continuing education courses for real estate licensure. The bureau will accept a degree in real estate in lieu of the qualifying courses; also acceptable is a course taken in New York or elsewhere, if the bureau deems it equivalent in form and content to New York qualifying courses. Applicants who wish to apply for equivalency credit should send official transcripts indicating successful completion of coursework and an outline of the course to the Bureau of Educational Standards at the address given earlier for DOS.

The New York licensure examination   `You Should Know`

All applicants must pass the New York exam to obtain a license. The exams are walk-in (no appointments are necessary) and can be taken at any time during the licensure process. It is preferable to take the exam upon completing the qualifying courses. The passing grade for both exams is 70 percent. You will need to bring two No. 2 pencils, a silent calculator, and a check or money order payable to the New York Department of State for $15. You also *must* bring a photo ID to the exam. A government issued photo ID includes a driver's license, state issued identification (example: non-driver ID), military ID, U.S. passport, U.S. INS issued ID, or certificate of U.S. citizenship. You will also be thumb printed before the exam. Cash is not accepted at the exam site. You will receive the exam results within approximately two weeks. If you don't pass, you may retake the exam as many times as necessary. The $15 fee will be charged each time. Exam applicants who take the test at the Albany, New York City, and Rochester test centers have an opportunity to receive the results of the examination and obtain their license on the same day. To receive same-day licensure, applicants must bring their completed applications with them. For broker applicants, the application will be reviewed for compliance with the license law including education, experience, business name approval, etc. If the information is acceptable, a broker license will be issued. For those who do not become licensed immediately, the exam pass grade is valid for two years.

Figure 1.2 lists the 12 statewide test centers. The DOS has a current schedule of exam dates and times online. Table 1.2 summarizes New York's licensure requirements.

THE SALESPERSON AND BROKER APPLICATIONS

The Salesperson Application

In most cases, salesperson applicants obtain the form from the school or organization where they complete the 45-hour qualifying course. (The school must certify directly on the application that the applicant successfully completed the course.) The salesperson application must include the following: the name and address of the applicant, the name and principal business address of the broker with whom the salesperson is to be associated, a statement of association and signature by the sponsoring broker, and a certificate

FIGURE 1.2
Written examination sites.

ALBANY
State Office Building
84 Holland Avenue, "A" Wing Basement
Albany, NY 12208-3490

BINGHAMTON
State Office Building
44 Hawley Street, 15th Floor
Binghamton, NY 13901-4053

BUFFALO
State Office Building
65 Court Street
Main Floor Hearing Room Part 5
Buffalo, NY 14202-3471

HAUPPAUGE
State Office Building
250 Veterans Highway
Basement Conference Room 1
Hauppauge, NY 11788-5501

FRANKLIN SQUARE
VFW Hall - Basement
68 Lincoln Road
Franklin Square, NY 11010

NEW YORK CITY
123 Williams Street, 19th Floor
New York, NY 10038-3813

NEWBURGH
Newburgh Orange Ulster BOCES
Adult Educational Center
Federal Building
471 Broadway, 2nd Floor
Newburgh, NY 11788-5501

PLATTSBURGH
Clinton County Community College
Lake Shore Drive, Route 9 South
Plattsburgh, NY 12901

ROCHESTER
Monroe Developmental Center
620 West Fall Road
Rochester, NY 14604-1197

SYRACUSE (broker only)
State Office Building
333 East Washington Street, Main Floor
Hearing Room A
Syracuse, NY 13202-1418

SYRACUSE (salesperson only)
American Postal Workers Union Hall
407 East Taft Road
North Syracuse, NY 13212-3734

UTICA
State Office Building
207 Genesee Street, 1st Floor, Room 110C
Utica, NY 13501-2812

WATERTOWN
State Office Building
Department of State Office
317 Washington Street, 11th Floor
Watertown, NY 13601-3744

TABLE 1.2
Licensure requirements.

REQUIREMENT	SALESPERSON	BROKER/ASSOCIATE BROKER
Age	at least 18	at least 19
Citizenship/permanent residency	yes/other choices	yes
Qualifying course	45 hrs.	90 hrs.
Experience	none	1 yr. as a salesperson or 2 yrs. equivalent
Fee and term of licensure	$50 every 2 yrs.	$150 every 2 yrs.
Number of exam questions	50	100
Continuing education	22.5 hrs. every 2 yrs.	22.5 hrs. every 2 yrs.
Broker sponsorship	yes	associate broker only

of completion indicating that the applicant has successfully completed the 45-hour salesperson qualifying course. This section of the application is signed and sealed by representatives of the school or organization that offers the course. Both the salesperson and broker applications ask whether the applicant is responsible for child support. This question reflects a screening process by the state to assist parents who are owed child support payments.

A finalized salesperson license application should include the following: the completed front of the form, including the name and address of the sponsoring broker; the completed back of the form, including certification that the 45-hour course has been completed, with the school's name, date of course completion, authorized signature by a school official, and the school seal; the applicant's signature and that of the sponsoring broker; the exam "Passed" slip; and a $50 check made out to the New York Department of State. Figure 1.3 illustrates the salesperson application.

The Broker Application

The application is divided into several parts. After filling in their name, home address, and business name and address, applicants must then provide background data regarding age, criminal offenses, if any, and whether they are an attorney, a corporate officer, and so on. Associate broker applicants must have their sponsoring broker sign the application; all applicants must sign an applicant affirmation.

Supplements detailing the accumulated points for applicant experience follow. (The point system is discussed in more detail later in this chapter.) Salesperson experience applicants must fill out Supplement A and provide relevant employment history. The salesperson's sponsoring broker at the time he attained the experience must verify the information and sign the application. Supplement B is completed by individuals claiming equivalent experience in general real estate along with information about relevant employment history; Supplements A, B, and C are filled out by applicants claiming combined salesperson and general real estate experience.

Although applicants do not have to submit proof of experience with the application, DOS reserves the right to investigate applicants prior to or after licensure. It is important that salespersons take note of the *scope* of the broker application. *Salespersons should keep detailed chronological records of all of their real estate activity so that this material will be available if they decide to become a broker.*

A completed broker application should include the following: the completed application form (incomplete applications will be returned); original certificate of completion for the 45-hour qualifying courses (salesperson applicants need not submit salesperson certificates of completion since these documents are already on file with DOS); d/b/a, corporate, or partnership certificates, if applicable; the "Passed" broker exam slip; and a check made out to New York Department of State for $150.

The broker application details all necessary information for receiving a broker or associate broker license. Figure 1.4 shows Supplement A of the broker application, which illustrates the point system for experience credit.

Classes of Licensure for Brokers

Before applying for a broker license, applicants must decide the class of licensure they wish to obtain. DOS offers several classes of licensure for brokers:

Individual broker (Class 35). This class is for individuals who will be doing business under their individual name *only*. For this license, brokers may add the words "licensed real estate broker" after their name for use on signage, business cards, or other forms of advertising. This class of licensure does not allow brokers to represent

FIGURE 1.3   The salesperson license application.

OFFICE USE ONLY	CLASS	KEY	UNIQUE ID NUMBER	CASH NUMBER	FEE
	4				$ 50

E W S | / | | B | / | |

Real Estate Salesperson Application
Read the Instruction Sheet for details before completing this application form. You must answer each question and TYPE or PRINT responses in ink.

APPLICANT'S LAST NAME _____   FIRST NAME _____   M.I. _____   SUFFIX _____

HOME ADDRESS -NUMBER AND STREET (P.O. BOX MAY BE ADDED TO ENSURE DELIVERY) _____   APT/UNIT _____

CITY _____   STATE _____   ZIP+4 _____   COUNTY _____

SPONSORING BROKER OR FIRM NAME (EXACTLY AS IT APPEARS ON THE BROKER/S LICENSE) _____

OFFICE ADDRESS WHERE APPLICANT WILL BE PERMANENTLY STATIONED - NUMBER AND STREET _____

CITY _____   STATE _____   ZIP+4 _____   COUNTY _____

DAYTIME TELEPHONE NUMBER   (   )   _____   SOCIAL SECURITY NUMBER OR FEDERAL ID NUMBER (*SEE PRIVACY NOTIFICATION*)

E-MAIL ADDRESS (IF ANY) _____

1   BACKGROUND DATA

1. What is your date of birth? _____

	YES	NO

2. Have you ever been convicted in this state or elsewhere of any criminal offense that is a misdemeanor or a felony? ....   ___   ___
    →**IF "YES,"** submit a written explanation giving the place, court jurisdiction, nature of the offense, sentence and/or other disposition. You must provide a copy of the accusatory instrument (e.g., indictment, criminal information or complaint) and a Certificate of Disposition. If you possess or have received a Certificate of Relief from Disabilities, Certificate of Good Conduct or Executive Pardon, you must provide a copy of same.

3. Are there any criminal charges (misdemeanors or felonies) pending against you in any court in this state or elsewhere? ....   ___   ___
    →**IF "YES,"** you must provide a copy of the accusatory instrument (e.g., indictment, criminal information or complaint).

4. Has any license or permit issued to you or a company in which you are or were a principal in New York State or elsewhere ever been revoked, suspended or denied? ....   ___   ___
    →**IF "YES,"** you must provide all relevant documents, including the agency determination, if any.

5. Have you ever applied for or been issued a real estate broker's or salesperson's license in this state?   ___   ___
    →**IF "YES,"** in what year? _____   Under what name? _____

    UID # (if applicable) _____

(continued)

FIGURE 1.3   Continued.

Real Estate Salesperson Application

2   Certification of Satisfactory Completion

(Name of School)

Real Estate Salesperson Course (Code) #S-_____

This certifies that _____ has satisfactorily completed a 45-hour salesperson
(Name of Student)
qualifying course in real estate approved by the Secretary of State in accordance with the provisions of Chapter 868
of the Laws of 1977; that attendance of the student was in compliance with the law and that a passing grade was
achieved on the final examination. The course was completed on _____ .

Authorized Signature

X_____   *Date* _____

(School Seal)

3   Child Support Statement — *You must complete this section. If you do not complete it, your application will be returned.*

"X" A or B, below

I, the undersigned, do hereby certify that (You *must* "X" A or B, below):

A. [ ] **I am not under obligation to pay child support.** (SKIP "B" and go directly to **Applicant Affirmation**).

B. [ ] I am under obligation to pay child support (You must "X" any of the four statements below that are true and apply to you):

    [ ]   I do *not* owe four or more months of child support payments.

    [ ]   I am making child support payments by income execution or court approved payment plan or by a plan agreed to by the parties.

    [ ]   My child support obligation is the subject of a pending court proceeding.

    [ ]   I receive public assistance or supplemental social security income.

4   Applicant Affirmation — I affirm, under the penalties of perjury, that the statements made in this application are true and correct. I further affirm that I have read and understand the provisions of Article 12-A of the Real Property Law and the rules and regulations promulgated thereunder.

Applicant's Signature

X_____   *Date* _____

DOS-0022 (Rev. 11/02)   PAGE 2 OF 3

(continued)

FIGURE 1.3   Continued.

Real Estate Salesperson Application

5   Association Statement — I am sponsoring this application in accordance with the Real Property Law, §441.1(d).

Broker Name _____   Date _____

Broker Signature _____

Broker Print Name _____

Please remember to include with this application any required explanations and statements along with your application fee (payable to NYS Department of State).

It is important that you notify this division of any changes
to your business address so you can continue to receive renewal
notices and any other notifications pertinent to your license.

Source: New York Department of State.

FIGURE 1.4   The broker point system.

Category	Point Value X	Number of Transactions Performed	=	Total Points Earned
Residential Sales:				
1. Single Family, condo, co-op unit, multi family (2 to 8 unit), farm (with residence, under 100 acres)	250 X	_____	=	_____
2. Exclusive listings	10 X	_____	=	_____
3. Open listings	1 X	_____	=	_____
4. Binders effected	25 X	_____	=	_____
5. Co-op unit transaction approved by seller and buyer that fails to win Board of Directors approval	100 X	_____	=	_____
Residential Rentals:				
6. Rentals or subleases effected	25 X	_____	=	_____
7. Exclusive Listings	5 X	_____	=	_____
8. Open Listings	1 X	_____	=	_____
9. Property Management - Lease renewal	2 X	_____	=	_____
- Rent collections per tenant/per year	1 X	_____	=	_____
Commercial Sales:				
10. Taxpayer/Storefront	400 X	_____	=	_____
11. Office Building	400 X	_____	=	_____
12. Apartment Building (9 units or more)	400 X	_____	=	_____
13. Shopping Center	400 X	_____	=	_____
14. Factory/Industrial warehouse	400 X	_____	=	_____
15. Hotel/Motel	400 X	_____	=	_____
16. Transient garage/parking lot	400 X	_____	=	_____
17. Multi-unit commercial condominium	400 X	_____	=	_____
18. Urban commercial development site	400 X	_____	=	_____
19. Alternative sale type transaction	400 X	_____	=	_____
20. Single-tenant commercial condo	250 X	_____	=	_____
21. Listings	10 X	_____	=	_____
Commercial Leasing:				
22. New Lease - aggregate rental $1 to $200,000	150 X	_____	=	_____
23. New Lease - aggregate rental $200,000 to $1 million	250 X	_____	=	_____
24. New Lease - aggregate rental over $1 million	400 X	_____	=	_____
25. Renewal - aggregate rental $1 to $200,000	75 X	_____	=	_____
26. Renewal - aggregate rental $200,000 to $1 million	125 X	_____	=	_____
27. Renewal - aggregate rental over $1 million	200 X	_____	=	_____
28. Listings	10 X	_____	=	_____
Commercial Financing (includes residential properties of more than four units):				
29. $1 to $500,000	200 X	_____	=	_____
30. $500,000 to $5,000,000	300 X	_____	=	_____
31. Over $5,000,000	400 X	_____	=	_____
Miscellaneous:				
32. Sale vacant lots, land (under 100 acres)	50 X	_____	=	_____
33. Sale vacant land (more than 100 acres)	150 X	_____	=	_____
34. Other, must be fully explained	___ X	_____	=	_____
Total Qualifying Points	➤			

Source: New York Department of State.

themselves as being associated with any firm or company. Even though brokers may be licensed in their own names, they still must have a business address even if the business is operated from their homes. Home offices, however, must comply with zoning requirements as to use and signage (discussed later).

Associate broker (Class 30). Individuals applying for an associate broker license must be sponsored by a broker and therefore must have their supervising broker sign the association statement contained in the broker application.

Trade-name broker (Class 37). Trade-name *brokers conduct business as a sole proprietorship, using a name other than their personal name.* A certificate to do business under an assumed name (d/b/a certificate) must be filed with the county clerk in the county where the applicant does business. For example, the certificate might state: *Alinda Rodriguez doing business as (d/b/a) Own Your Home Realty.* A copy of the business certificate must be submitted with the application.

Applicants who plan to do business as a sole proprietorship have the advantage of making their own business decisions and generally have less complicated record keeping for taxes and other purposes than do other types of business organizations. A disadvantage of a sole proprietorship is that the owner is personally financially liable for debts and lawsuits against the business whereas a corporation generally protects its shareholders from personal financial liability.

Partnership broker (Class 33). A *partnership* is a form of business organization that is owned by two or more partners. A partnership is created by contract between the partners. The partners do not have to have the same degree of interest in the partnership or the same extent of management authority. The partners may be of two categories: general or limited. In *general partnerships,* the partners are personally liable for partnership debts exceeding partnership assets. Partners are jointly (together) and severally (separately) liable for these debts. A *limited partnership* consists of one or more general partners who are jointly and severally liable, and one or more silent, or limited partners, who contribute money or other assets of value to the extent of their ownership interest. Limited partners are not liable for the debts of the partnership beyond the amount of money they have contributed.

A partner or partners in a partnership may apply for the broker license under the partnership name. Each partner who wishes to be licensed as a real estate broker must file an application and individual fee. A partnership certificate must be filed with the county clerk in the county where the business is located, and a copy of the certificate must be filed with the application.

Corporate broker (Class 31). A *corporation* is an artificial being, invisible, intangible, and existing only pursuant to law. A corporation is a taxable legal entity recognized by law with tax rates separate from individual income tax rates. It is created by a charter granted by the state of incorporation. The bylaws may expressly state which officers, directors, or other persons carry out the various duties of the corporation.

An officer of a corporation may be issued a license to conduct business as a real estate brokerage under a corporate name. A copy of the corporate filing receipt must be submitted with the application for new corporations only. Each officer of a corporation or member of a co-partnership who is involved in any form of the real estate brokerage must be licensed as a broker. Salesperson licenses are not issued to officers of corporations or members of co-partnerships. Salespersons and associate brokers may not be principals in the brokerage firm and may not own voting stock in the licensed brokerage corporation. Individuals who are not licensed brokers *can* be principals in a real estate brokerage firm. They cannot, however, perform any of the duties allowed by licensure; for example, listing and selling real estate for others. Unlicensed principals of a brokerage corporation may hold up to 100 percent of the shares of voting stock; however, at least one of the corporate principals must be a licensed real estate broker.

All business names, including trade, partnership, and corporate names, must be submitted for approval in writing to DOS, Division of Licensing Services, prior to filing a certificate of partnership and/or incorporation. Established business names that will be submitted for licensure must go through the same clearance process. In the case of a corporation, once a name is cleared by the Division of Licensing, the corporation must be set up (if it is not an existing corporation). Name clearance is also required by DOS, Division of Corporations. Once the name is cleared, the corporate papers may be filed with NYS Department of State, Division of Corporations, 41 State Street, Albany, NY 12231; (518) 473-2492.

Limited Liability Company (LLC) or Limited Liability Partnership (LLP) (Class 49). A member or manager of an LLC or LLP who meets the qualifications for licensure, may be issued a license to conduct real estate brokerage under the LLC or LLP name. Applicants must be members or managers prior to licensing. New limited liability companies *only* must file a copy of the articles of organization with the Division of Corporations or the company filing receipts must be submitted with the broker application.

Franchises. A franchise is the right to use the name of a parent company along with certain operating procedures. Generally, this right must be paid for by the franchisee through a percentage of the profits or outright fees or a combination of both. In some franchise firms, the franchise fee portion is deducted from the final commission due the sales associate. (Some brokers use an incentive program, raising the proportion paid to the sales associate in relationship to the dollar volume produced by the sales associate.)

Real estate franchises are popular because they offer name recognition, referral services on a nationwide level, and methods of operation that have proven track records. In many cases, a real estate firm can keep its own name in conjunction with the franchised name.

The point system. DOS has implemented a point system to clarify real estate experience required for the broker license. A certain number of points is allotted for various types of experience. For example, 250 points are allotted for the sale of a single family house, a condo, co-op unit, multifamily (two to eight units), or a farm (with residence under 100 acres). The applicant must multiply the allotted points in each category by the number of completed transactions per category and then total the points from each category. *Experience for a broker license may be obtained through one type of experience only, such as residential sales, or a variety of experiences such as residential and commercial sales, property management, rentals, and leasing.* The three types of acceptable experience are one year as a salesperson and the accumulation of 1,750 points; two years' equivalent experience in general real estate and the accumulation of 3,500 points; and combined experience that includes work as a salesperson and general real estate activity, as well as the accumulation of 3,500 points. For the combined experience licensure, the applicant multiplies by two the experience gained as a salesperson. Salesperson experience requires only half the time in the business as equivalent experience.

MAINTAINING A LICENSE

All licensees are expected to be familiar with license law, rules, and regulations. If DOS officials deem that a licensee has violated some part of the license law, they do not accept ignorance of wrongdoing as an excuse.

License and Pocket Card

When licensure is approved, DOS issues both a license and a pocket card. The broker license must be displayed conspicuously in the principal place of business and at branch offices at all times. A broker may not display an expired license. Salesperson licenses need not be displayed, but must be stored by the broker in a safe and accessible place. Salespersons and brokers receive a *pocket card,* which includes their name and business address. The pocket card also includes the name and business address of the broker with whom the salesperson or associate broker is affiliated. Pocket cards must be carried at all times and be shown on demand. Pocket cards may be laminated. If the card is lost or destroyed, DOS will issue a duplicate card for a $10 fee.

Change of Address, Status, or Name

If the broker moves a principal or branch office to a different address, the broker must notify DOS within five days. Failure to do so renders the broker subject to license suspension. It is prudent, in some cases, to have the location preapproved, especially if the location is in a cease and desist zone. Brokers must first cross out the former address on their license and the licenses and pocket cards of the salespersons and associate brokers who are employed by them, and the new address must be printed on all licenses and pocket cards. Then the broker must complete a broker change of address form and send it to DOS with a $10 fee. Each salesperson or associate broker affiliated with the broker must also submit a salesperson/associate broker change of address form and pay a $10 fee.

If salespersons or brokers decide to change the *status* of their license from, for example, associate broker to broker, the fee is $150. Changes of *name* may be filed for a fee of $50 for a salesperson and $150 for individual or company broker name changes. (Example: A woman who marries during a licensure term may wish to have her married name, if different, appear on the license.)

Responsibility of Brokers

Business Sign

Brokers must post a *business sign* conspicuously outside of their place of business that is easily readable from the sidewalk. The sign must include the name and business address and indicate that the individual or corporation is a licensed real estate broker. If the brokerage office is located inside a building where the sign would not be visible from the street, the sign must be posted in the building directory where the names of businesses are displayed, and it must include the broker's name and the words "licensed real estate broker." In many towns and municipalities, various zoning ordinances exist that prohibit or restrict signage, and also designate certain areas for either residential or business use, but not both. *A broker is not allowed to violate license law in order to comply with local zoning ordinances,* and conversely, a broker may not violate zoning laws to comply with the license law.

Fees, Branch Office Requirements, and Term of Licensure

A broker must pay a $150 fee and a salesperson a $50 fee for each licensure term. If a broker license is issued to a corporation or co-partnership, the officers or co-partners must also pay $150 for their individual licenses. Additional licenses for each branch office cost $150. Both the salesperson and the broker license must be renewed every two years. If licensees fail to renew by the expiration date, they have a two-year grace period during which they may renew the license. If applicants do not renew within this time period, DOS requires them to retake and pass the exam. Table 1.3 summarizes most of the fees charged by DOS.

Termination or Change of Association

When salespersons or associate brokers *terminate* association with their broker, the broker must forward a salesperson/associate broker *termination of association notice* to DOS along with a $10 fee and return the license to the salesperson or associate/broker. If desired, the broker may send a letter to DOS stating the reason for termination.

To *change* association, the new sponsoring broker must send a salesperson/broker *new record of association notice* signed by the salesperson or associate broker and the new broker to DOS along with a $10 fee. The salesperson or associate broker must cross

LICENSURE	FEE	
Salesperson license	$ 50	**TABLE 1.3** Summary of licensure fees.
Associate broker/broker license	$150	
Each broker branch office	$150	
Exam fee	$ 15	
Change of salesperson name	$ 50	
Change of broker name or status	$150	
Change of address	$ 10	
Termination of association	$ 10	
New association	$ 10	
Duplicate license/pocket card	$ 10	

Many forms required for salespersons and brokers may be downloaded from the DOS website.

out the name and address of the former broker and print the name and address of the new broker on the front of the license. DOS will issue new licenses and pocket cards. (See Figure 1.5)

Dual Licensure—Broker and Salesperson

Licensees may hold more than one license at a time. A separate application and fee must be submitted to DOS for each license. For example, a broker may hold two broker licenses. A licensed broker may also become an associate broker with another firm. A salesperson or an associate broker can work under the association and supervision of more than one broker. Associate brokers and salespersons who wish additional licenses must submit a statement to DOS from each sponsoring broker indicating acknowledgment of each licensure.

FIGURE 1.5   Salesperson/Associate Broker Termination of Association form.

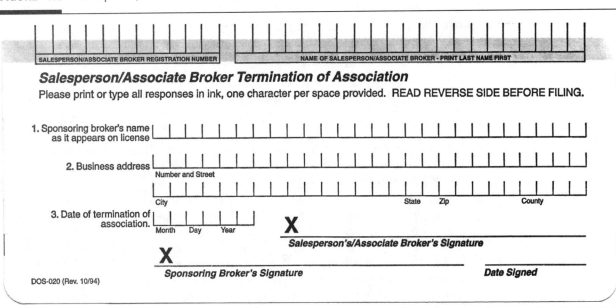

Source: New York Department of State.

Renewal Requirements of Sponsoring Brokers

Approximately one to two months before the two-year renewal deadline, DOS sends a renewal application. Licensees may renew their licenses online at the DOS website using their registration number and a password obtained through calling the Department of State. If the licensee is a salesperson or an associate broker, the renewal application *must be signed by the broker attesting to the fact that the licensee is sponsored by that broker.* The renewal application also asks if continuing education requirements have been completed. Although DOS does send the licensee the renewal application, it is still the licensee's responsibility, *before* license expiration, to complete the renewal form and pay the appropriate fees (see Table 1.3). A licensee who does not receive a renewal application should call DOS to obtain one.

You Should Know | **Continuing education requirements**

Unless exempt, licensees must complete the required *continuing education* courses within the required time frame. Licensees must successfully complete 22.5 hours of approved continuing education every two years upon license renewal. The salesperson qualifying course may not be used for the 22.5-hour continuing education requirement. Salespersons must complete an additional 22.5 hours of continuing education during their two-year license period. Salespersons may use the broker qualifying course for *one* two-year period to fulfill this requirement. New York allows alternative distance learning formats for continuing education such as online delivery, CD–ROM, and other applications. Check with your course provider for more information on these learning choices. Individuals *exempt* from completing continuing education requirements are licensed brokers who are engaged in the real estate business full-time and who have been licensed with no lapse in licensure for 15 years. The licensed broker need not have been a broker during the entire 15 years but could have been licensed as a salesperson for part of that time. Attorneys are also exempt from continuing education requirements.

DOS REGULATIONS

The regulations governing real estate licensees must reflect and be subject to a combination of laws in Article 12-A of the Real Property Law; other sections of the Real Property Law; codified DOS rules and regulations; and other New York laws, such as agency, contract, and human rights.

Violations of Real Estate License Law

The following summarizes possible violations submitted as complaints to DOS:

1. Making a material misstatement in the application for a license. Examples include not checking the appropriate spaces that ask about age, criminal records, or previous license revocations.

2. Committing fraud or engaging in fraudulent practices. *Fraudulent practices are acts meant to deceive or misrepresent resulting in giving one person an advantage over another.* One example is if a broker does not disclose his knowledge of a high level of radon in a given property to prospective customers. Another includes a broker who has knowledge of a new zoning variance allowing industrial activity in a residential neighborhood and not passing this information on to prospective home buyers. (See Chapter 6 Section 1 for a discussion of seller property condition disclosure.)

3. Demonstrating untrustworthiness or incompetency to act as a real estate broker or salesperson.

4. Failing to account for and remit funds belonging to others that have come into the licensee's possession. *All brokers must maintain a separate trust* or **escrow account** in a federally insured bank. The broker must deposit any monies as promptly as practicable. A broker need not have an interest-bearing account. If there is such an account, accrued interest may *not* be retained for the benefit of the broker. However, with the consent of all the parties to the transaction, this interest may be applied toward monies owed to the broker for the commission.

Brokers are prohibited from **commingling,** or *mixing the funds or property of others with their business or personal funds.* They must maintain adequate records regarding the deposit and disbursement of funds. A broker should have at least two accounts: an office escrow account for client deposits and an operating account for business expenses. If a broker uses deposit money which is not yet his, places it into the operating account and spends it, he may be guilty of *conversion.* Conversion is the apportionment of other people's money from one use to another. In the above example, it is illegal and may be classified as a felony. Article 36–C of the General Business Law further clarifies that the broker need not establish a *separate* escrow account for each transaction deposit as long as he keeps adequate records of each individual deposit in the one separate escrow account.

The General Business Law also addresses deposits for new residential construction. The vendor, for example, the builder, can either: (1) post a bond in the amount of the deposit with the chief fiscal officer in the locality where the property is located; or (2) establish a separate interest-bearing account in the name of each of the vendees (purchasers) in the amount of the deposit.

Although most offers to purchase are accompanied by an **earnest money deposit,** it is not legally required for a valid offer to purchase. *An earnest money deposit (a) shows the sincerity of the buyer, (b) demonstrates financial capability to raise the money called for in the agreement, and (c) serves as possible liquidated damages to the seller in the event of default by the buyer.* Salesperson licensees are required to promptly remit to their supervising broker all funds belonging to others that come into their possession.

5. Failing to notify DOS of a change of address and/or office location and also an agent's status.

6. Failing to supervise the activities of salespersons.

7. Allowing unlicensed agents to conduct activities that require licensure.

8. Being a party to an exclusive listing contract that contains an automatic continuation of the listing beyond the specified termination date. Listing contracts must be renewed by the signing of a written renewal agreement. This agreement must be signed by the seller and the agent. If the property is listed through a multiple listing service (MLS), the broker must notify MLS of the renewal.

9. Soliciting for business in a nonsolicitation area. *If the secretary of state determines that some homeowners within a certain geographic area have been subject to intense and repeated solicitation by real estate agents, this area can be declared a cease and desist zone.* Upon establishment of the cease and desist zone, homeowners may file a request with DOS that they *do not desire to sell, lease, or list their residential property and do not wish to be solicited by real estate agents.* These homeowners are then put on a *cease and desist list.* If real estate agents solicit these homeowners, DOS can take disciplinary action.

A *nonsolicitation order* is a directive from DOS prohibiting all real estate licensees to refrain from soliciting listings for the sale of residential property in a certain designated geographical area to stop the practice of blockbusting. Examples of prohibited solicitation are letters, leaflets, telephone calls, door-to-door calls, and postings in public places. In general, newspaper advertisement is allowed in a non-solicitation area. However, in a lawsuit brought by the NYS Association of REALTORS® against DOS, the court found that nonsolicitation orders violated the constitutional rights of licensees.

10. Failing to renew the license of salespersons.

11. Engaging in the unauthorized practice of law: drawing up legal documents such as deeds or mortgages; giving an opinion as to the legal validity of any document, or the legal rights of others; or performing a title examination or rendering an opinion as to the quality of the title. In essence, a *licensee may not perform any service that must be performed by an attorney.* In all legal matters affecting buyers and sellers, the licensee should recommend that the parties retain the services of a competent attorney.

   In 1978 a landmark decision by the New York Appellate Division, entitled *Duncan & Hill Realty, Inc. v. Department of State* (62 AD2d 690, NYS 2d 339), determined that real estate brokers may not insert detailed legal agreements into contracts and must alert buyers and sellers to see an attorney before signing a contract. In the *Duncan & Hill* case, the brokerage firm, which represented the seller, described the terms of a purchase money mortgage into a contract of sale. The court found that this activity constituted an unauthorized practice of law. Also, the purchase form contained no warning alerting the parties that, when signed, the instrument became a binding contract. The form did not caution the parties that it would be preferable for them to consult an attorney before signing.

12. Collecting an unearned commission.

13. Collecting a commission if the broker was not the *procuring cause* of the sale and/or did not procure a "ready, willing, and able purchaser." The broker's entitlement to commission is determined by two tests:

   (a) *Ready, willing, and able.* If the broker brings to the seller a buyer who is ready to buy, is willing to buy, and is able (financially) to buy under the terms and conditions of the listing contract, the broker is legally entitled to the commission. The broker has done the job he was hired to do in the listing contract—find a buyer who will pay the listed price in cash or other specified, accepted terms. When the broker does this, the commission has been earned under the ready, willing, and able test. Whether the owner actually agrees to sell the property to the prospective buyer does not matter. The seller may reject any offer, but rejection of an offer that conforms to the terms of the listing contract does not remove the duty to pay the commission.

   (b) *Acceptance.* If the broker brings a buyer that the seller accepts, the broker is legally entitled to the commission, as he has been instrumental in *procuring* a buyer for the property. Acceptance is based on some price or terms other than the listed price in cash. For example, the listing contract may specify $80,000 to be payable in cash. A broker may bring an offer to the seller of $78,500. This offer may not be for payment in cash, but instead may be subject to the buyer's assuming the seller's existing mortgage. If the seller accepts this offer, the broker is legally entitled to the commission on the basis of acceptance. The broker has brought the seller a buyer who is acceptable to the seller.

   Another term for offer and acceptance is *meeting of the minds.* This concept further clarifies commission entitlement. The broker or brokers who are the procuring cause of the meeting of the minds as evidenced by the parties reaching agreement on the terms of the contract are the ones who are entitled to the commission.

   Both these tests are not required—it is an either-or situation. The broker earns a commission either on the basis of having brought a ready, willing, and able buyer, or on the basis of having brought an offer that the seller accepts.

14. Failing to provide adequate disclosure regarding any one or more of the following: (a) if licensees purchase property listed by their firm, they must make their position clear to the seller; and (b) if licensees buy or sell property for a client and they have an ownership interest, the licensees must disclose their interest to all parties.

    In addition, licensees must make clear their position regarding the party for whom they are acting in a residential real estate transaction: seller, buyer, or both. In the sale or rental of 1–4 unit residential properties, licensees must have all prospective buyers and sellers read, understand, and sign specific disclosure forms mandated by Section 443 of the Real Property Law, explaining the position of each salesperson or broker in the real estate transaction. (See Chapter 2 for a full explanation of agency and disclosure.)

15. Entering into a **net listing** contract. A net listing occurs *when a seller authorizes a broker to procure a specified amount for the property and then allows the broker to keep as a commission any money above this specified amount obtained from the sale. This type of listing is illegal in New York.*

16. Negotiating the sale or lease of any property with an owner or a lessor if the licensee knows that the owner or lessor has an existing exclusive written contract with another broker.

17. Inducing *breach of contract.* In some cases a *party to a contract fails to complete the contract or fails to perform, with no legal cause.* This is known as a **breach of contract.** The breach, however does not terminate the contract obligations of the breaching party. The nondefaulting party may seek legal remedies against the defaulting party by filing a lawsuit. A licensee may not induce any party to a contract of *sale or lease to break the contract for the purpose of substituting a new contract with another principal.*

18. Violating laws and regulations regarding signs and advertising. Licensees may not place a sign of any kind on a property without the consent of the owner. Guidelines for advertising are discussed later.

19. Failing to deliver duplicate instruments relating to any type of real estate transaction in which the broker is a participant.

PUTTING IT TO WORK

Licensees must follow certain prescribed rules in handling purchase offers and other documents. Licensees must:

- Always give the seller a copy of the listing contract.
- Present all offers, whether they are written or not, to the seller. It is the seller's prerogative to accept or reject any offer.
- Immediately deliver duplicate copies to all parties who sign the documents.
- Provide the buyer and seller with copies of all documents executed by buyer, seller, or both. The buyer must receive a copy of the offer, and both buyer and seller must receive copies of the executed contract.
- Copies of any other documents, such as options, contracts for deed, or contracts for lease must be provided to the parties.

---

20. Failing to provide definitions of *exclusive right to sell* and *exclusive agency* listings. This requirement is necessary in the sale of one- to three-unit dwellings but does not apply to condominiums and cooperatives. In all listing agreements the broker must provide a printed explanation of the difference between the two listings. The explanation must be initialed or signed by the homeowner. (See the exclusive right to sell agreement form in Chapter 2.)

21. Failing to provide a list of **multiple listing service** (MLS) members. A *multiple listing service is a system that pools the listings of all member companies.* If listing brokers are members of MLS, they must provide this list. In addition, the listing contract should give the homeowner the option of having all offers to purchase submitted through the listing or selling broker.

22. Making any substantial and willful misrepresentations. It is illegal for a licensee to make an intentional false statement regarding an important matter in a real estate transaction for the purpose of inducing someone to sign a contract. Although it is not the duty of the broker to verify all representations made by the owner, if the broker knows or has reason to know that the owner has made misrepresentations or has failed to disclose material defects, then the broker must not perpetuate these misrepresentations. Moreover, if representation could be considered crucial to the sale, the broker has a duty to verify the accuracy of the representation.

23. Receiving compensation from more than one party in a real estate transaction without the knowledge and consent of all parties.

24. Offering a property for sale or lease without the authorization of the owner.

25. Accepting the services of any salesperson employed by another broker. A broker may not compensate another broker's salesperson without the knowledge of that salesperson's broker. In addition, the salesperson may not represent another broker without the knowledge and consent of the broker with whom the salesperson is associated.

Remember 26. Retaining listing information upon termination of association. If licensees terminate their association with a real estate broker, they must turn over all listing information obtained during their association with the broker whether the information was given to them by the broker, copied from the broker's records, or acquired by the licensee.

27. Discriminating because of race, creed, color, national origin, age, disability, sex, or familial status in the sale, rental, or advertisement of housing or commercial space covered by law. (New York City and other municipalities in New York have additional discrimination restrictions.) Licensees also are prohibited from engaging in the practice of *blockbusting;* that is, the solicitation or the sale or lease of property initiated by a change in the ethnic composition of a neighborhood.

28. Failing to maintain records. In the sale or mortgage of one- to four-unit properties, brokers must maintain records of transactions for three years. Records must include the names and addresses of the seller, buyer, mortgagee, if any, the purchase price and resale price, if any, the amount of deposit paid on the contract, the commission paid to the broker or the gross profit realized by the broker if purchased by her for resale. Instead of other types of records, the broker can keep, for each transaction, a copy of the contract of sale; commission agreement; closing statement; and statement showing disposition of the proceeds of the mortgage loan.

PUTTING IT TO WORK   One of the most important duties of a broker is to handle other people's money in compliance with New York laws and regulations. Respond to the following scenario.* Then compare your response with the model in the Answer Key at the end of the chapter.

We are about to place an offer on a house through a broker. He told us our offer should be accompanied by a deposit. What happens to that money?

---

*Source: James A. Ader, "Real Estate Spotlight." Copyright ® *The Albany Times Union.* Reprinted by permission.

Guidelines for Advertisements

Advertisements placed by real estate brokers must be truthful and not mislead the public. *All ads placed by a broker must indicate that the advertiser is a broker and give the name and telephone number. Ads that do not contain this information are called* **blind ads.** In addition, advertising stating that a property is in a certain geographical vicinity must identify the exact name of the geographical area. Figure 1.6 includes examples of correct and incorrect copy.

FIGURE 1.6

DOS guidelines for broker advertising.

Blind Ad. 19NYCRR RULE 175.25(a) requires that all advertisements placed by a broker must indicate that the advertiser is a broker and give the name and telephone number of the broker.

Correct copy

House, 1/2 acre, $90,000
John Doe, Broker (or)
John Doe, XXX Realty
518-XXX-1000

Incorrect Copy

House, 1/2 acre, $90,000
518-XXX-1000

Geographical Locations. 19NYCRR Rule 175.25(b) requires that all advertisements placed by a broker that state that property is in the vicinity of a geographical area or territorial subdivision must include as part of such advertisement the name of the geographical area or territorial subdivision in which such property is actually located.

Correct copy

House, 1/2 acre, $90,000
New Concord
John Doe, Broker
518-XXX-1000

Incorrect Copy

House, 1/2 acre, $90,000
Vicinity Berkshire Mts.
John Doe, Broker
518-XXX-1000

PUTTING IT TO WORK

The following sample ads illustrate the elements of correct ad copy. Analyze them to understand why they adhere to DOS regulations.

SUNRISE
Overlooking beautiful Lake George. 3 bedroom, 2 bath bungalow with full view of lake. Includes boat slip. 1/4 acre lot, Bolton Landing. $200,000.
Rustic Realty, Inc.
Glens Falls, New York
Ahmad Mir, Salesperson
(518) 678–9999

Cityscape Properties
Prime Location
East 80s, Fifth Avenue
Gorgeous 3 bedroom condo; 2.5 baths. Full service building. $450K.
Contact Richey Riche, Broker
891–2222

New beginnings
Near schools and shopping. Adorable cape. 2 bedrooms, front porch, AC, screened sunroom. Must see. Yonkers, New York. $150,000
J. C. Meckler, Broker
call and ask for
Byung Lee, Salesperson
(914) 943–4444

Buyer Representation Only
Let us find you the best properties for the lowest price. We negotiate price and terms for you.
Buyer Brokerage Unlimited
Bill Blue, Broker
370–9472

GARDEN APARTMENT
(Duplex), Queens
Co-op in established community. Union Turnpike and Main Street. 2 bedrooms, 2 baths, A/C, hardwood floors.
103–24 Gardenway Road. $120,000
Shelly Duval, Broker
Gardenpark Management
(718) 383–9876

Advertisements should also state the exact name under which a license is issued. Confusion occurs when brokerage firms that are part of large franchises have the same name. Also, individuals in large communities may have a same or similar name. Advertising guidelines may be obtained from DOS. These guidelines also include the correct copy, typesetting, and other details necessary for licensee business cards.

DOS Hearings and Appeals

If DOS receives a complaint or has reason to believe that a licensee may be in violation of the law, it will investigate the allegations and notify the licensee in writing of the charge and the penalty. Licensees may then request a hearing to contest the charges and penalty. If all parties agree, the charge may go to voluntary mediation; if not, a hearing is scheduled. If DOS decides to deny a license application, the applicant will be notified in writing. The applicant may then ask for a hearing within 30 days of receiving denial. Applicants and licensees may bring an attorney to any DOS hearing. Administrative law judges preside over each hearing. DOS has its own attorneys.

An appeal of a decision made by DOS at a hearing may be heard through a proceeding under the NYS Civil Practice Law and Rules (CPLR) called an **Article 78 proceeding.** This proceeding is *the method for appeals against regulatory agencies.*

The *revocation* or *suspension* of a broker's license *suspends the licenses of the salespersons and associate brokers affiliated with the broker.* The suspension is lifted if the salesperson or associate broker affiliates with another broker or when the designated suspension period ends. If a salesperson or broker license is revoked, the licensee loses his license and must wait one year from the date of revocation to be eligible for relicensure.

You Should Know	**Liabilities and penalties for violations of the license law**

Unlawful acts committed by licensees violate Article 12-A and fall under the jurisdiction of DOS. Persons who violate any part of Article 12-A of the Real Property Law are guilty of a **misdemeanor.** *Under the Penal Law in New York, a misdemeanor is punishable by a fine of up to $1,000 and/or imprisonment for up to one year.* **Administrative discipline** *by DOS may include a reprimand to the licensee. DOS may also deny, revoke, or suspend the license of a salesperson or broker for as long as it deems proper,* and impose a fine not to exceed $1,000. Article 12-A empowers all state courts to hear and try, without indictment, anyone who violates the license laws.

New York State Real Estate Board

The new real estate board forming in New York consists of 15 members, including the Secretary of State and the Executive Director of the Consumer Protection Board together with 13 additional appointed members from the real estate brokerage community and the public at large. The board will have the power to promulgate rules and regulations affecting real estate licensees, with certain exceptions.

CASE STUDIES   The following examples of DOS cases brought to administrative hearings illustrate how DOS makes determinations regarding a real estate licensee's duties and responsibilities as an agent. (See "To the Student" at the front of this text, which explains the terms and format of the following DOS administrative hearings.)

Department of State, Division of Licensing Services, Complainant against John Droz, Jr., d/b/a Adirondack Real Escapes, Respondent.

Among other reasons, this complaint was brought about because of the alleged unlawful practice of law by a real estate broker.

Allegations. Respondent Droz allegedly failed to place a deposit in a special account, engaged in the unlawful practice of law by drafting preprinted terms of and addenda to a contract of sale lacking an attorney approval clause, and failed to make clear for which party he was acting in a transaction.

Findings of fact. Respondent was the listing agent for Mr. and Ms. Grygiel in the purchase of an apartment house. A Mr. Wallace made an offer to purchase. Respondent Droz used an offer to purchase form for the transaction, which he had created with the advice of two attorneys, and which he subsequently printed and copyrighted. This form did not have the approval of a bar association or board of REALTORS® and did not contain a provision making it subject to attorney's approval. With Wallace's verbal authorization, Respondent signed Wallace's name to the contract.

At a later date, Wallace decided that he did not wish to go through with the purchase at the stated price of $190,000 as the property had been appraised at $180,000. Respondent then drew up a new contract and addendum. In an addendum to the contract, Respondent agreed to accept a $35,000 second mortgage as his compensation instead of the previously agreed-upon 10 percent commission. The addendum also provided that the purchaser would receive a credit in the amount of the second mortgage against the purchase price and that purchaser Wallace had the option of buying the mortgage back. Respondent did not discuss with the Grygiels how his participation would affect his fiduciary relationship with them.

Opinion. Real estate brokers are permitted to prepare purchase offer contracts subject to very definite limitation. In *Duncan & Hill Realty, Inc. v. Department of State* (cited previously), it was decided that "the personal interest of the broker in the transaction and the fact that he is employed by one of the opposing parties are further reasons to require that . . . the contract entail legal advice and draftsmanship . . . only lawyers be permitted to prepare the document, to ensure the . . . consideration and protection of the rights and interests of the parties. The law forbids anyone to practice law who has not been found duly qualified." In preparing a purchase offer contract, real estate salespersons and brokers may not insert any provision that requires legal expertise. "Legal terms beyond the general description of the subject property, the price and the mortgage to be assumed . . . may readily protect brokers from a charge of unlawful practice of law by inserting in the document that it is subject to the approval of the respective attorneys for the parties. The decision also states that the form should be recommended by a joint committee of the bar association and the local board of REALTORS®. The form in this action was not recommended. Although it was prepared with the assistance of two attorneys, it was fundamentally the Respondent's creation. Respondent also attached contract addenda that he drafted, which included language regarding recording of a mortgage. Such language requires legal expertise.

The evidence in the case, however, establishes that Respondent was clearly acting for the sellers. While the complainant alleges the Respondent failed to disclose the possible conflict of interest inherent in his agreeing to accept a second mortgage from the buyer, that agreement was the result of a suggestion by the seller attorney, who no doubt understood the implication.

Conclusions of law. Respondent with regard to the drafting of the legal document violated Judiciary Law Section 478 and demonstrated incompetency.

Determination. Respondent shall pay a fine of $250 and shall also file an affidavit with the complainant stating that he will no longer make use of any contracts for purchase and sale in violation of legal precedent defined in the *Duncan & Hill* case.

Department of State, Complainant, against Jayson Realty, Leon J. Sloane and Bruce T. Sloane, Respondents.

In this case, among other allegations, charges were brought against the Respondent for failing to deliver duplicate documents.

Allegations. First, Respondents violated NYCRR 175.12 (New York Codified Rules and Regulations) by failing to give a prospective tenant a duplicate original involving a rental. Second, Respondents violated NYCRR 175.7 in failing to make it clear which party for whom they were acting as an agent and in representing both the landlord and prospective tenant, thereby acting as undisclosed dual agents. Third, Respondents extracted a fee from the prospective tenant for the rental of housing while they were acting as the rental agent of the managing agent of the landlord. Fourth, Respondents applied pressure tactics and harassment against the tenant.

Findings of fact. Apartment rentals for the building in question were handled by Respondents. Respondents were the rental agent for the managing agent and subagent of the landlord. Ms. Ramirez signed a Jayson Realty form application for a lease and a credit application form with Respondent. She gave them a rental deposit in the amount of $694.47 and a commission check payable to Respondent Sloane for $1,833.40. Ramirez was not given a copy of these documents at the time of signing. The next day, Ramirez called Respondent and told them that she wanted to withdraw her rental application. Respondent Leon Sloane informed her that she had been accepted by the landlord and was obligated to take the apartment. Ramirez stopped payment on the check. Ten days later, Respondents procured another tenant for the apartment and collected a commission. Respondent Leon Sloane obtained a judgment against Ramirez for $1,548.64, which Ramirez then paid.

Opinion. Respondent prepared and had the prospective tenant execute documents without giving copies to Ramirez. NYCRR 175.12 states that "a real estate broker shall immediately deliver a duplicate original of any instrument to any party or parties executing the same . . . when prepared by a broker or under his supervision . . . to any matter pertaining to the consummation of the lease or purchase, sale or exchange of real property."

Respondents also made an illegal charge in excess of the lawful stabilized rent in that Respondents collected a fee from a tenant for a rent-stabilized apartment as subagents of the landlord. A broker fee for leasing an apartment in a rent-stabilized building in which the broker is the subagent of the owner constitutes an illegal charge in excess of lawful stabilized rent.

The evidence does not establish that Respondents failed to make it clear for which party they were acting or that they acted as undisclosed dual agents, nor does it establish that Respondents committed dishonest and misleading acts.

Conclusions of law. Respondents violated NYCRR 175.12 in failure to deliver duplicate copies and extracted an illegal charge as subagents of the landlord–owner in the rental of a rent-stabilized dwelling.

Determination. Respondents' licenses are suspended for a period of three months. Respondents must pay Ramirez the sum of $1,548.64, including interest accrued from the day she canceled the lease.

memorize

THE REAL ESTATE BROKERAGE BUSINESS

This section deals with antitrust laws, court cases, and the independent contractor relationship between broker and sales associates.

Antitrust Law

Under federal and New York antitrust law, brokerage firms, franchises, real estate boards, and multiple listing services *cannot combine to fix commission rates.*

Elements That Define an Antitrust Violation

In general, antitrust violations include any business activity in which there is *a monopoly, a contract, a conspiracy, or a combination* that negatively impacts an individual's or a company's ability to do business. The negative impact is called restraint of trade. To violate antitrust law, the restraint of trade must unreasonably restrict competition and function against the public interest. For example, if all the broker members of a particular real estate board agreed to charge a commission of not less than 15 percent of the purchase price of a property, they would be violating antitrust law.

A History of Antitrust Laws—Common-Law Era

 *Memorize*

As the United States grew into an industrial power during the nineteenth century, large monopolies formed that controlled business and commerce in various sectors of the economy. By the end of the century, the status of common law, that is, nonstatutory general public policy regulations, was not broad enough to protect the public from the power and control of these monopolies. Sanctions were needed to define, regulate, and control antitrust activity. The Sherman and Clayton Antitrust Acts and the Federal Trade Commission Act (Table 1.4), enacted over a span of 24 years at the turn of the century, provided the necessary legislation and control.

The **Sherman Antitrust Act** was enacted July 2, 1890, to preserve a system of free economic enterprise and *to protect the public against the activities of monopolies, contracts, or other combinations that tend to be an unreasonable restraint of trade.* The focus of the act was to allow small businesses to compete effectively with larger companies. The Sherman Act covers trade and commerce with foreign countries and

TABLE 1.4   Federal antitrust regulations.

REGULATION OR AGENCY	PURPOSE	ENFORCEMENT
Sherman Act (1890)	Protects public from monopolies or combinations that restrain trade	corporate fines up to $10,000,000 individual fines up to $350,000 possible felony up to 3 years in prison
Clayton Act (1914)	Supplements sanctions in Sherman Act	allows for individual or group (class-action) lawsuits for antitrust violations
Federal Trade Commission (1914)	Declares applicable trade procedures unfair	no penal sanctions but can provide monetary relief for victims enforces Sherman Act and indirectly enforces Clayton Act
U.S. Department of Justice	Has antitrust division that enforces the Sherman and Clayton Acts	federal court system

between states (interstate commerce). Congress can exempt public agencies and selected industries from the provisions of the act. An example of an exemption is the baseball industry.

The **Clayton Antitrust Act,** enacted October 15, 1914, supplements the Sherman Act and has the same general purpose. It was designed to cover restraints on interstate trade or commerce not covered by the Sherman Act. The *Clayton Act made it unlawful for any individual engaged in commerce to lease or sell goods or machinery on the condition that the lessee or purchaser would then not deal with the goods or machinery of another competitor of the lessor or seller.* If this was allowed, it would decrease competition in the marketplace and create monopolies.

The **Federal Trade Commission (FTC)** was formed through an act of Congress in 1914. *The FTC is an administrative body and has the broad power to declare trade practices unfair, particularly with regard to practices that conflict with basic policies of antitrust legislation.* The FTC has the authority to enforce compliance with the Sherman Act and certain sections of the Clayton Act.

In creating antitrust legislation, Congress did not intend that the statutes themselves would decrease the practice of unfair methods of competition and the tendency to monopolize. Ultimately, it would be up to the FTC and, more importantly, the courts, to resolve these questions.

Legislative Action

Over the years, congressional regulatory power has been expanded to include *intrastate* (within a state) trade and commerce as well as interstate. Most states, including New York, have statutes against monopoly, restraint of trade, and unfair trade practices, as well as other laws that protect the consumer. Although more private antitrust lawsuits have been filed in recent years, Congress and the courts are still deciding whether an individual has legal standing to sue under antitrust law. State enforcement is generally considered synonymous with federal law. It focuses on local and intrastate offenses. If antitrust activities occur on the state or local levels, violators may be subject to both federal and state laws.

You Should Know | **Antitrust liability under the law**

The Antitrust Division of the Department of Justice enforces the Sherman and Clayton Antitrust Acts. Violators of the Sherman Act can be subject to both criminal liability and monetary damages. A 1990 amendment to the Sherman Act provides that corporations can be fined up to $10 million and individuals up to $350,000. Violators of the Sherman Act can be found guilty of a felony and can be imprisoned for a term of up to three years. The Department of Justice can also impose other fines for antitrust violations.

The FTC has no penal sanctions; it has the power to enforce only the Sherman Act and to enforce the Clayton Act indirectly. The commission may stop practices that violate antitrust laws and can act as a court of equity and apply monetary relief for violations. A court of equity decides matters of law and makes judgments based on these laws.

Section 4 of the Clayton Act allows private parties, either individually or as a group (class-action lawsuit), *to sue antitrust violators.* Injured parties can recover three times the damages sustained plus court costs and attorney's fees. Proving damages in antitrust lawsuits is difficult. Specific or certain proof of the injury is not required; however, the lawsuit must include facts that go beyond speculation. Even if individuals are damaged, they may not have the legal standing to sue unless it can be proved that they were directly injured by the actions.

RULE OF REASON VERSUS PER SE ILLEGALITY

In antitrust lawsuits, the courts have to determine *if the restraints of trade are unreasonable and therefore illegal.* If the activity *is* reasonable, then it is allowable under law; this is called the *Rule of Reason.* Certain kinds of restraints of trade, however, were so inconsistent with free competition that they were found to be per se illegal, that is, absolutely not allowable under the law. Under the Rule of Reason, the following considerations apply:

1. Was the act a reasonable restraint with a compelling rationale?
2. What are the surrounding circumstances that led to the presumption of restraint of trade?
3. What is the nature or character of the contracts involved in the restraint of trade?

A restraint of trade is per se illegal if it is arbitrary in application and is potentially harmful to free competition. Per se illegal restraints of trade include price-fixing agreements between competitors, group boycotts, market allocation agreements between manufacturers and distributors, and tie-in arrangements between sellers and buyers.

Price Fixing

Illegal **price fixing** occurs *when competitors in a group or an industry conspire to charge the same or similar price for services rendered.* Price fixing can be engaged in by competitors at the same level, such as retailers, or by members of different levels of production, such as manufacturer and retailer. Price fixing decreases competition between businesses, when for example, all brokerage firms in a community agree to charge a six percent commission.

Group Boycott

A **group boycott** is *a conspiracy wherein a person or group is persuaded or coerced into not doing business with another person or group.* An example of a group boycott might be if an MLS directs that all broker members do not do business with a certain real estate related company.

Market Allocation Agreement

A **market allocation agreement** is *an agreement between competitors who are dividing or assigning a certain area or territory for sales.* For example, two large business franchises agree that one will sell goods or services in Albany County only and the other will sell in Schenectady County only. They agree not to compete with each other in the same county.

Tie-in Arrangements

Tie-in arrangements are *agreements between a party selling a product or service with a buyer that, as a condition of the sale, the buyer will buy another product from the seller or the buyer will not buy a product or use a service of another.* If a buyer brokerage firm, for example, tells a buyer that the buyer must use a certain mortgage company as a condition of the Exclusive Buyer/Purchaser Agency Agreement, this would be illegal.

ANTITRUST LAWS AND THE REAL ESTATE BROKERAGE INDUSTRY

The increase in antitrust lawsuits has included those filed in the real estate industry. The federal and New York cases discussed below have defined the legal standard of conduct for real estate brokers.

United States v. National Association of Real Estate Boards (339 U.S. 485, 1950).
This case was initially an action brought by the U.S. government against the Washington, D.C., Real Estate Board. They were accused of fixing the commission rate for services rendered by association members. The National Association of Real Estate Boards joined in defense of the lawsuit. The board was accused of violating the Sherman Antitrust Act, and the case was brought before the United States Supreme Court. The issues to be decided in the case were:

1. Was the jurisdiction of the Sherman Act limited to interstate and not intrastate commerce?
2. Under the Sherman Antitrust Act, did the word "trade" encompass the real estate profession?
3. Did the suggesting or fixing of commission rates constitute per se illegal price fixing?

The Supreme Court found that the Sherman Act could be applied to local conduct within a state as well as to interstate antitrust violations.

The Court also found that the concept of "trade" as used in the phrase "restraint of trade" encompassed the real estate brokerage business. The finding stated that "trade" referred to occupation, employment, or business conducted for the purpose of profit or gain. The fact that no goods are sold, manufactured, or bought is irrelevant. The real estate brokerage sells services rather than commodities; antitrust law applies nevertheless.

Price fixing was condemned in the sale of services as well as goods and was deemed per se illegal. Schedules of fixed or mandatory real estate commission or fees established by real estate boards violate the Sherman Antitrust Act.

Parens Patriae Lawsuits

Parens patriae lawsuits are permitted under the Hart-Scott-Rodino Antitrust Improvement Act of 1976 (15 U.S.C.A. Sections 15c–h). Literally translated, the Latin phrase *parens patriae* means "parent of the country." The legal definition of the term refers to the right of government to litigate and therefore protect in the name of the public good. The doctrine of parens patriae can be applied to different types of lawsuits, such as when the state wishes to protect the property of a minor or of incompetent persons. The doctrine has also been used by states to litigate antitrust claims. It provides a class-action means by which a state attorney general can recover for monetary damages suffered by individuals residing in the state.

Antitrust Crisis of the 1970s

In the early 1970s, Assistant U.S. Attorney General for Antitrust Richard W. McLaren decided to investigate professional service providers and their industries to discover whether they were violating antitrust laws. The occupations that he investigated included architects, accountants, and real estate brokers.

United States v. Prince George's County Board of REALTORS®, Inc. (Maryland) 1970 WL 546 (D.C. MD.). As a result of Assistant Attorney General McLaren's investigation, a number of lawsuits were decided that affected the real estate industry. One of them was the *United States v. Prince George's County Board of REALTORS®, Inc.* This lawsuit involved a *consent decree* by the county board of REALTORS® to stop the following activities: price-fixing commission rates, suggesting commission rates, punishing members for violating suggestions, publishing schedules of commission rates, and boycotting members who did not follow suggestions. The court found that all of these activities violated antitrust law.

A *consent decree* (called nolo contendere in criminal cases) is used by the government in civil cases. The consent decree is a compromise in which the accused party agrees to stop the alleged illegal activity without admitting guilt or wrongdoing. This action must be approved by the court. A court-ordered injunction is issued to the accused party and the government action is then dropped. An injunction may include the directive that if the illegal activity continues, fines will be levied.

United States v. Long Island Board of REALTORS®, Inc. (1972 WL 584 E.D.N.Y.). → Read
The court-ordered sanctions in this case were the same as in the Prince George case. The importance of this lawsuit is that it took place in New York and therefore set legal precedent there. The parties to the actions agreed to a consent decree that precluded the Long Island board from engaging in:

1. fixing the rate or amount of a commission
2. urging or recommending board members to adhere to any prescribed schedules of commission rates or publishing prescribed commission rates or amounts
3. including a suggested commission rate or amount in an educational course
4. limiting the right of a board member to negotiate and agree to a commission with a client
5. taking any punitive action against a person for not adhering to a rate or schedule of commission
6. fixing, suggesting, or enforcing a recommended percentage division of commissions between selling and listing brokers
7. adopting any rules that would prohibit a member from doing business with another
8. conducting or publishing any survey relating to prevailing commission rates or amounts when the purpose or effect is to establish or maintain a certain rate or amount of commission
9. establishing fees for membership in the board or MLS that are not related to the cost of maintaining or improving the organization
10. refusing to accept for multiple listing any listing because of the rate or amount of commission set forth in the listing

United States v. Foley (598 F.2d 1323 4th Cir. 1979). In this case, six corporations and three individuals were convicted of a felony by a federal district court for conspiracy to fix real estate commissions. The parties to the lawsuit were real estate brokers who set a fixed commission rate among themselves and then divided the commission among all the firms in a shared commission arrangement.

The issue raised in this lawsuit was the question of whether intrastate antitrust activities *have an impact on interstate commerce*. It was found that illegal antitrust activities, even though carried on intrastate, can directly impact interstate commerce. Therefore, the activities in Foley were in violation of the Sherman and Clayton Acts.

Other Antitrust Lawsuits

As antitrust lawsuits are heard in court, legal precedent is created. The courts decided in 1980 that the fixing of real estate commissions may affect the demand for interstate financing and title insurance and therefore have interstate effects. (See *McLain v. Real Estate Board of New Orleans, Inc.* 444 U.S. 232 [1980].) The courts have also found that charging net commissions and sharing commissions with brokers who provided no services in the sale and listing of the property or with nonlicensed companies are also violations of antitrust law.

Under antitrust law, not only can offenders be fined but the fixing of real estate commissions can also be a criminal act. By the end of the 1970s, the courts were imposing a record level of jail terms for violations. The antitrust division of the Department of Justice acts as an advocate for competition. Vigorous prosecution and criminal sanctions as well as large fines for violations continue to date.

United States v. Realty Multilist, Inc. (U.S.D.C. 1982). In this lawsuit, decided in federal district court, the government brought an antitrust action against multiple listing service requirements, which stated that members must have a favorable credit rating and business reputation, maintain an active real estate office during customary business hours, and pay a $1,000 fee for a share of stock in the MLS. The purpose of the Multilist organization was to provide a multiple listing service for its members, help increase sales, apply lock boxes containing door keys to listed properties, and keep members aware of new occurrences in the real estate market. The rules of Multilist, however, prohibited nonmember access to listing books, did not allow a direct response to nonmembers' inquiries regarding listed property, and did not disclose information regarding listed properties to nonmembers.

The federal government filed a lawsuit claiming that the members of Multilist had conspired together to restrain interstate commerce. The court found that the requirement to have a good credit rating and business reputation, have the office open during customary business hours, and purchase shares of stock were not *per se unreasonable* but could be found to be unreasonable. The court also found that when a broker is excluded from a multiple listing service without reasonable justification, the broker and the public are harmed. The court held:

1. The multiple listing service is prohibited from refusing access to MLS to any licensed broker who complies with MLS requirements that are reasonable and nondiscriminatory.
2. MLS charges are to be equal to the cost of setting up the participant in the MLS.
3. The cost of operations are to reflect the pro rata share of operating expenses, including accumulation and maintenance of reasonable reserves.
4. MLS must establish reasonable and nondiscriminatory per listing fees.
5. Part-time brokers can be admitted to MLS.
6. MLS cannot regulate office hours.
7. MLS cannot prohibit membership in any other multiple listing service.
8. MLS cannot apply restrictions as to advertising types of property.
9. MLS is prohibited from restricting participants' cooperation with a nonmember.

Thompson v. DeKalb County Board of REALTORS® (934 F.2D 1566). This case deals with the admission of nonREALTORS® to REALTOR® multiple listing services. This 1991 Georgia lawsuit was decided in the eleventh Circuit Court of Appeals, which has jurisdiction over the states of Florida, Georgia, and Alabama. The case concerned a board of REALTORS® that insisted a real estate broker must be a member of a *real estate association branch* to obtain access to MLS. Members of local REALTOR® association branches hold the title of REALTOR® or REALTOR®–Associate, which stems from the branch association's connection to the National Association of REALTORS®. The court ruled that this requirement is an illegal group boycott because the MLS had sufficient marketing power to affect the ability of nonREALTORS® to conduct business and, therefore, restrain their trade.

Real Estate and Antitrust Law

The real estate brokerage industry in New York must adhere to both the Sherman and Clayton antitrust laws, New York law, and court decisions based on those laws. The lawsuits discussed in this chapter outline most of what is *not permissible* under antitrust law. The court decree in *United States v. Long Island Board of REALTORS®, Inc.,* furnishes guidelines for proper conduct within the real estate industry:

1. Commission rates must be negotiable between board members and their clients.
2. MLS may circulate information concerning the commission that a broker has agreed upon with a client. MLS may also give out information as to the percentage division that a listing broker has agreed to pay a selling broker.
3. The commission rate can be altered only with the consent of both the listing and selling broker.
4. The recipient of the commission must pay the listing or selling broker the agreed-upon percentage division of the commission.

INDEPENDENT CONTRACTOR VERSUS EMPLOYEE

It is sometimes difficult to classify whether a worker is an independent contractor or an employee. From the standpoint of the Internal Revenue Service (IRS) and New York law, the most important aspect of an independent contractor relationship is a worker situation in which the employer does not have the right to control the details of a worker's performance. Other issues that are considered when determining independent contractor status are whether the worker (a) receives any instructions or training from his employer, (b) has work hours set by his employer, (c) is required to do the work at a specific location, (d) is paid by the job, (e) is required to do the work in a set order, (f) must pay his own expenses, and (g) must have his own tools.

The issue of whether a worker is an independent contractor or an employee affects how the worker is paid. If the worker is classified as an employee, then the worker's employer(s) must withhold federal, state, and social security taxes (FICA). The employer also must pay federal unemployment (FUTA) and state unemployment taxes, prepare quarterly reports (941) and annual reports (W-2, W-3, and Form 940), and make required deposits of income taxes withheld and FICA taxes. The employer also must pay workers' compensation and disability insurance.

However, if a worker is classified as an independent contractor, none of these taxes or deposits must be made, and no money is withheld from the worker's paycheck. If the worker earns more than $600, the employer must file only a Form 1099 misc. with the IRS to report the worker's earnings for the year. The worker must also pay self-employment taxes. In addition, a worker classified as an employee may receive other benefits that an independent contractor does not, such as pension plans, paid vacation and sick days, and health care premiums.

Case Law, IRS, and New York

The classification of an employee versus an independent contractor has evolved through a combination of what is in the IRS code (federal law); New York, which generally follows the guidelines set forth by IRS; and case law, in which statutory law is interpreted through lawsuits and legal precedent is set through the courts.

For federal employment tax purposes, four categories of workers exist:

1. **Independent contractor.** This is *a worker who does not work under the direct supervision of his employer and holds nonemployee status under the law.*
2. *Common-law employee.* The trade or profession of this worker has generally been accepted as holding employee status.
3. *A statutory employee.* The work, trade, or profession of this worker is written into legal statutes as holding employee status.

4. *A statutory nonemployee.* The trade or profession of this worker is written into legal statutes as holding *nonemployee* status. *Workers who hold nonemployee status under the law are classified as independent contractors.*

Internal Revenue Code Section 3508 (a)(b)

According to the IRS code, real estate agents are statutory nonemployees and are therefore independent contractors. To be qualified under this category, the real estate agent must be licensed, and all monies received for services rendered must be related to sales or other output, not to the number of hours worked. The code also states that *there must be a written contract between the broker and the sales associate and the contract must state that the licensee will not be "treated as an employee for federal tax purposes."*

1986 New York Independent Contractor Laws

In 1986 additions to the New York labor law and workers' compensation law further defined the role of the salesperson in the independent contractor relationship. In addition to the definition outlined above in the IRS code, the 1986 law requires that the contract between broker and sales associate not be executed under duress. Note that both federal and state law require a written contract between broker and sales associate. The salesperson and his broker must review the independent contractor agreement once every 12–15 months. This is to ensure that the activities of the salesperson fall within the parameters of independent contractor guidelines. Figure 1.7 illustrates an independent contractor agreement.

You Should Know   **The salesperson–broker independent contractor relationship**

1. Commissions are paid without deductions for taxes and are directly related to output.
2. There is no remuneration for the number of hours worked.
3. Salespersons are permitted to work any hours they choose.
4. Salespersons can work from home or a broker's office.
5. Salespersons are free to engage in outside employment.
6. Brokers can provide office facilities and supplies, but salespersons are responsible for expenses.
7. The broker supervises but does not direct and control the activity of the salesperson.
8. Either party may terminate the relationship at any time.

Consequences of Noncompliance

Classification of a worker as an independent contractor rather than an employee can save the employer a large sum of money that would otherwise go toward employment taxes. Thus an employer can incur tax penalties if a worker is incorrectly classified as an independent contractor. Salespersons who are deemed independent contractors must work in compliance with the rules stated above. If the broker-sales associate relationship becomes one of employer-employee, then the broker must pay all federal and state taxes and insurance premiums, as discussed earlier.

If the sales associates are not deemed independent contractors, they will not be able to file Schedule C of the federal income tax Form 1040 or deduct the expenses incurred during the year. The lump-sum compensation received during the year would also be subject to withholding taxes.

important information / Review every 12 to 15 months

FIGURE 1.7

An independent contractor relationship agreement form.

INDEPENDENT CONTRACTOR RELATIONSHIP AGREEMENT

THIS AGREEMENT, (hereinafter "Agreement") made and entered into this _____ day of _____, 200___, by and between _____ (hereinafter "Salesperson") and _____ (hereinafter "Broker").

WHEREAS, the Salesperson and the Broker are both duly licensed pursuant to Article 12-A of the Real Property Law of the State of New York; and

WHEREAS, the Salesperson and Broker wish to enter into this Agreement in order to define their respective rights, duties and obligations.

NOW THEREFORE, in consideration of the terms, covenants, conditions and mutual promises contained herein, and other good and valuable consideration, it is hereby stipulated and agreed as follows:

1. The Salesperson is engaged as an independent contractor associated with the Broker pursuant to Article 12-A of the Real Property Law and shall be treated as such for all purposes, including but not limited to Federal and State taxation, withholding, unemployment insurance and workers' compensation; and

2. The Salesperson (a) shall be paid a commission on his or her gross sales, if any, without deduction for taxes, which commission shall be directly related to sales or other output; (b) shall not receive any renumeration related to the number of hours worked; and (c) shall not be treated as an employee with respect to such services for Federal and State tax purposes; and

3. The Salesperson shall be permitted to work any hours he or she chooses; and

4. The Salesperson shall be permitted to work out of his or her home or the office of the Broker; and

5. The Salesperson shall be free to engage in outside employment; and

6. The Broker may provide office facilities and supplies for the use of the Salesperson, but the Salesperson shall otherwise bear his or her own expenses, including but not limited to automobile, travel and entertainment expenses; and

7. The Broker and Salesperson shall comply with the requirements of Article 12-A of the Real Property Law and the regulations pertaining hereto, but such compliance shall not affect the Salesperson's status as an independent contractor nor should it be construed as an indication that the Salesperson is an employee of the Broker for any purpose whatsoever; and

8. This contract and the association created hereby may be terminated by either party hereto at any time upon notice give to the other; and

9. This Agreement is deemed to have been entered into in, and will be construed and interpreted in accordance with the laws of the State of New York; and

10. BY SIGNING BELOW THE UNDERSIGNED STIPULATE AND AGREE THAT THEY HAVE COMPLETELY READ THIS AGREEMENT, THAT THE TERMS HEREOF ARE FULLY UNDERSTOOD AND VOLUNTARILY ACCEPTED BY THEM AND THAT THIS AGREEMENT IS NOT SIGNED UNDER DURESS.

IN WITNESS WHEREOF, the parties hereto have executed this Agreement as of the day and year first above written.

_____
SALESPERSON

_____
BROKER

Review of Recommended Forms

Sales associates should track earnings and expenses and should file yearly federal and state tax returns. The broker must prepare and file IRS Form 1099 misc. for all sales associates who earn $600 or more. The sales associate should receive a copy of Form 1099 misc., which reports the total of earnings for the year. A copy of this form must be filed with the IRS. To protect the independent contractor relationship, all brokers and sales associates should enter into an independent contractor agreement.

Supervision of Salespersons by Broker

DOS Regulation 175.21, based on subdivision 1(d) of Section 441 of the Real Property Law, states that the supervision of a salesperson by a broker "shall consist of regular, frequent, and consistent guidance, instruction, oversight and superintendence." Although no legal duty exists to supervise an independent contractor, it is nevertheless required by New York license law and regulations. Moreover, even though entering into an independent contractor agreement fulfills one of the legal requirements to maintain independent contractor status, license law maintains that the broker must still supervise a salesperson's activities.

Records of Transactions to Be Maintained

DOS Regulation 175.23 states that "each licensed broker shall keep and maintain for a period of three years records of each transaction effected through his office concerning the sale or mortgage of one- to four-family dwellings." In addition to keeping records of the parties to the transaction and other items, the broker must maintain records showing the amount of commission or gross profit realized through the transaction as well as the *net profit* or *commission "and the disposition of all payments."* These payments include commissions or fees paid to salespersons. Again, this regulation may imply activities such as recording and tracking earnings, which are considered employer-employee activities. However, in abiding by license law and regulations, this activity must still be a part of the salesperson-broker relationship.

Implications for the Future—Will Licensees Become Employees?

Many considerations are involved in evaluating the employee versus the independent contractor relationship and the different interests involved. For the licensee, although the employer saves money in an independent contractor relationship, the licensee bears some of the burden because she must pay a social security self-employment tax to make up for the FICA (social security taxes) not withheld from her pay. The licensee also gives up (in most cases) other benefits of an employee relationship, such as pensions, sick pay, and so on.

The broker, within the context of the independent contractor relationship, still has a duty to supervise and can be held accountable by New York law and regulations for the activity of sales associates.

As previously discussed, the IRS code allows independent contractor status for sales associates despite the fact that boundaries have crossed into an employer-employee relationship. It is possible, therefore, that the status quo will be maintained in the future unless the statutory legal definition of the independent contractor–real estate associate is changed by federal law or regulation.

MULTIPLE LISTING SERVICES

In most counties in New York, a multiple listing service (MLS) operates to offer a pooling of listings from a number of real estate firms for member brokers and their agents. MLS members are authorized to show any of the properties in the pool, an arrangement that greatly expands the offerings available to prospective buyers and the marketing of their own listings. Pooling listings is an offer of cooperation and compensation that benefits all MLS members.

Membership in MLS is not a requirement of licensure. A broker may choose to access this service or not. MLS members fill out a data sheet on the subject property which is reprinted in MLS books together with a picture of the property. Expired, withdrawn, pending, and sold listing information is also available.

Advantages

Multiple listing services offer a greater exposure for a listed property, which could allow for a faster sale and generally a better price due to the wider market range. Most MLS organizations are now computerized and therefore all information about the listed property, including updates, can be accessed online by member brokers and their sales agents. This computerized method also facilitates the creation of the comparative market analysis. The broker need only key in certain relevant information and the computer does the search of comparable properties within the service.

Generally, MLS listings allow the listing broker to compensate buyer brokers. Therefore, if the buyer broker is a member of the MLS, she does not have to be a sub-agent (of the seller and listing broker) but can still be reimbursed through the commission paid by the seller.

Disadvantages

MLS charges a fee for its services and every broker or agent who accesses the service must pay it. The MLS cannot charge fees above that which enables it to operate. However, the individual broker must be able to justify this expense by the volume of business incurred. In New York, brokers must generally pay a fee that covers both Board of REALTOR® membership together with MLS membership. In some areas of the country (but not in New York; see *Thompson v. DeKalb County Board of REAL-TORS®*, discussed earlier in this chapter), the courts have challenged the MLS requirement that allows only real estate board members to become members of MLS.

One of the most obvious disadvantages of MLS is that a listing sold through a broker from another firm and the resulting commission split reduces the commission dollars for the listing broker and his sales agents. (See Chapter 2 for a discussion of compensation.)

INTERACTION WITH OTHER BROKERAGE FIRMS
Sharing Commissions

Salespersons may not accept any compensation except from their sponsoring broker. Brokers may share compensation only with salespersons employed by them or with other New York brokers and brokers from another state. Brokers may, however, share compensation with individuals described previously who are exempt from the license law; for example, attorneys.

An unlicensed person, co-partnership, or corporation cannot bring about a lawsuit to collect compensation for real estate services rendered because only a licensed real estate broker or salesperson is entitled to a judgment by the courts. *If brokers improperly pay any part of a compensation to anyone who is not licensed or who is not exempt from the license law, then they are in violation of the license law.* This payment is called a **kickback**. An example of a kickback might be a situation in which a broker pays an unlicensed person for procuring a listing.

Relocation Companies and Referral Fees

Referral fees involve receiving compensation for services rendered to another party in the transaction. Brokerage firms often pay a referral fee to licensees from other localities when the licensee refers prospective buyers or sellers. In New York, however, such fees may be payable to the broker only with the informed consent of the party being referred. Referral fees are then distributed to the licensee who originated the referral in accordance with the in-house policy of commission split. Certain franchises offer a referral fee for relocation. Some real estate firms seek referral through offerings made through the directory published by the National Association of REALTORS® or the New York State Association of REALTORS®.

Mortgage brokers, especially those affiliated with the firm originating the referral, must sign a disclosure to dual agency and acknowledgment of prospective buyer and seller.

Licensure of Nonresident Licensees and Reciprocity

In order to be licensed in New York, salespersons and brokers who live in other states (nonresidents) must take the New York exam and work in or maintain an office in New York. Under reciprocity regulations, however, nonresident licensees who live in states that do *not* require New York salespersons and brokers to have an office in their state or pass their exam do not have to do so in New York. This arrangement is called **reciprocity.** New York has reciprocal licensure arrangements with seven other states. For a list of the states with which New York has reciprocity arrangements, see Table 1.5. The states listed allow licensees from New York to obtain a nonresident license, and New York allows residents from these states to obtain licensure here in New York.

All nonresident applicants must adhere to and complete the following guidelines:

1. Maintain a current (dated within six months) certification from the real estate authority where they obtained their license.
2. Submit a New York application with the appropriate fees.
3. Submit a signed **uniform irrevocable consent and designation form.** *This form gives the New York courts jurisdiction over unlawful actions of applicants who conduct business in New York and allows the courts to serve a summons or other legal documents on the New York secretary of state in place of personal service on the applicant.*

TABLE 1.5 New York reciprocity with other states.		
	Arkansas	Broker only—two years licensure and current. (Business and Residence must be in Arkansas.)
	Connecticut	Broker and Sales—current licensure only. (Business and Residence must be in Connecticut.)
	Georgia	Broker and Sales—current licensure only (business and residence must be in Georgia). Must have obtained their license by passing Georgia exam.
	Massachusetts	Broker only—two years licensure and current. (Business and Residence must be in Massachusetts.)
	Nebraska	Broker and Sales—two years licensure and current. (Business and Residence must be in Nebraska.)
	Oklahoma	Broker and Sales—two years licensure and current. (Business and Residence must be in Oklahoma.)
	West Virginia	Broker and Sales—current licensure. (Business and Residence must be in West Virginia.)

Source: New York Department of State.

4. Applicants seeking a reciprocal salesperson's license must be sponsored by their home-state broker who must hold a current New York State broker's license.

5. Applicants seeking a corporate real estate broker license must file the corporation with the New York DOS, Division of Corporations, as a foreign corporation. (See address earlier in this chapter.)

6. Broker applicants from nonreciprocal states must also submit Supplement B of the New York broker application, two character witness statements, a New York resident's reference, licensing requirements from the state where the broker is licensed, and real estate course transcripts.

IMPORTANT POINTS

1. License laws are an exercise of the police power of New York. Much of license law pertaining to salespersons and brokers is contained in Article 12-A of the Real Property Law.

2. A real estate broker is a person or an organization who, for compensation of any kind, performs or offers to perform aspects of real estate transactions for others.

3. Real estate salespersons perform acts that a broker is authorized to perform, but salespersons do so on behalf of a broker with whom they are associated.

4. Associate real estate brokers must fulfill the same requirements as a broker, but their status in the firm is equivalent to that of a salesperson.

5. Other licenses related to real estate including mortgage bankers and mortgage brokers, apartment information vendors and sharing agents, and licensed and certified appraisers. Individuals engaged in the initial offering of condominiums or the initial offering and resale of cooperatives must register with the New York attorney general.

6. Attorneys do not have to be licensed to engage in real estate brokerage unless they employ licensees to work under their supervision.

7. The term of licensure for both real estate salespersons and brokers is two years. All salespeople must successfully complete the 45-hour licensing course. Brokers must complete 90 hours of qualifying education.

8. Real estate salespersons and associate brokers may not be officers of real estate brokerage corporations, hold voting stock in the company, or be a partner in the company.

9. Brokers have a responsibility to comply with sign requirements and change in status notices, change of address notices, and termination notices, which must be filed with DOS, along with a fee.

10. Violations of license law include net listing arrangements, kickbacks, and commingling of funds.

11. DOS has specific guidelines for real estate advertising by brokers and also for the employment and duties of unlicensed real estate assistants.

12. DOS has the power to deny, revoke, fine, or suspend a license.

13. Violation of the license law is a misdemeanor and is punishable by a $1,000 fine and/or a maximum sentence of one year in jail.

14. The revocation or suspension of a broker real estate license also suspends the license of the salespersons and associate brokers in the broker's employ.

15. Antitrust violations are any business activities in which a monopoly, contract, or conspiracy negatively impacts an individual's or a company's ability to do business. The negative impact is called restraint of trade.

16. Antitrust laws are important to the real estate profession because it is unlawful for brokerage firms, real estate boards, franchises, and MLS services to conspire to fix commission rates.

17. The Sherman (1890) and Clayton (1914) antitrust acts and the Federal Trade Commission (1914) established legislation to control and regulate antitrust activity.

18. The antitrust division of the Department of Justice enforces the Sherman and Clayton Acts. Violators are subject to criminal liability and monetary damages.

19. Antitrust laws prohibit price fixing, group boycotts, market allocation agreements, and tie-in arrangements.

20. A series of lawsuits, heard in federal district courts, in both New York and out of state, set forth activities that are prohibited under antitrust law and defined those activities that are allowable under the law.

21. Real estate salespersons and brokers are classified under the IRS code as independent contractors. The salesperson and his broker must review the independent contractor agreement once every 12–15 months.

22. Although there is a fee for services and the possibility of less commission, multiple listing services generally offer a greater exposure for listed property, perhaps rendering a faster sale and a better price.

23. New York has reciprocal arrangements with seven other states for the licensure of nonresident licensees.

CHAPTER REVIEW   How Would You Respond?

Analyze the following situations and decide how the individuals would handle them in accordance with license law and regulations. Check your responses using the Answer Key at the end of the chapter.

1. Dmitrios, a salesperson, has sold a $750,000 waterfront home in Lake George, New York, listed with his firm, Vacation Properties, Inc. Not only will he receive a commission from his broker, but the sellers, Mr. and Ms. Richards, had promised him a bonus of $5,000 to sell the property within three months (which he did). Dmitrios has promised his girlfriend, Tessie, that he will give her $1,500 upon the sale of the home, because she referred the Richardses to him. Should Dmitrios engage in these activities? Is he violating the license law?

_____

_____

_____

_____

2. Juan is a Staten Island, New York, real estate broker who represents Triad Corp., a company that needs 10,000 square feet of office space and wants to pay about $14 per square foot for a five-year lease. Juan has a broker colleague, Steve, who has a listing for 10,000 square feet. Steve tells Juan that his client wants to receive $650,000 for the whole deal; their commission would be the amount over and above the negotiated lease obligation. Can Juan accept this type of commission arrangement? Explain.

_____

_____

_____

_____

KEY TERM REVIEW

Fill in the term that best completes the sentence and then check the Answer Key at the end of the chapter.

1. Most of the law pertaining to salespersons and brokers is contained in _____ _____ of the Real Property Law.

2. A(n) _____ is licensed by the Department of State to bring together individuals who wish to share apartment space.

3. A person who is licensed by the New York Banking Department to make residential mortgage loans is a(n) _____. A person who is registered by the New York Banking Department to negotiate and solicit residential loans is a(n) _____.

4. In holding money for others, brokers may not _____ deposit funds for real estate transactions with their personal or other business operating accounts.

5. If a seller authorizes a broker to procure a set amount for a property and keep all funds above that amount, the broker has entered into an illegal _____ arrangement.

6. Ads for real property placed by a real estate broker that do not indicate that the person advertising the property is a broker are known as _____.

7. A legal procedure for appeal of a determination of a Department of State hearing is called (a)n _____.

8. Aviva Green is the sole proprietor of a real estate brokerage firm which does business under the name of AGB Realty. AGB is the _____ for Aviva's firm.

9. When competitors in a group or industry conspire to charge the same or similar price for services rendered, illegal _____ has occurred.

MULTIPLE CHOICE

Circle the letter that best answers the question and then check the Answer Key at the end of the chapter.

1. Which of the following does NOT require real estate licensure?
   A. listing real property for sale for other people
   B. auctioning real property for others
   C. arranging placement of real estate ads in the local newspaper
   D. renting apartments for a number of different owners

2. Eugene is an attorney who, in his role as a broker, sold a subdivision that a client had listed with him. Which of the following is not allowable under the law?
   A. collecting a commission
   B. representing his client as his attorney in the transaction
   C. appearing at the closing
   D. advising his client of flooding problems that he is aware of in connection with the subdivision

3. Kim has decided to put her condominium up for sale. She contacts her friend Kendra, who is a real estate salesperson, to take the listing. Which of the following is true?

    A. Kendra needs to register with the attorney general's office to sell the condo

    B. only Kendra's broker needs to register with the attorney general's office

    C. condominiums can be sold only by owners

    D. the resale of condominiums can be handled by real estate salespersons and brokers

4. Which of the following statements about broker licensure is FALSE?

    A. a broker license may be issued in the name of a partnership

    B. an associate broker may hold shares in a real estate brokerage corporation

    C. a broker license may be issued as a sole proprietorship

    D. DOS must approve the name of trade, partnership, and corporate brokerage firms prior to licensure

5. The ultimate responsibility of notifying DOS about a change of address of a branch office is up to the:

    A. principal broker of the firm, who must make the notification within five days of moving

    B. principal brokers, who can wait until the time of their license renewal to notify DOS

    C. manager of the branch office

    D. salespersons working in that branch

6. When licensees terminate an association with their broker:

    A. the broker need not do anything except bid a final farewell

    B. the licensee who leaves the firm must file a termination of association form with DOS

    C. the broker must file a termination of association form with DOS and return the license to the licensee

    D. the licensee must ask the new broker she associates with to file a termination of association form for her

7. Applebee Real Estate Brokers, Inc. wishes to relocate in a large residential house on a main road. Because of town zoning ordinances, the company may not place a sign outside of the house identifying the business. Applebee brokerage:

    A. must look for a different location

    B. need not worry about a sign because their location will spread through word of mouth

    C. may open up as long as the zoning ordinance allows a business in the house

    D. may open up and inform clients and customers when they come into the office as to the nature of the business

8. Carole is principal broker of Go-Your-Own-Way Realty. She decides she needs a vacation and leaves her company in the hands of two salespersons for three months. While she is gone, one of her deals falls through, but she cannot return the deposit as one of the salespeople inadvertently commingled the deposit with the office operating account and spent the money. Carole is:

    A. probably guilty for failure to supervise, but is not responsible for the deposit money

    B. not at all responsible for any of these activities as she wasn't there

    C. only accountable to the Department of State and not to the prospective purchasers who placed the deposit with her company

    D. vicariously liable for the activities of her salespeople in violation of license law, rules, and regulations and is guilty of failure to supervise

9. Noreen, a real estate broker, is about to close a deal on the rental of an apartment in a building that she manages. The deal takes place at the home of the prospective tenant. Noreen has forgotten the preprinted lease agreement, so she hastily draws one up from memory so as not to lose the deal. She has the tenant sign the lease and tells him that he can sign the preprinted one tomorrow and she will throw away this one. Which of the following is correct?

    A. Noreen's quick thinking saved the deal and there is nothing wrong with her actions

    B. Noreen has engaged in the unauthorized practice of law and is in violation of license law

    C. Noreen's actions are not exactly appropriate, but she will not be held responsible as she intends to replace the lease the next day

    D. the tenant is at fault for signing the lease, which in turn absolves Noreen of all liability for her actions

10. The Whitefaces are willing to give Jennie the listing on their house, but they do not want to sell to a family with children. They claim that noisy children will ruin the nice, quiet neighborhood. Jennie:

    A. can accept the listing if it is in a nonsolicitation area

    B. can accept the listing without any reservation

    C. cannot accept the listing as it is in violation of federal and state fair housing and human rights laws

    D. can apply for special permission to accept the listing to her board of REALTORS®

11. Mattie, a real estate salesperson, placed an ad that read, "Luxury home in beautiful mountain area of upstate New York." There were no more specifics as to geographic location. On the basis of this geographic description only, the ad is:

    A. perfectly fine

    B. unacceptable as it does not include the name of the specific geographic area

    C. allowable for rural areas only and not populated cities

    D. allowable for in-house advertisements but not for newspaper advertising

12. The revocation or suspension of a broker license:

    A. suspends the licenses of the salespersons and associate brokers affiliated with this broker

    B. does not affect the broker license

    C. suspends the licenses of the salespersons only

    D. suspends the licenses of the associate brokers only

13. The federal law whose purpose is to protect the public against the activities of monopolies is the:

    A. Federal Fair Housing Law

    B. Federal Trade Commission Act

    C. Sherman Antitrust Act

    D. Federal Penal Code

14. If a restraint of trade is inconsistent with free competition, it:

    A. may still be allowable under the Rule of Reason

    B. is per se illegal

    C. may be still allowable under the Sherman Antitrust Act

    D. is a violation of Article 12-A of the license law

15. All of the members of a certain board of REALTORS® agree to refrain from showing properties belonging to members of another board of REALTORS®. This is an example of illegal:

    A. price fixing

    B. market allocation agreement

    C. tie-in arrangement

    D. group boycott

16. Which of the following is an allowable activity for multiple listing services?

    A. refusing to admit part-time brokers

    B. prohibiting membership in any other multiple listing service

    C. charging a reasonable fee for services rendered

    D. restricting a participant's cooperation with a nonmember

17. Which of the following guidelines governing the activities of MLS is correct?

    A. MLS may refuse any listing lower than 7% of the sales price

    B. MLS can dictate commission rates between REALTOR® board members and their clients

    C. MLS may not circulate information regarding the commission that a broker has agreed upon with his client

    D. MLS may limit membership to individuals who are licensed real estate brokers and salespersons

18. In order for salespersons to qualify for independent contractor status under the IRS code, there must be:

    A. an oral agreement between salesperson and broker as to the arrangement

    B. a written agreement between salesperson and broker that the salesperson will not be treated as an employee for federal tax purposes

    C. no agreement necessary

    D. an agreement in writing if desired by the broker

19. Although real estate salespersons are independent contractors, brokers:

    A. still have a duty to supervise their activities

    B. have no duty to supervise the activities of sales agents under the law

    C. are not required to keep records of commissions

    D. may, at their own discretion, choose to supervise, if they desire, in spite of the independent contractor arrangement

20. Which of the following is NOT required for a salesperson to qualify as an independent contractor?

    A. to have his broker file a W-2 with IRS if he earns over $600 per year

    B. to be licensed

    C. to receive monies for services rendered, which must be related to sales, not to hours worked

    D. to have his broker file a 1099 misc. with IRS if he earns over $600 or more per year

ANSWER KEY

Putting It to Work*

If your offer is not accepted by the owner of the property, your deposit will be returned to you by the broker. If your offer is accepted, the deposit will be placed in the broker's escrow account, which cannot be used for any other purpose. The broker is holding the funds pending completion of the transaction. If the deal falls through by no fault of either party (an example would be the inability of the buyer to obtain financing), the contract between the parties will spell out what happens to the deposit. If the deal falls apart for some other reason, the broker will hold the deposit until the parties involved agree to the disposition or until some other resolution is made, such as a court order. If the deal goes through, the deposit is applied against the purchase price. Handling of deposits is generally spelled out in the contract of sale.

How Would You Respond?

1. Dmitrios is not legally allowed to accept any compensation in a real estate transaction except from his supervising broker, so he must not accept a $5,000 bonus directly from the Richardses. His broker also may not give Tessie a bonus of $1,500 as this constitutes a kickback, which is in violation of the license law.

2. Juan cannot accept this commission arrangement. The commission that Steve is talking about is a net listing, which is illegal in New York. The proper compensation could be a flat fee or a percentage of the gross amount of the lease.

Key Term Review

1. Article 12-A
2. apartment sharing agent
3. mortgage banker; mortgage broker
4. commingle
5. net listing
6. blind ads
7. Article 78 proceeding
8. trade name
9. price fixing

---

*Source: James A. Ader, "Real Estate Spotlight." Copyright © The *Albany Times Union.* Reprinted by permission.

Multiple Choice

1. C	6. C	11. B	16. C
2. B	7. A	12. A	17. D
3. D	8. D	13. C	18. B
4. B	9. B	14. B	19. A
5. A	10. C	15. D	20. A

Supplemental Reading

Salesperson and Broker License Law Pamphlet, printed by New York DOS, which may be obtained by written request.

Exam information, frequently asked questions, forms, and other information can be accessed through the DOS website at: *http://www.dos.state.ny.us*

Chapter 2

agency disclosure form

agent

broker's agent

buyer agent

buyer brokerage

client

cooperating agent

customer

disclosure

dual agency/dual agent

estoppel

exclusive right to sell

express agency

fiduciary

fiduciary duties

first substantive contact

general agent

implied agency

informed consent

misrepresentation

open listing

principal

ratification

seller agent

single agent

special agent

subagent

undisclosed dual agency

undivided loyalty

vicarious liability

LEARNING OBJECTIVES   *Classroom hours: 4*

1. Describe the duties of a real estate agent.
2. Define the word *agent*.
3. Understand the difference between a client (principal) and a customer.
4. List the different forms of agency alternatives and discuss the roles of each.
5. Define vicarious liability. Discuss liability of all parties in all types of agency.
6. Understand the forms of listing agreements a client may sign and indicate the responsibility of the broker for each type.
7. Discuss the rights a client has concerning a request to be released from a listing agreement. Discuss the right a broker has concerning the granting of a release.

Ginette

Real Estate Agency Disclosure

8. Understand the agency disclosure document and discuss the steps that must be taken to properly disclose agency.
9. Define what is meant by the first substantive contact.

IN THIS CHAPTER   A real estate broker in New York not only has the personal legal obligation to comply with the law of agency governing real estate transactions, but has a duty to supervise associate brokers and salespersons to ensure that they too are in compliance. This chapter covers the creation of agency, types of agencies, obligations of a licensee as agent, and New York disclosure requirements.

AGENCY RELATIONSHIPS

When one person is hired to act on behalf of another person, an agency relationship is created. The *person hired on another's behalf* is the **agent.** An agency relationship is consensual; the parties willingly enter into the agreement. Upon creation of the relationship, the agent is placed in a position of trust and loyalty to the principal.

The *person who selects the agent to act on his behalf* is the **principal** or the **client** *of the agent.* The **customer** of an agent is *the party whom the agent brings to the principal as a seller or buyer of the property.* For example, an agent can represent a seller in a real estate transaction. The seller then becomes the client of the agent. If the seller agent finds a prospective purchaser for the seller's property, the purchaser is the agent's customer. This particular example raises the issue of a dual agency relationship, which is allowable in New York with disclosure and informed consent. The issue of dual agency is discussed later in this chapter.

SCOPE OF AGENT'S AUTHORITY

Most agency relationships are contractual relationships. Few are simply implied by law. Therefore, the authority must be expressed in the brokerage contract. The principal controls the extent of authority delegated to the agent through the language in the brokerage contract.

Two important classifications of agents exist: general and special. The differences between each type of agency revolve around the authority given to the agent by the principal and the services to be provided.

General

A **general agent** is *someone authorized to handle all affairs of the principal concerning a certain matter or property,* usually with some limited power to enter into contracts. An example is a person who has been appointed property manager of an apartment complex by its owner. The property manager may collect rent, evict, enter into leases, repair the premises, advertise for tenants, and perform a range of activities on behalf of the principal concerning the specified property. This type of agency also may be established through power of attorney, but this is not always required. Someone given the complete power of attorney over another's affairs is called an attorney-in-fact. A power of attorney, which allows one individual to handle the affairs of another within the scope of a predetermined arrangement, can be either a general or special agency relationship.

Special

A **special agent** is *someone who has narrow authorization to act on behalf of the principal.* An example is a real estate broker who has a property listing. The broker can market the property for sale but cannot make decisions about price, repairs, financing, and so on. A special agent cannot bind a principal to a contract. The range of authority is specialized and limited, and the services provided are specifically defined.

FIDUCIARY RESPONSIBILITIES

An agency relationship is basically a contractual relationship to provide services. The person hired is the agent. The person who hires is the principal. As a result of the agency agreement, a fiduciary relationship then exists between the agent and the principal. The term **fiduciary** means *a position of trust.* Fiduciary responsibilities should not be taken lightly by licensees. *A breach in fiduciary duties can jeopardize an agent's commission as well as render the agent liable for his acts or omissions.*

Agent's Responsibilities to Principal

Every agency creates a fiduciary relationship between principal and agent. The agent has certain obligations to the principal as required of every agent by law. The agent's **fiduciary duties** and responsibilities include *obedience; loyalty; disclosure of information; confidentiality; accountability; and reasonable care, skill, and diligence.*

Obedience

The agent must act with *obedience* and obey reasonable and legal instructions from the principal. For example, a seller, as principal, may specify that the property be shown only during certain times of the day or, for instance, not on a seller's religious holiday. The buyer being represented may instruct the broker not to disclose the buyer's identity to the parties without the buyer's consent. Of course, the principal cannot require the agent to perform any illegal acts, such as violating fair housing laws. If the principal insists that the broker commit an illegal act, the broker must withdraw from the relationship.

Loyalty

An agent must demonstrate *loyalty* to the principal and must work diligently to serve the best interests of the principal under the terms of the employment contract creating the agency. The agent may not work for personal interest or for the interest of others adverse to the principal's interest. The agent cannot legally represent any other person who directly affects the principal without disclosing this fact to the principal and obtaining the principal's consent in writing. A real estate agent cannot represent both buyer and seller in the same transaction and the broker cannot receive a commission from both without the knowledge and consent of both buyer and seller.

Disclosure of Information

Agents are required to keep the principal fully aware of all important matters through *disclosure of information.* They must promptly communicate to the principal all information material to the transaction for which the agency is created. As an example, the requirement for disclosure of information requires that a broker present every offer to the seller (principal) with information about all circumstances surrounding the offer, even after a contract exists or is believed to exist. The seller has the prerogative to decide whether to reject or accept any offer for purchase of the property. If the agent is a buyer agent, the agent should indicate to the buyer the property's market value and use all possible negotiating techniques to obtain the most favorable terms and price for the buyer.

New York also has specific disclosure and informed consent requirements regarding whom the agent represents in a real estate transaction. (This subject is explored in more depth later in this chapter.)

Confidentiality

Because of the fiduciary relationship, the principal is owed faith, trust, and confidentiality by the agent hired. For example, if a seller's agent represents principals who are selling their home because of a divorce, this information should not be given to prospective purchasers without the seller's permission.

Accountability

Accountability generally refers to *financial accountability.* An agent must account for and promptly remit as required all money or property entrusted to the agent for the benefit of others. The agent is required to keep adequate and accurate records of all receipts and expenditures of other people's money in order to provide a complete accounting. For example, a real estate broker must maintain a special account for depositing other people's money. This account should be labeled either "trust account" or "escrow account" and be maintained in an insured banking institution. An agent is violating the law of agency for real estate brokers if the agent commingles funds or property, held in trust for others, with the agent's own personal or corporate money or property, or with the operating account of the business. Handling other people's money is one of the most serious fiduciary responsibilities of licensees.

Agent's fiduciary responsibilities to the principal   `You Should Know`

It helps to remember them if you think of the words OLD CAR:

O Obedience

L Loyalty

D Disclosure of Information

C Confidentiality

A Accountability

R Reasonable Care, Skill, and Diligence

Reasonable Care, Skill, and Diligence

In offering services to the principal, agents assert that they possess the necessary skill and training to perform the requested services. Agents must exercise the *reasonable skill, care, and diligence* to which the public is entitled in all real estate transactions. If an agent's principal incurs a financial loss as a result of the agent's negligence and failure to meet the standards of skill, care, and diligence, the agent is liable for any loss the principal incurs.

Agent's Responsibilities to Third Parties

The broker and the principal are the first two parties in an agency relationship. Other individuals who are involved in any way with the principal and broker are called *third parties.*

Even though one of the agent's obligations to the principal is not to disclose certain confidential information to other parties that could be injurious to the principal, the agent may not engage in any way in *misrepresentation* of fact to a third party. Agents must disclose any material facts of which they have knowledge or should have had knowledge regarding the condition of any service or item provided. For example, a seller broker must disclose to prospective buyers any information about any aspect of the property that may be defective, such as a wet basement or an unresolved boundary dispute. Liability may be imposed upon the agent for concealing defects in the property or for failing to disclose the existence of defects that they know about.

The basis for imposing liability in a case of misrepresentation consists of (a) a false representation of a material fact, (b) the fact that the person making the false representation *knew or should have known it to be false,* (c) the fact that the misrepresentation was made with an intent to induce the party to act or refrain from acting in reliance upon the misrepresentation, (d) the fact that the party relied upon the misrepresentation in acting or failing to act, and (e) the fact that there was damage to the party who relied upon the misrepresentation in acting or not acting.

A *positive misrepresentation* by a seller broker occurs when the broker conceals a defect in the property from the buyer or misrepresents to the buyer the existence of a defect. A positive misrepresentation occurs by omission of facts about the property even if the buyer does not ask. Positive misrepresentation may also occur when an agent engages in *self dealing.* Illegal self dealing can occur when a broker has an undisclosed interest in a property.

An *unintentional misrepresentation* occurs when the seller broker makes a false statement to the buyer about the property and the broker does not know whether the statement is true or false. In either of these situations, the broker is liable to a customer who suffers a loss as a result of the broker's acting or failing to act in reliance upon the misrepresentation. The broker is not excused from liability for making a misrepresentation based upon statements the principal makes to the broker. The broker is required to make a personal, diligent investigation before passing on any information. Brokers are liable for what they know from disclosure by the principal, what they should know because of their skill and training, and what they should know by an inspection of the property.

Principal's Responsibility to Agent

Under an agency agreement, the principal is obligated to the agent for cooperation, compensation, and indemnification. The agency agreement should clearly set out the amount of compensation to be paid and the conditions that must be met to earn the compensation.

Because an agency agreement is for providing services to the principal by the agent, the principal must not hinder the agent's efforts in providing services. For example, the seller of listed property must not refuse to allow the broker to show the property to prospective buyers in accordance with terms of the listing.

For compensation, a typical listing agreement might provide that the seller will pay the broker a set percentage of the accepted sales price of the property when a ready, willing, and able buyer is produced. If the broker brings a buyer with an offer completely in accordance with the listing agreement, the broker is entitled to a commission whether the seller does or does not accept the offer or is later unable to close the transaction.

Finally, the agent is entitled to be free from liability if the principal has withheld information that causes the agent to make incorrect representations to third parties. If the agent is found liable to the third parties for the principal's misrepresentation, the agent is entitled to repayment from the principal for all monies paid. The repayment from the principal is indemnification to the agent and makes the agent financially whole.

For instance, the seller of listed property may know of a *latent defect*. Latent defects are generally structural problems that a seller may know about but are not obvious to the purchaser. Examples include hidden water damage, faulty wiring, a malfunctioning heating system, or termites. If the seller fails to disclose this information to the agent, legal action may be brought by an innocent buyer against the broker and then the broker may in turn bring action against the seller for failure to disclose.

Principal's Responsibility to Third Parties

The principal in an agency agreement has no express contract with anyone except the listing broker and agent. The principal, however, does have a common-law duty of disclosure and fairness to any third parties. This duty complements the duty the principal has to the agent for *revealing all information that affects the agency agreement*. This duty is owed to any person who may be affected directly or indirectly by any of the terms of the agency agreement. This duty also requires that the principal disclose completely all information that has a bearing on the subject of the agency agreement. For example, brokers may encounter hidden defects that can be problematic, especially if not disclosed, such as an easement in the form of a public path through a back yard.

The seller's duty to disclose to the broker knowledge of any and all hidden defects also runs to any buyer brokers, prospective buyers, and subagents of the listing broker. A property condition disclosure form (discussed in Chapter 1) completed by the seller is a means through which defects may be disclosed. If sellers fail to disclose correctly, they can be held liable for the statutory penalties.

REAL ESTATE BROKERAGE AND AGENCY ⟶ Same

Real estate brokerage refers to the business of bringing buyers and sellers together and assisting in negotiations for the terms of sale of real estate. A brokerage contract is created when the principal, usually the owner of real estate, hires a broker (agent) to perform services relating to the real estate. The services typically involve selling or renting real estate that the principal owns. Under the listing agreement the principal and the agent have expressly agreed to the terms of the agency relationship. Although the real estate listing contract is the most common brokerage contract, a brokerage contract also can be created between a prospective buyer and the broker. Under that agency agreement, the buyer is the principal. Under buyer brokerage, the services typically involve finding a suitable property for the buyer to purchase, as well as assisting the buyer through all phases of the transaction and closing. The typical brokerage contract is a special agency with narrow authority.

The Brokerage Firm

A brokerage firm, or company, may be owned by a single licensed broker (sole proprietor) or by more than one licensed person, such as in a partnership or corporation. A brokerage firm is considered an independent broker if the brokerage is not associated with a national or local real estate franchise organization. Association with a real estate franchise organization licenses the brokerage firm to use the franchise's trade names, operating procedures, reputations, and referral services. The franchisee still owns and operates the brokerage firm. Brokerage firms usually employ or have other licensed salespersons or brokers working there. The listing contracts are shared between the sellers and the brokerage firm. The brokerage firm owns the listing contracts.

The sales associates affiliated with the brokerage firm are agents of the broker and subagents of the brokerage firm's principals (clients). The fiduciary duty of sales associates therefore extends both to their employing brokerage firm and to the firm's principals. Therefore, the broker has two separate agency relationships. The broker is the agent under the listing agreement. The broker is also the principal of the sales associates under a subagency agreement in the brokerage firm. The broker is responsible for the actions of the sales associates even though the sales associate almost always is an independent contractor. As subagents of the broker in reference to the listing agreements, the sales associates are required to comply with the terms of the listing and all rules of the brokerage firm.

Vicarious Liability

In any study of employment arrangements in the brokerage business, it is important to understand the meaning of **vicarious liability.** The term means that *one person is responsible or liable for the actions of the other.* According to Section 442-c of the New York Real Property Law, a broker is vicariously liable for a salesperson's actions only if "the broker had actual knowledge" of such violations or if "the broker retains the benefits from the transaction after he knows that the salesperson has engaged in some wrongdoing." If, however, while acting as an agent (salesperson), the agent is negligent and causes damage and/or injury to another, the employer (broker) can be held liable and be reprimanded or required to pay damages even if the broker did not know of the wrongdoing.

Agency and Brokerage—Are They Synonymous?

With the advent of strict disclosure regulations in New York, real estate agents must clearly define to buyers and sellers whom they represent in the real estate transaction. It is possible, in some situations, for buyers or sellers to request that a licensee *not* represent them as an agent. Under certain conditions, a licensee may also suggest this relationship. The licensee then may become a *finder* or *facilitator* in the real estate transaction. In this role, the licensee may bring together individuals who will communicate, negotiate, and contract directly. This relationship is permissible under New York agency and disclosure law. However, in any kind of relationship between a licensee and a buyer or seller, it is easy for a licensee to cross the line into the role of agent/fiduciary. Finders are not common, in residential real estate particularly. Agency and brokerage are generally synonymous.

DETERMINATION OF COMPENSATION

The fee or rate of commission paid to a real estate broker is strictly negotiable between the broker and the seller or buyer. Brokers are typically paid by a percentage commission of the final sales price or less often by a flat fee for services rendered.

Percentage of Final Sales Price

The most common type of commission arrangement in listing contracts is for the broker to receive a specified percentage of the final sales price of the property. For example, the contract may call for the broker to be paid 7 percent of the property's sales price. Real estate firms generally establish their own individual office policy regarding the level of commission charged. The fee decided upon by the broker is frequently tied to the amount of services being offered, such as in-house services, agent support systems, or advertising.

Flat Fee

Under the flat fee listing arrangement, the broker takes the listing based on a specified payment by the seller at the time of the listing. This is called an up front fee. The broker is entitled to retain this fee for efforts to market the property. Compensation under this listing does not depend on the sale of the property; therefore the flat fee typically is substantially less than it is compared with the fee for percentage of the final sales price. Under this arrangement, the broker usually advertises the property but may not be involved in showing the property or negotiating terms of the sale between seller and buyer. Under a flat fee arrangement, if a seller wants a broker to open the listing to other brokers, the commission usually becomes a combination of a flat fee (to the listing broker) and a small percentage (to cooperating brokers).

Flat Fee to Buyer Brokers

When representing buyers, brokers may charge a flat fee for a full range of services that include negotiations for the buyer. This arrangement may be in the buyer's best interests since the total commission paid to the buyer broker is not always determined by the purchase price of the property but by the services provided by the broker.

In addition, the flat fee arrangement is generally a better choice for all parties since the commission arrangement may contain a conflict of interest. This is because the higher the purchase price of the property, the more the buyer broker will make for his commission. A flat fee arrangement precludes buyers from believing that their brokers did not show them less expensive properties because of the percentage commission arrangement. The flat fee can be paid partially at the initial buyer agency agreement (upfront) and the balance can be paid at closing.

Commission for Sales Associates

Commission splits paid to sales associates in real estate brokerage firms are established by the owner of the firm and the sales associates. Under the usual commission split agreement, a portion is paid directly to the broker, who then pays a portion to the sales associate who listed the property and a portion to the sales associate who sold the property. If a sales associate sells a listed property, the associate will receive both portions.

Commission for Cooperating Brokers

Upon the sale of real estate through the cooperating efforts of two real estate firms, the commission paid pursuant to the listing agreement is paid to the listing broker by the property owner. This commission then is shared by the listing broker and the seller broker on a prearranged basis. Through the publication of cooperative commissions reflected in multiple listing services, some listing offices offer two forms of cooperating commission. One amount is payable to a subagent of the seller and another amount is payable to a buyer agent as a cooperative agent who does not represent the seller.

CREATION OF AGENCY

Express Agency

An *agency relationship created by an oral or a written agreement between the principal and agent* is called an **express agency.** A typical example is the written listing agreement between the seller of real estate and the broker.

Implied Agency—Ratification and Estoppel

An agency also may be created by the words or actions of the principal and agent indicating that they have an agreement. This is called an **implied agency.**

> EXAMPLE: Juanita, a real estate agent, places an ad in the paper for the sale of her friend Savannah's house, even though she has no express agreement with Savannah. This could be construed as an implied agreement.

Let's take this implied agency a step further:

> Juanita has an implied agency with Savannah. It is not in writing. Savannah does not stop Juanita from advertising and marketing the house. Juanita later brings her a written offer to purchase the property. Savannah finds the contract acceptable and signs it. The signature on the contract *ratifies* or *confirms* the previously understood implied contract. This is known as *agency by ratification.* Ratification should restate an earlier understood contract, including an agreement or contract of sale.

Ostensible and estoppel agency refer to the principal in the relationship. *Ostensible agency* occurs when a principal allows a third party to believe that an agency relationship exists; there is an appearance of relationship between the parties.

> EXAMPLE: Assume that Savannah needs to rent her house and Juanita takes the liberty to show the house to a prospect. Savannah does not want to be represented by Juanita, but she does not mention this to her. Juanita brings Savannah an offer to rent. Juanita begins to negotiate some of the points in the offer. Neither Savannah nor Juanita disclose to the tenant (third party) that Juanita is not representing Savannah, the owner/landlord. The tenant (third party) believes that Juanita is Savannah's representative. Later, the case goes to court and Savannah claims that Juanita was not her representative. The court may declare that an ostensible agency existed because the tenant believed that Juanita was Savannah's representative. Ostensible agency can be intentional or unintentional.

An agency by **estoppel** *exists when a principal does not stop an individual from representing his interests, thus creating an agency relationship between the two.*

> EXAMPLE: Through their recent discussions, Juanita knows that Savannah wants to rent her house. Savannah allows Juanita to bring prospects to her property and does not make it clear to the prospect that she is not represented by Juanita. In this relationship, the principal, Savannah, fails to estop an individual, Juanita, from representing her interests.
>
> In New York, implied real estate agency agreements are not easily enforced by the courts because, according to the Statute of Frauds, all real estate contracts, except listings contracts and leases of less than one year's duration, must be in writing. However, other New York laws may affect the determination of the courts.

AGENCY ALTERNATIVES

Agents, as fiduciaries, cannot offer absolute loyalty to both seller and buyer in the same transaction, yet New York law does not prohibit dual agency (discussed later). Once agents choose, they must always fully represent the principal, whether that is the seller or buyer. The different roles that agents may assume are shown in Table 2.1.

SELLER AGENCY AND SUBAGENCY

Subagency can be created when a seller and broker agree, usually by means of a multiple listing service, that other agents will also work for the seller.

TABLE 2.1   Possible roles of real estate agents.

TYPE OF AGENT	REPRESENTATION	DEFINITION	LIMITATIONS
1. Single agent	Buyer or seller	The agent works for the buyer or seller.	The agent never represents both. Firms that represent solely the buyer or seller may reject subagency and dual agency. The broker should counsel, but not advise the principal as to the limitations of this relationship. If a situation arises to compromise the relationship, the broker could suggest that another broker from a referral firm be utilized.
2. Seller agent	Seller	A listing agent who acts alone or cooperates with other agents as a subagent or broker's agent.	The agent works in the best interests of the seller but must deal fairly and honestly with buyers.
3. Subagent	Seller or buyer	An agent of the principal under the agency relationship of the primary broker.	The agent must be hired with the principal's informed consent. The principal may be vicariously liable for the acts of the subagent.
4. Buyer agent	Buyer	The agent represents the buyer as principal and enters into a listing agreement with the buyer. Locates a property and negotiates for the buyer.	The agent works in the best interests of the buyer but must deal fairly and honestly with sellers.
5. Dual agent	Buyer and seller	Represents both buyer and seller in the same transaction; undisclosed dual agency is a breach of fiduciary duty and violation of license law.	This arrangement is allowable only with disclosure and written informed consent. The agent cannot give undivided loyalty to either party.

(continued)

TABLE 2.1   Continued.

TYPE OF AGENT	REPRESENTATION	DEFINITION	LIMITATIONS
6. Broker's agent	Broker (who may represent either buyer or seller)	An agent is hired through a broker to work for that broker. The broker alone has hired the agent and accepts liability. Although a broker's agent does not work directly for the principal, the agent still owes a fiduciary duty to that principal because an agency relationship has been established through the broker that hired the broker's agent.	The agent owes a fiduciary duty to the broker's principal.
7. Cooperating Agent	Buyers or sellers	Representation includes seller agents, subagents, buyer agents, and broker's agents. These agents work to assist the listing broker in the sale of the property. Cooperating agents may or may not work through MLS.	The principal can designate those agents that work as broker's agents, subagents, or buyer agents. The principal may choose to reject subagency arrangements.

Real estate agents, in cooperation with the principal, may assume different roles within the agency relationship. The principal can designate those agents that work as broker's agents, subagents, or buyer agents. One or more defined roles may apply to an agent within the transaction. For example, a seller agent may also be a subagent and a cooperating agent.

In the distant past, placing a property in MLS automatically created subagency. In other words, all the agents showing the listed property became subagents for the listing broker and principal. Today, however, primarily because of the prevalence of buyer brokerage and other choices, the listing in MLS does not create a blanket unilateral offer of subagency. The principal can agree to accept or reject the option of subagency when signing the listing agreement.

A buyer agent cannot be a subagent of the seller broker. Licensees acting as buyer agents must make their agency status clear to the listing broker before showing the property. Brokerage, therefore, can be conducted without a unilateral offering of subagency by using the services of an MLS and offering a commission share to all cooperating agents even when the cooperating agents have been employed by buyers.

When cooperating brokers accept the offer of subagency associated with a seller's listing, however, they work through the listing broker and are therefore the principal's subagent, as are the sales associates in the listing agency's office. Cooperating subagents have the same responsibility to work for the best interests of the seller. The advantage to this arrangement is that cooperating subagents from other firms and in-house subagents have more offerings, and sellers have more licensees working on their behalf.

EXAMPLE: Melissa, who works for Sellquick Realty, shows the Millers' house, which is listed by Tom, another agent at Sellquick. Tom is the subagent of the seller (principal), the Millers. Melissa is also the Millers' subagent because both Melissa and Tom are employed by the same broker, the primary agent listing the property. The Millers' house is also listed in the multiple listing service. Matthew, an agent for Payless Realty, also shows the Millers' house to some of his customers. Because Matthew's firm, through the MLS, has agreed to a subagency arrangement, Matthew, although an agent from another firm, is also the subagent of the Millers. All the individuals who have accepted subagency owe the same fiduciary responsibilities to the principal and to the primary seller agent. The principal, however, may be held liable for the action of agent and subagent alike in cases of misrepresentation or any acts that result in damages to any other party in the real estate transaction. Subagents must also deal honestly and ethically with the buyer or customer and must disclose any pertinent information that may affect the value of the specific property.

Broker's Agent

The concept of the broker's agent can be understood if it is compared with that of the subagent. In the case of the subagent, the principal accepts vicarious liability for the acts of the agents and subagents. In the case of the broker's agent, the broker accepts vicarious liability for the acts of the agents working for his principal through him.

> EXAMPLE: Ricardo hires Sellquick Realty to market his house. However, he does not want to accept vicarious liability for the acts of agents working on his listing. Avita, his broker, still wants to list the property and have the cooperation of other agents. Avita agrees to take any responsibility for liability problems that may arise because of other agents' activities. The agents who assist with the sale of the property according to this arrangement are known as broker's agents.

Cooperative Sales

Cooperative sales, either those handled by a seller agent from another real estate firm as subagent of the listing broker and owner (seller) or those handled by a buyer agent from another real estate firm, are either processed through MLS or between cooperating offices. When a cooperating office arranges to show a listed property, the role of the cooperating agent must be identified immediately. The cooperating agent must indicate if the prospective buyer is a client or a customer.

When the seller real estate firm takes a listing, the owner must be informed that some agents will be acting as representatives of the buyer. Arrangements can then be made in advance of any showing as to whether or not the owner wants the listing agent to accompany any appointments made by the buyer agents to protect the best interest of the seller.

Who Represents the Buyer in Seller Agency?

In dealing with seller agents, buyer customers may gain the mistaken impression that their broker is representing them against the seller. However, the broker is working for the seller; this should be made clear to the buyer at the outset. The buyer customer can tell nothing to the selling broker or agent in confidence, such as how much the buyer is willing to pay for the property, since the broker is required to pass on all pertinent information to the seller client or seller's broker.

When the broker represents the seller, the buyer customer does have rights. Although the broker is working on behalf of the seller, the buyer can expect honest disclosure from the broker, including full property disclosure outlining any problems the seller has experienced. The broker must accurately and completely answer any and all questions from the buyer concerning the property. Furthermore, the buyer can expect that the broker will comply with all local, state, and federal discrimination laws. The buyer, however, cannot expect the broker to disclose confidential information concerning the seller's reasons for selling, the seller's lowest sales price, the seller's original purchase price, or any other information that might give the buyer an enhanced negotiating position with the seller. Conversely, the buyer customer's duties should include fair and honest dealings with the seller and seller agents.

DUAL AGENCY

A **dual agency** exists when *a real estate firm or agent attempts to represent both the buyer and seller in the same transaction.* Dual agency can occur not only when one sales associate is involved with both buyer and seller but also when the salesperson representing the seller and the salesperson representing the buyer both work for the same broker. In such cases, only one firm (one agent) is involved despite the fact that two separate associates are working independently with the two parties.

Single licensee dual agency occurs when a sales agent attempts to represent the interests of both a seller client and a buyer customer in the same transaction. A licensee may not engage in any form of dual agency without the informed consent of the listing broker and of all other parties to the transaction.

Broker dual agency can occur in several ways if agents of the broker represent both buyer and seller in the same transaction, as stated above, or if the broker offers services to a buyer such as finding or negotiating a mortgage for the buyer, when the broker already represents the seller. Another example of broker dual agency would be if the broker who represents the seller offers to negotiate the purchase agreement for the buyer. Dual agency may be intended or unintended.

Intended Dual Agency

An *intended dual agency* can arise when a listing broker acts as a buyer broker and shows an in-house listing with the seller's full knowledge and consent. The real estate firm then represents both the buyer and the seller in a dual agency capacity and owes both the seller and the buyer confidentiality. In this situation, it is important to convey to both buyer and seller that neither can receive full representation. In certain cases, maintaining neutrality may be difficult because the responsibilities to both buyer and seller are complex and multifaceted.

Unintended Dual Agency

An *unintended dual agency* occurs if the *buyer believes by the agent's actions and representations that the buyer is being represented by that broker.* This implication can arise, for example, when a broker gives the buyer advice on negotiations or suggestions of what price to offer when in fact the broker is representing the seller. Confusion may occur when a seller successfully sells her property with the broker as the agent and then enters the market as a buyer. The seller may assume that the broker then automatically represents her in the new transaction, but this is not the case unless this individual establishes a new agency relationship in her new role as buyer.

Obligation of Informed Consent

Dual agency must be disclosed to both buyer and seller, and both must agree to that dual relationship in writing. Undisclosed dual agency is a breach of a broker's fiduciary duty and is a violation of New York license law. In the sale or rental of certain residential property (defined later) in New York, licensees must present a written disclosure form at the first substantive meeting with prospective sellers or purchasers (discussed later).

Undisclosed Dual Agency

Undisclosed dual agency *occurs when a subagent or seller agent is working with a buyer customer and agrees to negotiate for that buyer customer rather than working in the best interests of the other client, the seller.*

Consensual Dual Agency and In-House Sales

The law of agency in New York permits consensual dual agency with **disclosure and informed consent** of all parties to the transaction. The New York DOS generally interprets dual agency as a lawful alternative as long as informed consent is coupled *with timely and complete disclosure of the nature and consequences of dual agency.*

In certain circumstances, consensual dual agency may pose problems since both the seller and purchaser must release the portion of the fiduciary agent relationship known as undivided loyalty. The goals of the seller and purchaser are adverse. The sellers want to receive the highest price for their property under the best financial terms while the buyers want to pay the lowest price for a property under the most favorable financial terms for them. In many instances, however, with proper disclosure and informed consent, the agent may effect an agreement that is acceptable to all parties.

Company Policies

New York real estate offices can provide consensual dual agency representation for in-house sales. A seller client should be made aware when the listing agreement is signed that a dual agency could occur if a buyer agent affiliated with that same firm has a buyer client who might be interested in purchasing the seller's particular property. Because a dual agency situation must be disclosed at the time that it arises and informed consent must be obtained at that time, the seller client should not agree to dual agency at the date of the listing but has the option to agree to it should it occur. Brokerage firms whose primary business is representing buyers will, at the time of listing buyer clients, inform them that a prospective property may be available through an in-house listing. At that time, the buyer clients may choose to relinquish their roles as client principals and choose one of the alternatives discussed next.

- The broker and buyer could dissolve their agency relationship. The buyer can then retain another broker, an attorney, or represent himself. The broker then would continue to act as the agent for the seller.
- The broker and the seller could dissolve their agency relationship. The seller could find another broker or attorney, or represent himself. The broker then would continue to act as the agent for the buyer.
- With informed consent, the buyer and seller may elect to continue with the brokerage firm serving as consensual dual agent.

The Designated Agent

Recently, DOS has defined an alternative for handling a dual agency with a brokerage firm. With full disclosure and informed consent, one sales agent in the firm can be designated to represent the buyer and another agent designated to represent the seller.

For example, if a buyer expresses interest in a property listed with a firm, consent must be obtained by both parties to proceed as a dual agent. The agency disclosure form is used for that purpose. At the same time, the benefits of appointing a *designated agent* for the buyer and another for the seller is explained. If, after full disclosure, the buyer and seller agree to this arrangement, designated agents may be appointed. The firm continues as dual agent representing both the buyer and the seller in the same transaction. The designated agents, however, by virtue of the new agreement with the

FIGURE 2.1
A designated agent
agreement.

Central New York's
#1 Residential Real Estate Company

DESIGNATED AGENT AGREEMENT

We, the undersigned, Buyer and Seller, regarding the purchase and sale of premises known as
_____, New York, acknowledge our consent to _____("Broker")
acting as a dual agent with respect to this transaction. We acknowledge that the Broker will be working
for both the Buyer and the Seller in this transaction and we understand that we are giving up our
respective rights to the Broker's undivided loyalty. We have carefully considered the possible
consequences of a dual agency relationship and understand that instead each of us could have engaged our
own agent as a seller's agent or buyer's agent, respectively.

We hereby agree that _____ is appointed to represent only the Buyer
(the "Buyer's Designated Agent") and _____ is appointed to represent only the
Seller (the "Seller's Designated Agent") in this transaction. We understand that the Broker continues to
be a dual agent representing both of us in this transaction with honesty and fairness, but that the Buyer's
Designated Agent and the Seller's Designated Agent will each function as a single agent providing each of
us, respectively, with undivided loyalty.

SELLER: **BUYER:**

_____ Date _____   _____ Date _____

_____ Date _____   _____ Date _____

FormD002 - 5/98

buyer and seller, function as single agents giving undivided loyalty to their respective
clients. If proper procedures are carried out, this arrangement does not violate Article
12–A or any other DOS regulations. While not mandatory, both DOS and NYSAR recommend that the buyer and the seller enter into a Designated Agent Agreement. A form
has been drafted by NYSAR and adopted by many real estate firms (see Figure 2.1).

Consequences of Undisclosed Dual Agency

An undisclosed dual agency can result in a violation of the Real Property Law and regulations. Violators may be guilty of a misdemeanor. DOS may reprimand a licensee, or
deny, revoke, or suspend the license of a salesperson or broker for as long as DOS
deems proper. DOS may elect to impose a fine not to exceed $1,000. Article 12-A also
empowers all courts of the state to hear and try, without indictment, anyone who violates the license laws. A civil court may also require that monetary damages be paid to
a buyer or seller or other injured party. The legal process may also result in a rescission of any contracts involving the real estate transaction.

Obtaining Informed Consent of Both Parties

Section 443 of the Real Property Law specifically provides for informed consent and written acknowledgment of dual agency by a prospective buyer or tenant and seller or landlord. Certain procedures must be carefully undertaken in the presentation of the disclosure form when listing the seller's property or entering into a buyer agency agreement. When the listing takes place, the licensee should give a full explanation of dual agency and neither party should sign, at this time, an acceptance of dual agency.

If at any time in the transaction, an in-house listing results in the possibility of a dual agency, it should be clarified with all parties. If the seller and the buyer both agree to accept dual agency, then the acknowledgment of prospective buyer or tenant and seller or landlord to dual agency sections of the disclosure form must be signed and acknowledged. *The dual agency relationship applies to only one singular transaction at a time.*

TERMINATION OF AGENCY

An agency relationship ends in accordance with the terms of the agency contract. An example is the expiration of a listing contract for the sale of real estate. When the contract terminates, so does any authority of the agent to act on behalf of the principal. Another means of terminating an agency relationship is by completing the terms of the agency; for example, the sale of listed real estate is complete and the seller has paid the commission. In some cases, an agency relationship may be terminated by operation of law. For instance, a power of attorney terminates automatically at the death of either principal or agent. Another example is the termination of a listing contract held by a broker whose license is revoked.

Release From Contracts

The parties to real estate contracts may wish to terminate before the listing agreement or contract of sale is fulfilled. Generally accepted practice is the use of prescribed forms outlining the terms of the release. Basically, there are three types of release agreements: conditional, when some obligation must be met; unconditional, in which no condition need be met; and consideration, when compensation is paid. Samples of release agreements are as follows:

Conditional Release from Exclusive Listing Agreement

This *conditional* agreement between the listing broker and the owner is used when the owner decides to withdraw his property from the market prior to the expiration or fulfillment of the exclusive listing contract. In this contract, depicted in Figure 2.2, the owner agrees that if he sells the property, or another agent in MLS or any other agency sells the property, within a certain designated timeframe (determined by agreement of the parties), the terms of the original listing can be extended beyond the termination date of the exclusive listing contract as additional consideration for the release.

Cancellation and Release from a Contract for Purchase and Sale

This *unconditional* agreement may be used when the parties to a contract mutually agree to end their contractual obligations. The contract depicted in Figure 2.3 releases the parties from any liability and directs the distribution of the deposit money.

Other types of contractual problems may arise during the term of a real estate contract. Generally, release agreements that involve consideration may be drawn up by attorneys depending on the particular facts and circumstances. Litigation may be required to resolve contract disputes.

Exclusive Right to sell - you pay any way

FIGURE 2.2 A conditional release from exclusive listing agreement.

CONDITIONAL RELEASE FROM EXCLUSIVE LISTING AGREEMENT-1

THIS IS A LEGALLY BINDING CONTRACT. IF NOT FULLY UNDERSTOOD, WE RECOMMEND CONSULTING AN ATTORNEY BEFORE SIGNING.

Supplemental agreement to Exclusive Listing Agreement dated —————————————— of property at —
——.

Dated: ——————————————, 20————

TO ALL MEMBERS OF THE CAPITAL REGION MULTIPLE LISTING SERVICE

1. OWNER'S REPRESENTATIONS

   The undersigned owner represents:

   (a) That said owner has decided in good faith to withdraw the property described in the above captioned listing contract from the sales market, and

   (b) That there are now no negotiations pending or contemplated with anyone for the sale, exchange, or rental of the property described in the above-captioned listing contract.

2. CONDITIONS OF RELEASE

   The undersigned owner hereby requests that the property be withdrawn conditionally from the above-captioned exclusive listing agreement and agrees to the following conditions of the release:

   (a) If the above-captioned property shall again be offered for sale, exchange or rent at any time in the period from date hereof to within ————— months after the expiration date of said exclusive listing contract and/or

   (b) If the above-captioned property shall be sold, exchanged or rented either directly by said owner or through any broker member of said Multiple Listing Service or through any other agency or inducement whatever; then and in the event it is agreed as follows:

   That all the terms listed in the above-captioned listing contract shall remain and continue to remain in full force and effect except that the listing period will be executed ————— months from the originally agreed termination date.

3. WHEN EFFECTIVE

   This conditional withdrawal shall become effective upon proper execution of this agreement.

   Owner hereby acknowledges receipt of a copy of above conditional release form.

———————————————————————————
Owner

———————————————————————————
Owner

Approved and consented to:

this ————— day of ——————————, 20—————
by ——————————————————————————————
Listing Broker

Appendix X 3/22/91 [C-CONDIT]
Capital Region Multiple Listing Service, Inc.

FIGURE 2.3   A cancellation and release form.

ADDENDUM #———— CANCELLATION AND RELEASE—all parties

THIS IS A LEGALLY BINDING CONTRACT. IF NOT FULLY UNDERSTOOD, WE RECOMMEND CONSULTING AN ATTORNEY BEFORE SIGNING.

WHEREAS, ————————————————————————— as Purchaser,

and as ————————————————————— Seller, entered into an agreement

dated ————————————— for the Purchase and Sale of premises known as ————————

————————————————————————————— .

copy of which agreement is attached hereto.

It is mutually agreed as follows:

1. Said agreement for the Purchase and Sale of the aforesaid premises is hereby cancelled.

2. The principal parties hereto and the undersigned brokers hereby release and discharge each other from any and all liability arising out of said agreement and;

3. The parties direct that the deposit in the sum of $ ———————————— paid on the signing of the said agreement be distributed to ————————————————————————

————————————————————————————————————

————————————————————————————————————

————————————————————————————————————

————————————————————————————————————

Purchaser	Date	Seller	Date
Purchaser	Date	Seller	Date
Selling Broker (authorized signature)	Date	Listing Broker (authorized signature)	Date

Appendix I 3/22/91 [C=CANREL]

Capital Region Multiple Listing Service, Inc.

BUYER BROKERAGE: BUYER AS PRINCIPAL

Although some buyers are most comfortable with customer status, real estate buyers increasingly are hiring real estate brokers to represent them. This relationship is referred to as **buyer brokerage.** In such cases, *an agency relationship exists between the buyer and the broker;* the buyer is the principal and the broker is the agent.

Why Is Buyer Brokerage So Popular?

Buyers moving into a new area recognize the advantages of broker representation in locating a house for purchase: using the broker's technical expertise to negotiate a better price and gaining the broker's fiduciary confidentiality and trust. Buyers naturally want assurance that they are paying a reasonable and fair price for a property. A buyer broker may perform a market analysis and advise the buyer on an offer. A buyer broker also may be able to suggest creative financing that is in the buyer's interests.

A buyer-broker relationship is common in commercial real estate, in which a buyer employs a broker to locate a certain type of property for purchase. Today this approach is common in residential real estate. With the establishment of buyer agency, the direction of agency responsibility is reversed from the typical seller agency situation. When a buyer hires a broker, the broker owes all duties of loyalty and disclosure to the buyer, not to the seller. A written buyer broker agreement signed by both buyer and broker is used to prevent any disputes; however, verbal agreements are common in a certain percentage of cases. A disclosure of this relationship is made to the seller prior to any showing of the property.

Does Everyone Need an Agent?

Buyers represented by their own agent may encounter properties listed by sellers who have a real estate agent and sellers who do not. A buyer agent may arrange to show properties that may or may not be listed with MLS but in which a seller agent represents the property owner. A buyer agent may also arrange to show a buyer property that is for sale by owners. These owners may or may not have representation.

Who Pays the Buyer Broker?

The buyer broker is compensated through a variety of methods. The buyer broker may be paid directly by the buyer upon the purchase of property through terms in the buyer/purchaser listing agreement. In this case, the buyer broker must inform the seller and the seller broker that compensation is being directly paid; therefore the buyer broker rejects any offer of a cooperative agency commission.

The more common method of compensation, however, is when a broker shares in the commission according to the traditional arrangement between listing broker and cooperating broker. This method occurs when the seller offers a commission upon sale through MLS. The seller is notified and agrees to splitting the commission between the listing broker and the buyer broker. The buyer in this scenario does not pay an additional fee, which keeps the transaction simple and avoids any restructuring. Should the broker receive any up front guarantee of compensation, then the buyer is credited on purchase; therefore the transaction requires some restructuring. An example is a buyer listing agreement that reflects a payment due to the buyer broker on completion of the agency transaction, a sum equal to 3 percent of the purchase price. The cooperating commission offered through MLS is 2.75 percent. The balance then due from the buyer client is 0.25 percent. A buyer broker commonly accepts a fee equal to the cooperating offer in MLS thereby allowing the buyer to have client representation without any additional cash outlay.

In some cases, the buyer broker can receive a nonrefundable upfront fee that would not be credited at the closing to the monies owed to the buyer broker. In this case, the buyer broker is paid the balance due according to the arrangement between the buyer broker and the principal.

Buyers as Clients

Once the purchaser accepts a role as the client of a firm, a buyer/purchaser listing agreement is signed (Figure 2.4). As in all consensual contracts in real estate, both parties must agree to the terms of the listing agreement, including the services provided by the broker. The agreement also delineates the obligations of the broker and affiliated agents as well as the client (principal), the means of compensation, and the length of time of the listing. Legal obligations are outlined in a standard listing contract. Most other terms are negotiated, established, or determined by the office policy of the buyer broker firm with the acceptance of the buyer client. As in seller agency, the client of the buyer broker now has a fiduciary relationship with the broker and agent.

Buyers as Customers

Some agencies specializing in buyer brokerage do accept listings from seller clients. After disclosure, a prospective buyer may elect customer status regarding the properties listed with that firm. As in other examples, this arrangement is a consensual agreement. Company policy determines whether or not a buyer brokerage firm will agree to work with a customer rather than working for a buyer client.

DISCLOSURE AND LISTING FORMS

In New York, all real estate listing agreements for the sale or rental of one- to four-unit residential property must be accompanied by the disclosure regarding real estate agency relationships form illustrated later in Figure 2.9. The disclosure form must be explained by the agent, read, acknowledged, and signed by the principal prior to signing the listing agreement.

The Exclusive Right to Sell Agreement

Under the **exclusive right to sell** listing contract (Figure 2.5), the *property is listed with one broker only.* If anyone else sells the property during the term of the listing contract, the broker is legally entitled to the commission. As discussed above, this form must contain or have an addendum attached that includes a statement regarding in-house sales that offer options available to a principal should dual agency occur.

The Exclusive Agency Agreement

In an **exclusive agency** listing (Figure 2.6), the *property is listed with one broker only as the agent.* If the broker effects sale of the property, the broker is legally entitled to

The difference between exclusive right to sell and exclusive agency	You Should Know
EXCLUSIVE RIGHT TO SELL	**EXCLUSIVE AGENCY**
Property listed with one broker	Property listed with one broker
Broker is paid commission no matter who sells property	Broker receives no commission if owner sells property

FIGURE 2.4   An exclusive buyer/purchaser agency agreement form.

CAPITAL REGION MULTIPLE LISTING SERVICE, INC.

THIS IS A LEGALLY BINDING CONTRACT. IF NOT FULLY UNDERSTOOD,
WE RECOMMEND CONSULTING AN ATTORNEY BEFORE SIGNING.

EXCLUSIVE BUYER/PURCHASER AGENCY AGREEMENT

AGREEMENT

The BUYER/PURCHASER _____ (hereinafter called the "CLIENT")

retains and authorizes as Buyer's Broker (hereinafter called the "BROKER") _____

_____ (firm) represented by _____ (agent)

to locate and/or negotiate for the purchase of real property of the general nature shown below.

AGREEMENT PERIOD

This Agreement begins upon signing and ends on _____, 19_____ or upon closing of a property purchased
under this Agreement.

BROKER'S OBLIGATIONS

The BROKER will:

(1) use diligence in locating a property on price and terms acceptable to the CLIENT;

(2) use professional knowledge and skills to negotiate for CLIENT's purchase of the property;

(3) assist CLIENT throughout the transaction and act in the CLIENT's best interest at all times; and

(4) personally present the purchase offer to the Seller unless otherwise directed by the CLIENT.

CLIENT'S OBLIGATIONS

The CLIENT will:

(1) work exclusively with the BROKER during the period of this Agreement in all matters pertaining to the purchase of real property located
within the Capital Region market area with the following exceptions:

_____

_____

_____ ; and

(2) furnish the BROKER with all requested personal and financial information necessary to complete this transaction.

COMPENSATION

The CLIENT agrees to compensate the BROKER if the CLIENT, or any other person acting on the CLIENT's behalf, buys, exchanges for,
or obtains an option on any real property.

The amount of compensation shall be:

(1) If the property is listed with a real estate company or licensee, BROKER will accept a fee equal to the fee being offered to cooperating agents; but in any event not less than _____ % of the purchase price of the property, or a flat fee of $ _____.
If such fee, or any portion thereof, is paid by the Seller or the Seller's agent as a convenience of the transaction, then CLIENT will be
credited by BROKER for the amount so paid.

(2) If the property is not listed with a real estate company or licensee, a fee of _____ % of the purchase price, or a flat fee of
$ _____ will be paid.
If such fee, or any portion thereof, is paid by the Seller as a convenience of the transaction, then CLIENT will be credited by BROKER
for the amount so paid.

(3) Other Compensation Agreement: _____

_____

_____ .

NOTE: If the CLIENT within _____ months of the termination of this Agreement, without the services of a licensed agent, purchases
real property shown to the CLIENT by the BROKER during the term of this Agreement compensation as set forth in this Agreement shall
apply and a fee shall be due the BROKER.

ADVICE ON TECHNICAL MATTERS

BROKER will not counsel CLIENT on legal, home inspection, public health, surveying, tax, financial or other technical matters. Upon
request, BROKER will assist CLIENT in engaging qualified professionals to consult in such fields.

FAIR HOUSING

BROKER is committed to the philosophy of Fair Housing for all people. Therefore, BROKER will present properties to CLIENT in full
compliance with local, state and federal fair housing laws against discrimination on the basis of race, color, religion, sex, national origin,
handicap, age, marital status and/or familial status, children, or other prohibited factors.

PROPERTY LISTED WITH BROKER

If CLIENT becomes interested in acquiring any property for which BROKER has a listing contract, CLIENT may:

(1) elect customer status as to the property for which there is a conflict; or

(2) terminate this contract as to the property for which there is a conflict; or

(3) with knowledge and informed consent in writing of both CLIENT and Seller, CLIENT may agree to dual agency. CLIENT understands
that in such a dual agency situation, the agent will not be able to provide the full range of fiduciary duties to the CLIENT and Seller and
that by consenting to the dual agency relationship, CLIENT and Seller are giving up the right to undivided loyalty.

BROKER_____   CLIENT _____

By _____   CLIENT _____

[C–BUYERAGENCY] 1/15/92   Date _____

Source: Reprinted courtesy of the Capital Region Multiple Listing Service, Inc.

FIGURE 2.5   An exclusive right to sell contract form.

Greater Rochester
Association of REALTORS®, Inc.

EXCLUSIVE RIGHT TO SELL CONTRACT

THIS FORM IS FOR USE BY MEMBERS OF THE GREATER ROCHESTER ASSOCIATION OF REALTORS®, INC. ("GRAR") ONLY FOR THE PLACING OF PROPERTY LISTINGS IN THE GENESEE REGION REAL ESTATE INFORMATION SERVICES, INC. MULTIPLE LISTING SERVICE ("GENRIS MLS").

REALTORS® EXCLUSIVE RIGHT TO SELL, EXCHANGE OR LEASE CONTRACT. COMMISSIONS OR FEES FOR REAL ESTATE SERVICES TO BE PROVIDED HEREUNDER ARE NEGOTIABLE BETWEEN REALTOR® AND OWNER. IT IS UNDERSTOOD THAT GRAR AND THE GENESEE REGION REAL ESTATE INFORMATION SERVICE, INC. ("GENRIS") IS NOT A PARTY TO THIS LISTING AGREEMENT.

1. OWNERSHIP OF PROPERTY AND POWER TO SIGN CONTRACT. I, _____, am the Owner(s) of the property located at _____ (the "Property"). I have complete legal authority to sell, exchange or lease the Property. I have not entered into any other agreement which would affect the sale, exchange, lease, or transfer of the Property; except as follows: (name or specify agreement) _____. For purposes of this Contract, any reference to a "sale" or "purchase" of the Property shall be deemed to include any "exchange" of the Property.

2. EXCLUSIVE RIGHT TO SELL OR LEASE. (Check and complete either (a) or (b), or both).

(a) ____ I hereby hire _____ (REALTOR®) to sell the Property and I hereby grant to REALTOR® the Exclusive Right to Sell the Property for the price of $ _____ or any other price that I later agree to, and upon such terms and conditions as I may agree to.

(b) ____ I hereby hire _____ (REALTOR®) to lease the Property and I hereby grant to REALTOR® the Exclusive Right to Lease the Property for a rent of $ _____ per _____ or any other rent that I may later agree to, and upon such terms and conditions as I may agree to.

3. MULTIPLE LISTING SERVICE/INTERNET. I authorize REALTOR® to submit the information contained in this listing agreement and the applicable GENRIS Data Sheet relating to the Property to the GENRIS MLS. REALTOR® will submit such information to GENRIS **within 24 hours** of my signing this Contract. REALTOR® shall retain this listing agreement and the Data Sheet for at least six years. I agree that REALTOR® will provide GENRIS with information, including the selling price, about the Property upon final sale of the Property. I further agree that REALTOR® will provide GENRIS with information, in addition to the list price, prior to final sale of the Property. All information submitted becomes the property of GENRIS and may be published by GENRIS including, without limit, on the Internet.

4. PAYMENT TO REALTOR®. (Check and complete either (a) or (b), or both).

(a) _____ I will pay REALTOR® a commission of ___ % of the gross sale price of the Property as set forth in the purchase and sale contract that I sign, or $ _____ .

(b) _____ I will pay REALTOR® a commission of ___ % of the gross rent for the Property as set forth in the lease contract that I sign, or $ _____ .

5. AUTHORIZATION REGARDING OTHER BROKERS. I authorize REALTOR® to cooperate with other brokers, including brokers who represent buyers (with the understanding that such "buyer's brokers" will be representing only the interests of the prospective buyers), to appoint subagents, and to divide with other licensed brokers such compensation in any manner acceptable to REALTOR® , such other brokers and me. In the event that there is a participating subagent broker or buyer's broker, I authorize that the following compensation be paid out of the commission provided in Paragraph 4 above to such subagent broker or buyer's broker: (Complete both)

Subagent broker will be paid _____% of the gross sale or rent price, or $_____.

Buyer's broker will be paid _____% of the gross sale or rent price, or $_____.

6. PAYMENT OF COMMISSION. I agree to pay to REALTOR® the commission set forth in Paragraph 4 on the "closing date" specified in the purchase and sale contract or when I sign a lease for the Property. I will pay this commission to REALTOR® whether I, REALTOR® , or anyone else sells or leases the Property during the life of this Contract. REALTOR® has earned the commission when I am provided with a written purchase offer which meets the price and other conditions I have set or when the purchase and sale contract becomes a binding legal commitment on the buyer, or when I sign a lease for the Property.

7. SUBMISSION OF OFFERS TO PURCHASE. I agree that any offers to purchase or lease the Property shall be submitted through REALTOR® or, with my REALTOR® 's consent, through any cooperating broker.   **Check One**

8. FOR SALE, FOR RENT SIGN. I authorize REALTOR® to install a "**For Sale**"/"**Sold**" or "**For Rent**" sign on the Property.   _____ Yes   _____ No

9. LOCKBOX. I authorize REALTOR® to use a lockbox. I understand that neither REALTOR® , any cooperating broker, the GRAR nor GENRIS shall be responsible for any theft, loss or damage attributed to the use of a lockbox.   _____ Yes   _____ No

10. DUTIES OF REALTOR® . REALTOR® will use best efforts to procure a buyer. REALTOR® will physically inspect the interior and exterior of the Property prior to submission of the listing to the GENRIS MLS. REALTOR® will list the Property in full compliance with local, state and federal fair housing laws against discrimination on the basis of race, creed, color, religion, national origin, sex, familial status, marital status, age, or disabilities. REALTOR® will bring all offers to purchase or lease the Property to me. REALTOR® will assist in negotiating any and all offers to purchase or lease the Property.

_____

Owner's Initials

_____

Broker's/Salesperson's Initials

Revised GRAR 11/00   **Exclusive Right to Sell Contract**   **Page 1 of 2**

(continued)

FIGURE 2.5
Continued.

11. OBLIGATIONS OF OWNER/PROPERTY INFORMATION. To the extent within my possession, I agree to furnish to REALTOR® complete information reasonably necessary for processing this listing in the GENRIS MLS and for closing the sale or lease of the Property. All information about the Property I have given REALTOR® is accurate and complete, and REALTOR® assumes no responsibility to me or anyone else for the accuracy of such information, except as otherwise provided by law. I authorize REALTOR® to obtain other information about the Property. REALTOR® will use sources of information REALTOR® believes to be reliable, but is not responsible to me for the accuracy of the information REALTOR® obtains, except as otherwise provided by law. I authorize REALTOR® to disclose to prospective purchasers and any other persons, including other brokers, any information about the Property REALTOR® obtains from me or any other source. I understand that New York law requires me to give certain information about heating and insulation to prospective purchasers if they ask for it in writing before a purchase and sale contract is signed. I agree to refer all inquiries about the Property to REALTOR® and conduct all negotiations through REALTOR®. I agree to cooperate with REALTOR® in showing the Property to possible buyers or renters at any reasonable hour. I agree that REALTOR® and GENRIS may photograph the Property listed for sale or lease and may use the photographs in promoting its sale or lease. If the Property becomes vacant, I understand it is my obligation to continue to maintain the Property, including but not limited to, lawn care, snow plowing, utility service continuation, interior and exterior maintenance, until transfer of title unless otherwise agreed in the purchase and sale contract.

12. AUTHORIZATION OF REPRESENTATIVE TO PAY COMMISSION. Without in any way limiting any provision of Paragraph 6 above, I authorize my closing representative (such as my attorney) to pay to REALTOR® the commission agreed to in Paragraph 4 from the proceeds of the sale of the Property upon recording of the closing of the sale of the Property. If the proceeds of sale are insufficient to pay the entire commission due, I agree to pay the balance of commission to REALTOR®.

13. LIFE OF CONTRACT; SALE OR LEASE OF PROPERTY AFTER CONTRACT ENDS TO A PERSON WHO WAS SHOWN THE PROPERTY DURING THE LIFE OF CONTRACT. This Contract will last until midnight on _____, 20 ____. However, if I sell or lease the Property within _____ days after this Contract ends (the "Effective Period") to a person who was shown the Property by Owner(s). REALTOR®, or anyone else during the life of this Contract, I will pay REALTOR® the same commission agreed to in Paragraph 4 of this Contract. I will not owe any commission to REALTOR® if such sale or lease occurs during the life of another Exclusive Right to Sell Contract I enter into with another REALTOR® after this Contract ends but before the expiration of the Effective Period.

14. NON-DISCRIMINATION. I understand that the listing and sale or lease of the Property must be in full compliance with local, state and federal fair housing laws against discrimination on the basis of race, creed, color, religion, national origin, sex, familial status, marital status, age, or disabilities.

15. RENEWAL AND MODIFICATION OF CONTRACT. I may extend the life of this Contract by signing another Exclusive Right to Sell Contract. If I renew this Contract, REALTOR® will notify GENRIS of the renewal. All changes or modifications of the provisions of this Contract must be made in writing, signed by Owner(s) and REALTOR®.

16. OWNER'S LIABILITY FOR CONTRACT TERMINATION. In the event this Contract is terminated prior to the time specified in Paragraph 13 for any reason other than REALTOR®'s fault, I will be liable for and agree to pay all damages and expenses incurred by REALTOR®, including without limitation costs for advertising the Property and any commission due hereunder.

17. ATTORNEY'S FEES. In any action, proceeding or arbitration arising out of this Contract, the prevailing party shall be entitled to reasonable attorney's fees and costs.

18. RESPONSIBILITY OF OWNER(S) UNDER THIS CONTRACT. All Owners must sign this Contract. If more than one person signs this Contract as Owner, each person is fully responsible for keeping the promises made by the Owner.

19. OTHER. _____

In consideration of the above, REALTOR® and Owner accept this Contract and agree to its terms and conditions as of _____, 20____.

Owner(s) Signature	Owner(s) Signature
Print Owner(s) Name	Print Owner(s) Name
Property Address	Broker or Salesperson Signature
Print Name of REALTOR® Firm	Print Name of Broker or Salesperson

EXPLANATION

The Secretary of State, State of New York, requires that the following explanation be given to homeowners and acknowledged by them in the listing of property:

An *"exclusive right to sell"* listing means that if you, the owner of the property, find a buyer for your house, or if another broker finds a buyer, you must pay the agreed commission to the present broker.

An *"exclusive agency"* listing means that if you, the owner of the property find a buyer, you will not have to pay a commission to the broker. However, if another broker finds a buyer, you will owe a commission to both the selling broker and your present broker.

Owner(s) understands that this Contract grants REALTOR® the exclusive right to sell the Property.

Owner(s) Signature	Owner(s) Signature

Revised GRAR 11/00   Exclusive Right to Sell Contract   Page 2 of 2

the commission agreed upon, but if the owner sells the property, the broker earns no commission. Again, the agreement should include or have an addendum attached with a statement regarding in-house sales.

Upon listing with either the exclusive right to sell contract or the exclusive agency agreement, the agent must fully disclose the difference between the two contracts and allow the sellers to choose. In addition, a termination date for the listing must be assigned. New York prohibits automatic extensions of listings. All listings last for a specific time and are renegotiated or renewed after the contract expires.

The Open Listing Agreement

Under an **open listing** (Figure 2.7), the *seller allows a property to be shown by one or more brokers.* The broker effecting the sale is entitled to the commission. If the owner sells the property to a prospect not generated by any broker, however, the owner owes no commission. In an open listing, the same rules of disclosure apply as in other listing contracts.

EXCLUSIVE AGENCY CONTRACT
Approved as to form by the Multiple Listing Service
OTSEGO-DELAWARE BOARD OF REALTORS, INC.

_____
Listing No.

FIGURE 2.6
Exclusive agency listing agreement form.

COMMISSIONS OR FEES FOR REAL ESTATE SERVICES TO BE PROVIDED ARE NEGOTIABLE BETWEEN REALTOR AND CLIENT.
THIS IS A LEGALLY BINDING CONTRACT. IF YOU HAVE QUESTIONS CONCERNING THIS CONTRACT,
YOU SHOULD CONSULT AN ATTORNEY BEFORE SIGNING IT.

DATE:_____, 19 _____

GRANT OF EXCLUSIVE AGENCY/TERM OF LISTING
TO_____
I the undersigned OWNER(the word OWNER refers to each and all parties who have an ownership interest in the property) hereby give you the
Broker the exclusive agency to sell my property located at:
_____

more fully described as:
_____
for $_____ until 12:00 o'clock midnight on _____. It is understood and agreed that you will submit this
listing within 48 hours to the MULTIPLE LISTING SERVICE of the Otsego-Delaware Board of Realtors, Inc., (MLS) for circulation to all member participants in the MLS and to make an offer of subagency and cooperating agency to all members of the Otsego-Delaware Board of Realtors MLS, and
any other cooperating agent authorized under the law to receive a commission. The Owner grants the Broker exclusive For Sale Sign privileges on
said property, consents that said property may be shown at any reasonable hour, and agrees to refer any and all inquries concerning said property to
Broker.

COMPENSATION/BROKER PROTECTION PROVISION
I agree that if my property is sold to or exchanged with any person during the term of the listing I will pay broker a commission of _____percent (%)
of the gross selling price, or _____dollars ($), unless I am the procuring cause for the sale or exchange of my property, then no commission
is due.
If within_____ days after the expiration of the term of this listing, my property shall be sold to or exchanged with any person to whom the
property has been shown by a Broker, subagent, or cooperating Broker during the term of listing, I will pay broker the commission stated in this
agreement as if broker, subagent or cooperating Broker had made the sale.
If, during the term of said protection period, a valid exclusive agency agreement is entered into with another licensed real estate broker, any payments
made thereunder may be offset against the sums owing pursuant to this agreement.
If the Owner must remove the above described property from the market during the duration of this agreement and subsequently the property is sold
within _____days or within the original duration of this agreement, whichever is longer, the Broker will be entitled to a full commission,unless the property is sold or exchanged by the owner to a person or persons who previously had not viewed the property during the the term of
this agreement.
Should the owner desire to rent the property during the period of this agreement, the Broker is hereby granted, irrevocably, the sole and exclusive right
to rent the property, the exclusive "for rent" sign privilege and the Broker rental commission of $_____.

ONE COMMISSION
In utilizing subagency, cooperating agency, and/or buyer agency as described below, I will not be liable for more than one (1) commission totaling
_____percent (%) of the gross selling price.

SUBAGENCY
I am aware that this MLS listing is an offer of subagency made by me through you to the participants in the MLS. I am further aware that I could be liable for the misrepresentations, if any, of subagents. If I incur a loss,as a result of misrepresentations of subagents, I may be entitled to bring legal action against the responsible subagents, for reimbursement of such loss.

I agree with you that the compensation to the selling subagent or cooperating broker in a transaction shall be_____percent (%) of the gross selling
price or _____dollars ($).

BUYER AGENCY
I authorize you to cooperate with brokers who represent buyers with the understanding that such buyers' brokers will be representing only the
interests of the prospective buyers, unless I agree otherwise in writing.

I agree with you that the compensation to the buyer's agent in a transaction shall be_____ percent (%) of the gross selling price or
_____dollars ($).

TERMINATION
I understand that if I terminate the listing Broker's authority prior to expiration of its term, that the listing Broker shall retain its contract rights to a commission and recovery of advertising expenses and any other damages incurred by reason of my early termination of this agreement.

PROPERTY INFORMATION
I direct you to furnish a copy of the signed profile sheet (Schedule A), which you have completed, to participants of the MLS.
I have___ or have not ____completed and delivered to you a signed Seller's Disclosure of Property Condition Statement, and I certify that the informa-
tion furnished is accurate to the best of my knowledge, and may be disseminated to interested customers.

NON-DISCRIMINATION
It is agreed that my property is listed in full compliance with local, state and federal fair housing laws against discrimination on the basis of race,
creed, color, religion, national origin, sex, familial status, marital status, age, or disabilities.

SUBSEQUENT PURCHASE OFFERS
Owner should consult an attorney regarding subsequent purchase offers becasue a binding contract for the property may already exist and owner
could incur additional liabilities to buyers and/or Brokers.

LOCKBOXES, PHOTOGRAPHS, FOR SALE SIGN (Please initial for authorization)

_____ I authorize the photographing of my property and the use of such photographs in promoting its sale.
_____ I hereby authorize the use of a lockbox, and I accept any responsibility for any damage or loss arising from the use of the lockbox
_____ I authorize the placement of a " For Sale" sign on my property.
_____ I authorize the above mentioned property to be placed in the Multiple Listing Service.

MLS COMPANIES
I also confirm that I have received a list containing the names and addresses of all MLS companies.

ACCEPTANCE
By signing this contract, each party agrees to be bound by all of the terms of this contract and each party further acknowledges that he or she received
a fully signed duplicate of this contract.

Owner _____   Broker _____

Owner _____   By _____

An_"Exclusive Right to Sell"_ listing means that if you, the owner of the Property, find a buyer for your house, or if another Broker finds a buyer, you
must pay the agreed commission to the present Broker.

An_"Exclusive Agency"_ listing means a contract under which the owner appoints a real estate broker as his or her exclusive agent to sell the property
on the owner's stated terms for a commission. The owner reseves the right to sell without paying anyone a commission.

ODMLS-12/92

FIGURE 2.7   An open listing agreement.

OPEN NON-EXCLUSIVE LISTING AGREEMENT

Owner(s) have engaged _____ Pathfinder Realty to act as agent for the sale of property known as _____ and located at _____ New York.

In return Agent will use his/her best efforts to sell the property. The Owner(s) agree to grant the agent the Open Listing to sell this property under the following terms and conditions.

1. Time Period of Agreement: This agreement shall be in effect from _____ until the property is sold or Agent is notified that the property is no longer available.

2. Price of Property: The property will be offered for sale at the list price of $ _____ and shall be sold subject to negotiations at such price and terms which the Owner(s) may agree.

3. Commission to be Paid to Agent: The agent shall be entitled to one commission of _____ % of the selling price. Agent is due one month's rent if property is rented by Agent for Owner. All commissions are Negotiable.

4. Owner(s) Obligation after Expiration of Agreement: Owner understands and agrees to pay commission of _____ % if this property is sold or transferred, or is the subject of a contract of sale within 120 days of this agreement, expiring to anyone who was offered, quoted, shown the property by the Agent or subagent during the time period of this Agreement. Owner will not however be obligated to pay such a commission if the owner enters into an Exclusive Listing Agreement with another licensed real estate broker after the expiration of this agreement or if the owner(s) sells the property themselves without any assistance from the Agent.

5. Negotiations and Deposits: Owner(s) agree to have all negotiations submitted by this Agent with buyers shown the property with this agent or subagent. Further, all deposits shall be held by _____ Pathfinder Realty in its escrow account at _____ Bank in _____ New York. Any forfeiture of the deposit by the buyer shall go 1/2 to Owner, 1/2 to _____, Pathfinder Realty not to exceed the commission due in #3.

6. Marketable title owners shall cooperate with the marketing of this property and shall provide at the time of sale a good marketable title. All information given by the owners is correct to the best of their knowledge and they give authorization to the Agent to place a For Sale sign on the property; to take interior and exterior photos of the property; and to give listing information to buyers and subagents.

7. Nondiscrimination: It is agreed that the property is listed in full compliance of all local, state and federal fair housing laws against discrimination on the basis of race, color, creed, religion, national origin, sex, familial status, marital status, age, or disabilities.

8. Acceptance: This is a legal and binding contract. No change, amendment, or termination of this agreement shall be binding unless in writing and signed by both parties. By signing this agreement each party agrees to be bound by the terms of this agreement and acknowledges that they have received a copy.

Owner _____   Date _____

Owner _____   Date _____

Address _____

Phone# _____   Attorney _____

Acceptance by Pathfinder Realty _____ Agent   Date _____

An "Open Listing" means that if you, the seller of the property, find a buyer for your property without assistance from the broker you will not owe the agreed commission to the present broker. However if a purchase offer is accepted by you from anyone that has been sent to you, told about your property, or shown your property by the broker you must pay the agreed upon commission to the broker.

Further, you agree that if you, or another broker, find a buyer and enter into a purchase agreement, you will notify _____ Pathfinder Realty immediately.

Source: Pathfinder Realty, Inc. East Springfield, New York. Reprinted by permission.

FIGURE 2.8
Exclusive right to rent
contract form.

Exclusive Right to Rent Contract

Approved as to Form by the Multiple Listing Service

Greater Syracuse Association of REALTORS®

Commissions or fees for real estate services to be provided are
negotiable between REALTOR® and Client

—————————— , 20 ———

TO: ————————————————————

I hereby give you the exclusive right to rent my property located at ——————————
———————————————————— for $———————— per month. This
exclusive right to rent agreement will expire at 12:00 midnight on ———————— , 20 ———— .

It is understood that you will submit this contract to the Multiple Listing Service of the Greater
Syracuse Association of REALTORS®, Inc., for circulation to all members of the service.

It is agreed that my property is listed in full compliance with local, state and federal fair housing
laws against discrimination on the basis of race, creed, color, religion, national origin, sex,
familial status, marital status, age, or disabilities.

I agree to pay $———————— rental fee to you if my property is rented to any person to
whom it has been shown during the term of this listing agreement.

In the event a contract to purchase and an offer to rent are presented simultaneously, the contract
to purchase shall take precedence, and, in such case, there will be no rental fee deemed earned.

I agree with you that the compensation to the rental agent in a cooperative transaction shall be
————— % of the rental fee or $———————— , unless other arrangements have been made
between the cooperative brokers.

———————————————————————————————————————
Owner   Real Estate Company

———————————————————————————————————————
Owner   By

Signed original to owner; signed original to broker; copy to MLS.

Source: Copyright © Greater Syracuse Association of REALTORS®, Inc. Reprinted by permission.

The Exclusive Right to Rent Agreement

This contract (Figure 2.8) is between an owner or a lessor and an agent in the rental
of residential property. This contract is similar to the exclusive right to sell listing
agreement discussed earlier. The rental fee is paid to the listing agent even if the
owner or another party rents the property. In New York, disclosure is required with
listing agreements for rental or lease just as it is with listing agreements for the sale
of residential property.

AGENCY DISCLOSURE

Section 443 requires that licensees present a written **agency disclosure form** that
details consumer choices about representation at the **first substantive contact** *with a
prospective seller or buyer* (Figure 2.9). This contact is defined as when some detail

FIGURE 2.9   A written disclosure form.

Disclosure Regarding Real Estate Agency Relationships

Section 443 of Article 12-A of the Real Property Law requires the real estate industry to provide the following information to prospective buyers, tenants, sellers and landlords: *Before you enter into a discussion with a real estate agent regarding a real estate transaction, you should understand what type of agency relationship you wish to have with that agent. New York State law requires real estate licensees who are acting as agents of buyers or sellers of property to advise potential buyers or sellers with whom they work of the nature of their agency relationship and the rights and obligations it creates.*

1

Seller's or Landlord's Agent

If you are interested in selling or leasing real property, you can engage a real estate agent as a seller's agent. A seller's agent, including a listing agent under a listing agreement with the seller, acts solely on behalf of the seller. You can authorize a seller's or landlord's agent to do other things including hire subagents, broker's agents or work with other agents such as buyer's agents on a cooperative basis. A subagent, is one who has agreed to work with the seller's agent, often through a multiple listing service. A subagent may work in a different real estate office.

A seller's agent has, without limitation, the following fiduciary duties to the seller: reasonable care, undivided loyalty, confidentiality, full disclosure, obedience and a duty to account. The obligations of a seller's agent are also subject to any specific provisions set forth in an agreement between the agent and the seller.

In dealings with the buyer, a seller's agent should (a) exercise reasonable skill and care in performance of the agent's duties; (b) deal honestly, fairly and in good faith; and (c) disclose all facts known to the agent materially affecting the value or desirability of property, except as otherwise provided by law.

2

Buyer's or Tenant's Agent

If you are interested in buying or leasing real property, you can engage a real estate agent as a buyer's or tenant's agent. A buyer's agent acts solely on behalf of the buyer. You can authorize a buyer's agent to do other things including hire subagents, broker's agents or work with other agents such as seller's agents on a cooperative basis.

A buyer's agent has, without limitation, the following fiduciary duties to the buyer: reasonable care, undivided loyalty, confidentiality, full disclosure, obedience and a duty to account. The obligations of a buyer's agent are also subject to any specific provisions set forth in an agreement between the agent and the buyer.

In dealings with the seller, a buyer's agent should (a) exercise reasonable skill and care in performance of the agent's duties; (b) deal honestly, fairly and in good faith; and (c) disclose all facts known to the agent materially affecting the buyer's ability and/or willingness to perform a contract to acquire seller's property that are not inconsistent with the agent's fiduciary duties to the buyer.

3

Broker's Agents

As part of your negotiations with a real estate agent, you may authorize your agent to engage other agents whether you are a buyer/tenant or seller/landlord. As a general rule, those agents owe fiduciary duties to your agent and to you. You are not vicariously liable for their conduct.

4

Agent Representing Both Seller and Buyer

A real estate agent acting directly or through an associated licensee, can be the agent of both the seller/landlord and buyer/tenant in a transaction, but only with the knowledge and informed consent, in writing, of both the seller/landlord and the buyer/tenant.

In such a dual agency situation, the agent will not be able to provide the full range of fiduciary duties to the buyer/tenant and seller/landlord. The obligations of an agent are also subject to any specific provisions set forth in an agreement between the agent and the buyer/tenant and seller/landlord.

An agent acting as a dual agent must explain carefully to both the buyer/tenant and seller/landlord that the agent is acting for the other party as well. The agent should also explain the possible effects of dual representation, including that by consenting to the dual agency relationship the buyer/tenant and seller/landlord are giving up their right to undivided loyalty.

A buyer/tenant or seller/landlord should carefully consider the possible consequences of a dual agency relationship before agreeing to such representation.

5

General Considerations

You should carefully read all agreements to ensure that they adequately express your understanding of the transaction. A real estate agent is a person qualified to advise about real estate. If legal, tax or other advice is desired, consult a competent professional in that field. Throughout the transaction you may receive more than one disclosure form. The law requires each agent assisting in the transaction to present you with this disclosure form. You should read its contents each time it is presented to you, considering the relationship between you and the real estate agent in your specific transaction.

6

(continued)

and information about the property is shared with interested parties. The law became effective as of January 1993 and is part of Article 12-A of the New York Real Property Law. *Section 443 applies to the sales and rental of residential one- to four-unit properties.* The law does not cover vacant land or condominium and cooperative apartments in buildings containing more than four units. The law's purpose is to make consumers aware of the agency relationship of a real estate agent with whom they come into contact and of the choices available to them. For example, a prospective buyer may attend an open house and discuss matters regarding the property with the

FIGURE 2.9   Continued.

Acknowledgment of Prospective Buyer/Tenant. (1) I have received and read this disclosure notice. (2) I understand that a seller's/landlord's agent, including a listing agent, is the agent of the seller/landlord exclusively, unless the seller/landlord and buyer/tenant otherwise agree. (3) I understand that subagents, including subagents participating in a multiple listing service, are agents of the seller/landlord exclusively. (4) I understand that I may engage my own agent to be my buyer's/tenant's broker. (5) I understand that the agent presenting this form to me, *(name of licensee)* _____ of *(name of firm)* _____ is *(check applicable relationship)* _____ an agent of the seller/landlord   _____ my agent as a buyer's/tenant's agent

Buyer/Tenant Signature _____   Date _____

7   Buyer/Tenant Signature _____   Date _____

Acknowledgment of Prospective Seller/Landlord. (1) I have received and read this disclosure notice. (2) I understand that a seller's/landlord's agent, including a listing agent, is the agent of the seller/landlord exclusively, unless the seller/landlord and buyer/tenant otherwise agree. (3) I understand that subagents, including subagents participating in a multiple listing service, are agents of the seller/landlord exclusively. (4) I understand that a buyer's/tenant's agent is the agent of the buyer/tenant exclusively. (5) I understand that the agent presenting this form to me, *(name of licensee)* _____ of *(name of firm)* _____ is *(check applicable relationship)* _____ my agent as a seller's/landlord's agent   _____ an agent of the buyer/tenant

Seller/Landlord Signature _____   Date _____

Seller/Landlord Signature _____   Date _____

Acknowledgment of Prospective Buyer/Tenant and Seller/Landlord to Dual Agency. (1) I have received and read this disclosure notice. (2) I understand that a dual agent will be working for both the seller/landlord and buyer/tenant. (3) I understand that I may engage my own agent as a seller's/landlord's agent or a buyer's/tenant's agent. (4) I understand that I am giving up my right to the agent's undivided loyalty. (5) I have carefully considered the possible consequences of a dual agency relationship. (6) I understand that the agent presenting this form to me, *(name of licensee)* _____ of *(name of firm)* _____ is a dual agent working for both the buyer/tenant and seller/landlord, acting as such with the consent of both

8   buyer/tenant and seller/landlord and following full disclosure to the buyer/tenant and seller/landlord.

Buyer/Tenant Signature _____   Date _____

Buyer/Tenant Signature _____   Date _____

Seller/Landlord Signature _____   Date _____

Seller/Landlord Signature _____   Date _____

Acknowledgment of the Parties to the Contract. (1) I have received, read and understand this disclosure notice. (2) I understand that *(name of real estate licensee)* _____ of *(name of firm)* _____ is *(check applicable relationship)* _____ an agent of the seller/landlord   _____ an agent of the buyer/tenant _____ a dual agent working for both the buyer/tenant and seller/landlord, acting as such with the consent of both the buyer/tenant and seller/landlord and following full disclosure to the buyer/tenant and seller/landlord. I also understand that *(name of real estate licensee)* _____ of *(name of firm)* _____ is *(check applicable relationship)* _____ an agent of the seller/landlord   _____ an agent of the buyer/tenant

9   _____ a dual agent working for both the buyer/tenant and seller/landlord, acting as such with the consent of both the buyer/tenant and seller/landlord and following full disclosure to the buyer/tenant and seller/landlord.

Buyer/Tenant Signature _____   Date _____

Buyer/Tenant Signature _____   Date _____

Seller/Landlord Signature _____   Date _____

Seller/Landlord Signature _____   Date _____

DOS-1565 (9/01)

Source: New York State Department of State.

agent who is present and who holds the listing on the property. This agent represents the seller. However, the prospective purchasers may erroneously think that this agent is considering *their* best interests. The duty of the agent, when details are discussed about the property, is to inform the prospective purchasers that she represents the seller. A disclosure form must be acknowledged and signed to verify that disclosure has taken place.

Section 443 of the Real Property Law includes the actual text of the New York required disclosure form. Brokers may copy this text and use it. Most of the real estate boards in New York have printed copies available to members.

In addition to the Real Property Law, New York also has codified rules and regulations that govern the behavior of licensees. *Regulation 175.7* states: "Compensation. A real estate broker shall make it clear for which party he is acting and he shall not receive compensation from more than one party *except* with the full knowledge and consent of all the parties."

This regulation bears a direct relationship to Real Property Law Section 443 covering one- to four-unit residential properties. This regulation states that licensees must disclose whom they represent in a real estate transaction. This mandatory disclosure reveals the party whom the agent represents, explains the choices available to the consumer, and provides written proof of the disclosure.

You Should Know   **When the agency disclosure form should be used**

The disclosure form must be utilized in the following transactions involving the sale or rental of one- to four-unit residential properties:

1. A listing agent must obtain a signed acknowledgment from a seller prior to entering into a listing agreement with the seller.
2. A seller agent must present the disclosure form to a buyer or buyer agent *at the first substantive contact* and the buyer must sign and acknowledge the form.
3. An agent must provide the disclosure form to a buyer prior to entering into an agreement to act as a buyer agent.
4. A buyer agent must present the disclosure form to the seller or seller agent at the first substantive contact with the seller and must obtain a signed acknowledgment from the seller or the seller's listing agent.
5. When the real estate transaction reaches the point where the contract of sale is signed, all parties to the contract must sign the acknowledgment of the parties to the contract section of the disclosure form.
6. The agent must provide a copy of the disclosure form to the buyer or seller and maintain a copy for a minimum of three years.

The Agency Disclosure Document

The licensee should first explain to the prospective buyer or seller that by law they have certain consumer rights. The licensee should then thoroughly explain each section of the document. The prospective clients should be given some time to read through the document fully and ask the licensee any questions. The roles of the agent, seller, buyer, client, and customer should be defined, and the consumers should be offered a choice about which position they prefer.

The form covers the following information:

- *Section 1* notifies consumers that brokers must disclose for whom they are working in an agency relationship.

- *Section 2* pertains to seller or landlord agency and the fiduciary duties inherent in this relationship. The agent owes allegiance to the seller or landlord; however, in dealing with the buyer, the agent must use reasonable skill and care and must disclose all known facts affecting the property.

- *Section 3* defines the role of the buyer or tenant agent and the fiduciary duties inherent in this relationship. The agent owes allegiance to the buyer or tenant; however, in dealing with the seller, the agent must exercise care and skill and must disclose all known facts that may affect the buyer's ability to execute the contract that are inconsistent with the agent's fiduciary duty to the seller.

- *Section 4* states that the consumer may authorize the agent to engage other agents (broker's agents) and that these agents are bound by the same fiduciary duties. The agents must be loyal to the consumer, but the consumer has no vicarious liability for the agent's actions.

- *Section 5* defines dual agency with informed consent and warns that a dual agency causes the consumer to give up the fiduciary right of undivided loyalty.

- *Section 6* explains that other kinds of advice, such as legal advice, should be obtained as necessary from other professionals. It also clarifies that the disclosure form may be presented on more than one occasion.

- *Section 7* is the acknowledgment by the parties to the transaction. It asks the buyer or tenant or the landlord or seller to confirm an understanding of the disclosure form.

- *Section 8* is an acknowledgment by a prospective buyer or tenant and/or seller or landlord to a dual agency relationship.

- *Section 9* is a reaffirmation that both the buyer and the seller have been introduced to the agency relationship. This section is used when the buyer and seller go to a contract for purchase and sale.

When disclosure should take place   **You Should Know**

Whether or not a written disclosure form is required, the following typical situations require the agent to clarify who he represents.

1. *Open houses.* Prospective buyers express a sincere interest in a property and want additional time with the agent to discuss a possible offer. Disclosure must be made prior to any substantive contact.

2. *Walk-ins.* A prospective buyer or seller may walk into a real estate office, meet an agent, and want to discuss listing or purchasing a property. At this point, disclosure must be made.

3. *Appointments.* An agent meets with a seller to discuss the possibility of listing a property for sale. Disclosure must take place at the meeting and/or before a listing agreement is signed.

4. *Viewing the property.* When the prospective purchaser and the agent meet to view the property, disclosure must be made.

1 To 4 Family

Is the Licensee's Role Clear?

It is imperative that licensees thoroughly discuss the agency that they represent and their relationship with the agency. Agents must clarify client and customer roles and enumerate the agent's responsibilities to the client. It is equally important for licensees to explain to the client their services and define their obligation to deal fairly and honestly with the customer.

Refusal of Buyer or Seller to Sign Disclosure Form

If a buyer or seller refuses to sign the disclosure form, the agent should determine the reason for that decision, reinforce the idea that the document is intended to protect the consumer, and explain that the form is a notice of consumer rights and not a binding contract. Sellers are more likely to sign as a part of the listing process than buyers, who may be reluctant. Buyers often state, "I never sign anything without the approval of my attorney." If this occurs, the agent should make notes in an appointment book of the names of the prospective buyers, the time, date, and reasons for refusal. At this point, the property may be shown. However, after returning to the office or at the earliest possible moment following this substantive contact, the agent must complete a declaration form stating all of the facts, have it acknowledged, retain a copy for the records, and provide a copy to the broker to be kept on file for a period of three years. Figure 2.10, Declaration by Real Estate Licensee Pursuant to Section 443(3)(f) of the Real Property Law, indicates that this declaration must be completed if either a seller or buyer refuses to sign the mandated disclosure form. Additional information may be appended to the form.

You Should Know | **Agent record keeping**

As illustrated above, agents will have opportunities to record information relevant to their daily activities. The recorded information can be used as factual reminders of past, present, and future activities, and is useful should dispute arise. Diaries, journals, notebooks, and appointment books are generally admissible in court as evidence should disputes arise. Documented statements, directives, and interactions with customers, clients, prospects, and other agents can be particularly useful, but should not be limited to, the areas of license law, agency relationships, and human rights.

Record keeping should include:

- Properties shown
- Communication log; parties who call and nature of their call
- Properties suggested to prospects
- Copies of contracts and other documents
- Correspondence on offers and contracts
- Refusals to sign the agency disclosure form
- Other relevant business

Can Buyer Agents and Seller Agents Change Roles?

With the written consent of the principal, an agent may change roles after having established a relationship with the seller as client, a seller subagent relationship, or a buyer client relationship. Some examples follow:

Change in role from buyer–client agent to dual agent. An agent employed to represent a buyer client may have another agent at the same firm show a listing on a property in which the buyer might have an interest. The buyer agent could then approach the buyer client, review and discuss the disclosure form, and receive an acceptance by the buyer client to revert to customer status for that particular property, or, with disclosure and informed consent, permit the firm to be a dual agent. In either case, both the seller and the buyer must sign the disclosure form and can also sign the informed consent to dual agency form (Figure 2.9) indicating acceptance of the new role.

FIGURE 2.10   A declaration form for use if buyers or sellers refuse to sign disclosure form.

CAPITAL REGION MULTIPLE LISTING SERVICE, INC.

DECLARATION BY REAL ESTATE LICENSEE
PURSUANT TO SECTION 443(3)(F) OF THE REAL PROPERTY LAW

STATE OF NEW YORK   )
) ss.:

COUNTY OF   )

_____ (name of licensee), do hereby swear and affirm under

penalties of perjury:

1. I am a principal broker/associate broker/licensed salesperson affiliated with _____

_____(name of firm). I make this statement in compliance

with Section 443(3)(f) of the New York State Real Property Law.

2. On_____, _____, I presented to_____

_____(name of buyer or seller) the disclosure notice required

under Section 443 of the Real Property Law. A true copy of the actual disclosure form presented to

him/her is attached to this affirmation.

3. Although I indicated to the buyer/seller that New York State Law required that I request that

he/she sign to acknowledge receipt of the disclosure notice, he/she refused to sign the acknowledge-

ment to the disclosure form when presented. The reason given for this refusal was as follows:

_____

_____

_____

Dated: _____ , New York

_____ , _____ .

_____
Print Name Below Signature of Licensee

PUTTING IT TO WORK   Choose a partner to enact the following role-playing exercises. These situations may have a number of alternatives. Your discussion should consist of alternative choices, solutions, and procedures for legally enacting these choices. Compare your role playing with the model in the Answer Key at the end of the chapter.

a. *Sally is a prospective seller; Betty is a listing agent. Sally Seller is about to list her house with Betty Best broker. Betty explains subagency and the liability responsibility that Sally will be accepting. Sally trusts Betty and her firm; however, she does not want any responsibility for agents in other firms although she does want the services of Betty.*

b. *Harry is a listing agent; Helen is a prospective seller. Harry Hoosier goes to a listing appointment. Helen Homeowner likes Harry and his qualifications; however, she tells Harry that two other agents have offered to list the property for less commission. She also states that because all commissions are negotiable in New York, she would like to negotiate with Harry.*

c. *Bill is a customer; Dan is a subagent of the seller. Bill BestBuy has been working with Dan Dealer for several months. Bill has signed a disclosure form and has remained as a buyer customer. Dan has shown the same property to Bill three times as a subagent of the seller and listing agency. Now Bill wants to submit an offer as a buyer client.*

d. *Molly is a seller; Valerie is the listing agent. Molly Maysell has had her house listed for sale with Valerie Value, an agent with Top Sale Real Estate. The listing period is eight months and the house has been on the market for three months. Valerie is resigning from Top Sale and moving her license to High Hat Homes. Molly calls the broker at Top Sale, explains that Valerie is her cousin, and asks the broker to release the listing to High Hat Homes.*

e. *Nathan is a listing agent; the Buynews are customers. Nathan Newhouse is the listing agent and on-site representative for Happy Homes Builders. Ben and Birdy Buynew have signed a disclosure form as buyer customers. Nathan has explained that he represents the builder but can work well with the Buynews. The Buynews, however, choose representation from a buyer agent who presents an offer for the new construction on their behalf. Since Nathan's firm has a registration policy, and since the buyer agent had not registered the Buynews, Nathan claims that the home cannot be purchased without him as the selling agent.*

Change in role from seller client—agent to dual agent. An agent employed by a seller client to represent that client may have another agent in the same brokerage firm who has been employed by a buyer client. This prospective buyer may have a sincere interest in the property listed by the seller agent in the same firm. Since all agents of the listing firm are now subagents of the seller, the listing agent must approach and discuss with the seller a possible dual agency relationship for that particular buyer. The seller and the buyer may then accept the dual agency arrangement and the brokerage firm becomes the dual agent for buyer and seller. Designated agents may be assigned as discussed earlier. Disclosure and informed consent must be made and accepted by all the parties.

OTHER TYPES OF DISCLOSURE

New York laws provide for other types of disclosure and notice to prospective purchasers.

Stigmatized property disclosure. Article 443-a of the Real Property Law deals with stigmatized property disclosure. The law covers all residential property for sale or lease and addresses properties that have: (1) occupants who have AIDS or other illnesses not transmitted through occupancy or (2) properties that were a site of death due to natural causes, accidents, suicide, homicide, or other crime, and other reasons. Under this law, sellers and seller agents do not have to disclose this information and may or may not disclose upon written request of the buyer or buyer agent. A seller agent can only disclose with permission of the seller. A buyer or buyer agent may provide written request for disclosure to the seller or seller agent during negotiations for purchase.

Electrical service. An individual or a company must provide written notice to a purchaser or a purchaser agent if there is no public utility electrical service available at the property being purchased.

Utility surcharge. Also in New York, any individual or company who sells a property where there is a gas or an electric utility surcharge imposed to defray the costs of extending the service to that particular property must provide written notice to a purchaser or purchaser agent. The exact wording must be: "This property is subject to an electric and/or gas utility surcharge." The notice must include the amount of the surcharge and the terms of payment.

Agricultural districts. At or before a purchase offer is made for property located partially or entirely within a state-mandated agricultural district, a specifically worded notice must be given to the purchaser. An agricultural district disclosure form, when necessary, is appended to the contract for purchase and sale.

CASE STUDIES

The following examples of DOS cases brought to administrative hearings will illustrate how DOS makes determinations regarding a real estate licensee's duties and responsibilities as an agent. As you will see from the following case studies, charges alleged by DOS do not always prevail at the hearing.

Department of State, Division of Licensing Services, Complainant, against Chetiara Realty, Inc., and Walt H. Bonar, representative real estate broker, Respondents.

This case deals with alleged undisclosed dual agency.

Allegations. The Complainant alleges that the Respondents acted as an undisclosed double agent by representing simultaneously the diverse interests of both the landlord and the tenant and in so doing, the Respondents: (1) breached the fiduciary duties of full and fair disclosure and of good faith and undivided loyalty owed to a principal, and (2) collected and retained an unearned commission.

Findings of facts. Respondent Bonar is the representative broker of Chetiara Realty and owner of 16 and 2/3 shares of Jhobe Realty Estate Associates, Inc. Chetiara Realty was the rental agent for Jhobe Realty, which owned a building containing three storefronts. Jhobe Realty was not licensed as a real estate broker. A Mr. Reed, of John Reed Realty, a licensed real estate broker, asked Respondent Bonar about the rental of one of the storefronts. In April 1990, Chetiara Realty, as rental agent of and in the same name of Jhobe Realty, rented one of the storefronts to Reed Realty. Reed Realty paid Chetiara Realty a commission of $1,050. Reed claimed that at the time of the rental, he was unaware and not informed by Respondent Bonar that Bonar was the president and principal owner of Jhobe Realty, the building in which the leased premises are located. In an interview with a DOS investigator, Bonar stated that he was not required to and did not inform Reed of his ownership shares in Jhobe Realty. Respondent Bonar claims that Reed was a longtime acquaintance, was aware that Bonar was a minor stockholder with four others in Jhobe Realty, knew that Jhobe Realty owned the property, and knew that Chetiara Realty was the rental agent for the property. Because of that knowledge, Reed came to Chetiara Realty when he wanted to rent the storefront.

Opinion. The evidence is insufficient to establish that the Respondents: (a) acted as an undisclosed double agent and (b) breached the fiduciary duties of full and fair disclosure and undivided loyalty to a principal. The evidence offered in support of the charge that the Respondents failed to make a full and fair disclosure to the tenant is minimal and conflicting. The evidence did not establish what Reed knew or did not know about the legal relationship that existed between Respondent Bonar and Jhobe Realty. The Complainant failed to prove that an agency existed between the real estate broker and the tenant at the time the rental transaction occurred. Consequently, the fiduciary obligations of an agent were not imposed by law on the Respondents. The argument of the Complainant that 19 NYCRR, Section 175.6, is applicable in this case is incorrect; the rule applies to the sale of property in which a broker owns an interest. This rule states that "before a broker sells a property in which he owns an interest, he shall make such interest known to the purchaser." The charge that the Respondents obtained and retained an unearned commission is not supported by the evidence.

Conclusions of law. The evidence is insufficient to support the alleged charges against the Respondents.

Determination. The complaint against the Respondents is dismissed.

Department of State, Division of Licensing Services, Complainant, against Chong S. Piper, as Representative of B. F. Lotus Realty, Inc., Respondent.

Among other issues, this case deals with a broker's alleged failure to disclose to a principal whether Respondent's firm would be acting as the principal's agent.

Allegations. Respondent failed to file a change of address with the Department of State, engaged in the real estate business under an unlicensed trade name, failed to separate the exclusive agency listing agreement explanation from a form given to a seller and failed to disclose to that seller whether or not her firm would be acting as his agent, failed to file a change of association card for an associate broker, and employed an unlicensed salesperson.

Findings of fact. The Respondent notified the Department of State by letter of a change in address, which was the address on the letterhead. The letter was accompanied by a fee and advised that three licensees were relocating to the new address, but it did not include the required change of address forms. It appears that rather than submit the cards, Respondent relied on the license renewal procedure to effectuate the change of address for her individual license. Since Respondent's license did not become due for renewal since the move, Lotus had been conducting business at the new address.

Also, a Mr. Parviz entered into an exclusive right to sell agreement with Respondent, who was acting as representative broker of Lotus, for Lotus to act as his agent in the sale of a vacant lot. Subsequently, Respondent executed a document releasing Parviz from the agency agreement. In both cases, the document listed the name of the broker as simply "Lotus Realty." Printed on the bottom of the agency agreement signed by Parviz and the Respondent is the explanation of exclusive listings mandated by 19 NYCRR 175.24 (b). That explanation, which is signed by Parviz, was not detached from the bottom of the form agreement. Based on the unrefuted testimony of Respondent, the facts show that Respondent told Parviz that Lotus could act as his agent.

An individual associated with Lotus as an associate broker for about one month had never been licensed in association with Lotus. Also, during a period of approximately nine months, Respondent employed a salesperson whose license had expired and had not been renewed.

Opinion. Real Property Law Section 441-a (5) describes that changes of business address shall be in writing "in a manner and form prescribed by the department. . . ." While Respondent sent a letter to DOS advising it of the move, she never responded to the DOS letter telling her that she must file change of address cards even though DOS had supplied them. Although her conduct does not establish an intentional intent to evade the mandate of the statute, it does show a negligent disregard to comply with the specifics of the law.

Pursuant to RPL Section 440-a and 441 (1), a real estate broker may conduct business only under the exact name appearing on the broker license. Respondent also conducted business under the name "Lotus Realty," while in fact licensed to represent B. F. Lotus Realty. While such a departure may seem to be minimal, it can significantly interfere in a search of license records.

19 NYCRR 175.24 provides that any exclusive agency agreement for the sale of residential property (defined as one- to three-family dwellings) must have attached to it or printed on the reverse side an explanation of the terms *exclusive right to sell* and *exclusive agency*. Such an explanation was printed on the bottom of the agreement between Lotus and Parviz. The complaint seems to allege that the regulation is violated since the explanation was printed on the front of the document, rather than being printed on the back or on a separately printed attached sheet. Whatever the merits of the argument might be, the Parviz property was a vacant lot, and therefore not the residential property that is the subject of the regulation. The Complainant, DOS, failed to offer any evidence, other than the testimony of Respondent, that Respondent failed to disclose to Parviz that she would be acting as his agent. The employment of the associate broker who is not licensed in association with that broker is a violation of RPL Section 440-a, which requires "that associate brokers must be licensed under the name and supervision of another broker." Respondent admitted employing a salesperson whose license had expired. RPL Section 442-c provides that a broker who has associated with her as an unlicensed salesperson shall be guilty of a misdemeanor.

Conclusions of law. By relocating her office without proper filing, Respondent demonstrated incompetency; by conducting business under an unlicensed name, the Respondent violated RPL Section 440-a and 441 (1). The charge that involved the agency explanation was dismissed because the property was not residential. The Complainant also failed to establish that Respondent did not disclose to Parviz that she was acting as his agent. By employing an associate broker who was not licensed in association with Piper or Lotus, Respondent violated RPL Section 440-a and 442-c. By employing an unlicensed salesperson, the Respondent violated RPL Section 442-c and demonstrated incompetency.

Determination. Respondent must pay a fine of $750 to the Department of State.

IMPORTANT POINTS

1. When one person is hired to act on behalf of another, an agency relationship is created. Agency is usually created with an agreement (express agency) but also can be implied by the agent's conduct. A position of trust, which is a fiduciary relationship, exists between every principal and agent in an agency relationship.

2. Real estate agents are special agents with specific authority.

3. The agent's fiduciary duties and responsibilities include obedience; loyalty; disclosure of information; confidentiality; accountability; and reasonable care, skill and diligence.

4. A brokerage contract is created when the principal, usually a real estate owner, hires a broker (agent) to perform services relating to the real estate. Every agency relationship is consensual.

5. The principal may authorize the agent to use other people to assist in accomplishing the purpose of the agency. These people are subagents.

6. An agency relationship is not determined by the nature of the compensation (commission or flat fee) or who pays it.

7. An agent may decide to represent either the seller or the buyer in a real estate transaction.

8. A single agent is an agent who works only for the buyer or seller directly and who may elect to reject subagency.

9. A seller agent represents the owner of real property and accepts the employment contract of a listing agreement establishing a client relationship that works in the best interests of the seller.

10. A buyer agent represents the buyer or purchaser of real property and accepts the employment contract of a listing agreement establishing a principal or client relationship working in the best interests of the buyer or purchaser.

11. A dual agent is an agent who attempts to represent both the buyer and the seller in the same transaction. It can occur in real estate companies when the firm attempts to represent both the buyer and seller in the same transaction.

12. A multiple listing service (MLS) offers cooperation and compensation to participating members. It does not create an automatic subagency.

13. Cooperative sales, with seller agents from another real estate firm as subagents of the listing broker and seller, or with buyer agents from another real estate firm, are processed through the usual system of offerings published within MLS.

14. In New York, in the sale or rental of one- to four-unit residential properties, a dual agent must have the *written* approval of both parties after the agent's informed disclosure. The buyer and seller each agree to relinquish the individual, undivided loyalty in the fiduciary relationship.

15. An undisclosed dual agency can result in a violation of New York Real Property Law.

16. Currently, New York real estate firms can provide consensual dual agency for in-house sales.

17. All agents must disclose what party they represent in the real estate transaction.

18. In New York in the sale or rental of one- to four-unit residential properties, the mandatory disclosure regarding real estate agency relationships form must be presented to all parties signing listing agreements and at other meetings and discussions between prospective buyers and sellers at the time of the first substantive contact or meeting.

How Would You Respond?   CHAPTER REVIEW

The following scenarios describe aspects of a real estate transaction in which you will need to define and explain your role and offer supporting documentation. Check your responses using the Answer Key at the end of the chapter.

1. Stella, an associate broker, is on floor duty when Stanley walks in to inquire about a For Sale sign placed by her company on the lawn of a home in his neighborhood. How should Stella handle this situation?

   _____

   _____

   _____

   _____

2. Scarlett, a real estate broker, has interested a prospective buyer in the property she is showing at an open house. She is the listing agent for the house. The prospective buyer refuses to sign the disclosure forms but wants to discuss the property further. What must Scarlett do?

   _____

   _____

   _____

   _____

3. Lois is the listing agent on a property owned by Mr. and Ms. Clark. Another agent in Lois's company has prospective purchaser clients interested in this property. The only trouble is that Lois's sellers refuse to accept dual agency on an in-house sale transaction. How can this sale be handled?

   _____

   _____

   _____

   _____

KEY TERM REVIEW

Fill in the term that best completes each sentence and then check the Answer Key at the end of the chapter.

1. The _____ of the agent is the party who the agent brings to the principal as a seller or buyer of the property.

2. A(n) _____ is someone authorized to handle all affairs of the principal concerning a certain matter or property.

3. A(n) _____ has narrow authorization to act on behalf of the principal.

4. A(n) _____ relationship, that is, a position of trust, exists between agent and principal.

5. _____ may be agents of both the seller and the broker who lists the property.

6. An agency relationship created by an oral or written agreement between the principal and agent is known as a(n) _____.

7. If the words and actions of a broker are accepted by a seller indicating that an agency relationship exists, then they may have created a(n) _____.

8. A broker places an ad to sell a house without the seller's written consent and the seller accepts the actions of the broker after the fact. The agency arrangement created is called _____.

9. A(n) _____ is one who is hired through a broker to work for that broker.

10. One who works only for the seller or buyer directly and who may reject subagency is called a(n) _____.

MULTIPLE CHOICE

Circle the letter that best answers the question and then check the Answer Key at the end of the chapter.

1. From the standpoint of both the agent and the seller, the best type of listing contract is:
   A. open
   B. exclusive agency
   C. net
   D. exclusive right to sell

2. A seller or principal gives a listing to one broker but still retains the commission (instead of the broker) if he (the seller) sells his property during the listing term. Which type of listing is this?
   A. net
   B. open
   C. exclusive agency
   D. exclusive right to sell

3. A real estate salesperson, who is agent of the seller, is asked by a prospective buyer if the household wastewater treatment system works well. The salesperson knows it does not and tells this to the prospective buyer. This disclosure constitutes which of the following?
   A. disloyalty to principal
   B. misrepresentation
   C. required disclosure to buyer
   D. violation of disclosure of information by agent

4. After inspecting a property, the prospective buyers tell the listing salesperson that they like the property but will not pay the listed price of $200,000. Knowing that the owners are going through a divorce and are anxious to sell, the salesperson tells the prospective purchasers about the divorce and suggests they act accordingly. Which of the following statements is correct?
   A. the salesperson is violating his fiduciary duties as agent of the principal
   B. because the salesperson knows the owner is anxious to sell, he is acting correctly
   C. the salesperson is violating his obligations as a universal agent
   D. the prospective buyer can be found guilty of conversion

5. Frances is a property manager for Lakeview Apartments only. In that role she collects rents, advertises, enters into leases, and oversees maintenance. Frances is a(n):
   A. special agent
   B. ostensible agent
   C. general agent
   D. universal agent

6. Because of their religious beliefs, the Goods instruct their agent not to show their home on Friday evenings or Saturdays. On a particular Saturday morning, while the Goods are out, and without their knowledge, the sales agent showed their property to prospective purchasers. This agent:

   A. has violated the fiduciary relationship between himself and the Goods

   B. is working in his clients' best interests because it is almost impossible to sell a house if it cannot be shown during the weekend

   C. has not violated their rights as this arrangement was not specified in the listing contract

   D. has not violated their rights because the prospective purchasers were anxious buyers and could not see the house at any other time

7. Under a special agency agreement with respect to real property, the agent has which of the following rights?

   A. to bind the principal to the contract even if this is not specified in the listing contract

   B. only to market the property

   C. to advise as to the legality of documents that need to be signed by customers and clients

   D. to make decisions on behalf of the principal if the principal is not available to give him direction when needed

8. Karen is a buyer broker representing a couple who are relocating to Hornell, New York, and are very anxious to buy. They decide to purchase a 70-year-old colonial. They ask Karen if she knows of any problems with "this old house." Karen knows that the house has a termite problem. Karen:

   A. need not disclose this to her prospective buyers because only the sellers are liable if there is a problem

   B. need not disclose this to her prospective buyers because both the listing agents and sellers are liable, not her

   C. need not disclose this because the house is not her listing; she is simply representing the buyers

   D. must disclose this to her buyer clients because she has knowledge of the problem

9. Marie and Don work with a buyer agent in purchasing a new raised ranch. They move in the winter and then discover that in the spring the downstairs floods every time it rains. They sue the builder, the listing broker, and their buyer agent. Their buyer agent claims that he talked about the house extensively with the builder and the selling broker and was not informed of this problem. Which of the following is correct? The:

   A. buyer agent is probably not liable as he was never informed of the problem

   B. buyer agent is probably liable whether he was informed or not

   C. house is bought "as is" and none of the parties can ever be found liable

   D. builder is the only party that is not liable as he was not an agent of the buyers

10. Desiree wants a list of apartment houses available and asks her friend, John, a real estate broker, to give this list to her. He gives her the list and does nothing more. Which of the following has been established between the two?

    A. a special agency

    B. agency by ratification

    C. single agency

    D. no agency relationship

11. Benny, a broker, represents the sellers and has found a buyer for their property. Benny tells the buyer that he will find him a mortgage company to finance his purchase and will also assist him in negotiating the purchase offer. Which of the following applies to this scenario?

    A. Benny still represents the sellers only

    B. Benny's assistance in finding a mortgage company has nothing to do with an agency relationship

    C. a broker dual agency has arisen

    D. once Benny has found a ready, willing, and able buyer, he can do whatever is necessary to close the deal without violating his fiduciary relationship with the seller

12. A broker may NOT share compensation with which of the following?

    A. salespersons who work in her firm

    B. unlicensed individuals who are not exempt from license law

    C. licensed real estate brokers from another state

    D. buyer agents

13. Which of the following payment arrangements are unacceptable in New York? Payment:

    A. of a percentage of the sales price

    B. of a prearranged flat fee

    C. of a net amount above the sales price that has been specified and prearranged between broker and principal

    D. by both the seller principal and buyer principal

14. Salespersons may receive compensation from which of the following?

    A. their sponsoring broker

    B. a cooperating broker from another company who is sharing the compensation

    C. sellers in the form of a bonus

    D. buyers in the form of a bonus

15. In New York, dual agency is:

    A. a violation of the law of agency and license law under all circumstances

    B. legally allowable with disclosure and informed consent of all parties to the transaction

    C. only permissible if two different real estate firms represent the seller and buyer respectively

    D. only allowable if the transaction takes place outside New York State

16. With regard to MLS, which of the following is correct?

    A. properties placed in MLS are limited as to commission rates

    B. both cooperating agents and buyer agents may work through MLS

    C. placing a property in MLS automatically creates subagency

    D. properties listed in MLS must be placed by brokers who work full-time

17. Lisa is an agent of the seller; however, she is showing a property to buyer customers. She advises her buyer customers that they should not offer less than the listed price as she is sure the sellers will take no less. The buyers are desperate for the house and take Lisa's advice. In this scenario, which of the following may have happened?

    A. an unintended dual agency may have arisen

    B. Lisa is simply doing her job; that is, working in the best interests of all parties to the transaction

    C. a dual agency cannot exist in this situation if the buyers purchase the house since the deal is closed and the agency relationship is terminated

    D. Lisa's advice was in the best interests of the sellers; her role is the same as agent for the seller

18. Selma lists her property with several different brokerage firms. She retains the right to sell the property herself, in which case she would not owe a commission to any of the listing brokers. This kind of listing contract is known as a(n):

    A. exclusive agency

    B. net listing

    C. exclusive right to sell

    D. open listing

19. Marilyn has completed her listing presentation to sell a home and has the signed listing agreement in hand. This is the only document that was signed. What important document is Marilyn forgetting that must be signed and must accompany all listing agreements according to New York law?

    A. informed consent to dual agency form

    B. disclosure regarding real estate agency relationships form

    C. power of attorney form

    D. contract for purchase and sale

20. A written listing agreement is an example of which of the following?

    A. implied agency

    B. ostensible agency

    C. general agency

    D. express agency

21. Which of the following is FALSE regarding buyer broker relationships?

 A. they occur in residential real estate transactions

 B. a buyer broker may perform a market analysis and advise the buyer about offers

 C. they are not used in commercial transactions

 D. a buyer broker may be paid through a percentage of the selling price of the property that his buyer customers are buying

22. In which of the following situations is disclosure and informed consent NOT necessary?

 A. at the first substantive contact, when some detail about the property is shared with parties who express interest

 B. when setting up a phone appointment to view a property even though no other specific information is shared

 C. when a meeting and viewing of the property take place

 D. when a prospective buyer or seller walks into a real estate office and wants to discuss listing or purchasing a property

23. Which of the following is NOT a type of disclosure mandated by law in New York?

 A. electrical service

 B. radon

 C. utility surcharge

 D. agricultural districts

24. In New York, the use of the disclosure form covers which of the following?

 A. the sales and rental of all residential and commercial property

 B. the sales of all property used for residential purposes only

 C. the sales and rental of all residential property

 D. the sales and rental of all one- to four-unit residential properties, excluding condominiums, cooperatives containing more than four units, and vacant land

25. If a prospective client or customer refuses to sign the disclosure form, the sales agent must sign and keep on file a Declaration by Real Estate Licensee pursuant to Section 443 (3)(f) for a period of:

 A. one year

 B. two years

 C. three years

 D. five years

ANSWER KEY

Putting It to Work

The following responses are only suggestions; other variations are possible.

a. Betty must first explain to Sally the traditional procedure of MLS and why Betty might want to change her mind about the responsibility issue. Subagents will work hard to sell her property as there is generally a higher commission split for subagency, which provides agents with more incentive. Other choices, however, are available. The agents in Betty's firm can be the only subagents and Sally may have cooperating agents through MLS to market her property. These cooperating agents may be buyer agents who will, however, be working in the best interests of buyers. Sally may also designate her broker to hire broker's agents. The broker who hires these broker agents will accept vicarious liability for their actions and Sally will not be liable for the activities of the broker's agents.

b. Helen is correct about the fact that commissions are negotiable in New York. However, Harry explains that they are generally part of individual office policies which Harry, in his position in his firm, does not have the power to negotiate. Harry should focus on what he has to offer in the way of marketing Helen's property and suggest that if she is interested in his company, she can arrange to discuss any deviation from office policy with the principal broker.

c. In this case, Dan must switch from a subagent representing the best interests of the seller to a buyer agent representing the best interests of Bill, the prospective purchaser. New disclosure forms would have to be signed and, as a courtesy, Dan should notify the listing agent about the change in his agency role. In confronting the sellers with his buyer client, Dan should also disclose his role as buyer agent and make written disclosures.

d. A listing is the property of the broker who obtains it. However, if the broker chooses to release the listing, she must explain to the homeseller that the company has had expenses to date in marketing the property. Written agreements regarding compensation for time, money, and effort already expended would have to be drawn and paid either immediately or upon the sale of the property by the seller. Other types of financial agreements are possible.

e. Many firms that have on-site construction offer registration so that prospective purchasers automatically become customers of the firm. However, since the customers have no one representing their best interests, they are entitled to go to an agent in another firm for representation. A registration of this type is not a written and signed listing agreement, and therefore the registration with Nathan and his firm is not enforceable.

How Would You Respond?

1. Stella should respond to questions asked about the property and give Stanley any available information. If he expresses further interest in the property, Stella should bring out the disclosure regarding real estate agency relationships form. She should give Stanley some time to read the form, explain it to him, and then they should both sign it.

2. Scarlett should document the facts and circumstances of the prospective buyer's refusal. Scarlett can further discuss the details of the property. However, at the earliest possible moment, she must complete the declaration by real estate licensee pursuant to Section 443(3)(F) of the Real Property Law form, stating all of the facts; have it notarized; retain a copy for her own records; and provide a copy to the broker to be kept on file for three years.

3. Several alternatives are available. The purchaser clients could dissolve the agency relationship with the firm. Then Lois's clients could continue with the same representation as they now have. The purchaser clients may elect customer status in the firm without representation and choose to represent themselves. They may also ask an attorney for representation, or may go to an agent in another firm. If the purchaser clients refuse, the seller clients could be given the same alternatives.

Key Term Review

1. customer
2. general agent
3. special agent
4. fiduciary
5. subagents
6. express agency
7. implied agency
8. ratification
9. broker's agent
10. single agent

Multiple Choice

1. D	8. D	15. B	22. B
2. C	9. A	16. B	23. B
3. C	10. D	17. A	24. D
4. A	11. C	18. D	25. C
5. C	12. B	19. B	
6. A	13. C	20. D	
7. B	14. A	21. C	

Chapter 3

KEY TERMS

adjustable rate mortgage

amortized mortgage

bridge loan

buydown

construction loan

conventional loans

convertible mortgage

Department of Veteran Affairs (VA)

depression

disintermediation

Federal Housing Administration (FHA)

gap financing

ground lease

home equity loan

inflation

installment land contract (contract for deed)

loan-to-value ratio

mortgagee

mortgagor

primary mortgage market

recession

redlining

release clause

sale leaseback

secondary mortgage market

stagflation

State of New York Mortgage Agency (SONYMA)

subordinate lease

underwriting

usury

LEARNING OBJECTIVES   *Classroom hours: 5*

1. Define *mortgage* and describe the various types of mortgages.
2. Discuss the methods of underwriting construction loans.
3. Discuss the use of the lease as a form of financing property.
4. Describe the history and development of FHA financing.
5. Discuss how the economy affects the real estate market.
6. Explain how various lending policies affect the real estate market.
7. Recognize the various real estate cycles.

Real Estate Finance II

IN THIS CHAPTER Appropriate financing is at the backbone of every successful transaction; without financing, there is no sale. Prospective purchasers need to be presented with a variety of options to bring about the desired goal. This chapter discusses types of mortgages and financing, the economy and its effect on real estate cycles, and an update of lending policies.

LENDING PRACTICES

The two main lending practices, or theories of financing, are:

1. *Title theory (granting theory),* in which a disinterested third party holds legal title to the property in security for the loan through a *deed of trust.* The mortgagor (borrower) conveys title to the property to a trustee, a type of third-party referee. When the mortgagor completes paying off the debt, the trustee is required to return title to the trustor, the borrower, by executing a deed of release. If the borrower defaults, the lender (mortgagee) may instruct the trustee to sell the title to recover the lender's funds. Because the lender therefore benefits from the trust title, the lender is also known as the beneficiary. The deed of trust is not generally used in New York.

2. *Lien (or mortgage) theory,* in which the loan constitutes a lien against the real property. The mortgage is a two-party instrument between the lender and the borrower. This theory is the basis for mortgages in New York.

THE MORTGAGE

Cash sales of real property are certainly the exception, not the rule. Without the mortgage, there would be comparatively few real estate transactions. Mortgages are not limited to banks. Lending possibilities include insurance companies, private mortgage companies, real estate investment trusts, syndicates, and seller financing. Other types of financing include lease arrangements (discussed later). Special types of mortgages are available for a variety of purchaser needs.

DEFINITION OF A MORTGAGE

A *mortgage* is a two-party legal document pledging a described property as security for the repayment of a loan under certain terms and conditions. *The borrower who gives the mortgage is called the* **mortgagor.** *The lender who receives the mortgage is known as the* **mortgagee** (Figure 3.1). The borrower (mortgagor) retains title (ownership) to the property, but this title is encumbered by the lien created by the mortgage in favor of the lender (mortgagee). If the lender is not paid according to the terms of the mortgage and note, the lender can foreclose the lien.

Typically, the borrower's personal promise to pay the debt is not enough security for the large amount of money involved in a mortgage loan. The lender therefore requires the additional security of the property itself as collateral for the loan. Pledging property as security for the loan (hypothecating) is accomplished through the mortgage. Therefore, every mortgage loan has two instruments: (a) the note (a personal IOU), and (b) the mortgage. Pledging the property does not require the borrower to give up possession except in case of default.

Mortgage Clauses and Covenants

Examples of the various clauses and covenants that may be included in a mortgage are as follows:

1. The mortgage is dated and contains the names of mortgagor and mortgagee.
2. The note or bond executed by the (mortgagor) borrower is reproduced in the mortgage. The note includes an *acceleration clause* enabling the lender to declare the entire balance remaining immediately due and payable if the borrower is in default.
3. The note may provide a *prepayment penalty clause* stating either that the borrower is permitted to pay off the loan any time prior to expiration of the full mortgage term without incurring a financial penalty for the early payoff, or that a prepayment penalty will be imposed on the borrower if the debt is satisfied prior to expiration of the full term. Most loans, however, including FHA and VA loans, cannot have a prepayment penalty; therefore this clause is more often found in owner financing or commercial loans. However, residential mortgages given to institutional lenders may provide for a prepayment penalty if the mortgage is paid within the first year.
4. The mortgage contains a *defeasance clause* giving the borrower the right to defeat and remove the lien by paying the indebtedness in full.

FIGURE 3.1
An illustration of a mortgage transaction.

MORTGAGOR
The *borrower gives* a mortgage to the lender.

MORTGAGEE
The *lender receives* a mortgage from the borrower.

The borrower (mortgagor) must give the lender (mortgagee) a mortgage lien and a promissory note or bond in return for the borrowed funds.

5. The mortgage provides the right of foreclosure to the lender if the borrower fails to make payments as scheduled or fails to fulfill other obligations as set forth in the mortgage.

6. In the mortgage, a covenant always specifies that the mortgagor has a good and marketable title to the property pledged to secure payment of the note.

7. The mortgage may contain an *alienation clause* (due-on-sale clause) entitling the lender to declare the principal balance immediately due and payable if the borrower sells the property during the mortgage term and making the mortgage unassumable without the lender's permission. Permission to assume the mortgage at an interest rate prevailing at the time of assumption can be given at the discretion of the lender. The alienation clause may provide for release of the original borrower from liability if an assumption is permitted. This release is sometimes referred to as a *novation*.

8. The mortgage always provides for execution by the borrower.

9. The mortgage provides for acknowledgment by the borrower to make the document eligible for recording on the public record for the lender's protection. (See Figure 3.2, which defines various mortgage clauses.)

Note or Bond

In making a mortgage loan, the lender requires the borrower to sign a *promissory note,* or bond. The note, which must be in writing, provides evidence that a valid debt exists. The note contains a promise that the borrower will be personally liable for paying the amount of money set forth in the note and specifies the manner in which the debt is to be paid. Payment is typically in monthly installments of a stated amount, commencing on a certain date. The note also states the annual rate of interest to be charged on the outstanding principal balance. The note and mortgage are generally part of the same document. See Figure 3.3 for an example of a bond and mortgage.

FIGURE 3.2   A summary of note and mortgage clauses.

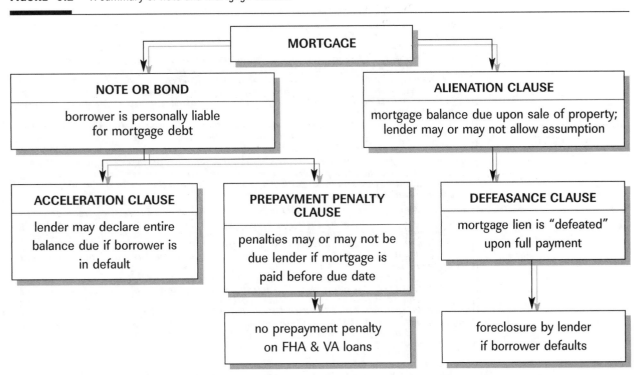

FIGURE 3.3
Bond and mortgage.

FORM 547X N. Y. BOND AND MORTGAGE, FULL COVENANT AND LIEN

TUTBLANX REGISTERED U. S. PAT. OFFICE
TUTTLE LAW PRINT, PUBLISHERS, RUTLAND, VT. 05701

This Bond and Mortgage.

Made the day of

Nineteen Hundred and

Between

the mortgagor , and

the mortgagee

Witnesseth, *That the mortgagor , do hereby acknowledge to be indebted to the mortgagee in the sum of Dollars,*
(*$*) *lawful money of the United States, which the mortgagor do hereby agree and bind to pay to the mortgagee*

to secure the payment of which the mortgagor hereby mortgage to the mortgagee

AND the mortgagor

covenant with the mortgagee as follows:

1. *That the mortgagor will pay the indebtedness as hereinbefore provided.*
2. *That the mortgagor will keep the buildings on the premises insured against loss by fire for the benefit of the mortgagee ; that will assign and deliver the policies to the mortgagee ; and that will reimburse the mortgagee for any premiums paid for insurance made by the mortgagee on the mortgagor default in so insuring the buildings or in so assigning and delivering the policies.*

3. *That no building on the premises shall be removed or demolished without the consent of the mortgagee*

4. *That the whole of said principal sum and interest shall become due at the option of the mortgagee : after default in the payment of any installment of principal or of interest for days; or after default in the payment of any tax, water rate or assessment for days after notice and demand; or after default after notice and demand either in assigning and delivering the policies insuring the buildings against loss by fire or in reimbursing the mortgagee for premiums paid on such insurance, as hereinbefore provided; or after default upon request in furnishing a statement of the amount due on the bond and mortgage and whether any offsets or defenses exist against the mortgage debt, as hereinafter provided.*
5. *That the holder of this bond and mortgage, in any action to foreclose the mortgage, shall be entitled to the appointment of a receiver.*

6. *That the Mortgagor will pay all insurance premiums, taxes, assessments or water rates, and in default thereof, the legal holder of this mortgage shall have the right to cause such property to be so insured in the owner's name, and to pay such taxes and assessments, adding the proper expense thereof to the principal sum secured under this mortgage.*

7. *That the mortgagor within days upon request in person or within days upon request by mail will furnish a written statement duly acknowledged of the amount due on this bond and mortgage and whether any offsets or defenses exist against the mortgage debt.*
8. *That notice and demand or request may be in writing and may be served in person or by mail.*
9. *That the mortgagor warrant the title to the premises.*
10. *That, in Compliance with section 13 of the Lien Law, the mortgagor will receive the advances secured by this mortgage and will hold the right to receive such advances as a trust fund to be applied first for the purpose of paying the cost of improvement, and that the mortgagor will apply the same first to the payment of the cost of improvement before using any part of the total of the same for any other purpose.*

Source: Reprinted with permission of Tuttle Law Print, Inc., Rutland, VT 05701.

Principal, Interest, and Payment Plans

Interest is the money paid for using someone else's money. The mortgage principal is the amount of money borrowed on which interest is either *paid or received.* In the case of an interest-bearing note, *principal* is the amount of money the lender has lent the borrower and on which the borrower will pay interest to the lender.

The note can be an interest-only note on which interest is paid periodically until the note matures and the entire principal balance is paid at maturity. Construction notes are usually of this type. Or the note can be a single-payment loan that requires no payments on either principal or interest until the note matures, and the entire principal and interest are paid at maturity. This occurs more frequently with short-term notes. The note also can be an amortized note in which periodic payments are made on both principal and interest until such time as the principal is completely paid. Most mortgage loans are of the latter type. The original principal is the total amount of the note. This amount remains the same in an interest-only or a one-payment loan until the entire principal is paid. *Tax deductible* expenses involved in home ownership are *mortgage interest* (not principal) and ad valorem real property taxes paid to local taxing authorities.

MORTGAGE REQUIREMENTS

Duties and Rights of the Mortgagor (Borrower)

In addition to paying the debt insured by the mortgage, the mortgage requires the borrower to pay all real property taxes and assessments on a timely basis; keep the buildings in proper repair; and protect against loss by fire or other casualty by an insurance policy written in an amount at least 80 percent of the value of the structure. Many lenders also require insurance for 100 percent of the loan value minus the lot value.

Rights of the borrower include:

1. The right to possession of the property during the mortgage term as long as the borrower is not in default.
2. The defeasance clause, which gives the borrower the right to redeem the title and have the mortgage lien released at any time prior to default by paying the debt in full.

Rights of the lender include:

1. The right to take possession of the property (after foreclosure) if the borrower defaults in mortgage payments and the lender is the purchaser at the sale.
2. The right to foreclose on the property if the borrower defaults on the payments.
3. The right to assign the mortgage. This enables the lender to sell the mortgage and thereby free up the money invested. The right of *assignment* provides liquidity to mortgages because the lender can sell the mortgage at any time and obtain the money invested rather than wait for payment of the loan over an extended time.

Lenders' Criteria for Granting a Loan

Investment Quality of the Property

Some of the considerations the lender must include in the evaluation process are neighborhood and location, site analysis, condition of the property, improvements, economic life, and comparable value to other similar properties. The *sales price* that

LTV = loan / value

Appraisal ← value
Lesser of ← sale price

the purchaser has agreed to pay should be comparable with the recent sales prices of other similar properties in an area or neighborhood as close to the subject property as possible. An appraisal is performed for the subject property. Based on the gathered data, the appraiser makes a final reconciliation of value. This is the appraised value, and the lender, after reviewing the appraisal, makes a conclusion as to value.

Loan-to-Value Ratio

The loan-to-value (LTV) is the ratio of the loan amount to the property value. The *loan-to-value ratio compares the loan amount to the property value.* The value of the property for mortgage purposes is either the appraised value or the purchase price, whichever is less. For example, a loan of $200,000 on a property valued at $400,000 is at an LTV of 50%. Loan-to-value ratios are determined by the primary lender, Fannie Mae, or the secondary mortgage market. The importance of a prevailing loan-to-value ratio is in determining the down payment amount. A down payment is the difference between the purchase price and the amount the lender will loan. In New York, if the loan-to-value ratio is greater than 80 percent, a purchaser must obtain private mortgage insurance (PMI).

Borrower's Ability to Repay Loan

The buyer's ability to pay consists of the following considerations:

Income/Salary. Even if employment is stable, income may not be. Borrowers must submit signed federal income tax returns for the most recent two years. Income reported on past tax returns is averaged with current verified income to reflect a stable income figure. In reaching a stable income figure, self-employed or commissioned employees with declining incomes are evaluated against offsetting factors.

Overtime and bonus income usually are not counted unless the borrower verifies stability over the prior two years. Part-time income can be counted if the borrower has held the job continuously for the past two years and seems likely to continue. Seasonal employment is counted if it is uninterrupted over a two-year period and prospects for continued employment are evident.

Qualifying ratios. The underwriter must calculate the borrower's two debt ratios: (a) monthly housing expense to income, and (b) total payment obligations to income. These ratios determine the borrower's ability to meet home ownership responsibilities. The ratios most lenders in the secondary market recognize are:

	Monthly housing expense	Total obligations
Conventional loans		
Fixed-rate	28%	36%
Adjustable-rate	28%	36%
FHA loans	29%	41%
VA loans	None	41%

Monthly housing expense includes: principal and interest of mortgage payment plus escrow deposits for hazard insurance premium; real estate taxes and mortgage insurance premium; owners' or condominium association charges, less the utility charge portion; any ground rents or special assessments; and payments under any secondary financing on the subject property. These ratios do not constitute absolute requirements. A borrower who has an excellent credit history or the capability for future increased earnings and savings may be considered.

Mortgage Loan Origination, Application Review, and Loan Underwriting

Once a borrower has contracted to purchase a home, the process of arranging for mortgage financing commences. The main document in the loan origination process is the loan application. Customarily, the borrower's and the lender's representatives meet, and the borrower completes the loan application at this initial meeting. The first step in loan processing is to order an appraisal and a credit report.

Application Review

The purpose of loan processing is to verify all data the borrower presents in the loan application. The involved parties compare the verified information with the application data. The borrower must explain items that do not match and must obtain additional verification or data. For example, employment income, bank deposits, and outstanding debts must be the same on the credit report as on the loan application. Although the loan processor is not the loan underwriter, the processor sometimes may decline the loan before submitting to underwriting if the borrower clearly will not qualify because of excessive debts or insufficient income, or if the property fails to meet the lender's standards of condition or value.

Loan Underwriting

Once all information has been verified and the loan documentation assembled, the loan processor submits the loan to **underwriting.** The underwriter is responsible *for reviewing the loan documentation and evaluating the borrower's ability and willingness to repay the loan and the sufficiency of the collateral value of the property.* The underwriter may be someone on the lender's staff or, in the case of a loan designated for sale, someone on the investor's staff. For FHA and VA loans, the relevant agencies have delegated underwriting responsibility to the lender. For conventional loans over 80 percent loan-to-value and requiring mortgage insurance, an underwriting submission also must be made to the private mortgage insurance company. Many factors govern loan underwriting. Basically, however, loan underwriting can be divided into three categories: buyer's ability to pay, buyer's willingness to pay, and property evaluation.

Discount Points

Lending institutions may charge *discount points* in making mortgage loans. Each point that the lender charges costs someone (either the buyer or the seller, depending upon the situation) 1 percent of the loan amount, paid at the time of loan closing. Lenders may charge discount points in conventional loans. At times of high interest rates and short supply of money for making mortgage loans, lenders often charge one or two points in making 90 percent and 95 percent conventional loans. New York has **usury** laws that fix a maximum allowable interest rate. (*Usury refers to charging a higher interest than that allowable by law.*) This maximum rate is subject to fluctuation. Borrowers sometimes volunteer to pay discount points to **buy down** or *reduce a mortgage interest rate at the time the loan is made.*

TYPES OF MORTGAGES

The Single-Family Home Mortgage

Home mortgage loans that may be obtained from lending institutions are divided into two groups: conventional loans and government loans. **Conventional loans** involve *no participation by an agency of the federal government.* Many kinds of conventional mortgage loans exist that are either uninsured or insured. Government loans are guaranteed, insured, or funded by a government agency, such as the Federal Housing Administration (FHA) (discussed later), Department of Veteran Affairs (VA), Rural Housing Service (RHS), and the State of New York Mortgage Agency (SONYMA). See Table 3.1, Summary of government mortgage loans.

- The **Department of Veteran Affairs** Guaranteed Loan Program offers a guaranteed loan program that *guarantees repayment of the top portion of the loan to the lender in the event the borrower defaults.* Unlike the FHA, the VA does not set maximum loan amounts. The VA-guaranteed loan is a 100 percent loan; therefore, no down payment is generally required.
- The Rural Housing Service (RHS) is an agency of the Department of Agriculture (USDA). RHS makes direct loans, guarantees loans made by private lenders, and provides a limited number of grants.
- The **State of New York Mortgage Agency (SONYMA),** also known as Sonny Mae, *raises money from the sale of New York tax-free bonds, which then is used for mortgage loans.* Sonny Mae mortgages are available through participating lenders at lower interest rates than most conventional loans.

The following describes some of the types of home mortgages:

Fixed Rate Loan

This loan carries the same rate of interest for the entire term of the loan.

Straight-Term Mortgage

In a straight-term mortgage, the borrower pays interest only for a specified term and, at the end of the term, the borrower is required to pay the principal. This type of mortgage was primarily used before and during the depression in the 1930s.

TABLE 3.1   A summary of government mortgage loans.

NAME	AGENCY	WHAT IT DOES	SPECIAL REQUIREMENTS
Federal Housing Authority (FHA)	U.S. Department of Housing and Urban Development	insures loans	buyer qualification upfront mortgage insurance premiums maximum loan amounts
Department of Veteran Affairs (VA)	Department of Veteran Affairs	guarantees loans	buyer must be veteran guarantees up to 100% of appraised value on sales price no maximum loan amount no down payment
Rural Housing Service (RHS)	U.S. Department of Agriculture	makes direct loans guarantees loans makes some grants	borrowers must reside in rural areas loan up to 100% appraised value
State of New York Mortgage Agency (SONYMA)	State of New York Mortgage Agency	makes loans	percentage of loans go to buyers in target areas nontarget area loan can be made to first-time buyers or borrowers who have been nonowners for 3 years, insured by private mortgage insurance

Adjustable Rate Mortgage (ARM)

With the **adjustable rate mortgage (ARM)**, the *parties agree to float mortgage rates based on the fluctuations of a standard index.* Common indices include the cost of funds for savings and loan institutions, the national average mortgage rate, and the more popular one-year rate for the government's sale of Treasury bills.

For an ARM, the lender designates an index and then adds a *margin* (*measure of profit*) above this index. For example, if the Treasury bill (T-bill) index was 7 and the lender's margin was 2.50, the ARM would call for an interest rate of 9.5. (Margins sometimes are expressed in terms of basis points. Each basis point is 1/100 of a percent, or 250 basis points in the above example.) Some mortgages may contain an *escalator clause,* which gives the lender the right to increase monthly payments or interest rates based on the T-bill index or other economic fluctuations.

ARMs are structured with *rate caps* (ceilings) that limit both the annual adjustment and the total adjustment during the lifetime of the loan. For example, annual increases could be limited to perhaps 1 or 2 percent interest, and the lifetime of the loan cap might be no higher than perhaps 5 or 6 percent.

A payment cap may also be offered by the lender. If the interest rate on the loan changes and therefore the monthly payments increase, the lender allows a payment cap, in which the monthly payment remains the same and the money for the higher interest rate is added to the principal. This interest then accumulates onto the principal that eventually will have to be paid. This is an example of *negative amortization.* Many modern ARMs prohibit negative amortization.

A significant concern in an ARM is the possibility of negative amortization. When the index rises while the payment is fixed, it may cause payments to fall below the amount necessary to pay the interest required by the index. This shortfall is added back into the principal, causing the principal to grow larger after the payment.

Balloon Mortgage

The *balloon mortgage* provides for installment payments that are not enough to pay off the principal and interest over the term of the mortgage, so the final payment (called a balloon payment) is substantially larger than any previous payment, to satisfy the remaining principal and interest. If this balloon payment is to be a substantial amount, the note may provide for refinancing by the lender to provide the funds to the borrower if he cannot otherwise make the final payment.

Amortized Mortgage

FHA will insure only **amortized mortgages;** *that is, mortgages that retire the debt.* As a result of this and of the potential hardship for borrowers under the term mortgage, the typical home mortgage loan today is the amortized mortgage, whether the loan is FHA, VA, or conventional. As previously explained, amortization provides for paying a debt by installment payments. A portion of each payment is applied first to the interest and the remainder to the principal. The interest always is applied against only the outstanding principal balance unpaid at the time of an installment payment. The rate of interest is an annual percentage rate as specified by the note and mortgage. The interest rate is calculated by multiplying the annual percentage rate by the unpaid principal balance and dividing the result by 12 (months) to determine the amount of interest that is due and payable for any monthly installment.

After deducting the interest, the remainder of the payment goes to reduce the principal balance. Therefore, the amount of interest paid with each installment declines because the interest rate is applied against a smaller and smaller amount of principal.

In this way, the loan is amortized, so the final payment in a fully amortized mortgage will pay any remaining interest and principal.

Reverse Annuity Mortgage

The *reverse annuity mortgage* is often used by older people who need additional income and want to take advantage of the equity in their homes. The lender makes payments to the borrower for a contracted period of time. Upon the death of the homeowner or the sale of the property, the lender recaptures the equity or amount paid during the mortgage term.

Installment Land Contract (Contract for Deed)

The **installment land contract (also known as contract for deed)** is both a contract of sale and a financing instrument. The seller provides a method of purchasing the property, and the buyer makes installment payments. *Under this type of contract, the purchaser has equitable title; that is, ownership right to the property being purchased even though the title is still in the name of the seller.* Once all payments are made and all contractual obligations are met, title is transferred to the purchaser. Under equitable title, if the seller refuses to transfer title once the terms of the contract have been met and the purchase price has been paid, then the purchaser can sue for *specific performance* to force the seller to transfer the title. In some instances, an installment contract may contain a clause that provides for *liquidated damages* if the purchaser defaults on the contract. For example, if the purchaser does not make the payments contracted for, the seller may claim that all payments previously made remain with the seller as the liquidated damages caused by purchaser's default. Unlike mortgages, installment land contracts cannot be foreclosed for nonpayment since the purchaser does not generally hold title until the final payment is made.

Blanket Mortgage

In a *blanket mortgage,* two or more parcels of real estate are pledged as security for payment of the mortgage debt. The blanket mortgage usually contains a **release clause** *that allows certain parcels of property to be removed from the mortgage lien if the loan balance is reduced by a specified amount.* The mortgage always should provide that sufficient property value remain subject to the mortgage lien to secure the remaining principal balance at any given time.

Real estate developers typically use blanket mortgages with release clauses. In this way, the mortgagor can obtain the release of certain parcels from the lien of the mortgage and convey clear title to purchasers to generate a profit and provide the funds to make future mortgage payments.

Shared Appreciation Mortgage

The shared appreciation mortgage (SAM) allows the lender to benefit from the appreciation of property value in exchange for a lower rate of interest to the borrower. Typically, for one-third share in appreciation, the lender makes the loan at a rate one-third less than the going rate for a first-term conventional loan at the time the loan is created. The increase in value that the lender shares is evidenced by the price for which the borrower sells the property, as compared to the price paid for the property. Federal regulations require that if the property is not sold within 10 years, the property must be appraised and the lending institution must receive its one-third share of the value increase as shown by the appraisal. This could result in a substantial hardship for the borrower who does not sell within the 10-year term. This borrower may have to refinance to obtain the money to pay the lender the one-third share of value increase.

Commercial Mortgage

A commercial mortgage is usually made to a business enterprise. Examples are residential subdivisions, shopping centers, apartment complexes, mobile home parks, recreational centers, and so on. To obtain a commercial mortgage, a portfolio fully describing the project and the financial strength of the borrower must be presented to the lender. The commercial mortgage may contain a number of contingencies before the loan will be made. These contingencies must be met by the borrower. Some examples of contingencies include a percentage lease for certain tenants, an audited financial statement, an appraisal of the property, and a cash flow projection for the property. A commercial mortgage usually will include an assignment of leases, personal guarantees, and a substantial down payment.

Package Mortgage

In a *package mortgage,* personal property in addition to real property is pledged to secure payment of the mortgage loan. Typical examples of these items are the large household appliances. The package mortgage is used in the sale of furnished condominium apartments and includes all furnishing in the unit. This method is also common in commercial real estate lending where the business assets are offered as collateral.

SPECIAL TYPES OF MORTGAGES

Purchase Money Mortgage

The *purchase money mortgage* is a mortgage given by a buyer to the seller to cover part of the purchase price. The seller becomes the mortgagee and the buyer becomes the mortgagor. The seller conveys title to the buyer, who immediately reconveys or pledges it as security for the balance of the purchase price. The seller is financing the sale of the property for the buyer in the amount of the purchase money mortgage. The purchase money mortgage may be a first mortgage, a typical junior mortgage, or a junior mortgage in the form of a wraparound.

Gap Financing

Gap financing is *usually a short-term loan, or one that provides funds over and above an already existing loan until more permanent financing is in place.* It can also provide necessary temporary funds to a purchaser until permanent financing is available. *One example of gap financing is a* **bridge loan.** For example, purchaser contracts on house sales often are written contingent upon sale of the buyer's property. However, the seller may be unwilling to accept such a contingency. Bridge financing provides a vehicle for the buyer to obtain the new house without having to sell her property. For this financing, usually the sum of the mortgage on the buyer's house plus the bridge loan must not exceed 85 percent of the appraised value of the buyer's house. Bridge loans typically run 90 days in maturity because of the prediction that the buyer's house will close soon. The 90 days can be rolled over. Banks have found bridge financing to be successful only in cases when the buyer's house is already under contract.

The *swing loan* is another example of gap financing. A swing loan (also sometimes known as a type of interim or bridge loan) is usually not secured by a mortgage. A borrower uses the equity that he has in one property to obtain the money necessary to buy another property. When the property borrowed against is sold, the money from the sale is used to pay back the loan. A solid credit background is generally needed to obtain this type of loan. In addition, gap financing is available for commercial projects.

Wraparound Mortgage

A wraparound mortgage is a type of seller financing. It is a subordinate mortgage that includes the same principal obligation secured by a superior mortgage against the same property. This mortgage "wraps around" the existing first mortgage, which stays in place. The seller of the property makes a wraparound loan to the buyer, who takes title to the property subject to the existing first mortgage. The seller continues to make the payments on the first mortgage, and the buyer makes the payments to the seller on the wraparound.

The wraparound mortgage can be beneficial to both seller and buyer. The seller makes payments on the existing first mortgage at an old and often lower interest rate and on a smaller initial loan amount. The seller receives the buyer's payments on a substantially larger loan amount at a higher rate of interest than the seller is paying on the existing first mortgage. In this way, the seller receives principal payments on the second mortgage and earns interest income on the amount by which the interest received on the wraparound exceeds the interest being paid on the existing first mortgage. In addition, the wraparound may enable the seller to effect a sale that otherwise may not have been accomplished in times of high interest rates and tight money. The benefits to the buyer in this situation include purchasing the property with a small down payment and obtaining seller financing at a rate usually several percentage points below the prevailing market rate for new financing at that time.

Subordinate Mortgage

A junior mortgage or *subordinate mortgage* describes priority rather than a type of mortgage. A junior mortgage describes *any mortgage that is subordinate (lower in priority) to another mortgage.* A junior mortgage may be a second mortgage, a third mortgage, or a fourth mortgage. Each of these is subordinate to any prior mortgage secured by the same property. Junior mortgages are usually for a shorter term and at a higher interest rate because they pose a greater risk to the lender than a first mortgage.

Second mortgages, the most common form of junior mortgages, are often used to finance part of the difference between the purchase price of a property and the loan balance being assumed in a purchase involving assumption of the seller's existing mortgage. The seller often offers a short-term (five-, seven-, or ten-year) purchase money second mortgage to the buyer for part of the difference when the buyer does not have the funds to pay the full amount.

Priority and Subordination

Priority of mortgage liens usually is established by the time (date and hour) the lien is recorded. In the event of a foreclosure sale, the holder of the first lien has the first claim against the sale proceeds, and that debt must be fully satisfied before the holder of the second lien is fully satisfied, and so on down the line of priorities. In some instances, the order of priority can be modified by a subordination agreement, whereby an earlier lender may be willing to subordinate (take a back seat) to a later lender. Typically lenders will only subordinate their mortgage to another mortgage if they are certain the property value is sufficient to pay off both mortgages should foreclosure become necessary. An example of subordination is the lien holder on a building lot subordinating a mortgage lien to the construction mortgage lien.

Convertible Mortgage—Converting Mortgage to Equity

The **convertible mortgage** is generally used in commercial type endeavors. *A provision in the mortgage gives the lender the option of converting the outstanding balance into an agreed-upon percentage of ownership in the property.* The date when this conversion will occur is specified in the mortgage along with the time frame in which this conversion may take place. This arrangement is helpful to a buyer who may otherwise not be able to obtain the financing necessary for the project. For tax purposes, until conversion takes place, the entire property belongs to the buyer. The lender also has an opportunity to turn what may have been a risky investment at the onset into actual equity at a given time in the project and reap the rewards of a project that has now increased in value.

The Home Equity Loan as a Second Mortgage

A **home equity loan** is *a loan against the equity in a home.* It can be a first mortgage if the property is owned free and clear or second (junior) mortgage if there is an existing first mortgage. Usually, the interest rates are higher on a home equity loan because the loan is for a shorter term than for other types of mortgages. Some home equity loans are term loans for which one pays interest only at first, and then the later payments are attributable to the principal. (One provision the Internal Revenue Service imposes upon home equity loans is that the loan amount cannot exceed the original purchase price of the house plus improvements. Interest on accounts exceeding that amount is not deductible.)

CONSTRUCTION LOANS

The **construction loan** is a form of *interim, or temporary, short-term financing for creating improvements on land.* The applicant for a construction loan submits, for the lender's appraisal, the plans and specifications for the structure to be built and the property on which the construction is to take place. The lender makes the construction loan based on the value resulting from an appraisal of the property and the construction plans and specifications. The loan contract specifies that disbursements will be made as specified stages of the construction are completed, for example, after the foundation is laid or upon framing. Interest is not charged until the money has actually been disbursed. Upon completion, the lender makes a final inspection and closes out the construction loan, which is then converted to permanent, long-term financing or replaced by financing obtained by the property's buyer.

Often the lender requires the builder to be bonded for completion of the property. The bond is made payable to the lender in the event the builder goes bankrupt and is unable to complete the construction. In this way, the lender can obtain the funds to complete the construction and have a valuable asset to sell and recover the monies extended under the construction loan.

If the mortgage commitment is strictly a short-term construction loan, permanent financing (for example, 30 years) will have to be established. *Permanent financing on a short-term construction loan is known as a take-out loan or an end loan.* The commitment is necessary to ensure long-term financing within the mortgagor's means.

A construction loan is considered one of the hardest loans to underwrite because of the risk involved for the lender. *The borrower is asking for funds to create a project that does not yet exist.* A lender strictly controls the terms of a construction loan so that the least amount of funds are paid over to the mortgagor.

Structured Payback and Inspection

The construction loan made to a developer is disbursed in progressive installments to finance each portion of the project completed. Disbursements are often made in stages based on percentage of work in place instead of completed structures.

Release Land Subdivision Financing

This type of financing is structured so that the borrower has a monetary stake in the land before a mortgage is given. The mortgage may be for 70 percent or less of the appraised value of the land and the borrower must then put up the remaining 30 percent. The security for the mortgage is the *total amount of lots* in the subdivision. The lender, in effect, has a mortgage lien on all the lots. In order to transfer title to any of the lots, a portion of the mortgage lien must be satisfied. When the borrower transfers title to a lot, the lender releases the mortgage lien (obligation) from that lot in exchange for a pre–agreed-upon amount of money to be paid by the borrower to the lender. For example, an approved subdivision is appraised for $400,000 and has 40 lots. A lender will lend $240,000 and demand $12,000 per lot released; the lender will be paid in full after 20 lots are sold.

THE LEASE AS A FORM OF FINANCING PROPERTY

Sale Leaseback

In real estate financing, long-term leases have greater significance than do short-term leases, such as renting an apartment or retail space. Some types of property are quite difficult to finance. An alternative way to obtain financing is to find a purchaser who would be interested in buying the property and leasing it back to the seller. A **sale leaseback** is *a transaction in which a property owner sells a property to an investor who immediately leases back the property to the seller as agreed in the sales contract.* This type of transaction normally is used by an owner of business property who wishes to free up capital invested in the real estate and still retain possession and control of the property under a lease.

The sale leaseback also offers an alternative to a mortgage. It, in effect, provides 100 percent financing, whereas the mortgage might provide 70 or 80 percent. The purchaser–investor in this arrangement obtains the income tax benefits of ownership and the security of owning the property. The seller pays rent, which may include real estate taxes, insurance, and maintenance, for a fixed, predetermined number of years.

Long-Term Leases

Another means of using a lease to obtain financing is to lease property to a "premium-type" tenant for a long period of time, perhaps 20 years. The owner–lessor obtains a mortgage on the property and assigns the lease payment to the lender. The owner then has a large amount of capital, tax free, to invest elsewhere and the lender has excellent collateral for the mortgage loan. For example, B leases a car wash to C for $4,000 per month. B then borrows $400,000 from a lender at a monthly payment of $3,500 per month. B now has $400,000 to reinvest and the lender is secured with the assignment of the lease and the mortgage against the car wash property.

Owner's Desire to Retain Land

Long-term leases often apply to land on which the lessee wants to construct a building and the owner–lessor wishes to retain his interest in the land. A **ground lease** is *a lease of unimproved land, usually for construction purposes.* The ground lease normally contains a provision that the lessee will construct a building on the land. Ownership of the land and improvements is separated. The ground lease is a long-term lease that allows the lessee sufficient time to recoup the cost of improvements. This type of lease also typically is a net lease in that the lessee is required to maintain the improvements, pay the property taxes, and pay the expenses of the property. Normally, under a ground lease the owner–lessee has a *right to retain* and to mortgage the land (if desired), and the lessee has a right to finance the leasehold improvements.

Major Obligations of Corporations

Many Fortune 500 companies and other large corporations do not wish to make the substantial capital outlay to purchase a property. Therefore, such companies enter into a long-term lease to fulfill their purposes. The lease payments are fully tax deductible, the lease obligation is fixed and predictable, and the corporation's capital can be used for other purposes. (For a corporation with a large amount of equity tied up in real estate, perhaps the home office building, the sale leaseback method also can be used to extract funds for more active use.)

The Subordinate Lease

A **subordinate lease** is *a lease that can be canceled by a lender if the borrower defaults on a mortgage loan.* If a lender loans money on a property that has a lease in place, the tenant cannot generally be evicted if the borrower defaults on the mortgage. Lenders, however, can insist that they can evict the tenant if the borrower defaults, or they will not make the loan. The borrower must then have the tenant agree to subordinate (place behind for purposes of enforcement) the lease to the lender's mortgage. The lessor may put the subordination clause in the lease, which the tenant must sign. Then the lender can evict the tenant if the borrower defaults on the mortgage payment.

HOW TO SECURE FHA FINANCING

The **Federal Housing Administration** (FHA) was created in 1937 for the purpose of *insuring mortgage loans to protect lending institutions in case of borrower default.* FHA is an agency of the U.S. Department of Housing and Urban Development (HUD).

FHA does not make mortgage loans. Instead, FHA-insured loans *protect lenders against financial loss.* The buyer pays for this insurance protection by paying an up-front *mortgage insurance premium* (UFMIP) at closing and an annual mortgage insurance premium prorated monthly and paid with the monthly mortgage payment. This insurance enables lenders to provide financing when the loan-to-value ratio is high. With a high ratio, the borrower has made only a small down payment. The amount of insurance protection to the lender always is sufficient to protect the lender from financial loss in the event of a foreclosure sale because these loans are insured for 100 percent of the loan amount.

The FHA 203(b) loan that allows an owner-occupant to purchase a one- to four-family home only requires a minimum of 3% from the borrower and permits 100% of their money needed to close to be a gift from a relative, non-profit organization, or government agency. It provides for insuring loans for the purchase or construction of owner-occupied one- to four-family dwellings. FHA does not set a maximum sales price, only a maximum loan amount. A buyer may purchase a home for more than the FHA maximum loan amount, but he will have to pay anything above the maximum loan amount in cash. Effective January 1, 2003, FHA is insuring single-family home mortgages up to $154,896 in low cost areas and up to $280,749 in high cost areas. There are also higher loan limits for two-, three- and four-unit dwellings. The maximum loan amount is based on acquisition cost, which is the combination of FHA-appraised price or sales price, whichever is lower, plus those buyer's closing costs that FHA will allow to be financed.

The FHA 203(k) mortgage allows homeowners and homebuyers to purchase or refinance existing homes and finance 110% of the costs needed to improve the home. The mortgagor can borrow up to 110% of the "after-completed" value and the borrowed amount must be a minimum of $5,000. Although the loan applies to many property types, it must be owner occupied.

Licensees must remain current regarding FHA guidelines as they are constantly changing. Figure 3.4 shows a sample qualifying income worksheet for an FHA loan.

FIGURE 3.4

Examples of FHA maximum loan amount calculation.

Example 1: Based on a $90,000 FHA appraisal and estimated closing cost of $2,000 to be paid by the buyer. Appraised value is the same as the sales price in this example.

Calculation 1

Lesser of sales price or appraised value	$ 90,000
Buyer's total closing cost	+ 2,000
Total	$ 92,000
97% of first 25,000, 95% of remainder	× 97/95%

97% × $25,000 = $24,250
95% × $67,000 = $63,650
Total = $87,900

Maximum loan amount (excluding UFMIP)	$ 87,900

Calculation 2*

Appraised value	$ 90,000
Maximum loan-to-value	× 97.75%
Maximum loan amount (excluding UFMIP)	$ 87,975

The maximum loan amount (excluding UFMIP) is $87,900, which is the lesser of calculations 1 and 2. Maximum loan amount is always rounded down to the nearest $50 increment.

Example 2: Based on a $45,000 FHA appraisal and estimated closing cost of $1,350 to be paid by the buyer. Appraised value is the same as the sales price in this example. Because adjusted acquisition cost and appraised value is under $50,000, only the 97% maximum loan-to-value ratio is used in calculation 1, and 98.75% maximum loan-to-value ratio is used in calculation 2.

Calculation 1

Lesser of sales price or appraised value	$ 45,000
Buyer's total closing cost	+ 1,350
Total	$ 46,350
	× 97%
Maximum loan amount (excluding UFMIP)	$ 44,959

Calculation 2

Appraised value	$ 45,000
Maximum loan-to-value (1990 housing legislation)	× 98.75%
Maximum loan amount (excluding UFMIP)	$ 44,437

The maximum loan amount (excluding UFMIP) is $44,400, which is the lesser of calculations 1 and 2, rounded down to the nearest $50 increment.

Although space does not permit an example of all variations, the above examples illustrate the basic method of calculating FHA maximum loan amounts. When calculating, consider the following factors and adjust calculations and loan limits as required:

(1) Maximum loan amounts on single-family homes vary by area from $154,896 to $280,749. (2) When the loan basis is above $154,896, use 97/95/90 percent in calculation 1. (3) Closing costs are never included in calculation 2. (4) Any part of normal closing costs paid by seller for buyer cannot be added to the sales price to determine mortgage basis. (5) If seller pays over 6 percent of sales price for financing concessions including closing costs for buyer, any amount over 6 percent must be subtracted from sales price before determining mortgage basis. (6) If seller pays prepaid items such as taxes and insurance for buyer, the amount of these items must be subtracted from sales price before determining mortgage basis.

*Note: Closing cost is never included in calculation 2.

FHA Mortgage Insurance

FHA insured mortgages require mortgage insurance. The mortgage insurance, referred to as mutual mortgage insurance (MMI), charges 0.5% per year of the loan amount. Fifteen-year mortgages where the homebuyer makes a down payment greater than 10% of the purchase price do not have to pay the monthly mortgage insurance.

In addition to the mutual mortgage insurance that is charged to the purchaser each month, FHA charges an upfront mortgage insurance premium (MIP) that is 1.50% for 30- and 15- year fixed rate mortgages originated after January 1, 2001. The upfront mortgage insurance premium is calculated on the base loan amount and paid at closing or added to the loan amount.

MORTGAGE MONEY FOR A ONE-FAMILY HOME
IN A CAPITAL-SHORT MARKET

The Secondary Mortgage Market

A capital-short market can occur when lenders do not have funds for underwriting mortgages. *Loans generated by lenders directly are known as the* **primary mortgage market.** The sale of these mortgages to the **secondary mortgage market,** *which buys and sells mortgages created in the primary mortgage market, frees the banks to have more available funds to lend.* A mortgage must be assignable to qualify. A mortgage is generally assignable if not stated otherwise. Assignability allows the original lender to assign or sell the rights in the mortgage to another; therefore, the money invested in the mortgage is freed without waiting for the borrower to repay the debt over the long mortgage term.

A sale of a mortgage by the lender does not in any way affect the borrower's rights or obligations. The original mortgagor may not even be aware that the mortgage has been sold because the original lending institution often continues to service the loan. The mortgagor continues to make the necessary mortgage payments to the same lending institution. If the purchaser of the mortgage prefers to service the mortgage itself, the original lender simply notifies the mortgagor to make payments to the new lender at a different address.

Secondary Market Activities

Some lending institutions limit their mortgage loans to their own assets (known as in-house loans) rather than participate in the secondary mortgage market. For lenders that do participate in the secondary market, two types of markets are available: (a) the purchase and sale of mortgages between lending institutions, and (b) the sale of mortgages by lending institutions to three organizations that provide a market for this purpose: FNMA, GNMA, and FHLMC (See Table 3.2).

Federal National Mortgage Association (FNMA) (Fannie Mae)

FNMA is the oldest secondary mortgage institution and the single largest holder of home mortgages. Fannie Mae was created in 1938 as a corporation completely owned by the federal government to provide a secondary market for residential mortgages. By 1968 it had evolved into a privately owned corporation. It is a profit-making organization, and its stock is listed on the New York Stock Exchange.

To create liquidity in the mortgage market, Fannie Mae purchases both conventional and government issued mortgage loans and mortgage backed securities (MBS). Mortgage-Backed Securities are securities backed by mortgage loans. MBS' entitle an investor to an undivided interest in the underlying mortgage loan pool. Thus, an investor receives a pro rata share of the interest and principal on the underlying mortgage loans.

TABLE 3.2 Secondary mortgage market organizations.

NICKNAME	FULL NAME	OWNERSHIP	TYPES OF LOANS PURCHASED
Fannie Mae (FNMA)	Federal National Mortgage Association	privately owned corporation	purchases VA, FHA, RHS, and conventional loans
Ginnie Mae (GNMA)	Government National Mortgage Association	U.S. Department of Housing and Urban Development	purchases VA, FHA, and RHS mortgages only
Freddie Mac (FHLMC)	Federal Home Loan Mortgage Corporation	owned primarily by savings and savings and loan banks	purchases loans from any member of the Federal Home Loan Bank or any bank where deposits are insured by an agency of the federal government

Government National Mortgage Association (GNMA) (Ginnie Mae)

An agency of HUD established in 1968, Ginnie Mae guarantees (insures) the timely payment of principal and interest from government insured mortgages including those insured by the FHA, VA and RHS. Although Ginnie Mae does not issue, sell, or buy mortgage-backed securities, or purchase mortgage loans, its primary function is to operate its mortgage-backed securities program that increases the liquidity and efficiency of mortgage loan funding.

Federal Home Loan Mortgage Corporation (FHLMC) (Freddie Mac)

FHLMC also exists to increase the availability of mortgage credit and provide greater liquidity for savings associations. FHLMC purchases mortgages and packages them into securities that can be sold to investors. Freddie Mac was created by Congress in 1970 primarily to establish a reliable market for the sale of conventional mortgages. Any member of the Federal Home Loan Bank and any other financial institution, whose deposits or accounts are insured by an agency of the federal government, are eligible to sell mortgages to Freddie Mac. These organizations, together with activity between lending institutions, special incentive programs, and individual investor activity, allow the continuous flow of mortgage money into the marketplace.

This secondary mortgage market benefits lending institutions and, in turn, the borrowing public, by providing *liquidity* to mortgages. The mortgage is a liquid asset because it *can be readily converted to cash* by the lending institution selling the mortgage in the secondary market. Sale of the mortgage by the lender is especially beneficial in low-yield mortgages—those mortgages for which the lender receives a lesser return on an investment in terms of both discount and interest rate, expressed as an annual percentage rate. The lender may recover the money from these mortgages to reinvest in new mortgage loans at current higher yields, which provides stability in the supply of money for making mortgage loans. Therefore, the secondary mortgage market benefits the borrowing public by enabling lending institutions to make money available for loans to qualified applicants.

Mortgage liquidity available in the secondary market reduces the impact of disintermediation on lending institutions. **Disintermediation** is the *loss of funds available to lending institutions for making mortgage loans, caused by the withdrawal of funds by depositors for investment in higher yield securities in times of higher interest rates.* Without the secondary mortgage market, disintermediation would result in funds available to lenders "drying up" to the extent that the loans would be practically unavailable.

Other Methods of Creating Mortgage Availability

Fannie Mae Incentives

Fannie Mae has programs that are beneficial to homesellers who are willing to finance the sale by holding a purchase money first mortgage. Under this program, the seller can have the mortgage prepared by a lending institution qualified to sell mortgages to Fannie Mae using uniform FNMA and FHLMC documents. The lending institution will close the transaction between seller and buyer and continue to service the loan for the seller for a fee. The institution collects the payments of principal and interest from the buyer and forwards them to the seller. In this way, sellers have an on-site expert to protect their interests and rights in the mortgage.

Individual Investors

Individuals in every area invest in mortgages. These investors usually are an excellent source for second mortgage loans. The seller of real property is definitely not to be over-looked as an individual investor. These sellers may finance the sale of their properties by taking a regular second mortgage, taking a second mortgage in the form of a wrap-around, taking a purchase money first mortgage, or financing by means of a contract for deed (installment contract). In times of extremely high interest rates, a sale often cannot be made unless the seller provides a substantial part of the financing for the buyer.

Activities Between Lending Institutions

Another major activity of the secondary mortgage market is the purchase and sale of mortgages *by and between lending institutions*. The market thus facilitates movement of capital from institutions with available funds to invest to lenders that do not have enough money for this purpose.

For example, at any given time, the demand for mortgage loans may be low in a given locality. Institutions with funds available for making loans in those areas are unable to invest these funds in the local market by making primary mortgage loans. Their funds should be invested in mortgages where they could earn interest instead of lying idle. At this same time, another part of the country may have a high demand for mortgage loans. A lender in that area may have a short supply of available funds to lend to qualified loan applicants. The problems of both of these lending institutions can be solved if the institution whose funds are in short supply sells its existing mortgages on hand to a lender in another area that has a surplus of available funds and a low demand for mortgage loans. As a result, the lender with otherwise idle funds may invest them in mortgages earning interest, and the lender in short supply of money frees up capital invested in mortgages to meet the high demand for new mortgage loans in that area.

TRUTH-IN-LENDING ACT (TILA)

The Truth in Lending Act (TILA), Title I of the *Consumer Credit Protection Act* (1980), is aimed at promoting the informed use of consumer credit by requiring disclosures about its terms and costs. TILA requires four chief disclosures: annual percentage rate, finance charge, amount financed, and total amount of money to be paid toward the mortgage in both principal and interest payments. The Federal Reserve Board implemented these regulations by establishing Regulation Z. *Regulation Z* does not regulate interest rates but instead provides specific consumer protections in mortgage loans for residential real estate. It covers all real estate loans for personal, family, household, or agricultural purposes. The regulation does not apply to commercial loans. Regulation

Z also standardizes the procedures involved in residential loan transactions and requires that the borrower be fully informed of all aspects of the loan transaction. In addition, the regulation addresses any advertisement of credit terms available for residential real estate.

Disclosure

At the time of application or within three days thereafter, the lender must provide the borrower with a *disclosure statement*. The disclosure must set forth the true, or effective, annual interest rate on a loan, called the annual percentage rate (APR). This rate may be higher than the interest as expressed in the mortgage. For example, when certain fees and discount points charged by the lender are subtracted from the loan amount, the result is an increase in the true rate of interest. As a result of the subtraction, the borrower receives a smaller loan amount and pays interest on a larger amount. Therefore, the effect is to increase the interest rate.

The disclosure statement must specify the finance charges that include loan fees and interest and discount points. Finance charges do not include fees for title examination, title insurance, escrow payments, document preparation, notary fees, or appraisals.

Cooling-Off Period

If the borrower is refinancing an existing mortgage loan or obtaining a new mortgage loan on a residence already owned, the disclosure statement must provide for a cooling-off period, or three-day right of rescission for the loan transaction. The borrower has the right to rescind, or cancel, the loan prior to midnight of the third business day after the date the transaction was closed. The three-day right of rescission *does not* apply to the purchase of a new home, construction of a dwelling to be used as a principal residence, or refinancing of an investment property.

Advertising

Regulation Z also applies to the advertised credit terms available. The only specific thing that may be stated in the advertisement without making a full disclosure is the annual percentage rate that must be spelled out in full, not abbreviated as APR. If any other credit terms are included in the advertisement, they must also be fully disclosed. For example, an advertisement mentioning a down payment triggers the requirement to make a complete disclosure of all of the following credit terms: purchase price of the property, annual percentage rate, amount of down payment, amount of each payment, date when each payment is due, and total number of payments over the mortgage term. If the annual percentage rate is not a fixed rate but is instead a variable rate, the ad must specify this variable or adjustable rate.

Effect on Real Estate Licensees

Statements of a general nature about the financing may be made without full disclosure. Statements such as "good financing available," "FHA financing available," and "loan assumption available" are satisfactory. Real estate licensees must take special care not to violate the advertising requirements of Regulation Z.

Penalties

Violators of Regulation Z are subject to criminal liability and punishment by a fine of up to $5,000, imprisonment for up to a year, or both. If borrowers suffer a financial loss as the result of the violation, they may sue the violator for damages under civil law in federal court.

In the past, areas populated by culturally diverse persons were "redlined." Prior to enactment of the Fair Housing Act, some lending institutions circled certain local areas with a red line on the map, refusing to make loans within the circled areas based upon some characteristic of property owners in the area. The act prohibits lending institutions from **redlining,** or *refusing to make loans to purchase, construct, or repair a dwelling by discriminating on the basis of race, color, religion, gender, national origin, handicap, or familial status.*

The prohibition against discrimination also applies to those who deny a loan or who deny financial assistance to a person applying for the purpose of purchasing, constructing, improving, repairing, or maintaining a dwelling. The prohibition also extends to individuals who discriminate in fixing terms of the loan, including interest rates, duration of loan, or any other terms or conditions of the loan.

The Community Reinvestment Act (CRA) (1977, revised 1995), also known as the Fair Lending Law, was enacted to encourage lenders to help meet the credit needs of communities where they are located, including low- and moderate-income neighborhoods. The CRA requires that each lender's record in helping meet the credit needs of its entire community be evaluated periodically. In a process known as *filtering down,* properties in formerly middle- or upper-income neighborhoods decline in value, thereby allowing people with lower incomes to purchase these properties. If lenders do not make loans available to lower-income purchasers, these communities can deteriorate rapidly.

THE ECONOMY AND HOW IT AFFECTS THE REAL ESTATE MARKET

The real estate market often is the first industry to feel the adverse effects of depressed conditions in the national and local economies. When supply substantially exceeds demand, existing properties cannot be withdrawn from the local market and relocated to an area with higher demand. Conversely, when the demand exceeds supply, new supplies of housing and business properties cannot be constructed rapidly. Therefore, the real estate industry takes longer than the economy as a whole to climb out of a recession because of the inability to react quickly to radical changes in supply and demand. Supply and demand are affected by many factors: money supply, interest rates, population migrations, zoning, planning and environmental concerns, and local and federal taxes. Table 3.3 illustrates how certain factors affect supply and demand. The following are some of these economic factors:

Employment. When employment levels are steady and wages keep up with inflation, the demand for housing increases. One of the problems with employment levels in recent years is that large companies are downsizing or combining several branches of their operations into one location. This has had a direct impact on people's job stability. High rates of unemployment have an extremely negative effect on the real estate market. If a local area has a high rate of unemployment, for example, the number of houses for sale will increase while the number of prospective purchasers will decrease.

Interest rates/indices. An index is a value estimate used by banks to adjust interest rates. The consumer price index expresses the difference among the value, price, or cost of a group of items at various times. Index figures (indices) are available through the Federal Home Loan Bank Board and the Treasury Bond Index (discussed earlier in this chapter). High interest rates cause the cost of purchasing housing to increase. When interest rates increase, the cost of borrowing mortgage funds increases. Not only does this negatively affect the cost of buying property but it also forces investors to look to other types of investments, other than real estate, where the purchasing terms are more favorable. High interest rates directly cause the sale of real estate to decline.

TABLE 3.3 Factors affecting housing supply and demand.

ECONOMIC FACTOR	HIGH LEVEL	SUPPLY	DEMAND	RESULT
employment	✓	less	more	creates more new construction and sales of existing housing
interest rates	✓	more	less	values go down; new construction slows
stock market	✓	more	less	investors invest more heavily in stocks and bonds than in real estate
valuation or price of housing	✓	more	less	prices may be too high; buyers of housing wait for moderation in price
affordability of housing	✓	less	more	affordable housing creates high demand; new construction increases
local taxes	✓	more	less	homeowners may be forced to sell; homebuyers are also reluctant to pay higher taxes

Note: Housing supply and demand is directly related to factors in the economy. In the above chart, all economic factors are at high levels.

Stock market. If the stock market is a *bull market,* in which the value of stocks is constantly rising, investment in real estate becomes less attractive. As a rule, investment in stocks are paper transactions requiring no physical work, no aggravation or dealing with other people (other than your stockbroker), and little risk when the market is on the upswing. Not only is a stock a more liquid investment than real estate but a bull stock market will produce more rapid rewards than real estate investment.

However, if the stock market is going down (a *bear market*), investment in real estate could increase as long as the decrease in the stock market is not caused by higher interest rates and/or inflation (discussed later).

Valuation of seller's property. When the economy is good, real estate values are higher and available properties for sale will always increase proportionately. One of the first rules for investments of any kind is to buy low and sell high. In a good economy, the seller will want to achieve the maximum return on an investment, and the valuation of the property will tend to be on the higher end. Even in a positive financial climate, however, sellers should not price their property unreasonably. In a slow economy, prospective sellers tend to hold on to their properties, if possible, until the "good times" return.

Affordability of property for buyers. In a slow economy, seller expectations are not as optimistic and real estate investments are lower in price and therefore more affordable. In a good economic climate, however, competition among sellers also serves to moderate real estate investment prices.

UPDATE OF LENDING POLICIES

Licensees should check with lenders in their area to verify lending policies. The following sections summarize some general trends.

Nonincome Verification Loans

This type of loan verifies the nature of the borrower's employment, *but not the dollar value of the income.* To qualify for this loan, a borrower would have to have higher

---

Terminology to understand real estate cycles   `You Should Know`

Because of reasons discussed earlier, the real estate industry traditionally has been subject to cyclical periods of recession and prosperity. Four important terms must be defined to understand the occurrence of these cycles. They are recession, depression, stagflation, and inflation.

Recession is *a moderate and temporary decline in economic activity* that occurs during a period of otherwise increasing prosperity. A recession often occurs in a recovery period following a depression.

Depression is *the lowest possible point in the economic cycle.* The cycle encompasses all facets of the economy, including real estate and business. During this period, unemployment is generally high, the demand for goods and services is low, and production levels are down. A depression has a devastating effect on the real estate market.

Inflation is *an increase in money and credit relative to available goods, resulting in higher prices.* Inflation causes governments to borrow more to meet current debts, businesses to borrow more to meet costs of operations, and individuals to borrow more to pay for the higher cost of goods and services. When there is a high demand for housing, causing a high demand for mortgages, and the demand is coupled with rapid inflation, the demand for credit then accelerates to abnormal highs. Inflation generally is not good for the real estate market because not only will the price of real estate be higher but the cost to borrow will also increase. However, real estate purchased prior to inflationary trends provides an attractive hedge against inflation as once inflation kicks in, the return on investment is greatly increased.

Stagflation is *an economic condition in which economic growth is at a stand-still (stagnant) but inflation still exists.* In this economic climate, production and employment levels go down. Properties, therefore, are overpriced for many buyers. People do not have the cash needed for down payments and, because of inflation, credit of all types, including the cost of mortgages, increases. Because of the negative effects of the economy on real estate, as discussed earlier, the secondary mortgage market is one way in which money becomes available for real estate purchases, and the time frame of a down period in the cycle can be shortened or moderated. In addition, the Federal Reserve Board has some degree of control to expand and contract the amount of money and credit available in the economy. Changes in the real estate market will continue as a result of changes in the economy. The goal of an effective real estate licensee is to read the market and act. Licensees should become aware of new industries coming to the community and keep abreast of new legislation and local ordinances affecting real estate. Licensees must recognize trends in interest rates and closing costs and learn to adapt to the ever-changing real estate market.

---

than average credit and have been employed in the same way for at least three to five years. Also, the borrower may have to accept a higher-than-normal rate of interest and/or pay more points. Nonincome verification loans are not generally prevalent and are definitely not offered by as many lenders as in the past because this loan does not always meet the best interests of the lender.

Loan-to-Value Ratios

The loan-to-value ratio currently can run from 80 percent to 98.75 percent, depending on the program (government-insured or conventional mortgages). Literally dozens of loan programs with differing ratios exist.

Income Ratios

Different lenders use different ratios for certain types of lending products. As of this writing most lenders are looking for mortgagors who have a stable income. Certain lenders are more flexible than others. Generally, however, lenders are becoming more stringent regarding a mortgage applicant's credit history. Even if the applicant has a good income, credit problems, including instances when a lender believes that an applicant is overextended or has not paid bills in a timely manner, will negatively affect the applicant's chances for a loan.

Cooperatives

For a cooperative purchase, the shares of stock in the cooperative corporation are used as collateral. These loans are called share loans. Before 1985, loans on cooperatives were hard to find and often carried high interest rates. Banks could not sell these loans to other investors in the same way as they did mortgages, and were compelled to sign agreements with the board of each cooperative to ensure that they could actually take the shares of stock if a purchaser defaulted on a loan. After 1985, FNMA began purchasing share loans, and treated them like regular mortgages. Other lenders reached agreements (called recognition agreements) with cooperative boards, facilitating the lending process. In New York, share loans are widely available. Lenders have different underwriting policies and origination fees, but the criteria and procedures are generally the same for share loans as for mortgages. Interest rates on share loans are slightly higher than on ordinary mortgages, but no more than a 1/4 or 3/8 of a point. The IRS also allows share loan interest to be treated as mortgage interest.

Condominiums

An important difference between the financing of a cooperative compared with a condominium lies in the financing. With a condominium, the owner purchases the apartment, and can finance the purchase with a mortgage in the same way that a single-family house is financed. A variety of lender products are available to purchase condominiums including first-time buyer programs.

Commercial Property

Financing for commercial property is still abundant although commercial mortgages are not as flexible as residential mortgages. Lenders will carefully evaluate cash flow. The maximum range for a commercial mortgage is 15 years, possibly 20, and in a few cases 25 years. However, it is current practice for a commercial mortgage to be split into three- to five-year periods, with a balloon payment due at the end of each period. At that point, the mortgage can be rolled over, but the rate may increase. Normally, commercial mortgages are at a fixed rate that is renegotiated at the end of each period, which benefits the borrower as well as lender. At the end of each period, the lender reviews the property's financial condition. Lenders may elect not to renegotiate the loan if they feel that a property cannot produce the funds to cover its expenses. The rate initially offered on a commercial mortgage is changeable on a daily basis.

Foreclosures

The number of residential and commercial bad debt and resulting foreclosures decreased in the last ten years, mainly as a result of more stringent lending policies. Currently, lenders sell foreclosures, most often at a loss, to rid their portfolios of the bad debt. Lenders would rather incur a partial loss than a total loss because the more bad debt lenders carry, the more cash reserves they must have.

Programs for First-Time Buyers

Programs for first-time buyers, especially in the low-to-moderate income range, currently are abundant and a variety of mortgage products is available. Community home buyer programs offer affordable home mortgage programs for low-to-moderate income families. Fannie Mae community home buyer underwriting guidelines offer more flexible qualifications.

SONYMA, for example, offers a below market interest rate program for the first time home buyer with low down payment requirements, flexible loan underwriting, interest rate lock-in periods that are longer than conventional lock-in periods, no prepayment penalties and no payment reserve. (Payment reserves are funds required by some lenders to be retained in a borrower's bank account after closing in an amount equal to a specific number of monthly mortgage payments.)

Applicants must use the property for their full time residence and may not have had any ownership interest in their primary residence during the three years before the application. In addition, applicants generally may not own a vacation or investment home. Income limits vary for different target areas and are based on the total household size including all children. Applicants should have a steady job; good credit background and sufficient cash, savings, or assets for at least a 3% down payment (10% on certain properties) plus approximately 7% for closing costs.

Length of Time for Loan Processing and Its Effect on Buyers and Sellers

Because of automation on the part of the lender and other parties to a loan application, such as appraisers, title companies, and credit reporting companies, loan processing is faster than ever. Currently, an average residential mortgage takes approximately two to six weeks to process as long as few or no negative factors exist. Commercial mortgages require different documentation, and environmental studies may be necessary, which can be extremely time consuming. Processing a commercial mortgage application can take anywhere from two to six months or longer. Sellers should be informed of the approximate loan application time frame when the contract for purchase and sale is negotiated.

IMPORTANT POINTS

1. Without the mortgage, comparatively few real estate transactions would occur.
2. The purpose of the loan process is to verify all data the borrower presents in the loan application. Loan underwriting reviews the loan documentation and evaluates the borrower's ability and willingness to pay.
3. Commercial mortgages are extremely dependent on the financial strength of the borrower and may include personal guarantees as well as a substantial down payment.
4. Gap financing usually is a short-term loan used until more permanent financing is in place. Bridge loans and swing loans are examples of gap financing.
5. A wraparound mortgage is a subordinate mortgage that includes the same principal obligation secured by a superior mortgage against the same property.
6. A provision in a convertible mortgage gives the lender the option of converting the outstanding balance into an agreed-upon percentage of property ownership.
7. A home equity loan is not necessarily a second mortgage. The amount of a home equity loan cannot exceed the original purchase price of the house.
8. A construction loan is a form of interim financing. The mortgage made to a developer is disbursed in progressive installments to finance each part of the project completed.

9. A sale leaseback is a transaction in which a property owner sells a property to an investor and the investor agrees to lease back the property immediately to the seller.

10. The long-term lease is a way of controlling property without buying it.

11. A capital-short market occurs when lenders do not have funds for underwriting mortgages. The secondary mortgage market, which purchases mortgages from lenders, frees up capital so that lenders have money available for mortgages.

12. FHA is an agency of the U. S. Department of Housing and Urban Development (HUD). Licensees should keep abreast of all FHA changes and procedures.

13. The sale and purchase of mortgages between lending institutions, Fannie Mae incentives, and private investors help to free up capital for mortgages.

14. Regulation Z of the Truth-in-Lending Act provides for disclosure by lenders and truth in advertising.

15. The real estate market is subject to cyclical changes in the economy and is often the first industry to feel the adverse effects of depressed conditions.

16. Factors such as employment levels, interest rates, the stock market, seller valuation of property, and buyer's ability to afford property affect changes in market activity.

17. The cycles in the economy can be defined by four main economic events: recession, depression, inflation, and stagflation.

18. Lender policies reflect the changing real estate climate. Some of the policies include nonincome verification loans, loan-to-value and income ratios, and condominium and cooperative loans.

CHAPTER REVIEW   How Would You Respond?

The following hypothetical questions address a number of concerns that clients may ask relative to financing.* Check your responses using the Answer Key at the end of the chapter.

1. What are the advantages and disadvantages of assuming a mortgage?

   _____

   _____

   _____

2. We've had some difficulties lately and expect our home to be foreclosed on shortly. It is worth much more than we owe on the mortgage. What happens to the extra money the lender obtains when the property is sold at foreclosure?

   _____

   _____

   _____

3. We are buying a new home and are considering an adjustable mortgage. We currently have a fixed-rate mortgage and are unfamiliar with the adjustable. What items should we consider?

   _____

   _____

   _____

*Source: James A. Ader, "Real Estate Spotlight." Copyright © The *Albany Times Union*. Reprinted by permission.

KEY TERM REVIEW

Reponse (P132)

Fill in the term that best completes the sentence and then check the Answer Key at the end of the chapter.

1. A(n) _____ is a lease of unimproved land that contains a provision for the lessee to construct a building on the land.

2. Loan _____ is the process of reviewing the loan documentation and evaluating the borrower's ability and willingness to repay.

3. A transaction in which a property owner sells a property to an investor and the investor agrees to lease back the property immediately to the seller is known as _____.

4. A form of interim financing used by residential developers that is not the final financing on the project is a(n) _____.

5. A provision in the mortgage of commercial projects that gives the lender the option of converting the outstanding balance into an agreed-upon percentage of ownership in the property is a(n) _____.

6. _____ is usually a short-term loan to provide funds over and above an already existing loan until more permanent financing is in place.

7. _____ is the loss of funds available to lending institutions for making mortgage loans; it is caused by the withdrawal of funds by depositors for investment in higher yield securities.

8. A(n) _____ lease can be canceled by a lender if the borrower defaults on a mortgage loan.

MULTIPLE CHOICE

Circle the letter that best answers the question and then check the Answer Key at the end of the chapter.

1. Which of the following is NOT a reason for the loan processor to decline the loan before submitting to underwriting?
   A. borrower has excessive debts
   B. neighborhood where the subject property is located
   C. borrower has insufficient income
   D. property fails to meet the lender's condition standards

2. Which of the following does NOT apply to loan underwriting?
   A. buyer's ability to pay
   B. buyer's willingness to pay
   C. fully researching other data not presented in the loan application
   D. property evaluation

3. A home equity loan:
   A. is always a first mortgage on a property
   B. is always a second mortgage on a property
   C. may exceed the original purchase price of the house
   D. may be the only mortgage on the property

4. Which of the following regarding a construction loan is FALSE? It
   A. is a form of interim financing
   B. is one of the most difficult loans to underwrite
   C. involves a structured payback on the part of the mortgagor
   D. is one of the easiest loans to underwrite

5. A commercial mortgage:
   - A. is greatly dependent on the financial strength of the borrower
   - B. is impossible to obtain for a small retail operation
   - C. always includes a structured payback
   - D. is an example of short-term financing

6. Regarding gap financing, which of the following is FALSE? It:
   - A. is usually a short-term loan
   - B. is used for commercial properties only
   - C. may be in the form of a bridge loan
   - D. may provide temporary funds until permanent financing is possible

7. Regarding a wraparound mortgage, which of the following is FALSE? It is:
   - A. a type of second mortgage with longer terms
   - B. not beneficial to the buyer
   - C. workable only when the existing first mortgage is assumable
   - D. an example of the theory of leverage

8. Which of the following does NOT apply to a junior mortgage? It is:
   - A. a subordinate mortgage
   - B. possibly a home equity loan
   - C. a second mortgage
   - D. a first mortgage

9. A convertible mortgage:
   - A. is the same as a home equity loan
   - B. is generally used in residential-type transactions
   - C. gives the lender the option of converting the outstanding balance into a percentage of ownership in the property
   - D. converts the mortgage into shares of stock, as in cooperative ownership

10. In regard to release land subdivision financing, which of the following is FALSE?
    - A. the lender has mortgage liens on all of the lots
    - B. in order to transfer title to any of the lots, a portion of the mortgage must be satisfied
    - C. the security for the mortgage is initially all of the lots in the subdivision
    - D. under this arrangement, the borrower always receives 100 percent financing

11. Polly needs financing on her motel complex in Lake George, New York, but still wishes to retain possession and control of the property. She doesn't care if she retains title to the property. An ideal financing solution for Polly would be a:
    - A. sale leaseback
    - B. home equity loan
    - C. construction loan
    - D. tax-free exchange

12. Frank wishes to retain ownership in his successful banquet house, for which he still has a mortgage, but he no longer wants to run it. He would like to obtain cash from the banquet house to reinvest in a marina. What would be the *best* option for Frank?
    - A. lease the banquet house for a long term, borrow against the building it's in, and secure the loan with an assignment of the lease to the lender
    - B. obtain interim financing
    - C. sell the property and lease it back from the purchaser
    - D. obtain a wraparound mortgage

13. Which of the following regarding a ground lease is FALSE?
    - A. it normally contains a provision that the lessee will construct a building on the land
    - B. the lessee has a right to finance the leasehold improvements
    - C. it typically is a short-term lease
    - D. it typically is a long-term lease

14. The secondary mortgage market:
    - A. does not exist in a capital-short market
    - B. is composed only of federal institutions and not private investors
    - C. is of no benefit to the borrowing public
    - D. provides liquidity to mortgages

15. Disintermediation:
    - A. is lack of communication among lending institutions
    - B. provides stability in the supply of money for mortgage loans
    - C. is the loss of funds available to lending institutions for making mortgage loans
    - D. is the gain of funds available to lending institutions for making mortgage loans

16. The FHA (Federal Housing Authority) is an agency of:

    A. Fannie Mae

    B. HUD

    C. Freddie Mac

    D. SONYMA

17. The reason why the real estate industry takes longer than the rest of the economy to climb out of a recession is because:

    A. the real estate industry is a minor factor in the economy

    B. real estate is affected adversely only when demand exceeds supply

    C. real estate is essentially recession-proof

    D. of real estate's inability to react quickly to changes in supply and demand

18. The lowest possible point in the economic cycle is known as:

    A. depression

    B. recession

    C. stagflation

    D. disintermediation

19. Which of the following is NOT a consideration for a nonincome verification loan? The:

    A. nature of the borrower's employment

    B. number of years the borrower has been employed

    C. borrower's credit history

    D. dollar value of borrower's income

20. Which of the following regarding recent lending policies is FALSE?

    A. bank automation has sped up loan processing

    B. there are fewer foreclosures because of more stringent lending policies

    C. cash-flow projections are not needed for commercial mortgages

    D. financing for cooperatives and condominiums is more difficult to obtain and may be more costly for the borrower

ANSWER KEY

How Would You Respond?*

1. The evident advantage would be a buyer's ability to obtain the benefit of the interest rate of the seller's mortgage loan. If the rate is lower than prevailing rates, the buyer might have a financial benefit. At the same time, the buyer will have to provide the seller with cash representing the difference between the sales price and the mortgage being assumed. This results in a higher down payment than many buyers have available. Both buyer and seller have other considerations, depending on whether the buyer takes the property subject to the mortgage or assumes the mortgage and agrees to pay the debt. A property sold subject to the mortgage does not create a personal obligation for the buyer to pay the debt. If buyers stop payment, they are subject to foreclosure, but not for the difference between the amount raised on foreclosure sale and the debt. The original borrower (seller) will still be responsible to the lender for the difference. When buyers assume and agree to pay the debt, they become personally responsible. A foreclosure sale, if not sufficient to satisfy the loan, can result in a judgment against the assumer and the original borrower. Few truly assumable loans exist. Many loans call for lender approval and for the total balance to be due on transfer of title.

2. If the property were to sell for more than the amount due the mortgage holder (the lender), then the excess proceeds would be received by the borrower (yourself). However, remember that there could be other claims against the property including

---

*Source: James A. Ader, "Real Estate Spotlight." Copyright © The *Albany Times Union*. Reprinted by permission.

other (junior) mortgage holders and taxing authorities. In addition, sales expenses are paid from the excess. In contrast, a property may sell for less than what is owed. In this case, the borrower is not relieved of additional debt, but the lender may request a deficiency judgment that can proceed against other assets of the borrower. You should obtain legal counsel. Perhaps you can work out an arrangement with your lender that allows you to restructure your debt and keep the house.

3. Because of relatively low rates on fixed-rate loans, most people select a fixed rate at this time. But the low initial rate on the adjustable is attractive to some buyers. The interest rate on ARMs is adjustable, and when the interest rate changes, so does the amount of your monthly payment. The following questions should be answered before proceeding: (1) How often will the rate be adjusted: every six months, yearly, biyearly, and so on? (2) Is there a maximum adjustment that can be made at any one time? (3) Is there a maximum rate that can be charged? Is there a cap? If so, what is that cap? (4) Adjustments are made based on increases (or decreases) in a selected index (for example, average rate on sale of existing homes from the Federal Home Loan Bank Board, Treasury Bond index). Which index will your mortgage use? You should establish the provisions for switching from the ARM to a fixed-rate instrument in the future. Can you convert? When? What is the cost? Your interest rate on an ARM could change based on the index, but adjustments are made only at adjustment periods. The lender must give you 30 days' notice before the new rate becomes effective.

Key Term Review

1. ground lease
2. underwriting
3. sale leaseback
4. construction loan
5. convertible mortgage
6. gap financing
7. disintermediation
8. subordinate lease

Multiple Choice

1. B
2. C
3. D
4. D
5. A
6. B
7. B
8. D
9. C
10. D
11. A
12. A
13. C
14. D
15. C
16. B
17. D
18. A
19. D
20. C

Chapter 4

LEARNING OBJECTIVES   *Classroom hours: 5*

1. Describe the fundamentals of real estate investments.
2. Discuss the various steps that must be employed to perform proper investment analysis.
3. Discuss the strategy that should be implemented before investing.
4. Describe the various types of investment properties and the advantages and disadvantages of each.
5. Discuss the analysis profile to be performed prior to investing.
6. List the tax considerations to review before an investment transaction is finalized.

Real Estate Investments

Real estate professionals are in a good position to observe potential investments as they come on the market. In addition to the marketing and sale of single family homes, licensees should consider investment in income-producing property for themselves and prospective clients and customers as another aspect of their real estate careers.

BACKGROUND OF INDUSTRY

Investment is the outlay of money for prospective income or profit. The investment objective may be varied. Some common objectives of investment property ownership are:

- as a hedge against an inflationary economic trend
- for the tax savings generated by passive losses or depreciation deductions
- as a means of providing regular income (cash flow)
- to build a strong portfolio of properties for resale at retirement or for other future needs

In addition to their personal investment objectives, investors must consider the physical and economic characteristics, the highest and best use, and any public or private restrictions to the property that may affect the investment goal.

People can invest individually, through partnerships, corporations, and real estate investment trusts (discussed later). Investors must work with a variety of support professionals such as builders, architects, municipal planners and other officials, attorneys, accountants, and landlord and tenant groups. Investment in real estate is challenging and involves a great deal of hard work. Realizing profits may take a while, sometimes several years. However, the payoffs can be worth the effort both in personal satisfaction and in monetary gain.

Breaking into the Real Estate Investment Field

As a real estate licensee, you have ample opportunities to become involved in real estate investment. Residential brokers may already be involved in the sale, management, and/or rental of a number of two- or three-family dwellings or apartment complexes. Commercial real estate brokers may be active in selling and leasing office and retail space. Essentially, a prospective investor should always be on the lookout for potentially good deals.

Fundamentals of Investments

To understand how real estate investments work, it is important to discuss several basic concepts concerning the profits realized on investments as well as the inherent tax benefits. They include the time value of money, positive and negative cash flow, rates of return, capital gain, tax depreciation, leverage, tax shelters, operating statements, refinancing versus selling, and tax-free exchanges. These and other fundamentals are discussed throughout this chapter.

Statistical Data

When considering large-scale projects such as residential subdivisions, shopping centers, office complexes, and industrial parks, prudent investors must first statistically analyze the market. They must analyze all facets of the project and compare the data with similar projects. This detailed statistical analysis is called a *feasibility study*. Factors considered are the cost of site development (including environmental factors), available financing, cost of financing (including prevailing interest rates), tax considerations, rates of return on similar-type investments, and the benefit to the community and its acceptance of the project. Feasibility studies include demographic information ranging from average income to traffic patterns.

Another factor figured through mathematical analysis is how long to hold an investment. The answer depends not only on the market but also on the investor's desired rate of return and other financial goals that consider the time value of money (discussed next). Sources of information are: commercial brokerage firms; commercial appraisers; local lenders, who may have a number of portfolios on similar projects; the municipality, which usually has detailed demographic information; and the local planning board, which may have information on similar projects.

The Time Value of Money

Before investing, investors must consider what return their money would produce in a safe, risk-free, fixed-return investment *as opposed to a real estate investment*. Then investors can measure the risk versus the reward of the investment. Money left alone in a Certificate of Deposit (CD) will multiply without risk, but the return may be insufficient for future needs. The *time value of money* is a process that calculates the value of an asset in the past, present or future and is based on the premise that the original investment or principal will increase in value over a certain time period.

The present value of the investment is the principal. For example, if an investor deposits $5,000 in a CD, that $5,000 is the present value. The future value is the interest together with the principal; $5000.00 left in a mutual fund for five years at 10% interest will yield $8052.55.

INVESTMENT ANALYSIS
Knowledge of Operating Statements

An *operating statement* for a property includes income, vacancy rates, and expenses. Examples of operating expenses are: accounting and legal fees, services, advertising, maintenance and repairs, property management fees, property insurance, taxes, licenses and permits, utilities, and wages and salaries. Figure 4.1 illustrates a sample operating statement.

Tax Implications and the Operating Statement

Unlike the expenses of operating property held for personal use, such as a personal residence, the costs of operating property held for use in business or as an investment are *deductible expenses*. These operating costs may be deducted from **gross income** to arrive at the net income for tax purposes. *Gross income is income received without deducting*

OPERATING STATEMENT

250 unit apartment complex with rent schedule of $450 per month per unit.

Potential Gross Income: 250 × $450 × 12		$ 1,350,000
Less Vacancy and Credit Losses (6%)		(81,000)
Plus Other Income		25,000
Effective Gross Income		$ 1,294,000
Less Expenses		
Fixed Expenses:		
Property Insurance	$ 24,500	
Property Taxes	95,300	
Licenses and Permits	1,200	($ 121,000)
Operating Expenses:		
Maintenance	$ 106,000	
Utilities	103,200	
Supplies	16,000	
Advertising	7,500	
Legal & Accounting	15,000	
Wages & Salaries	90,000	
Property Management	64,700	($ 402,400)
Replacement Reserve:		($ 25,000)
Total Expenses		$ 548,400
Net Operating Income		$ 745,600

FIGURE 4.1

A sample operating statement.

expenses. Before deducting operating expenses, *losses from vacancies and credit losses are deducted from* potential gross income *(gross scheduled rental income)* to arrive at effective gross income. Operating expenses are deducted from effective gross income. The *result of deducting operating expenses* is **net operating income.** *Mortgage principal and interest payments* are called **debt service.** The interest, which is an allowable deduction, is deducted from net operating income to arrive at net taxable income. This otherwise taxable income may be completely or partially sheltered from tax liability as a result of a depreciation allowance. Consequently, the building may have no taxable income.

Current Rent Roll

The current **rent roll** is the *number of rental units that are currently occupied in a building multiplied by the rental amount per unit.* The total figure is then multiplied by 12 to obtain the annual rental income. Investors would be wise to consider ways to increase rentals, thus increasing their income for a building. Table 4.1 illustrates a rent roll for an apartment building.

Proforma Schedule

A **proforma statement** or *schedule* is an *operating statement adjusted to reflect a potential change in income and expenses based upon the investor's knowledge of the real estate market.* For example, the operating statement in Figure 4.1, previously discussed, could be reanalyzed with some new projections, illustrated in Table 4.2.

Before investing, a prudent investor must create a proforma statement or have an expert create one. The proforma statement analyzes a property's potential (or possible lack of potential). A miscalculation of the value of the investment may occur without such an analysis.

TABLE 4.1 Sample rent roll for an apartment building.	2 four-bedroom apts @ $1,000/each per month	$ 2,000
	10 three-bedroom apts @ $800/each per month	$ 8,000
	20 two-bedroom apts @ $600/each per month	$12,000
	10 one-bedroom apts @ $400/each per month	$ 4,000
	Current rent roll	$26,000 per month

When multiplied by 12, the total is $312,000, which is the gross rental income per year based on current occupancy levels.

Valuation

Investors may require a valuation of a property prior to purchase. **Valuation** of a property establishes an opinion of value utilizing a totally objective approach. *It is the process of estimating the market value of an identified interest in a specific property as of a given date.* A valuation is usually done to determine the property's market value.

Market value is defined as the most probable price, as of a specific date, in cash, or in terms equivalent to cash, or in other precisely revealed terms, for which the specified property rights should be sold after reasonable exposure in a competitive market, under all conditions requisite to a fair sale, with the buyer and seller each acting prudently, knowledgeably, and for self-interest, and assuming that neither is under undue duress.

Market value is the most probable price a property will bring if:

1. Buyer and seller are equally motivated, however, the seller is not under duress to take the first offer that comes along.
2. Both parties are well informed or well advised, and each is acting in what the individual considers her own best interest.
3. A reasonable time is allowed for exposure in the open market.
4. Payment is made in cash or its equivalent.
5. Financing, if any, is on terms generally available in the community as of the specified date and is typical for the property type in its locale.
6. The price represents a normal consideration for the property sold, unaffected by special financing amounts or terms, services, fees, costs, or credits incurred in the transaction.

Market value implies nonrelated buyer and seller in an arm's-length transaction. Related-party sales or sales in which one party is in a distress situation obviously are not indicative of fair market value.

TABLE 4.2 Proforma schedule based on operating statement in Figure 4.1.	Rents could be increased by 10% adding	+	$135,000
	Vacancy factors could be decreased by 3% adding	+	$40,500
	Additional miscellaneous income increases, such as laundry facilities adding	+	$5,000
	Insurance could be decreased adding	+	$4,000
	Taxes will increase subtracting	−	$5,000
	Maintenance costs will be decreased adding	+	$6,000
	Utilities costs will be increased subtracting	−	$5,000
	Total additional income		$180,500

Types of Value

In addition to market value, the following values can be of interest to the investor.

Investment value. Investment value is determined by *the amount of return on a certain dollar investment a property will produce*. Therefore, if an investor requires a 20% return and a property returns $20,000, the investment value is $100,000.

Insured value. This value estimates the value of property as a basis for determining the amount of insurance coverage necessary to protect the structure adequately against loss by fire or other casualty. Insurance companies are concerned with the cost of replacing or reproducing structures. *Insured value* is *the cost of replacing or reproducing the structure in the event of a total loss because of an insured hazard.*

Value in use. Value in use is *the value of the property based on its usefulness to an owner or investor.* Value in use is defined more for its value to the owner and not for its value if placed on the market. Usefulness, in this case, is defined as its utility, income, or other amenities. For example, a second home used for vacation purposes for the owner's family is an amenity for the family only. Its usefulness is expanded if this owner also rents the second home when the family is not using it. Another value, income value, can then be attributed to the property.

Assessed value. The assessed value of real property is determined by a local or state official. It is *the value to which a local tax rate is applied to establish the amount of tax imposed on the property.* The assessed value, as set by statute or local ordinance, is normally a percentage of market value. This percentage may be up to 100 percent. A combination of the assessment and the tax rate as applied to the property determines the annual tax bill. Assessed value is calculated by using the formula market value $\times$ assessment rate = assessed value.

Mortgage loan value. In making a mortgage loan, the lender is interested in the value of the property pledged as security for the debt or loan. In the event of a foreclosure, the lender must recover the debt from sale of the property. Consequently, the *mortgage loan value* is *whatever the lender believes the property will bring at a foreclosure sale or subsequent resale.* Some lenders make a conservative value estimate; others are more liberal. Mortgage loan value almost always differs from the market value.

Evaluation

Rather than an appraisal, investors may also seek an evaluation of a property. *Evaluation* is a study of the nature, quality, or utility of certain property interests in which a value estimate is not necessarily required. Evaluation studies can be land utilization studies, highest- and best-use studies, marketability studies, feasibility studies, and supply-and-demand studies. Evaluation of a property does not result in an estimate of value as does valuation.

INVESTMENT STRATEGY

Ownership Planning

Before purchasing property for investment, investors must consider the method of ownership that works best for their goals. Methods of ownership of real estate available to the investor are discussed below. (See Chapter 5 for a fuller discussion of corporations and partnerships.)

Sole proprietorship. A *sole proprietorship* is a business owned by one individual either in his own name or using the business as a trade name (d/b/a).

Partnerships. A *partnership* is a form of business organization owned by two or more partners. A partnership is created by contract between the partners who need not have the same degree of interest in the partnership or the same extent of management authority.

Corporation. A *corporation* is an artificial being, invisible, intangible, and existing only pursuant to law. A corporation is a thing, a taxable legal entity recognized by law with tax rates separate from individual income tax rates.

Syndicates. *Syndicates* denote multiple joint participation in a real estate investment and may involve joining of assets and talents of individuals, general partnerships, limited partnerships, or corporations in some combination.

Joint venture. A *joint venture* is an organization formed by two or more parties for the purpose of investing in real estate or another type of investment. The joint venture may take the form of a corporation or a partnership, or the parties may hold title as joint tenants or tenants in common. Joint ventures usually are devised for one project only.

Investment Syndicates

To achieve maximum purchasing power, some investors pool their resources in a *real estate investment syndicate,* a joint venture typically controlled by one or two persons who hope for profitable return to all investors. Profit for investors is generated when the syndicate buys, sells, and develops real estate.

To protect investors from fraud by syndicate promoters, federal and state governments have enacted securities laws and regulations. These laws are designed to protect investors from buying "blue sky," (or nothing), therefore the term *blue sky laws.*

The Securities Act of 1933 was the first federal securities law. This law regulated companies' initial issuance of securities, outlined fraudulent practices, and required registration of securities prior to sale. Many additional laws have since been passed requiring further disclosure, regulating insider trading, and requiring disclosure of any conflicts of interest. If a pool of investors (syndicate) does not comply with federal and state securities laws, the group is fined up to $10,000 and punished with imprisonment of up to five years.

Holdings Period Planning

Before investing in a property, the investor must decide if the investment will be short- or long-term. Does the investor wish to hold the property permanently or, at the first available opportunity, sell and go on to a new project? The answer depends on the investor's personality, financial goals, borrowing power, the nature of the investment, and ultimately the success of the investment. Because real estate investments can fluctuate as a result of market trends, investors should analyze their goals carefully before embarking on a project. If the investor buys with the intention of selling, or if conditions develop that necessitate a sale, economic conditions might not be conducive. Investors should have reserves available to cover losses, if necessary, so that they can wait out a low period. Real estate is *not* a liquid asset and cannot be transferred, even at a loss, as quickly and easily as can stocks or other cash-type investments.

Property Disposition and Timing Planning

When investing in larger projects, such as a residential subdivision development, it is best to have a timetable for disposition and/or completing the project. Major subdivisions are often developed in phases that are scheduled at the inception of the project and a projected timetable for completion and sale of all the houses within each phase is created. When all phases are completed and all properties sold, the investor's role has been fulfilled.

Available Financing

Most investors do not have the means to finance fully an investment project. A complete portfolio of the investment is necessary to obtain financing. The portfolio generally includes the following: a description of the project; a feasibility study; a history of the investment, including an income and expense statement going back several years as well as a current one; investor goals; projections for the investment, including a proforma statement; tax implications of the project; a resume of the investor, which includes involvement with other projects; a personal financial statement; a credit history; and income tax returns. Financing for an investment may be derived from a combination of sources including lender financing together with the seller holding a portion of the financing.

Leverage

By using other people's money (OPM), the investor's buying power is increased. The *use of borrowed funds* is called **leverage.** The investor will want to put the least possible amount down and obtain the lowest possible available interest rate over the longest period of time. This allows the investor to accumulate the maximum amount of real estate with the minimum amount of personal funds.

However, for the investor expecting a cash flow, the expenses and mortgage costs may well exceed the returns if she uses too much leverage. The example in Table 4.3 takes a property and analyzes the difference on the rate of return when cash is paid versus leveraging with a mortgage.

The figures on investment/financing in Table 4.3 are predicated on the rate of return on the investment. To many investors, this method is more meaningful since it considers only the amount of cash they have invested. The investment will be growing in equity and, ideally, appreciating in value.

PROPERTY-TYPE SELECTION

Individuals who wish to invest in real estate should review all types of property and then decide which best suits their goals. Potential investors should consider their personal resources such as level of expertise, scope of their desired involvement in the project, and cash on hand.

Land Acquisition

Investment in undeveloped land is one of the more risky forms of investment. An investor may have to hold the property for a longer time than other improved investments before the land's potential is realized. It is often difficult to obtain lender financing for this type of investment.

Cash investment	$125,000 investment with a $15,000 net income $15,000 divided by $125,000 = 12% return annually	**TABLE 4.3** The difference between cash paid and leveraging with a mortgage.
Investment financed	$125,000 investment $93,750 mortgage (75%) = $31,250 equity invested Subtract one year's interest at 10% ($9,375.00) from $15,000 Net income = $5,625 $5,625 (net income) divided by $31,250 (initial investment) = 18% return annually	

Because there are no improvements on the land, the property cannot be depreciated for tax purposes. Land can be sold in many forms: large acreage tracts; approved or unapproved subdivision tracts; or small, single residential lots. Landowners will have to work with zoning regulations, master plans, and complex governmental approval processes. In addition to the cost of the land, investors who hold the land for development purposes must invest more dollars in the approval and development process. While the investor waits to see his profits realized, he also theoretically loses money, because the money invested in the land could be producing interest or profits if invested elsewhere. When evaluating an investment, an investor must consider the loss of income from the money invested and add that to the actual dollar cost of the investment to determine the rate of return.

Retail: Strip, Community, Neighborhood, and Regional Malls

Retail centers differ in size and can be utilized for a variety of investment projects. The strip mall can consist of anywhere from three to five or more storefronts offering a mix of services including convenience stores, cleaners, variety stores, and so on. This type of project is manageable for the investor who desires a small project and wants to deal with only a few tenants.

Community and neighborhood malls are larger and usually contain a supermarket and a drugstore. They offer a wider range of retail stores and are usually spread over several acres of land.

Regional malls offer a still larger mix of retail stores and services. They can contain a large *anchor store, such as Wal-Mart or Kmart, a supermarket, and clothing and furniture stores.* The regional mall attracts business from outside the immediate community. Both the neighborhood and regional mall are more complicated investments than is the strip mall. These projects usually require a full-time management team, as the mix of tenants, their differing needs, and a larger customer base are more demanding than an investment in a strip mall.

Offices: Urban or Suburban

Urban office buildings may consist of a one-story structure or a skyscraper. In some high-rise buildings, one tenant may occupy all of the space. In a smaller office building, a mix of tenants may have offices. Suburban office buildings and parks are popular because they offer accessible parking and less traveling time for workers and customers. In some areas excess office space has been available recently. Before investing in office space, the prudent investor should check the vacancy rates over the previous few years of the subject property as well as vacancy rates for neighboring properties. A careful analysis of the office needs of the area will prevent cash-flow problems later.

Apartment Rentals

One of the most popular forms of investment is apartment rental because it can be done on a small scale and is manageable for the beginning investor. Apartment rentals may range from the duplex (two-family unit) to the fourplex, or other multifamily dwellings. Many investors choose to live in one of the units they own. Thus they not only reduce maintenance costs but do not pay rent. Part of the investor–tenant's income (including rent) becomes allowable tax deductions for expenses associated with income property. Multifamily high-rise apartment buildings are another appealing option to the experienced investor. This type of investment requires a sophisticated management team and large-scale financing.

Mixed Developments

Mixed-development investment involves commitment to a project consisting of a variety of structures with different uses. One type of mixed development is known as a Planned Unit Development (PUD) and includes housing, businesses, retail, recreation, and even schools and places of worship. Creating and investing in a PUD involves community-based planning, zoning, and other municipal approvals, and a team of experts in land development, construction, environment, and financing. Other examples of mixed-development projects may include a combination office and industrial park or a housing subdivision bordering a golf course. A project of this scope is often built and financed through a team of investors who pool their money and expertise.

Because the development may take many years to finish, this project is best suited to experienced investors who have the financial means to carry the project through to completion.

Hotels/Motels

A motel investment may be as small as 10 or 15 units or as large as a high-rise multiroom hotel. Because the motel/hotel business is a specialized industry, an investor who has little or no experience in this type of business should hire a professional to help run the operation. Real estate professionals who sell motels and hotels should also be aware of the workings of this industry. The success of a hotel/motel investment is extremely dependent on the general economy. The motel/hotel, depending on where it is situated, typically relies on two types of customer: the business customer and the vacation traveler. Investors should have a knowledge of the customer base for this type of investment and investigate the cyclical nature of the business. One hotel/motel may be situated in a waterfront community and have business in the summer only. A hotel in a business district of a city may be busy only during the week and yield no income on weekends.

ANALYSIS PROFILE

Before embarking on an investment of any kind, investors must analyze their project. An analysis profile includes: risk/return analysis, pricing, rate of return, portfolio development and securitization, sensitivity analysis, special risks, and special financing. These criteria are discussed next.

Risk/Return Analysis

The **rate of return,** or *percentage of income per dollar amount invested that the investor gets back on an investment,* includes considering a *risk factor. The greater the risk of loss, the greater potential rate of return* the investor is entitled to expect. Often, after a careful analysis of all other factors, a prospective investor may decide that the degree of risk is not worth the potential return on a particular investment.

Pricing

Investment price analysis involves the determination of the price paid for a property or project that an investor feels warranted in paying in order to achieve the desired rate of return. The price must take into account a level of risk that the investor feels comfortable with, not only for the particular investment but also in light of its effect on the entire investment portfolio.

The *income capitalization approach* converts income into value so that an investor can look at an investment's validity and reasonableness. The income approach is the primary method that appraisers use for estimating the value of properties that produce rental income.

Rate of Return

To evaluate the feasibility of an investment, investors decide what percentage of return they want on their investment and examine the return on the actual investment. If they know they can receive 3 percent return on a certificate of deposit or treasury bonds, they will expect more from a real estate investment because of the risks involved. However, income tax must be paid on the interest earned from savings. With a real estate investment, the earnings can be sheltered since the buildings and equipment can be depreciated and that depreciated dollar amount can be deducted from the income.

In the income approach technique for evaluating property investments, one divides the property's income by the desired rate of return. If an investor requires a 12 percent annual return and the property has a $15,000 net annual income, he should pay no more than $125,000: $15,000 (income) = $125,000 (property value); 12% (rate of return). The rate of return relates net operating income to the investment.

Portfolio Development and Securitization

To obtain financing for a project, an investor must present a portfolio to a lender, including documentation of past and current investment projects, a description of the subject project (including feasibility studies and proforma statements), a financial statement, and a detailed presentation about how the investor intends to pay the loan. A lender will require that the subject investment property be security for a loan and may require that the equity an investor has in other investment projects be used as security for the current project.

Sensitivity Analysis

When considering a real estate investment, an investor examines a property's income and expenses and draws conclusions regarding projected figures for income from rents and other sources, tax depreciation, vacancy rates, and so on. *Sensitivity analysis* is a study of how a change in one factor can affect the income to the property. For example, if a vacancy rate is higher than predicted, then the rental income will decrease. An understanding of the relationship of one factor to another and a projection of best-case and worst-case scenarios helps the investor to decide if the investment is in his best interests.

Special Risks

Risk is not necessarily limited to just one factor. In addition to incurring the financial risk associated with debt, an investor also has to deal with other risk factors. These can include a downturn in the real estate market, an investment that is not liquid, and so on. For example, with respect to development projects, an investor initially may have to invest dollars into formulating an idea and having it approved. The approval process may involve multiple government agencies. The parcel of land under consideration may be environmentally sensitive. The complexity and duration of the SEQR process alone (discussed in Chapter 6, Section 2), combined with possible public opposition, may push back the timetable for development, or even terminate the concept entirely. After evaluating this type of risk, an investor may decide, in the initial stages, that the project is not worth the effort. Think of similar efforts in your locality in which a project was abandoned because of the special risks involved.

Special Financing

Certain types of mortgages and alternative sources of funds are available for investment projects. Through creative financing techniques, investors can borrow money against their current investment and use this money to buy other properties. Four special financing options are described below.

Participation Mortgage

A *participation mortgage* relates to two different types of mortgages: (a) *A mortgage in which two or more lenders participate in making the loan.* The participation agreement between the lenders may provide that each participating lender owns a pro rata share of the mortgage and each will receive his share of the mortgage payment of principal and interest as it is made. Another option would be for one lender to contribute a substantial portion of the loan and another lender to give a small amount of the loan. In this case, the lender who invested more would receive first priority in the security pledged in the mortgage. (b) *A mortgage in which the lender participates in the profits generated by a commercial property used to secure payment of the debt in the mortgage loan.* The borrower agrees to the lender's participation in the net income as an inducement for the lender to make the loan. This allows the lender to receive interest as well as a share of the profits.

Leasehold Mortgage

The *leasehold mortgage* pledges a leasehold estate rather than a freehold estate to secure payment of a note. The leasehold acceptable to the lender is a long-term estate for years. The usual case is a lease for vacant land whereon the lessee is to construct an improvement such as a shopping mall, a hotel, or an office building as an investment.

Life Insurance Companies

At one time, a number of life insurance companies were active in making loans directly to individual mortgage borrowers. Today, they provide funds to lending institutions to lend to individual borrowers and to provide funds for the purchase or construction of large real estate projects such as apartment complexes, office buildings, and shopping malls.

Refinancing Versus Selling

Equity builds up in an investment property through increased value of the property and principal reduction on the amortized loan. The owner can then refinance the property with a new loan and use the tax-free money to purchase another property. Since the money is borrowed, it is not taxable. By refinancing, the investor avoids taxes on gains since taxes are payable only on the sale of the property. The owner is now able to purchase additional properties with the money obtained through refinancing and therefore can compound the holdings.

PUTTING IT TO WORK

Real estate licensees who work with investors should have knowledge of financing options. Respond to the following scenario.* Then compare your response with the model in the Answer Key at the end of the chapter.

We own, but do not reside, in a two-family rental property. For some reason, we can't find a bank that will offer us a home equity line of credit on our investment property, which is preventing us from making some needed repairs. Do you know of a bank that will offer us a home equity program?

---

*Source: James A. Ader, "Real Estate Spotlight." Copyright © The *Albany Times Union*. Reprinted by permission.

TAX CONSIDERATIONS

The most recent changes affecting real estate are included in the Taxpayer Relief Act of 1997. This law made some major improvements for home sellers effective for sales taking place on or after May 7, 1997. Home sellers may be eligible to exclude up $250,000 if single or up to $500,000 if married, of the capital gain on the sale of the residence. In order to be able to claim the entire exclusion, the home seller must have owned and resided in his home for at least two years of the last five years prior to the sale of the residence. If eligible for the exclusion, it may be claimed once every two years.

If the home was sold because of a change in employment, health, or other unforeseen circumstance, the home seller may be eligible to claim a partial exclusion of capital gains even if he didn't live in the home for a total of two years of the last five before the sale. The portion of the partial exclusion is calculated based on how long the home seller lived in and owned the home.

This exclusion relates to the gain only, not to the gross sale price. A single taxpayer who sells her home for $725,000 after paying $560,000 five years ago, has a gain of $165,000 entirely excluded from her income. In addition, for those taxpayers with gains totaling over $250,000 for singles and $500,000 for married couples, they must pay the excess tax when the sale occurs. Gains from real estate are reported on Schedule D, Capital Gains and Losses, of the tax return.

Income Tax

Income tax is progressive, so that not all taxpayers are taxed at the same rate. The tax rate applied to income is called the marginal tax bracket. There are currently six tax brackets: 0, 15, 28, 31, 36, and 39.6 percent. Most taxpayers fall in the 15 and 28 percent tax brackets.

Three major classifications for income and examples of each include:

1. Active income: earned by salaries or in a business in which the taxpayer materially participates,
2. Portfolio income: interest, annuities, dividends, royalties and,
3. Passive activity income: invested funds. A passive activity involves conducting any trade or business in which the taxpayer does not materially participate. This includes most rental activities and limited partnerships.

Losses from passive investments generally may not be used to offset ordinary income. The taxpayer may deduct losses from passive investments only against income from passive investments; they may not be applied against active or portfolio income. Other tax rules, however, may defer capital gain, such as tax free exchanges (discussed later). Further, any tax losses from the operation of investment property are allowable only to offset income from passive activities, called passive income.

$25,000 Special Loss Allowance for Rental Real Estate

Rental of real estate is generally a passive activity. However, up to $25,000 in passive losses from rental real estate can be deducted each tax year against income from non-passive sources, such as wages or portfolio income, if the taxpayer meets certain rules. However, income and expenses from a rental activity carried on as a trade or business with the taxpayer meeting the material participation requirements renders the activity nonpassive and it is taxed as ordinary income subject to income and self-employment taxes.

Property Taxes

Taxes paid on non-investment real property may be deducted as an itemized deduction on the tax return. Taxes paid on investment property are deducted on Schedule E. Itemized deductions are those that appear on the tax return form on Schedule A. Property taxes may be deducted on any type of real property including the personal residence, second home, time share, vacant land, income property, or inherited property.

Mortgage Interest

The current limits of home mortgage interest deductions are $1,000,000 of acquisition indebtedness plus $100,000 of additional indebtedness used for any purpose. Acquisition refers to debt incurred to buy, build, or improve the personal residence, including refinancing of these debts. The mortgage debt must encumber the principal residence or second home and the loan cannot be unsecured or secured by other real estate. There is no limit to the number of mortgages for interest deduction purposes. Interest paid on investment property is generally fully deductible.

Capital Gains and Losses

Different types of income are taxed differently. Most income is taxed at the taxpayer's marginal bracket (see above.) Some income and gains are tax free. Some income is taxed at a lower rate than other types of income. This last category includes capital gains.

Capital gain is *the profit realized from the sale of a real estate investment.* Assets such as stock, real property, and collectibles fall into the category of capital assets. If these items are held over one year, they earn a potential tax break when sold. The longer the asset is held, the lower the rate can go. Gains on capital assets held less than one year (short-term capital gains) are taxed at the marginal rate for the taxpayer's income. Gains on capital assets held over 12 months (long-term capital gains) are taxed at a rate of 20 percent, or 10 percent if the taxpayer's marginal bracket is 15 percent.

Capital loss occurs *when investment or other types of property is sold at a loss.* Capital gains can be reduced by capital losses. Capital loss may be deducted from taxable income. Capital losses for tax purposes normally do not apply to non-business property.

Tax Depreciation

The two types of depreciation are (a) tax depreciation and (b) economic depreciation. Economic depreciation results from physical deterioration of property caused by normal use, damage caused by natural and other hazards, and failure to adequately maintain the property. **Tax depreciation** is a provision of the tax law, applicable to certain types of assets, that permits a property owner to take an ordinary business deduction for the amount of annual depreciation. *Tax depreciation is a deductible allowance* from net income of property when arriving at taxable income. It allows income on property to be sheltered from taxation.

This permits the owner to recover the cost or other *basis* of an asset over the period of the asset's useful life. The **adjusted basis** *consists of the price paid for the property, plus expenses incurred in acquiring the property, plus the cost of any capital improvements* (less depreciation if applicable).

Tax depreciation is an accounting concept only. The property being depreciated actually may appreciate in value. When the property is sold, tax may have to be paid on the "real" appreciation plus the recapture of the "artificial" tax depreciation. **Appreciation** *refers to an increase in value due to economic or other reasons.*

Currently, there are three depreciation schedules for real property acquired after December 31, 1986: 27.5 years for residential property (discussed further below), and 31.5 or 39 years for nonresidential property. The TRA of 1986 also limited the amount of claimed passive losses to an amount no more than the income received from similar passive activities. For example, if an investor loses $35,000 on his properties, but the properties' income is only $21,000, the investor can claim only $21,000 in losses that tax year. The excess loss of $14,000 ($35,000 − $21,000) cannot be claimed during the year of the loss. The excess loss may be carried over to future tax years. A limited exception to this rule applies to owners with an adjusted gross income of less than $100,000 who actively manage their own property. This exception phases out once the taxpayer's adjusted gross income exceeds $150,000. These owners may shelter up to $25,000 of other wages or active income in the same tax year. Passive investors who do not actively manage their own property cannot apply excess losses to other active income in the same tax year. In the above example, if the investor manages his own properties and has an adjusted gross income of $70,000, he can use the $14,000 excess loss to reduce the adjusted gross income to $56,000. Depreciable property includes assets such as buildings, equipment, machinery, and other items that are used in business to produce income (other than inventories) or that are held as an investment. Small businesses that invest less than $200,000 in depreciable property each year may depreciate $24,000 (in 2002) in equipment during the year purchased. The dollar limit is adjusted each year by the IRS.

Assets held for personal use, including a personal residence, are not depreciable assets. Land is not a depreciable asset because it does not "wear out." Therefore, the value of the land and the value of structures on the land must be separated to arrive at a basis for determining depreciation. The building and improvements are depreciable over 27.5 years for residential property (discussed earlier) on a **straight-line depreciation** basis. The basis normally is the cost of acquiring the property reduced by the estimated salvage value of the property at the end of its useful life. *Straight-line depreciation means that the portion allocated to the building is divided by 27.5 to determine the depreciation allowance each year.* This works out to be 3.636 percent (1 divided by 27.5 = .03636) for each full year. For example, if the building portion is determined to be $125,000, the depreciation per year is $4,545 ($125,000 × 3.636 percent). For the year the property is placed in service or returned from service, depreciation is prorated for the shorter year.

When a depreciable asset is sold, the basis of the asset used to compute the taxable gain from the sale is the depreciated value. For example, a depreciable asset is purchased for $100,000 and sold for $130,000. The purchaser had taken $40,000 of tax depreciation up to the time the property was sold. The taxable gain is $70,000 ($100,000 original basis minus $40,000 depreciation = $60,000 new basis; subtract the new basis from $130,000 selling price = $70,000 taxable gain). In essence, the basis of a depreciable asset is reduced by any depreciation deduction taken.

Cost Recovery

Cost recovery deductions are available for real estate and personal property used for business income and trade purposes. *Cost recovery allows the total cost of the property that is depreciable to be deducted over a certain timeframe.* Cost recovery is different from depreciation because it does not take into account the estimated *salvage* value of the property. The deduction begins when the property is put into service. The IRS has tables available to taxpayers to compute their deductions.

Pre-Tax and After-Tax Cash Flow

Ideally, an investment property will yield a positive cash flow. The **cash flow** represents *the net proceeds after all expenses are met and may be measured before or after taxes are considered.* If an investor has a property that generates an annual income of $44,000 and expenses total $35,000, he has earned a net return (cash flow) of $9,000. For example:

Rental income from office building	$44,000
Expenses	−$17,000
Mortgage principal	−$ 2,000
Interest on mortgage	−$16,000
Cash flow	$ 9,000

If the tax-deductible expenses, including depreciation of a property, are greater than the income, for tax purposes, a loss will result. To some investors, this loss is desirable because their main concern is to have a **tax shelter.** A tax shelter is best defined as *a paper loss; it is a phrase used simply to describe some of the advantages of real estate investments.* Since investment property can be depreciated as an expense when figuring income tax, it provides a tax shelter for its owner. For example:

Income	$44,000
Expenses	$17,000
Interest deduction	$16,000
Depreciation deduction	$13,000

$46,000 − $44,000 (income) = ($2,000) loss

The owner has a paper loss of $2,000 for tax purposes, but without including the depreciation deduction, the owner has a positive cash flow of $11,000.

Cash-Flow Income Shelter

Income shelters for taxpayer owners are deductible allowances from net income used to arrive at the amount of taxable income. Income shelters include tax losses allowed to offset passive and active income. Examples of expenses and allowances deductible from gross income include depreciation, operating expenses, real estate taxes, and mortgage interest.

To see the benefit of this concept, review the operating statement for the apartment building described in Figure 4.1. We assumed the subject property was purchased for $6,200,000. Because land does not depreciate, we have to make an allocation between the land and the improvement (the building). If we assume that 15 percent of the price is allocated to the land, the depreciable property becomes 85 percent times $6,200,000, or $5,270,000. Because the property can be depreciated over a 27½-year period, one year's depreciation could be 1/27th, or $191,636, which may be used to offset (shelter) income from the property itself. Further, interest on the debt service is deductible. The final figures are illustrated in Table 4.4. Viewed another way, we can see that if the property owner is in a 28 percent tax bracket, the deduction (sheltering) created by the depreciation allowance of $191,636 means that she saved 28% of this figure, or potentially $53,658, in federal income taxes, without having to write a check for the depreciation expense allowed by the tax law.

Net Operating Income	$ 745,600	**TABLE 4.4**
Less: Interest	− 463,836	Determination of net
Depreciation	− 191,636	taxable income.
Net Taxable Income	$ 90,128	

Tax-Free Property Exchanges

The Internal Revenue Code provides that, in cases of qualified exchange of property, some or all of the gain may not have to be recognized for tax purposes. The property exchanged must be investment property or business property. These requirements are not discretionary with the taxpayer or the government. If a transaction qualifies as a tax-free exchange, no gain or loss may be recognized in the year of the exchange. The basis of the property each exchangor received is the same basis as the property each owned prior to the exchange, plus any additional expenditures on the new property.

To qualify as a **tax-free exchange,** *the properties must be "like-kind."* Essentially, this involves exchanging personal property for other personal property or real property for other real property. *Exchanges of like-kind real property may be an office building for a shopping mall, an apartment house for a tract of land, or an office building for an apartment building.* Examples of personal property exchanges are a truck for a machine or an automobile for a truck. Personal residences and foreign property do not qualify for exchanges. Property held for personal use does not qualify. An exchange of residences by homeowners does not qualify as a tax-free exchange but is treated as a sale and a purchase. In addition, the property exchanged must not be held for sale to customers in the regular course of business, such as lots held for sale by a developer.

Boot

If an exchangor receives cash or some other type of nonqualifying property in addition to like-kind property, the transaction may still partially qualify as a tax-deferred exchange. The recipient of *the cash in the exchange,* called the **boot,** or other nonqualifying property incurs a tax liability on the boot or other unlike-kind property in the calendar year of the exchange. Unlike-kind property is property that is not similar in nature and character to the property exchanged.

Basis

The basis of the property an exchangor receives is the basis of the property given up in exchange plus new expenditures or debt incurred. Therefore, an exchangor does not change the basis of an asset as a result of the exchange. For example, Exchangor #1 trades a property with a market value of $100,000 and a basis of $20,000 for another property also worth $100,000. The property Exchangor #1 receives also is considered to have a basis of $20,000 plus any new debt assumed and cash paid, regardless of the other Exchangor's basis.

IMPORTANT POINTS

1. The primary purpose of the investor is to generate income (cash flow) without substantial risk.
2. Before investing, an investor must consider the time value of money, that is, where his investment funds would bring the greatest return on dollars invested for a given period of time.
3. An operating statement for a property includes the income and expenses for a property. The costs of business or investment property are tax-deductible expenses.
4. Valuation of a property estimates the market value of an identified interest in a specific property as of a certain date. Types of value include market value, investment value, value in use, assessed value, and mortgage loan value.

5. Forms of property ownership include sole proprietorship, partnership, corporation, syndication, and joint ventures.

6. The use of borrowed funds is called leverage, which allows the investor to accumulate the maximum amount of real estate with the minimum amount of personal funds.

7. Types of investment property include land, retail offices, offices, mixed developments, apartment rentals, and hotels and motels.

8. Analysis profile of a property includes the analysis of risk and return, special risks, timing, pricing, rate of return, portfolio development and securitization, sensitivity analysis, and special financing.

9. A feasibility study generally is used when considering large-scale projects. It is a statistical analysis of all facets of the market, including a comparison of other similar projects.

10. Under the Taxpayer Relief Act of 1997, single taxpayers may take up to a $250,000 exclusion from taxation on gain in the sale of their homes and married taxpayers may take up to a $500,000 exclusion.

11. Capital gain is the profit realized from real estate investment. Capital loss occurs when an investment is sold at a loss. The adjusted basis of a property is the cost of the investment combined with the cost of improvements.

12. Depreciation is a deductible allowance from net income in arriving at taxable income. It provides a tax shelter for the property owner.

13. Depreciation enables the owner of business or investment property to recover the cost or other basis of the asset. Land is not depreciable—only structures on the land.

14. Cash flow represents the net proceeds after all expenses are met and can be measured before or after taxes are considered.

15. Tax losses from investment property are allowed to offset income only from passive activities.

16. Deductible allowances from net income of property to arrive at taxable income and tax losses allowed to offset passive and active income are income shelters for investors.

17. To qualify as a tax-free exchange, like-kind property must be exchanged. The property exchanged must have been held for use in business (other than inventory) or as an investment.

How Would You Respond?   CHAPTER REVIEW

Analyze the following situations and decide how the individuals would handle them based on what you have learned. Check your responses using the Answer Key at the end of the chapter.

1. Andrea and Jeremy are considering the purchase of a duplex. They plan to live in one of the units and rent out the other. They are first-time investors and are getting cold feet. They ask their broker, Tamara, to outline the advantages and disadvantages of owning investment property. How should Tamara respond?

_____

_____

_____

_____

2. Raul and Sarah trade office buildings. In the trade, Raul receives $20,000 in cash in addition to Sarah's office building. Because cash is a part of the transaction, does this qualify as a tax-free exchange?

_____

_____

_____

_____

3. For five years Kendra has owned a small strip mall consisting of five storefronts. For the past year, the property has produced a negative cash flow because of two persistent vacancies. Since this is the only year that cash flow has been a problem, Kendra is reluctant to sell. She approaches a commercial broker, Dean, to explore her options. What advice might Dean give her? Even if Kendra decides not to sell the property, how can Dean turn this into business for himself?

_____

_____

_____

_____

KEY TERM REVIEW

Fill in the term that best completes the sentence and then check the Answer Key at the end of the chapter.

1. In a qualified _____, the tax on the gain is postponed and the deduction of a loss also must be postponed.

2. Mortgage principal and interest payments are known as _____.

3. _____ is the buying power of an investor through the use of borrowed funds.

4. The percentage of income per money invested that the investor receives back on an investment is known as the _____.

5. _____ is the profit realized from the sale of a real estate investment.

6. An IRS deduction, different from depreciation, that allows the total cost of a depreciated property to be deducted over a certain timeframe is known as _____.

7. A negative cash flow, called _____, is sometimes desirable to investors as it provides a paper loss on tax returns.

8. The _____ represents the net proceeds after all expenses are met and may be measured before or after taxes are considered.

MULTIPLE CHOICE

Circle the letter that best answers the question and then check the Answer Key at the end of the chapter.

1. Riverview Apartments is a small complex containing 10 units that rent at $800 per month. Based on 75 percent occupancy, the effective gross rental income per year is:

   A. $8,000

   B. $72,000

   C. $80,000

   D. $100,000

2. An operating statement adjusted to reflect a potential change in income and expenses based upon investor knowledge of the market is called a(n):

   A. income and expense statement

   B. rent roll

   C. proforma statement

   D. depreciation schedule

3. A form of real estate ownership that is a joint venture in which investors pool their resources is known as a(n):

   A. leasehold estate

   B. investment syndicate

   C. sole proprietorship

   D. tax shelter

4. If expenses and mortgage costs exceed the returns on an investment, it may mean that:

   A. too little leverage has been used

   B. the investment does not qualify as passive income

   C. expenses on this investment are not tax deductible

   D. too much leverage has been used

5. Investment in land is a more risky form of investment than other types of real estate investments because:

   A. it is always less valuable than improved property

   B. with no improvements on it, it cannot be depreciated for tax purposes

   C. it is always more liquid than other types of real estate

   D. it usually is more expensive to purchase than improved property

6. One of the main problems with an office building investment is:

   A. there is, in some areas, an oversupply of office space, which contributes to higher vacancy rates

   B. offices are usually located in deteriorating sections of cities or towns

   C. office building investment generally produces a lower return on investment than other types of property

   D. office building investment works only when the owner is a tenant in the building

7. Which of the following is NOT an advantage of apartment building investment?

   A. investors can live in one of the units, therefore saving on maintenance costs

   B. some of the expenses of the property in which a resident–investor lives are tax deductible

   C. smaller rental units are manageable for the beginning investor

   D. vacancy problems are almost nonexistent

8. Which of the following is FALSE regarding tax depreciation?

   A. it is a deductible allowance from the net income of a property for tax purposes

   B. the property being depreciated actually may appreciate in value

   C. it results from physical deterioration caused by normal use of property

   D. it is an accounting concept

9. If tax deductible expenses involved in a property are greater than the income, there will be, for tax purposes, a(n):

   A. negative cash flow

   B. positive cash flow

   C. increased debt service

   D. greater income

10. Investment funds from investors who do not materially participate in managing the investment are known as:

    A. active income

    B. passive income

    C. portfolio income

    D. partial income

11. Which of the following is a benefit that depreciation provides?

    A. tax credit

    B. tax deduction

    C. tax evasion

    D. tax basis

12. Which of the following is NOT a deductible expense for a business property?

    A. advertising

    B. utilities

    C. mortgage principal

    D. insurance

13. The basis of property received in a tax-free exchange is the:

    A. basis as it was to the prior owner at the time of the exchange

    B. average of the difference in the basis of all properties exchanged

    C. same basis as the basis of the property given up in the exchange plus any debt assumed and cash paid

    D. value of the property received in the exchange

14. If an investor has a property that generates an annual income of $100,000, and expenses total $25,000 and debt service equals $20,000, it generates a cash flow of:

    A. $20,000

    B. $25,000

    C. $55,000

    D. $100,000

15. The study of how, when one factor in an investment changes, it has a corresponding effect on another factor, which then affects the income of the property, is known as a:

    A. leverage

    B. feasibility study

    C. cash flow analysis

    D. sensitivity analysis

ANSWER KEY

Putting It to Work*

Home equity loans are available for owner and non–owner-occupied one- to four-unit properties such as yours. Home equity lines of credit, however, where an owner is given access to a limited amount of funds on an as-needed basis through a second mortgage, are allowed only on owner-occupied properties. Therefore, you can apply for a home equity loan; or consider a complete refinancing of the building, which allows you to take out some cash to make the repairs; a traditional property improvement loan, which can be unsecured; or the use of unsecured funds from credit card lines.

*Source: James A. Ader, "Real Estate Spotlight." Copyright © The *Albany Times Union*. Reprinted by permission.

How Would You Respond?

1. The advantages of a real estate investment include:
   a. the continual rise of property values, which is a hedge against inflation
   b. the potential high rate of return on the investment
   c. the leverage available, since the investor borrows money to finance the purchase and buying power thus is substantially increased
   d. the investor's equity buildup, since a portion of the payments apply to reducing the principal
   e. in Jeremy and Andrea's case, some of the expenses on the property where they live are tax deductible

   The disadvantages are:
   a. the nonliquidity. While stocks and bonds can be sold quickly through a stockbroker, it usually takes a period of time to find a buyer for real estate
   b. the risk. An investor must be a knowledgeable buyer and understand the risks involved, which include the importance of property location (its fixity and immobility); the ratio of rental returns to payments; the sum of money required; and maintenance requirements

2. The transaction does qualify as a tax-free exchange even though cash is also involved. The cash Raul receives is called boot and is taxable for the year in which the exchange occurs.

3. Dean might advise Kendra to refinance rather than sell the strip mall. It is possible that the downturn in business is only temporary. Not only does this prevent Kendra from having to pay capital gains tax on profits realized throughout the sale, but the influx of cash allows her the option of purchasing other investment property or using the cash to make improvements to the strip mall she now owns. Through proper approval, she may even use the money to create another store. Dean suggests that she hire him to analyze her vacancy problems and to lease the property for her.

Key Term Review

1. tax-free exchange
2. debt service
3. leverage
4. rate of return
5. capital gain
6. cost recovery
7. tax shelter
8. cash flow

Multiple Choice

1. B
2. C
3. B
4. D
5. B
6. A
7. D
8. C
9. A
10. B
11. B
12. C
13. C
14. C
15. D

Chapter 5

administrative law

arbitration

case law

commercial law

constitutional law

corporation

corporation law

criminal law

due process

general partnership

limited partnership

lis pendens

litigation

marital property

mediation

notice of pendency

partnership

partnership law

personal property law

procedural law

Real Estate Investment Trusts (REITs)

real property law

Statute of Frauds

Statute of Limitations

statutory law

torts

trusts and wills

trustee

Uniform Commercial Code (UCC)

LEARNING OBJECTIVES *Classroom hours: 5*

1. List the five sources of law that are associated with the study of general business law.

2. Explain the function of the Uniform Commercial Code.

3. Describe various negotiable instruments.

4. List the requirements that allow negotiable instruments to be valid.

5. List various business organizations and the advantages and disadvantages of each.

6. Identify elements of both the federal and New York court systems.

7. Describe the various types of dispute resolution.

8. Discuss the different types of bankruptcy that may be considered by businesses and individuals.

General Business Law

9. Understand the concept of marital property.

10. Understand the impact of marital litigation upon real estate ownership.

11. Understand the legal ramifications of the Statute of Limitations.

IN THIS CHAPTER   Many who obtain a broker's license do so because they wish to open their own brokerage firm. Others may find themselves in management positions in the real estate industry. These roles may involve various legal issues. Knowledge of general business law principles will assist the broker in evaluating choices pertaining to business decisions. Because of the many complicated regulations and paperwork in current real estate brokerage, a competent attorney and accountant are invaluable business assets.

SOURCES OF LAW

The basis of law in most states, including New York, is English *common law*. In earlier times, common law was a type of legal practice where judges decided legal issues and their predecessors abided by the decisions made by these judges. Common law as well as other modern laws are based on decisions which presumably required a careful, intelligent study of what is right and fair. The *United States Constitution* is the supreme law of our country. This means that other laws, federal, state, or local, that conflict with the Constitution are unenforceable. The Constitution lays out the branches of government (see Figure 5.1) and was designed as a broad-based law written to evolve with a changing society.

Various powers not specifically documented in the U. S. Constitution may be included in a *state constitution*. New York has its own constitution. State constitutions, including New York's, are generally patterned after the U. S. Constitution. State constitutions may not conflict with the U. S. Constitution.

The U. S. Congress is empowered by the Constitution to enact *federal laws* or statutes. Federal legislation includes such diverse areas as antitrust, securities, civil rights, mortgage lending, and environmental laws.

State governments also have legislative processes through which *state laws* or statutes are enacted. State laws include worker's compensation, real property, profes-

FIGURE 5.1
The structure of the federal government.

Congress Legislative	President Executive	Courts Judicial

Power to enact (make) the law	Power to enforce the law	Power to enforce, to interpret, and to determine the validity of the law

sional licensure, domestic relations (marital), human rights, and agency laws. In addition, states generally allow local governments to enact their own *local ordinances* since local governing authorities are most familiar with the needs of the region or community they govern. Types of local ordinances include zoning and traffic laws and building codes.

When a lawsuit occurs, interpretation of the statute has a direct bearing on future decisions by the court. *Interpretation by the court regarding these laws is known as* **case law** and is researched by attorneys to prepare their cases.

UNIFORM COMMERCIAL CODE

To keep up with the rapid growth of a nationwide and global economy, uniformity of business practices among and between parties from different states was needed. **The Uniform Commercial Code (UCC)** *is a state statute enacted by the State of New York and, in substantially the same form, by most other states, to simplify, clarify, and modernize the laws governing commercial transactions.* Article 3 of the Code, Negotiable Instruments, adopted by all of the states, was revised in 1990, and is the subject of this discussion. A **negotiable instrument** *is an unconditional promise or order to pay a fixed amount with or without interest. It must satisfy the requirements of negotiability defined in UCC Article 3 (discussed later).* Negotiable instruments are a substitute for money. Because the money the instrument represents can be transferred to others, laws governing its form and content are necessary to protect all parties in the transaction. Negotiable instruments include drafts, checks, promissory notes, and certificates of deposit. See Figure 5.2, which summarizes the types of negotiable instruments.

Drafts

A draft is a three-party negotiable instrument. The person who signs a draft and is identified as the one ordering payment is known as the *drawer*. The person ordered in a draft to make payment is known as the *drawee*. The drawee, instead of being obligated to pay the drawer, is obligated to pay a third party—the *payee*.

For example, Deana, a buyer, must pay a deposit of $5,000 as agreed upon in the offer to purchase. She decides to use the $5,000 owed to her by a friend, Beryl. Deana writes a draft that orders Beryl to pay this $5,000 to the sellers. Beryl agrees to this change of obligation (from paying Deana to paying the sellers instead) and accepts the draft. In this scenario, Deana is the drawer because she ordered the payment; Beryl is

INSTRUMENT	NUMBER OF PARTIES	PAYMENT	
Drafts	3	order to pay	**FIGURE 5.2**
Checks	3	order to pay	Types of negotiable instruments.
Promissory notes	2	promise to pay	
Certificate of Deposit (CD)	2	promise to pay	

the drawee because she accepted the draft, and the sellers are the payees because they received the $5,000 payment.

Checks

A *check* is a type of draft (also three-party) and is the most familiar negotiable instrument. The *drawer* is the signer of the check. The *drawee* is the financial institution through which it is drawn and the *payee* is the individual or entity to whom it is made out. A check is simply an order to pay.

Promissory Note

A promissory note (or note) expresses a promise to pay. The individual who makes the promise to pay is known as the *maker* or *borrower*. The person or entity to whom the promise is made is known as the *payee* or *lender*. The maker is then the person who obtained a loan and who is giving the lender a promissory note for repayment of the loan. Therefore, the promissory note is a two-party negotiable instrument. The terms of payment for the note, such as the interest rate and time frame for payment, are negotiable between the parties. A promissory note may be transferred to others. Lenders may require collateral along with the note. This serves as security for the payment. For example, when an individual obtains a loan, he signs a promissory note to evidence the debt.

Certificate of Deposit

A certificate of deposit (CD) is another type of note containing an acknowledgement by a bank that a sum of money has been received. The bank promises to repay the money together with interest at an agreed-upon rate when the CD matures. The time period for the CD is initially agreed upon by the parties. The CD is a two-party negotiable instrument. The bank is the *borrower* or *maker* because it is "making use" of the money of the depositor. The depositor is the *payee* or *lender* because the depositor is allowing the bank to "use" his money and also because the payee will receive his money back together with interest at a certain prescribed date.

Requirements for Negotiability

In order to be negotiable, a draft, note, or check must comply with the following:

- It must be in writing. Some or all of an instrument may be preprinted; however, an instrument entirely handwritten or typed is acceptable. Oral agreements are not negotiable instruments.
- It must be signed. If the negotiable instrument is a promissory note, it must be signed by the maker; that is, the borrower who promises to repay. If the instrument is a certificate of deposit, it must also be signed by the maker; that is, the bank that is the "user" of the money. A draft must be signed by the drawer, the one who makes the order. A check must be signed by the drawer, the one who has the

checking account. Under UCC regulations, the negotiable instrument may be signed by an authorized agent of the maker or drawer. Printed or stamped signatures are also valid.

- It must contain a promise or order to pay. According to the UCC, a negotiable instrument is a signed document that orders or promises payment of money. The instrument must be *unconditional;* that is, it may not contain conditions for payment. A check or draft is an unconditional *order* to pay. A promissory note or certificate of deposit is an unconditional *promise* to pay. If the promise or order is *conditional* on another factor, it is not a negotiable instrument.

For example, Nadine purchases a used car from Michael and gives him a promissory note for $10,000 agreeing to pay for the car only if the transmission holds up for 5,000 miles. This note is nonnegotiable because it is conditional on the transmission working for 5,000 miles.

- It must state a specific or fixed sum of money. The exact amount of money must appear on the instrument. Interest may be charged for the money owed and the rate written on the instrument or referenced to another document. Interest may be a fixed or variable rate.

- It must be payable on demand or at a definite time. Checks are payable on demand. The instrument may use language such as "payable on demand" or "payable on presentment." Other instruments such as drafts, promissory notes, and CDs may or may not be payable on demand. If no time for payment is stated, it is payable on demand.

Instead of on demand payment, an instrument may state a definite time for payment such as "on or before November 28, 2000." See Figure 5.3, Requirements for Negotiability.

Endorsements

An endorsement is a signature by other than a maker, drawee, or an acceptor that is placed on an instrument to *negotiate* (or transfer) it to another person. Endorsements may be written on the back of the instrument. For example, associate broker Russ Winter receives a commission check for $1000 and immediately takes it to the sporting goods store, endorses the check, gives it to the cashier and purchases a set of golf clubs. Winter has *negotiated* the check to the store. The person who endorses the check is known as the *endorser*. If the endorsement names a payee, this person is called the *endorsee*.

In one type of endorsement, the signature may appear alone. If so, this is known as a *blank endorsement*. For example, Russ Winter writes a check payable to the order of Sheldon Spring. Sheldon endorses the check by signing his name on the back. Sheldon Spring is the endorser.

In another type of endorsement, called a *special endorsement*, the instrument may name an individual to whom the instrument is to be paid. This contains the signature of the endorser together with the name of the person that is payable on the endorsement.

FIGURE 5.3 Requirements for negotiability.	To be negotiable (transferable) an instrument must meet these requirements: In writing Signed Promise or order to pay Specific or fixed sum of money Payable at definite time or on demand

Sheldon Spring writes "pay Langley Summer" on the back of the check and then signs his name: Sheldon Spring. Langley Summer would be the endorsee (see Figure 5.4).

Liability of the Endorser

By endorsing, the endorser makes various warranties. Therefore, if a holder (defined below) is not entitled to recover against the maker, he may be able to recover against the endorser.

Holder In Due Course

The person to whom an instrument is transferred becomes the holder. A *holder* is a person who is in possession of an instrument that is drawn, issued, or endorsed to him. The holder is subject to all of the claims and defenses (discussed later) that can be asserted against the transferor.

A *holder in due course (HDC)* is a holder who takes a negotiable instrument for value, in good faith, and without notice that it is defective or overdue. Negotiable instruments held by an HDC are virtually as good as money since the HDC makes an instrument free of all claims and most defenses that can be asserted by the drawer or maker. To qualify as an HDC, the transferee must meet UCC requirements as follows:

1. *Taken for "value."* The holder must give something of value for the instrument to qualify as an HDC. For example, Langley Summer endorses a check over to her daughter, Sunshine Summer. Sunshine does not qualify as a holder in due course because she gave nothing of value in receiving the instrument.

2. *Taken in good faith.* Good faith implies honesty in the conduct of the transaction.

3. *Without notice of defect.* With certain exceptions, persons cannot qualify as a holder in due course if the instrument is overdue, contains an unauthorized signature,

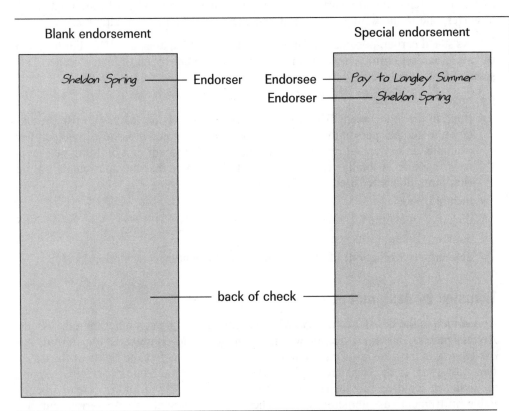

FIGURE 5.4
Blank and special endorsements.

is encumbered in any way such as a claim to it by another person, or if there is a known defense against it.

4. *Without any apparent evidence of forgery, alterations, or irregularity.*

Defenses

The creation of negotiable instruments may give rise to *defenses* against their payment. This means that individuals or entities involved in the payment of an instrument may claim that it is compromised in some way and therefore payment may be refused. There are two general types of defenses: *real defenses* and *personal defenses*. Real and personal defenses can be raised against a normal holder of a negotiable instrument. However, only real defenses and not personal defenses may be asserted against an HDC. Therefore, *real defenses* can be raised against both holders and HDCs. If a real defense is proven, the HDC cannot recover on the instrument against the drawer or maker. The HDC may be able to recover against the indorser. Real defenses include:

- instruments drawn by minors
- extreme duress such as force or violence; for example, an individual is forced to sign an instrument because of threats and intimidation
- mental incapacity
- illegality of the instrument; for example, a promissory note given for a gambling debt in a state in which gambling is illegal
- discharge in bankruptcy (discussed later)
- fraud in the inception. This occurs when a person is deceived into signing an instrument thinking it is something else. For example, a person might be led to fraudulently believe that a negotiable instrument is a contract or agreement to buy something when, in fact, it is a promissory note.

Other real defenses include forgery and material alteration, which might consist of adding to or removing any part of a signed instrument. Correcting a figure on a check to correspond to the written amount on the check is not a material alteration.

As stated earlier, personal defenses cannot be raised against an HDC, but they can be raised against enforcement of a negotiable instrument by an ordinary holder. Personal defenses include:

- breach of contract
- fraud in the inducement. This can occur when a wrongdoer makes a misrepresentation to another person to lead that person into a contract with the wrongdoer. For example, an individual purchases a cooperative apartment in a building that he is led to believe is totally residential, only to find later that the apartments on the first three floors are used for office space.
- mental illness
- illegality of contract
- duress or undue influence
- discharge (termination) of an instrument by payment or cancellation

Transfer by Assignment

Negotiation is the transfer of a *negotiable* instrument by a person other than the issuer. An assignment, however, occurs when a *nonnegotiable* contract is transferred. An *assignment* is the transfer of rights under a contract. It transfers the rights of the transferor (assignor) to the transferee (assignee). Because normal contract principles apply, the assignee acquires only the rights that the assignor possessed. In the case of a negotiable instrument, assignment occurs when the instrument is transferred but the transfer fails to qualify as a negotiable instrument under UCC Article 3. In this case, the transferee is an assignee rather than a holder.

BUSINESS ORGANIZATIONS

Business organizations can be structured in several different ways including sole proprietorships, partnerships, corporations, limited liability companies, limited liability partnerships, and joint ventures. Business organizations can receive, hold, and convey title to real property in the same ways as individuals. Refer to Chapter 1 for licensure requirements for real estate brokerage organizations.

Sole Proprietorship

This form of business organization is owned by one individual and uses a name other than the owner's personal name. The business title of a sole proprietorship could be, for example, Franklin Wonder doing business as (dba) Wondrous Heights Apartments. Title to real property may not be held in the name of the business alone, such as Wondrous Heights Apartments, but must be stated as Franklin Wonder doing business as Wondrous Heights Apartments.

Partnerships

A **partnership** *is a form of business organization that is owned by two or more partners and created by contract between the partners.* An agreement to be partners need not be in writing. The partners do not have to have the same degree of interest in the partnership or the same extent of management authority. The contract should contain the procedure for dividing ownership interest upon the withdrawal, death, or removal of a partner.

Under the Uniform Partnership Act, which has been adopted in New York, a partnership may hold title to real property in the name of the partnership as a tenancy in partnership. In addition, under common law, partnerships may hold title to real property in the names of the individual partners. The types of partners fall into two categories: general or limited. In the **general partnership,** *the partners are personally liable for partnership debts exceeding partnership assets.* Partners are jointly (together) and severally (separately) liable for these debts.

A **limited partnership,** which must be created by written agreement, *consists of one or more general partners who are jointly and severally liable, and one or more silent, or limited, partners who contribute money or other assets of value to the extent of their ownership interest.* Limited partners are not liable for the debts of the partnership beyond the amount of money they have contributed. To retain the protected status from partnership debts, a limited partner may not participate in managing the partnership and if he does, he may lose the protection beyond limited liability. Limited partners, therefore, may incur a general partner's liability merely by their actions.

The limited partnership organization is used frequently in real estate investments. Typically, a general partner conceives of the investment opportunity, then solicits monies from limited partners to purchase, construct, or improve a property. The general partners do all of the work and management necessary to create the investment. The limited partners provide the funds to purchase the investment. The return on the investment is divided among the partners—both general and limited—on a predetermined basis, as set out in the partnership agreement. The purpose of the investment may be to provide an income stream or to improve a property and sell the improved property at a higher price.

Corporations →you go online, to forme it

A **corporation** is an artificial being—invisible, intangible, and existing only pursuant to law. *A corporation is a taxable legal entity recognized by law, with tax rates separate from individual income tax rates.*

Creation

The formation of a corporation is subject to New York statutes governing its creation. It is formed by the filing of a certificate of incorporation. This is the basic governing document of the corporation. In order to pay for the operation of the business, a corporation issues and sells shares of stock. Purchasers of these shares are known as shareholders. Shareholders are owners of the corporation to the extent of their shareholdings.

Purpose

A corporation can be formed for any lawful purpose. The purpose of the corporation is defined in the certificate of incorporation. A corporation may have one purpose or diverse purposes. Corporations may be set up for profit or nonprofit. A profitmaking organization is created to do business and distribute profits to shareholders in the form of dividends. A nonprofit organization includes diverse organizations such as charities and colleges.

Rules

The corporate bylaws set out the method of operation for the corporation and the regulations that it must abide by. The bylaws also lay out the structure of the corporation as to officers, directors, secretary, treasurer, and so on.

Management

Essentially, the bylaws govern the operation and management of the corporation. They define the internal management structure. Shareholders, directors, and officers have different rights in managing the corporation. The shareholders elect the directors and may also vote on other important issues affecting the corporation. The directors are responsible for making policy decisions and employing officers. The bylaws may state expressly which officers, directors, or other persons may sign conveying documents.

Taxes

Corporations that are not subchapter S are known as *C corporations*. A *subchapter S corporation* is a type of corporate organization that is permitted to function as a corporation but is taxed as a partnership. A C corporation must pay corporate income tax to the IRS, and the shareholders are also taxed on their dividends that are profits of the corporation; therefore, a *double tax* is paid at the corporate level and the shareholder level.

An advantage of a subchapter S corporation is that since it is taxed as a partnership, it does not have not to pay corporate income tax, thereby avoiding the double tax a C corporation must pay. Subchapter S shareholders are taxed individually on their portion of the corporate income. The shareholders can deduct losses on their share of the corporation's losses on their individual tax returns.

A corporation franchise tax is a yearly tax levied on corporations by the state for doing business in New York. The minimum tax for all corporations including a subchapter S corporation is $325. Other charges apply to inactive corporations. The corporation franchise tax is calculated on the net profit of the corporation, and is a lien against the corporation's assets until paid. The corporation's assets may then be foreclosed by the state and the assets attached. Failure to pay a franchise tax will permit the state to dissolve the corporation, thus invalidating its right to do business legally in New York.

Advantages and Disadvantages

As separate legal entities, corporations are liable for their own contracts and debts. One advantage of a corporation compared with other forms of ownership is that, in most cases, when a liability issue arises, shareholders may be liable only to the extent of their investment. Under certain circumstances, a shareholder may be liable for unpaid wages owing to the corporation's employees. Another advantage is that stock ownership, compared with other forms of investment, such as real estate, is a *liquid investment*. If the stock is publicly traded, stockholders can freely buy and sell stocks at will. One of the main disadvantages of corporations is the double tax on income discussed above; that is, the tax on the corporate profit and the tax paid by shareholders on their dividends.

Termination and Dissolution

A corporation may be terminated in a number of ways and may be done voluntarily or involuntarily. If a corporation has not done business yet, it may be dissolved by a vote of the incorporators or directors. After doing business, it may be voluntarily dissolved if the board of directors recommends it and the majority of the voting shareholders vote for dissolution. In addition, the secretary of state can obtain administrative dissolution for a number of reasons such as failure to pay the franchise fee or failure to maintain registration. Corporations can also be dissolved by judicial decree. This might occur if the corporation engages in fraudulent activities, or for failure to pay judgment creditors.

Limited Liability Companies and Limited Liability Partnerships

Recently, other forms of business organizations have been made legal in New York. The *limited liability company (LLC)* may be formed by one or more persons. This form of business combines the most favorable attributes of both partnerships and corporations. Owners of an LLC (called members) are not personally liable for the obligations of the LLC; however, an LLC is taxed as a partnership.

A *limited liability partnership (LLP)*, typically formed by professionals such as attorneys and accountants, does not have to have a general partner. Instead, all partners are not personally liable for the obligations of the partnership, and may participate in management. An LLP is taxed as a partnership.

Joint Ventures

A *joint venture* is an organization formed by two or more parties for the purpose of investing in real estate or any other type of investment. The joint venture may be in the form of a corporation or a partnership, or the parties may hold title as joint tenants or as tenants in common. Joint ventures usually are devised for only one project. See Figure 5.5, Business Organizations.

PUBLIC AND PRIVATE SECURITY OFFERINGS

Purchase of a security earns the investor the right to participate in the profits of a company. These profits are realized through dividends paid to the investor and also by the sale of the securities after they have appreciated in value. The most common type of securities are stocks and bonds.

	TYPE	TAXATION
FIGURE 5.5 Business organizations.	Sole Proprietorship	Taxed as individual
	C Corporation	Double tax at corporate and shareholder level
	S Corporation	Taxed as a partnership
	General Partnership	Taxed as a partnership
	Limited Partnership	Taxed as a partnership
	Limited Liability Company	Taxed as a partnership
	Limited Liability Partnership	Taxed as a partnership

To protect investors from fraud on the part of securities dealers, federal and state governments have enacted securities laws and regulations. The Securities Act of 1933 was the first federal securities law. It was followed, in 1934, by the Securities Exchange Law, which focused on preventing fraud in the trading of securities. This law created the Securities and Exchange Commission (SEC) to administer federal securities laws. Together, these laws regulate companies' initial issuance of securities, outline fraudulent practices, and require registration of securities prior to sale. Amendments to these laws as well as additional laws have since been passed requiring further disclosure, regulating insider trading, and requiring disclosure of any conflicts of interest. The Securities Enforcement Remedies and Penny Stock Reform Act of 1990 granted authority to the SEC to further enforce its regulations. The SEC may order a cease and desist order to stop a certain activity that violates regulations. In addition, it imposes severe fines on offenders.

Public Offerings

The Securities Act of 1933 regulates the issuance of securities offered by a corporation, a general or limited partnership, an unincorporated association, or an individual. Securities offered through the mail or any other facility of interstate commerce must register with the SEC. This registration requires a registration statement and a prospectus (Figure 5.6). The registration statement must contain a description of the securities; the registrant's business; how the proceeds of the offering will be used; the degree of competition in the industry; government regulation; and any risk factors together with certain other information. The SEC does not decide upon the merits of the offering.

The *prospectus* is a disclosure statement that is used as a selling tool by the issuer. Much of the information in the prospectus can be found in the registration statement. The prospectus serves to help the investor in evaluating the risk of the investment. Certain securities are exempt from registration. They include securities issued by any U.S. government agency; securities issued by nonprofit organizations; securities of banking institutions that are regulated by banking authorities; insurance and annuity contracts by insurance companies; and stock dividends and stock splits.

Private Offerings

Securities that do not involve a public offering are exempt from the SEC registration requirement. This exemption is known as the *private placement exemption*. This exemption allows issuers to raise capital from an unlimited number of *accredited investors* without having to register with the SEC. There is no dollar limit on the amount of securities that can be sold pursuant to this exemption. An accredited investor may be one who: has a net worth of $1 million; a person who has had an annual income of at least $200,000 for the previous two years and reasonably expects to have a $200,000 income in the current year; any corporation, partnership, or business trust

FIGURE 5.6
A cover page of a prospectus.

PROSPECTUS

June 27, 2004   5,000,000 Shares

New Real Estate Investments, Inc.

COMMON STOCK

The common stock has been approved for listing on the New York Stock Exchange ("NYSE") subject to official notice of issuance.

This prospective does not contain all of the information regarding the stock. Further information is available in the registration statement that is filed with the Securities and Exchange Commission in Washington, D.C. pursuant to the Securities Act of 1933.

THESE SECURITIES HAVE NOT BEEN APPROVED OR DISAPPROVED BY THE SECURITIES AND EXCHANGE COMMISSION OR ANY OTHER STATE SECURITIES COMMISSION NOR HAS THE SECURITIES AND EXCHANGE COMMISSION OR ANY STATE SECURITIES COMMISSION PASSED UPON THE ACCURACY OR ADEQUACY OF THIS PROSPECTUS. ANY REPRESENTATION TO THE CONTRARY IS A CRIMINAL OFFENSE.

LB&C

Lattler, Brown & Company, Inc., New York

The prospectus cover contains brief information about the offering. The prospectus itself is developed for the public and details the investment objectives of the stock and the nature of the offering.

with total assets in excess of $5 million; insiders of issuers such as the executive offi-cers and directors of corporate issuers and general partners of partnership issuers; and certain institutional investors such as registered investment companies, pension plans, colleges, and universities.

No more than thirty-five nonaccredited investors may purchase securities pursuant to a private placement exemption. Nonaccredited investors must be sophisticated investors either though their own experience or through professional representatives such as accountants or attorneys. Advertising to the public is not permitted.

Small Offerings

Securities of a certain dollar amount are exempt from registration. The sale of securi-ties to either accredited or nonaccredited investors not exceeding $1 million during a twelve month period is exempt. The securities may be sold to an unlimited number of investors but general selling to the public is not allowed.

State Regulation

State laws are also designed to protect investors from buying "blue sky," (or nothing); therefore the term *blue sky laws*. In New York, the General Business Law addresses secu-rities offerings. The Department of Law is the agency that regulates these public and private offerings. Although a public securities offering is registered with the SEC, the company making the offering must still register in New York with the Department of Law.

Like the federal law, exemptions exist in New York as to registration requirements. Certain utility companies, not-for-profit organizations, savings banks, and trust funds may be exempt from registration. In addition, exemptions could include securities sold at judicial proceedings such as by an executor of an estate or a trustee in a bankruptcy. Securities sold in a limited offering of up to 40 people may also be exempt from reg-istration. In some cases, the Attorney General may grant an exemption to a securities offering of more than 40 people.

A type of public securities offering is the cooperative or condominium. In New York, no offering plan for the sale of co-ops or condos can be made public unless it is registered with the Attorney General's office in the Department of Law. (See Chapter 6 for a fuller discussion of condominium and cooperative offerings.)

REAL ESTATE INVESTMENT TRUSTS (REITs)

Real estate investment trusts (REITs) were created in 1967 stemming from changes in the Internal Revenue Code. *As a result, the beneficiaries of the trust were not taxed doubly on trust income. The trust can earn income from real estate investments without paying trust income tax.* Real Estate Investment Trusts make loans secured by real prop-erty. REITs are owned by stockholders and enjoy certain federal income tax advantages. To avoid the trust income tax, the trust must distribute 95 percent of the ordinarily tax-able income to the trust beneficiaries. Congress's stated purpose for creating this trust tax advantage was to allow and encourage small investors to pool their money to par-ticipate in larger real estate transactions and help make financing available for large real estate developments. The beneficiaries then report the income for tax purposes.

REITs provide financing for large commercial projects such as second-home developments, apartment complexes, shopping malls, and office buildings. The two major investment choices for REITs are whether (a) to lend or (b) to buy, rent, or sell property. If the REIT primarily lends money for the interest return, it is called a mort-gage REIT. If the REIT primarily owns, manages, rents, and sells property, it is called an equity REIT.

FEDERAL COURT SYSTEM

The federal court system (Figure 5.7) deals mainly with federal law enforcement issues. An exception is the Supreme Court, which may rule on appeals from the highest state courts if a federal issue is involved.

The U.S. Supreme Court is the nation's highest court. It is composed of nine Justices appointed by the President with the approval of the Senate. One of the Justices is appointed by the President as the Chief Justice. The Supreme Court does not hear evidence or testimony, as with the lower courts. The Supreme Court reviews the evidence and may reverse or modify the decision of the lower court. The Supreme Court hears appeals only from either federal circuit courts of appeals, sometimes from federal district courts, special federal courts and the highest state courts (in New York, the Court of Appeals.) The decision of the Supreme Court is final.

U.S. District Courts

These courts are federal trial courts. There is at least one federal district court in each state. The federal district courts are empowered to decide cases. Most federal cases originate in district courts.

COURT	FUNCTION
U.S. Supreme Court	Nation's highest court reviews and decides cases from lower courts
U.S. Court of Appeals for Territorial Circuit Courts	Hears cases from lower district courts, special courts, and federal agencies
U.S. Court of Appeals for the Federal Circuit	Hears cases from certain lower federal courts
U.S. District Court	Federal courts situated in 196 districts throughout the U.S.; at least one in each state
U.S. Bankruptcy Court	Located throughout U.S. to hear and try bankruptcy cases
U.S. Tax Court	Located throughout U.S. to hear and try tax cases
Federal agencies	Located throughout U.S.; agencies have internal administrative court system
U.S. Claims Court	Hears cases brought against the U.S.
U.S. Court of International Trade	Hears cases involving tariffs and international trade
U.S. Patent and Trademark Office	Hears patent and trademark cases

FIGURE 5.7
The federal court system.

Special Federal Courts

The following courts have limited jurisdiction. This means that they hear only certain types of lawsuits. They include the following:

- U. S. Tax Court, that hears cases involving federal tax laws
- U. S. Claims Court, which hears cases brought against the United States
- U. S. Court of International Trade, that hears cases involving tariff and international commercial disputes
- U. S. Bankruptcy Court, that hears cases involving federal bankruptcy laws

U. S. Courts of Appeals

The U. S. Courts of Appeals are the federal court system's intermediate appellate courts. There are 13 circuits in the federal court system. Circuits refer to the areas where the courts serve. The first 12 circuits are specific geographical areas. The 13th is located in Washington, D.C. Eleven of the circuits are designated by a number, such as the first circuit, second circuit, etc. These courts hear appeals from the district courts located in their circuit as well as from certain special courts and federal agencies. The courts review the decision of the lower federal courts to see if a reversal or modification of their decision is warranted.

NEW YORK COURT SYSTEM

New York's unified court system (Figure 5.8) was organized pursuant to a 1962 constitutional amendment and has been since modified. The New York court system handles a diversity of legal matters including:

- civil and family matters
- juvenile and criminal charges
- citizen-state disputes
- supervised administration of estates
- legal protection for children, the mentally ill, and others unable to manage their legal affairs
- regulation of admission to the bar and conduct of attorneys

Like the federal system, New York has trial courts that hear the cases first. These are known as courts of original jurisdiction. Then there are appellate courts that hear and determine appeals from decisions of the trial courts. Trial courts of limited jurisdiction decide matters such as misdemeanors, violations, and minor civil matters. In addition, they preside over arraignments and other preliminary proceedings in felony cases (which are then later prosecuted on the county level).

New York's court system is a multi-tiered system with courts beginning at the local or town level. New York City has a different system than that of upstate New York. The following explains the basic system from the lowest level (the town court) through to the Court of Appeal. Different modifications of jurisdiction may exist in various localities throughout the state.

City, Town, and Village Courts

City, town, village, and district courts handle minor civil and criminal matters. The jurisdiction of the city courts varies according to the terms of the city charter; some handle only civil cases, some only criminal cases, and some, both.

FIGURE 5.8   The New York Unified Court System.

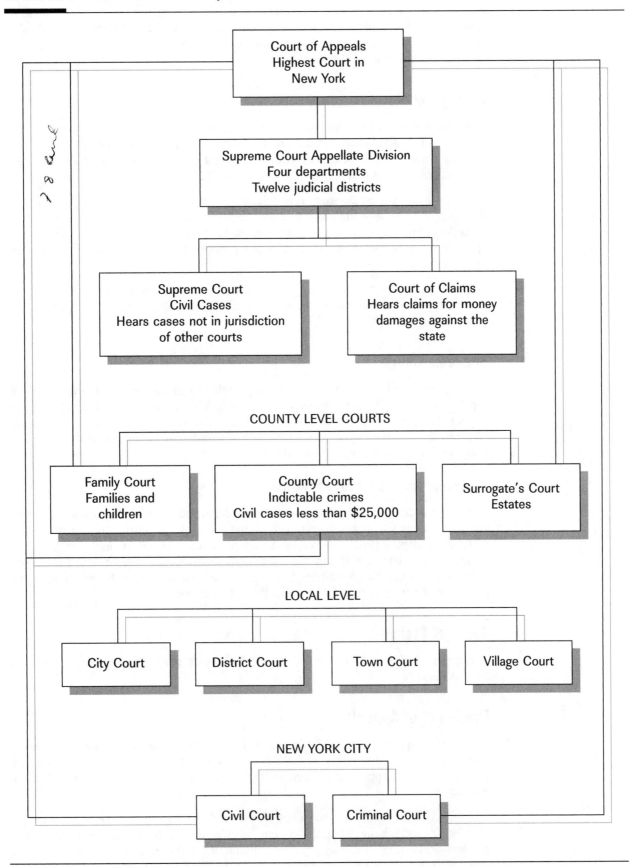

Court of Appeals
Highest Court in
New York

Supreme Court Appellate Division
Four departments
Twelve judicial districts

Supreme Court
Civil Cases
Hears cases not in jurisdiction
of other courts

Court of Claims
Hears claims for money
damages against the
state

COUNTY LEVEL COURTS

Family Court
Families and
children

County Court
Indictable crimes
Civil cases less than $25,000

Surrogate's Court
Estates

LOCAL LEVEL

City Court

District Court

Town Court

Village Court

NEW YORK CITY

Civil Court

Criminal Court

Court Appeals is Highest Court, Not supreme a

Court business law

New York City's system is divided into two courts: a civil court and a criminal court. Civil court decides civil matters involving amounts up to $25,000, including small claims and housing matters (for example, landlord–tenant disputes); and other civil matters referred to it by the Supreme Court. The criminal court rules on misdemeanor traffic infractions and violations.

County Courts

There are three county-level courts: county court, surrogate's court, and family court. County court, established in each county outside of New York City, has jurisdiction over indictable crimes committed within the county and has jurisdiction in civil cases in which the amount demanded does not exceed $25,000.

Family court is established in each county and in New York City. It has jurisdiction over matters involving children and families, including support of dependents, juvenile delinquency, persons in need of supervision, child protection, review and approval of foster-care placements, adoption proceeding, paternity determinations, and family offenses.

Surrogate's court is established in each county and has jurisdiction over cases involving affairs of decedents, including probate of wills, administration of estates, and adoption proceedings.

Supreme Court

The supreme court has both original and appellate jurisdiction. As a trial court, the supreme court possesses unlimited jurisdiction in law and equity, but it generally hears cases not falling under the jurisdiction of other courts. The supreme court exercises civil jurisdiction in every county. In New York City and some upstate counties, it also exercises jurisdiction over felony cases.

Supreme Court Appellate Division

The supreme court appellate division has four departments and twelve judicial districts and reviews cases from the supreme court and county level courts. The appellate division, third department, reviews cases from administrative tribunals such as the Workers' Compensation Board, the Commissioner of Education, and the Public Service Commission. The appellate division, first and second department (downstate), reviews cases from city and district courts in its jurisdiction.

Court of Claims

The court of claims is a statewide court that hears claims for monetary damages against the state.

The Court of Appeals

The court of appeals is New York's highest court. It hears cases on appeal from lower appellate courts, and in some capital cases, it may rule on questions of both law and fact. The court of appeals also reviews determinations of the commission on judicial conduct.

Various interest groups are calling for reform of the current New York court system. These groups believe that the system is not as unified as its name implies and will not answer the needs of a society in a millennium. New legislation would call for a statewide referendum and require a change to the state constitution.

In a lawsuit, the party bringing the action is known as the *plaintiff*. The party who must defend against the action brought by the plaintiff is known as the *defendant*. Lawsuits may involve one or more parties as either plaintiffs or defendants. Plaintiffs or defendants may be individuals, companies, or a combination of both.

SUBSTANTIVE AND PROCEDURAL LAW

From your experience in real estate, you are no doubt familiar with the many laws that come into play in various real estate deals. Law may fall into one of two categories: substantive or procedural. Certain bodies of law are a combination of both. **Substantive law** *is a body of law which addresses everyday behavior.* It governs the creation and exchange of assets. Also, it deals with conduct that can lead to punishment or result in one paying for bodily injury to another. Agency and torts (discussed below) are examples of substantive law.

Certain prescribed methods and regulations must be followed by all of those involved in the process of lawsuits, including the judges and attorneys. **Procedural law** *addresses the rules as to how a lawsuit proceeds through the court system and also deals with the functions of administrative agencies.* Civil procedure and administrative law (discussed below) are examples of procedural laws. The laws defined below are at least partially composed of **statutory laws.** *Statutory laws include all laws that are created by acts of the legislature in contrast to constitutional law (derived from the constitution) or laws generated by court decisions (case law) and other administrative bodies.* Criminal law and contract law, described below, include many statutory laws.

Types of Laws

In many lawsuits, more than one legal discipline may apply. For example, a dispute about an agency relationship may well include contract law elements. The following categorizes various legal disciplines.

Agency law. Agency law *embodies the laws pertaining to the relationship between parties to an agreement where one party in the agency relationship (agent) may act on behalf of another (the principal) and bind the principal by words and actions.*

Real property law. Real property law *deals with the acquisition, transfer, and possession of an interest in real estate and the rights attached to it.*

Administrative law. Administrative law *addresses administrative directives in the form of rules, regulations, and orders to carry out regulatory powers.* Its purpose is to define the duties of these agencies that must act upon these rules. Federal, state, and local government agencies rely on these administrative regulations to give form and shape to the statutes it must follow.

Commercial law. Commercial law *embodies statutes that are applicable to the rights and relations of persons engaged in commerce or trade carried on for profit.* An example of a commercial statute is the UCC (discussed earlier). —> *uniform commercial code*

Constitutional law. Constitutional law *covers the role of the Supreme Court and its authority as relates to the President, Congress, and the states.* Additionally, the law deals with the powers of Congress and the executive branch.

Contract law. Contract law *addresses the promises made by different parties to one another.* It defines the elements of contract validity and then examines remedies should there be a breach of contract. Real estate agents are prohibited from drawing contracts and may use only prescribed forms.

Corporation law. Corporation law *includes federal and state statutes and regulations that govern the formation and operation of corporations.* These laws include the Internal Revenue Code and the New York General Business Law.

Trusts and wills. Trusts and wills *addresses the succession to the ownership of an estate by inheritance or any act of law.* Title by descent is the title by which one person, upon the death of another intestate, acquires the deceased's property. Title may also transfer through a will, trust, or other method. A trustee is one who holds title to property for the benefit of another, called a beneficiary. The beneficiary is one who receives benefits or gifts from the acts of others given by, for example, a trust created by a will or a living trust.

When a person dies and leaves no valid will, the laws of intestacy determine the order in which the property is distributed to the heirs. The statute governing succession in New York is the Estates, Powers, and Trusts Law.

Civil law. Civil law *relates to the public. It addresses the private rights of citizens to sue and seek remedies through the courts for a wrongful action against them.* For example, if an individual sues another for breach of contract, this is a civil action. Civil law is different from criminal law where penal codes are applied.

Criminal law. Criminal law *declares what conduct is criminal and prescribes the punishment to be imposed for such conduct.* The purpose of criminal law is to create sanctions so as to prevent harm to the public. Criminal laws are codified into criminal or penal codes.

Personal property law. Personal property law is mainly addressed in the Uniform Commercial Code (discussed earlier). *Personal property, also known as chattel or personalty, is anything that is the subject of ownership other than real property.* According to the UCC, tangible personal property is known as goods. Goods include everything from crops to items removed from real property such as minerals and timber.

Partnership law. Partnership law *addresses the form of business organization composed of two or more individuals.* It is governed by the Uniform Partnership Act, which has been adopted in New York. Other laws, such as the New York General Business Law and the federal Internal Revenue Service code, deal with regulations regarding partnerships.

 Torts. Torts *deals with civil lawsuits; namely, wrongful acts that are committed either intentionally or unintentionally.* Intentional acts are known as *intentional* torts. Accidents, for example, car accidents, are a type of negligence known as unintentional torts. Assault and battery are examples of intentional torts that are also crimes. In such cases, the state can bring a criminal action and indictment. Victims can bring a tort (civil) suit against the wrongdoer.

You Should Know	**Due process of law**

Due process of law is inherent in the rights that are part of the American system of justice. It lies at the foundation of the legal system. *Due process mandates that anyone involved in a legal matter is entitled to have a legal proceeding according to established rules and regulations.* It implies the right of the person affected to be present in any court proceeding affecting his life, liberty, or property and to have the opportunity to defend himself.

Civil procedure. Civil procedure *defines the exact steps that must be followed in the development of a lawsuit.* These laws address legal pleadings such as complaints where the facts of the dispute are described. It also defines discovery procedures. Discovery seeks information pertinent to the lawsuit. In a matrimonial case, for instance, discovery would include financial disclosure by the parties. Civil procedure in New York can be found in the Civil Practice Law and Rules (CPLR).

DISPUTE RESOLUTION

Legal dispute may be resolved through one of three ways: litigation, mediation, or arbitration (see Figure 5.9).

1. **Litigation** *is another name for a lawsuit. It may involve a contest in court for the purpose of enforcing a law or seeking a legal remedy.* In a civil suit, it generally involves one or more plaintiffs and one or more defendants and the attorneys who represent each. Litigation may involve civil and criminal matters.

2. **Mediation** *involves the use of a neutral third party to discuss and attempt to resolve a dispute.* Mediation is an informal conference where the mediator, after hearing both sides, makes suggestions for reaching a solution. The mediator's role is one of persuasion.

3. Like mediation, **arbitration** *is a form of resolving a dispute between two or more opposing parties by a neutral third party. The neutral third party makes an award after hearing both sides.* Judgment can be entered in court based on the award and then enforced like any other judgment. The difference between arbitration and mediation is that an arbitrator makes a decision as to the dispute; a mediator does not. *Nonbinding arbitration* means that the arbitrator's decision is a recommendation and need not be complied with. Advantages of arbitration include the following:

- speed
- informality (the strict rules of evidence do not apply)
- expertise
- cost (the proceeding may cost less than a court proceeding)
- finality (there is no appeal from an arbitrator's award). The arbitrator may make error in law or fact but as long as he is honest and abides by the rules, the award is unimpeachable.
- confidentiality

Individuals cannot be compelled to give up their rights to have the dispute determined in a court unless they have agreed to arbitrate in writing.

MARITAL PROPERTY AND LITIGATION

The Domestic Relations Law is the statute that governs how marital property is divided should a couple divorce in New York. In community property states, all property acquired during the marriage is divided equally should there be a divorce.

TYPE OF REMEDIATION	METHOD	RESOLUTION
Litigation	Lawsuit	Through the courts
Mediation	Conference with neutral third party	Suggestion of mediator
Arbitration	Conference with neutral third party	Decision of arbitrator

FIGURE 5.9

Dispute resolution.

Because New York is not a community property state, property is not necessarily divided equally. The theory of *equitable distribution* is applied by the New York courts as to the division of marital property. There are generally four legal causes of action for divorce in New York. They are as follows:

1. Cruel and inhuman treatment which endangers the physical or mental well-being of the plaintiff.
2. The abandonment of the plaintiff by the defendant for a period of one or more years.
3. The confinement of the defendant in prison for a period of three or more consecutive years after the marriage of the plaintiff and defendant.
4. Act of adultery.

In New York, some marriages may be annulled under special circumstances defined in the domestic relations law. In addition, couples who live separate and apart for one or more years pursuant to a signed and filed separation agreement (usually drawn by an attorney) may divorce without cause provided that all of the terms of the separation agreement are strictly followed.

Divorces, in some ways, are similar to other civil litigation in the procedures that must be followed. Contested divorces, for example, when one of the spouses does not willingly enter the litigation, or if there are issues as to custody, alimony, child support, and property, may end up in court with a judge deciding the final terms of the action.

Marital Property

Generally, property acquired either before the marriage or inherited during the marriage is treated as separate property belonging solely to the spouse who acquired it. **Marital property** *is property acquired during the marriage and is distributed equitably taking into account numerous factors.* These factors include the number of years married, contributions of each of the partners, possible future circumstances, and projected tax consequences.

Division of Real Property

In some divorce actions, the spouse may jointly own land or other types of investment property. One or the other may bring legal action to have the property partitioned so that the spouses and possibly another owner of the property may have a specific and divided portion of the property exclusively. If this action can be done equitably, each party would receive title to a separate tract according to the share of interest allotted each of the parties. If this cannot physically be done to the land or other types of property, the court may order the sale of the property, distributing appropriate shares of the proceeds to the interested parties.

The Role of the Real Estate Broker

There are several instances where the real estate broker may be called upon to assist in the sale of the marital property during a divorce proceeding. Property involved in the litigation could include the family residence as well as other personal and investment property. For example, the court may order the spouses to sell the family residence because the spouses cannot agree on who will hold title to and/or continue to reside there. Even without a court order, the divorced couple may find that they can no longer afford or do not desire to keep the property the family lived in together. The broker may first have to assist the parties in arriving at a listing price as part of the settlement negotiation and then may be asked to place the property on the market.

If a broker is employed by either spouse involved in a divorce proceeding, the broker has a fiduciary duty to the client not to divulge to a buyer the circumstances through which the property is being sold.

BANKRUPTCY

Should an individual or business find that they can no longer pay their debts, bankruptcy may be chosen as an alternative. The purpose of the bankruptcy law is to allow the debtor to either continue doing business in a revised format or to start over completely. The decision to go bankrupt and the choices available should be carefully reviewed with an attorney should this become a desired option.

Federal Proceedings

Bankruptcy must adhere to the federal bankruptcy code and is filed in the federal district court. The most common bankruptcy options are Chapter 7, Chapter 11, and Chapter 13 of the bankruptcy code. The following discussion applies to Chapter 7, the most familiar bankruptcy option.

Chapter 7—Liquidation Bankruptcy

In this type of bankruptcy, the debtor's nonexempt property (discussed later) is sold for cash. The cash is distributed pro rata to the creditors, and any unpaid debts are discharged. Any person, partnership, or corporation may be debtors according to Chapter 7. A petition must be filed to commence a Chapter 7 bankruptcy. The petition may be filed by the debtor (voluntary) or one of the creditors (involuntary).

Trustee

A **trustee** must be appointed in a Chapter 7 filing. *Trustees are often lawyers or accountants who become the legal representative of the bankrupt debtor's estate.* The trustee must do a number of tasks, including taking immediate possession of the debtor's property; separating secured and unsecured property; setting aside exempt property; investigating the debtor's financial affairs; defending, bringing, and maintaining lawsuits on behalf of the estate; and employing others to assist in the administration of the estate.

Prior to selling the property of the debtor, real estate brokers must contact the bankruptcy trustee. The trustee will seek permission from the bankruptcy judge, who must approve the sale of the property.

Automatic Stay

The filing of a voluntary or involuntary bankruptcy petition automatically *stays;* that is, suspends certain actions of creditors against the debtor or the debtor's property. This is known as an *automatic stay.* The stay, which applies to collection efforts of both secured and unsecured creditors, is designed to prevent a scramble for the debtor's assets in a variety of court proceedings.

Secured and Unsecured Creditors ⟶ *Mortgage Bank* [handwritten]

In order for a creditor to possess a *secured interest* in the personal property of another, the creditor must comply with one of the following:

1. File a financing statement in a government office. Financing statements serve constructive notice that the creditor claims an interest in the specified personal property of the debtor. This filing is good for five years from the filing date and a continuation statement may be filed up to six months prior to its expiration and is good for another five years.

2. A creditor who extends credit to a consumer to purchase consumer goods under a written security agreement at the time of sale also serves as the creditor's security interest. A secured creditor's claims to the debtor's property has priority over the claims of unsecured creditors.

Unsecured creditors are those that do not have a security agreement or other collateral of the debtor. Collateral is property or something of value that can be used as security for repayment of the debt. According to the bankruptcy code, unsecured claims are to be satisfied out of the bankruptcy estate in the order of their statutory priority.

Exemptions

So that the bankruptcy does not completely wipe out the debtor, the federal code allows certain *exemptions;* that is, property or income that is not included in the bankruptcy. Exemptions include some of the following:

- interest in up to $10,000 in value of property used as a residence; this is known as the homestead exemption; husband and wife may double the exemption to $20,000
- interest in up to $2,400 in a motor vehicle
- interest in up to $200 per item in household goods, furnishing, clothing, and musical instruments totaling $5,000
- government benefits, including social security
- certain rights to receive income, including alimony, child support, and pension benefits

Claims Not Discharged

The term *discharged* refers to debts that are wiped out through the bankruptcy and are therefore no longer a debt of the bankrupt individual or entity. Claims not discharged refer to debts that, by statute, are not wiped out by the bankruptcy. The following debts are not discharged in a Chapter 7 bankruptcy:

- claims for taxes accrued within three years prior to the filing of the petition in bankruptcy
- certain fines and penalties payable to federal, state, and local governmental units
- claims based on the debtor's liability for causing willful or malicious injury to a person or property
- claims arising from the fraud, larceny, or embezzlement by the debtor while acting in a fiduciary capacity
- alimony, maintenance, and child support
- in general, liens such as mortgages and security interests in cars
- debts for luxury purchases (over $1,075) within 60 days before the petition is filed or cash advances (more than $1,075) within 60 days before the petition is filed
- student loans and grants made, guaranteed, or insured by a government agency or a non-profit institution
- judgment and consent decrees against the debtor for liability incurred as a result of the debtor's operation of a motor vehicle while legally intoxicated

Creditors who had nondischargeable claims against the debtor may participate in the distribution of the bankruptcy estate. The nondischarged balance may be pursued by creditors after the bankruptcy.

Discharge and Dismissal

After the property is distributed to satisfy the allowed claims, the remaining unpaid claims are discharged; that is, the debtor is no longer legally responsible for them. Only individuals may be granted a discharge. Discharge is not available to partnerships and corporations. These entities must liquidate under state law before or upon completion of the Chapter 7 proceeding. A debtor can be granted a discharge in a Chapter 7 once every six years.

Chapter 11 and Chapter 13 Bankruptcy

The other most common types of bankruptcy are Chapter 11 and Chapter 13. *Chapter 11—reorganization bankruptcy* provides a method for reorganizing the debtor's financial affairs under the supervision of the bankruptcy court. Its goal is to reorganize the debtor with a new capital structure so that the debtor will emerge from bankruptcy as a viable concern. This reorganization is in the best interests of the debtor and creditors. Chapter 11 bankruptcy is open to individuals, partnerships, corporations, and unincorporated associations.

Chapter 13—consumer debt adjustment is a rehabilitation form of bankruptcy for individuals. Chapter 13 permits the courts to supervise the debtor's plans for the payment of unpaid debts by installments. The debtor, under this plan, avoids the stigma of a Chapter 7 filing and also retains more property than is exempt under Chapter 7. Generally, this type of bankruptcy is less expensive and less complicated. The creditors also have a greater chance of being repaid than under Chapter 7. See Figure 5.10, Bankruptcy Options.

ESTATE AND GIFT TAXES

The subject of estates and wills is discussed in Chapter 7, Part II. This discussion addresses the current regulations on estate and gift taxes. The Internal Revenue Service Code regulates federal tax obligations. In New York, a combination of laws mentioned below addresses these issues. Currently, New York is in the process of making important changes to the estate and gift tax (discussed below).

Federal Estate and Gift Tax

If a person receives money or property from another, it may be subject to a federal *gift tax*. Money and property owned upon death may be subject to *estate tax*. Most gifts are not subject to federal gift tax and most estates are not subject to the estate tax. For instance, there is usually no tax if one makes a gift to one's spouse or if one's estate goes to one's spouse at death. If an individual makes a gift to someone else, the gift tax does not apply to the first $11,000 given that person each year.

The Economic Growth and Tax Relief Reconciliation Act of 2001 is a landmark law that amended the IRS code and changed the estate and gift tax. It is set to expire, however, in 2010. The law applies to those who are U.S. residents or citizens at the time of death. Under the law, for the years 2002 and 2003, an individual may transfer a total sum of $1,000,000 to a non-spouse or non-charity during lifetime or at death free of

TYPE	METHOD	AVAILABILITY
Chapter 7—Liquidation Bankruptcy	Property sold for cash to pay debts	Individuals and other business organizations
Chapter 11—Reorganization Bankruptcy	Reorganize with new capital structure	Individuals and other business organizations
Chapter 13—Consumer Debt Adjustment	Courts supervise debtor's plans for payment of debts by installment plan	Individuals

FIGURE 5.10

Bankruptcy options under the Federal Bankruptcy Code.

TABLE 5.1	CALENDAR YEARS	EXEMPTION AMOUNT
The new lifetime estate tax exemption amounts under the Tax Relief Act.	2002–2003	$1 million
	2004–2005	$1.5 million
	2006–2008	$2 million
	2009	$3.5 million

TABLE 5.2	CALENDAR YEARS	MAXIMUM RATE
The reduction in the federal estate tax rate under the Tax Relief Act.	2003	49%
	2004	48%
	2005	47%
	2006	46%
	2007–2009	45%

any estate and gift taxes. In 2004–2005, a total of $1,500,000 lifetime amount may be exempt from estate tax and $1 million from gift tax. The estate tax exemption will reach $3,500,000 by 2009. (See Table 5.1.) The gift tax exemption increased to $1,000,000 in 2002 with no other scheduled increases. These exemptions are known as unified credit equivalents and represent the amount by which a tax is eliminated or reduced.

The Act does not change the current right to pass the entire estate to a spouse tax-free. The estate tax is repealed for 2010, but the gift tax is retained.

For the year 2003, the maximum estate and gift tax rate is 49%; for 2004, 48%; and 2005, 47%. The Act gradually reduces the maximum estate and gift tax rate to 45% by 2007. (See Table 5.2.) The estate tax is repealed for 2010, while the maximum gift tax rate for 2010 will be 35%.

Exemptions to the Federal Gift Tax

The following are not taxable gifts:

- the annual exclusion of $11,000
- tuition or medical expenses for another
- gifts to a spouse
- gifts to a political organization
- gifts to a charity

A separate $11,000 annual exclusion applies to each person who receives a gift. Therefore, generally $11,000 can be given to any number of people. Married couples can each separately give up to $11,000 to the same person each year without making a taxable gift.

Gross Estate and Taxable Estate

The taxable estate is the *gross estate* less allowable deductions. The gross estate includes the value of all property in which the decedent had an interest at the time of death. This includes the following:

- the value of property sold or transferred for less than its full value while alive, if any interest was kept in the property
- property jointly owned with another
- life insurance policies payable to the estate, or if owned by the decedent, to the heirs of the estate

- value of certain annuities payable to the estate or heirs
- value of any property that decedent had power over
- gift tax paid by the decedent or his estate on gifts made to the decedent or spouse within three years before death of the decedent
- value of certain other property transferred within three years before death

The taxable estate is the gross estate reduced by:

- funeral expenses
- expenses of administering the estate
- debts owed at the time of death
- casualty and theft losses occurring during estate settlement
- charitable contributions made by the estate
- the marital deduction (generally, the value of the property that passes from the decedent's estate to the surviving spouse).

If a taxable estate plus the total amount of taxable gifts given during a lifetime will be more than $600,000, individuals may need a qualified estate tax professional. The IRS tax code includes payment schedules for taxes owed based on income, deductions, and other factors.

New York Estate and Gift Taxes

In 1997, amendments were added to the New York tax law, the Estates, Powers, and Trusts law, and other statutes as they relate to New York estate and gift taxes. These new changes were phased in over a prescribed time period.

Effective January 1, 2000, the New York gift tax was repealed. Effective February 1, 2000, the requirement to file a New York State estate tax return is essentially the same as the requirement to file a federal return. This means that as of February 1, 2000, if no federal return is required, no New York State return is required.

Also effective as of February 1, 2000, the estate tax payable to New York State is limited to the maximum amount allowed on the federal estate tax return as a credit for state death taxes. As a result, the total amount of the New York State estate tax paid is deductible from any federal estate tax return. New York also currently has an estate tax exemption for the value of a primary residence of up to $250,000.

LEGAL STATUTES AND NOTICES AFFECTING REAL ESTATE

Statute of Limitations

The **statute of limitations** *imposes time limits within which litigation may be commenced.* For example, if a party to a contract fails to bring a lawsuit against a defaulting party within a time period set by statute, the injured party loses the right to litigate the matter. The mere passage of time and expiration of the statutory time period affect the injured party's right to recover. In New York, the time limit by statute to bring legal action against a party arising out of a contract is six years from the date the right to sue arose.

Statute of Frauds

Because of the potential for misunderstandings in oral contracts, all states have adopted the **Statute of Frauds,** which in New York is codified in the General Obligations Law. Section 5-703 of the General Obligations Law *states that contracts involving the creation of an interest in real property or the conveyance of an interest in real property must be written to be enforceable.* The Statute of Frauds *requires that real estate contracts be written and contain all of the essential elements for a valid contract.* Oral testimony

You Should Know	**The difference between the Statute of Limitations and the Doctrine of Laches**

A Statute of Limitations can bar an action if it is not commenced with the specified period. The **doctrine of laches** *can bar an action even though the specified period has not yet run out if there has been any of the following:*

- unreasonable delay
- changes of position
- prejudice

Example: The Saga of Odessa. Avi sues Odessa for breach of contract five years and five months after the right to sue first arose. The suit is timely as the six-year statutory timeframe to sue has not yet expired. However, Odessa states the following:

"Avi, why did you wait this long? This is an example of *unreasonable delay.*"

"In fact," says Odessa, "during this delay, there has been a *change of position;* that is, the people who worked for me and who could help me disprove your case have moved away. On top of that, the records that would help me defeat your case were destroyed in a fire last month. By reason of the foregoing, I have been *prejudiced* in defending my case." The court, therefore, can discontinue this lawsuit under the doctrine of laches.

(parol evidence) is not sufficient to create a contract involving the transfer of title to real property. A primary purpose of the Statute of Frauds is to prevent presentation of fraudulent proof of an oral contract. The General Obligations Law also requires the use of "plain language" in consumer transactions.

Mechanics' and Materialmen's Liens

A "mechanic" does not refer to someone who works on vehicles but to a person who provides labor to a specific property, such as a carpenter. A "materialman" is a supplier, for instance, a lumber company that provides the wood for constructing a home. Therefore, a mechanic's lien is *a specific lien filed by a person who provides labor to a property;* a materialmen's lien is a specific lien filed by a supplier of products required in the construction or improvement of a building. New York law requires that a mechanic's or materialmen's lien for a single family dwelling be filed with the clerk of the county where the property is situated within four months from the date when the labor or materials were furnished. For other types of property, the liens must be filed in the public records within eight months after furnishing the labor or materials. This limitation allows title companies and buyers of property time to ensure that no unrecorded liens are outstanding upon the purchase of a newly constructed or remodeled home. The time and date of filing determines the priority of the mechanic's or materialmen's lien. An action to foreclose the lien must be commenced within one year of the filing and thereafter extended by order of the court.

Lis Pendens

The term **lis pendens** comes from Latin, and means *pending litigation.* A **notice of pendency** *is a legal notice that a lawsuit has been filed concerning title to specific property.* The notice is filed in the office of the county clerk. The notice is a warning to a prospective purchaser of the property that the pending lawsuit could result in an order that creates an enforceable claim against the property of the defendant. A court order resulting from the lawsuit will attach to the property even though the title was transferred to someone else prior to the final judgment in the suit as long as the transfer occurred after the lis pendens was placed on the public record. However, in an action to recover a broker's commission where the title to the property is not an issue, a lis pendens may not be filed.

IMPORTANT POINTS

1. The U.S. Constitution is the supreme law of our country. Federal, state, or local laws that conflict with the Constitution are unenforceable.

2. The Uniform Commercial Code (UCC) is a state statute enacted to simplify, clarify, and modernize the laws governing commercial transactions.

3. A negotiable instrument is an unconditional promise or order to pay a fixed amount with or without interest. It must satisfy the requirements of negotiability defined in UCC Article 3.

4. Negotiable instruments include checks and drafts (three-party instruments) as well as promissory notes and certificates of deposit (two-party instruments).

5. Negotiable instruments must comply with the following: be in writing; be signed; contain an order or promise to pay a fixed sum of money; and be payable on demand or by a definite date. If no date is specified, it is payable on demand.

6. An indorsement is a signature other than a maker, drawee, or an acceptor that is placed on an instrument to *negotiate* (or transfer) it to another person.

7. A holder in due course is one who takes a negotiable instrument for value, in good faith, and without notice that it is defective.

8. A partnership is a form of business organization that is owned by two or more partners and created by contract between the partners.

9. In a general partnership, the partners are personally liable for partnership debts exceeding partnership assets. Partners are jointly (together) and severally (separately) liable for these debts. A limited partnership consists of one or more general partners who are jointly and severally liable, and one or more silent, or limited, partners who contribute money or other assets of value to the extent of their ownership interest.

10. A corporation is a taxable legal entity recognized by law, with tax rates separate from individual income tax rates. Corporations have the power to receive, hold, and convey title to real property. Shareholders are owners of the corporation to the extent of their shareholdings.

11. A subchapter S corporation is a type of corporate organization that is permitted to function as a corporation but is taxed as a partnership.

12. A C corporation must pay corporate income tax to the IRS and the shareholders are also taxed on their dividends that are profits of the corporation; therefore, a *double tax* is paid; at the corporate level and the shareholder level.

13. The Securities Act of 1933 regulates securities offered by corporations, general or limited partnerships, unincorporated associations, or individuals.

14. Organizations offering securities must register with the Securities Exchange Commission (SEC). Registration includes a registration statement and prospectus.

15. Securities that do not involve a public offering are exempt from the SEC registration requirement. This exemption is known as the private placement exemption.

16. No more than thirty-five nonaccredited investors may purchase shares of stock in a private offering. Advertising to the public is not permitted.

17. In New York, companies offering securities to the public must register with the Department of Laws, including an offering of plans to sell condominiums or cooperatives.

18. Real Estate Investment Trusts allow small investors to pool their money to participate in larger real estate transactions. REITs make financing available for large real estate developments.

19. The U.S. Supreme Court is the nation's highest court. It is composed of nine justices appointed by the President with the approval of the Senate.

20. The federal court system includes federal trial courts. There is at least one federal district court in each state.

21. Special federal courts hear only certain types of lawsuits. They include the U. S. Tax Court; U. S. Claims Court; U. S. Court of International Trade; and the U. S. Bankruptcy Court.

22. The U. S. Courts of Appeals are the federal court system's intermediate appellate courts. There are thirteen circuits in the federal court system. Circuits refer to the areas where the court serves.

23. The unified court system in New York is composed of city, town, and village courts; county courts include county court, family court, and surrogate's court.

24. The New York Supreme Court hears civil cases and the New York Supreme Court appellate division reviews cases from the supreme court and county courts as well as administrative boards such as the Worker's Compensation Board. The court of appeals is the highest court in the state.

25. New York City's court system is divided into two courts: a civil court that decides matters up $25,000, including small claims and housing matters; and a criminal court that rules on misdemeanor and traffic violations.

26. Laws can be categorized into substantive laws dealing with everyday behavior and procedural law dealing with rules and regulations.

27. Bodies of law include, but are not limited to, agency law, real property law, administrative law, commercial law, contract law, corporation law, trusts and wills law, civil law, criminal law, personal property law, partnership law, torts, and civil procedure.

28. Litigation (lawsuit), mediation, and arbitration are methods to resolve disputes.

29. The theory of equitable distribution is applied by the New York courts as to the division of marital property.

30. Bankruptcies must adhere to the federal bankruptcy code and are filed in the federal district court. Bankruptcy options include Chapter 7, Chapter 11, and Chapter 13 of the bankruptcy code.

31. If a person receives money or property from another, the donor may be subject to a federal *gift tax*. Money and property owned upon death may be subject to an *estate tax*.

32. Under the Economic Growth and Tax Relief Reconciliation Act of 2001, for the years 2002 and 2003, an individual may transfer a total sum of $1,000,000 to a non-spouse or non-charity during lifetime or at death free of any estate and gift taxes.

33. The New York estate tax is limited to the maximum amount allowed on the federal estate tax return as a credit for state death taxes. There is no specific New York gift tax.

34. The Statute of Limitations imposes time limits within which litigation may be commenced. In New York, the time limit by statute to bring legal action against a party based on contract is six years.

35. The Statute of Frauds states that contracts involving the creation of an interest in real property or the conveyance of an interest in real property must be written to be enforceable.

36. A mechanic's lien for residential property must be filed with the clerk of the county where the property is situated within four months from the date when the labor or materials were furnished.

37. The term *lis pendens* comes from Latin, and means pending litigation. A notice of pendency is a legal notice that a lawsuit has been filed concerning title to a specific property.

How Would You Respond?   CHAPTER REVIEW

Analyze the following situations and decide how individuals would handle them. Check your answer using the Answer Key at the end of the chapter.

1. Courtney and Simon bought their house for cash three years ago. When they recently measured their boundaries in preparation for planting new landscaping, they found that the lot measured 150 feet × 250 feet. At the time of sale, they were assured by both the broker and the seller that the lot measured 175 feet × 275 feet. What, if anything, can they do?

   _____

   _____

   _____

2. Judy and Jermaine have found their dream house but they cannot obtain clear title because a mechanic's lien has been filed against the property. What must be done?

   _____

   _____

   _____

3. Broker Tony has been asked to market a two-family income property belonging to Ken, who is going through a Chapter 7 bankruptcy. How must Tony obtain authorization to sell the property?

   _____

   _____

   _____

KEY TERM REVIEW

Fill in the term that best completes the sentence and then check the Answer Key at the end of the chapter.

1. A document that is an unconditional promise or order to pay a fixed amount is known as a(n) _____ .

2. Laws created by acts of the legislature are known as _____ .

3. A body of law that deals mainly with civil lawsuits that arise because wrongful intentional or unintentional acts are committed is known as _____ .

4. The theory inherent in our civil rights that mandates that anyone involved in a lawsuit is entitled to a legal proceeding is known as _____ .

5. Another name for a lawsuit is _____ .

6. An individual who becomes the legal representative of the bankrupt debtor's estate is known as a(n) _____ .

7. The _____ is a law that claims that the conveyance of an interest in real property must be in writing.

8. The law that imposes time restraints on the imposition of lawsuits is known as the _____.

9. A legal doctrine that can be used to bar an action even though the specified period has not yet run out is known as the _____.

10. A Latin term that means pending litigation is called _____.

MULTIPLE CHOICE

Circle the letter that best answers the question and then check the Answer Key at the end of the chapter.

1. The supreme law of our country is contained in the:
   A. Uniform Commercial Code
   B. U.S. Constitution
   C. rulings by the Court of Appeals
   D. separate state constitutions

2. Which of the following is a negotiable instrument?
   A. deed
   B. notice of pendency
   C. promissory note
   D. security

3. A signature on the back of a check to transfer it to another is known as a(n):
   A. indorsement
   B. transfer of title
   C. estoppel
   D. discharge

4. A type of business organization that allows one or more silent partners to contribute money or other assets to the extent of their ownership is known as a:
   A. general partnership
   B. sole proprietorship
   C. C corporation
   D. limited partnership

5. A disadvantage of a corporation as a form of business organization is that it is:
   A. legal only in some states
   B. not allowed as a form of organization for real estate brokers in New York
   C. taxed on both the corporate and shareholder level
   D. not allowed to hold title to real estate

6. Which of the following is required by the SEC for securities registration? A(n):
   A. notice of pendency
   B. prospectus
   C. indorsement
   D. doctrine of laches

7. Entities that wish to sell condominiums or cooperatives in New York must register with the:
   A. Department of State
   B. Federal District Court
   C. Department of Law
   D. New York Real Estate Board

8. Which of the following is NOT a federal district court?
   A. U. S. Tax Court
   B. U. S. Claims Court
   C. U. S. Bankruptcy Court
   D. U. S. Court of Appeals

9. Which of the following is New York's highest court?
   A. Court of Appeals
   B. Supreme Court
   C. Supreme Court Appellate Division
   D. Surrogate's Court

10. Broker Hector sued his principal for failure to pay him a commission according to the terms of their contract. What two possible bodies of law apply in this situation?
    A. administrative and civil procedure laws
    B. agency and contract laws
    C. real property and constitutional laws
    D. tort and civil procedure laws

11. Interpretation by the court of a statute that may have a direct bearing on future lawsuits is known as:
    A. statutory law
    B. court law
    C. case law
    D. due process law

12. Substantive law is a body of law that is applicable to which of the following legal disciplines?
    A. procedural law
    B. agency law
    C. administrative law
    D. civil procedure

13. Which of the following applies to due process of law? It:
    A. is only applicable in criminal lawsuits
    B. has to do with constitutional law only
    C. is the right of a person to defend himself in a court of law
    D. does not apply to lawsuits regarding real estate transactions

14. Carrie was involved in a contractual dispute with her employer. She and the employer decided to allow a third party to resolve the dispute and agreed to abide by the decision. This describes what type of dispute resolution?
    A. arbitration
    B. mediation
    C. litigation
    D. estoppel

15. Should there be a divorce, marital property in New York is divided according to the theory of:
    A. community property
    B. equitable distribution
    C. civil procedure law and rules
    D. laches

16. A bankruptcy in New York is filed in which of the following courts?
    A. New York Supreme Court
    B. New York Court of Claims
    C. Federal District Court
    D. local town or city courts

17. A type of bankruptcy that calls for the reorganization of the debtor's financial affairs under the supervision of the bankruptcy court is in which chapter of the bankruptcy code?
    A. Chapter 7
    B. Chapter 11
    C. Chapter 13
    D. Chapter 21

18. Tamara recently sold a piece of land in Rye, New York and gave her friend, Sidney, a gift of $10,000 from the profits on the sale. Which of the following applies?
    A. Tamara must pay federal gift tax on the money
    B. Sidney must pay federal gift tax on the money she received from Tamara
    C. Neither Tamara or Sidney must pay federal gift tax
    D. Tamara must pay New York gift tax on the money

19. New York has an estate tax exemption for a primary residence valued at which of the following? Up to:
    A. $50,000
    B. $150,000
    C. $200,000
    D. $250,000

20. When the Contraries moved into Lazy Acre subdivision they parked their RV in the driveway in violation of the subdivision covenants and conditions. After three years, one of the neighbors decided to take court action to make the Contraries remove the RV. The court ruled against the neighbor because he did not make a timely complaint. This is an application of which of the following?
    A. doctrine of laches
    B. Statute of Frauds
    C. eminent domain
    D. escheat

ANSWER KEY

How Would You Respond?

1. The statute of limitations on contracts is six years in New York. Therefore, there is still time to bring suit against the broker and sellers.

2. Prior to closing, the sellers must pay or satisfy the lien. If, for some reason, the sellers cannot meet this obligation, the purchasers could pay the lien and deduct the sum from the purchase price of the house.

3. Broker Tony must contact the bankruptcy trustee who would then ask the bankruptcy judge for permission to sell the property.

Key Term Review

1. negotiable instrument
2. statutory laws
3. torts
4. due process of law
5. litigation
6. trustee
7. Statute of Frauds
8. Statute of Limitations
9. Doctrine of Laches
10. lis pendens

Multiple Choice

1. B
2. C
3. A
4. D
5. C
6. B
7. C
8. D
9. A
10. B
11. C
12. B
13. C
14. A
15. B
16. C
17. B
18. C
19. D
20. A

Chapter 6

KEY TERMS

amperage

area variance

Article 9-A of the Real Property Law

blueprint

building code

building permit

building specifications

certificate of occupancy (CO)

circuit breakers

completion bond

condemnation

cumulative zoning

defect

due diligence

eaves

eminent domain

exclusive-use zoning

flashing

footing

joist

outlots

percolation rate

pitch

platform construction

police power

property condition disclosure (PCD)

rafters

regulatory taking

sheathing

sill plate

slab-on-grade foundation

special-use permit

spot zoning

steep slope

subdivision

subdivision regulations

use variance

watts

wetlands

zoning ordinance

LEARNING OBJECTIVES   *Classroom hours: 4*

1. Discuss the various government agencies that regulate and oversee construction standards.

2. Explain how such standards affect real estate transactions and precontract building.

3. Explain how the failure to use due diligence may cause major faults and unsafe conditions.

Construction and Development

4. Describe the various steps with respect to construction and approved use of land.

5. Discuss the various needs for buyers and sellers to use building inspectors.

6. Discuss the steps prior to listing a property to determine preexisting problems in the basic construction of a structure.

7. Define the meaning of a subdivision.

8. Explain how an individual can determine the lawful use of any potential subdivision.

9. List the factors that determine the value of land.

10. Explain the steps to begin the development process.

11. List the steps in the acquisition of a subdivision.

12. Explain the requirements involved in the development and subsequent offering of condominiums and cooperatives.

SECTION 1   CONSTRUCTION

A major concern of licensees is liability regarding the condition of a structure upon transfer of title. This section discusses this issue as well as basic construction principles and the standards, rules, and regulations that the construction industry must adhere to in land development and building construction.

CONSTRUCTION BASICS

The following review of construction basics will acquaint you with the components of residential construction. As you read through this section, refer to Figure 6.1 in order to visualize the complete structure of the house.

Footings

The most important foundation building block is the **footing.** *The footing is the concrete base below the frost line that supports the foundation of the structure.* To construct the footings, the building lines are laid out with batter boards, temporary wood members on posts that form an L-shape outside the corners of the foundation.

FIGURE 6.1 The basic parts (structure) of a house.

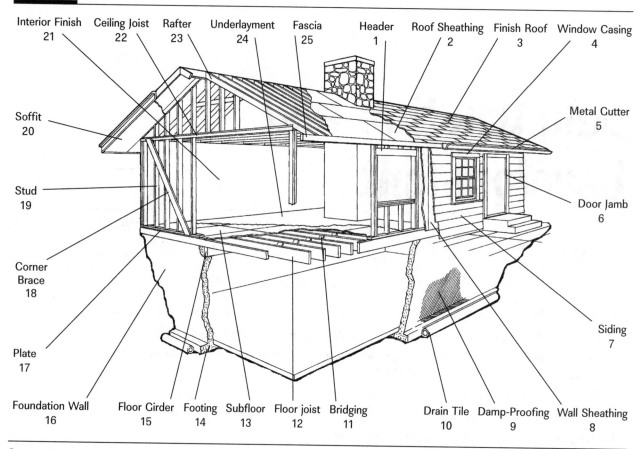

Source: From *The Home Inspection Book: A Guide for Professionals*, by Marcia Darvin Spada. © 2002. Reprinted with permission of South-Western Publishing.

The width of the footing has to be at least twice the width of the foundation wall erected upon it. The depth of the footing is usually a minimum of eight inches (one- and two-story homes) and should be as deep as the foundation wall is thick. The purpose of the footing is to support the foundation wall and, subsequently, the entire weight load of the structure. The footings must provide an adequate base for the structure so as to prevent settling of the house. Figure 6.2 illustrates a typical residential footing and foundation.

Foundation Walls

Foundation walls in New York are generally composed of poured concrete, masonry (concrete) block, or, sometimes, brick. The height of the foundation wall determines whether the structure has a full basement or a crawl space. In masonry block foundation walls, the block forms the back half of the wall and is sometimes covered with a brick veneer on the front. Vertical masonry piers are built inside these foundation walls to provide additional support for the house. Of the three types of foundations built in New York, full *basements* are most common (more than 80 percent), followed by slab-on-grade and crawl space.

The New York State Uniform Fire Prevention and Building Code requires that the foundation wall of the basement or crawl space and floors in contact with soil be treated for penetration of ground and surface water. These vapor barriers can be heavy-duty plastic. Also, depending on local conditions, the New York code requires these areas to be treated with termiticide.

FIGURE 6.2   Footing and foundation.

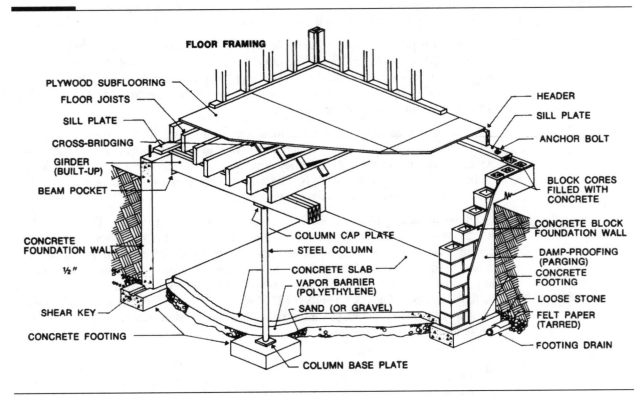

Source: *Houses, The Illustrated Guide to Construction, Design & Systems* by Henry S. Harrison, 3rd edition.

Slab-on-Grade Construction

On level terrain, **slab-on-grade foundation** is possible. The foundation, then, is a concrete slab instead of a foundation wall. The concrete slab is poured directly on the ground and therefore eliminates the crawl space or basement. *The slab provides the floor of the dwelling and the support for the exterior and interior walls.* Slabs can be constructed by pouring the footing first and then pouring the slab. This is called a floating slab. If the footing and slab are poured at the same time, it is called a monolithic slab. The concrete slab method is less expensive than the foundation wall system or basement but is not practical in all building situations.

Wood Framing

Framing refers to the wooden skeleton of the home. Wood-framing members are lumber with a nominal dimension of 2" thickness. For example, a 2" × 4" is a piece of lumber 2" inches thick by 4" wide. These framing members, known also as studs, are commonly 2" × 4"s, 2" × 8"s, 2" × 10"s, or 2" × 12"s and are used vertically for wall construction. These wooden framing members are also used as joists for floor and ceiling framing. Usually 2" × 6"s or 2" × 8"s are used as rafters in the roof framing system.

Flooring

The top of the foundation wall is finished off with a course of solid masonry. On top of this rests the foundation **sill plate.** The sill plate is usually made up of a pressure-treated 2" × 6" or 2" × 8" piece of lumber. The wooden sill is fastened to the foundation wall by anchor bolts. *The sill plate is the first wooden member of the house and used as the nailing surface for the floor system.*

The box sill, or banding, rests on the sill plate and is the same size wood member as the floor joists (2" × 8", 2" × 10", or 2" × 12"). The banding runs around the top of the foundation wall, attached to the sill plate.

The floor **joists** *span the distance between the foundation walls and the girder and provide support for the subfloor. The main carrying beam,* or **girder,** *is either a steel beam or several wooden members fastened together (usually with 2" × 10"s, 2" × 12"s, or larger) that spans the distance from one side of the foundation to the other.* The joists rest on the girder for support.

Lally columns may support the main carrying beam of the structure. They are round steel columns filled with concrete that vary in diameter and rest on a base plate, which is the column footing pad. They are placed in the basement or crawl space, and their height is adjusted accordingly. The spacing of the lally columns is determined by the size and material of the main carrying beam.

Typical framing places wooden members at 16 inches on center. The phrase "16-inches on center" means that the center of one 2" × 4" stud is 16 inches away from the center of the next. Depending upon the area to be spanned, the joists are doubled or even tripled to support the load. Some modern construction methods use wooden floor trusses in place of single floor joists. A truss is a support member constructed in a factory by nailing a number of smaller members (2" × 4"s or 2" × 6"s) together in a number of triangular patterns to provide maximum strength. A plywood or particle-board subflooring rests directly on top of the joists.

Walls

Wall framing forms the exterior and interior walls of the structure. The floor system serves as a stage or platform for the wall system. The walls are usually built of 2" × 4" studs, 16" on center. The bearing walls support the ceiling and/or the roof and include the outside wall frame. They are erected first. Nonbearing walls or partitions are walls that enclose interior space but do not support the structure.

A horizontal base plate, also called a sole plate, serves as the foundation for the wall system. A double top plate (Figure 6.3), also known as a flitch beam, is used to tie the walls together and provide additional support for the ceiling and roof system. The flitch beam is made of two or more structural timbers that are bolted together with a metal plate sandwiched between for additional strength.

FIGURE 6.3
A wall double top plate or flitch beam.

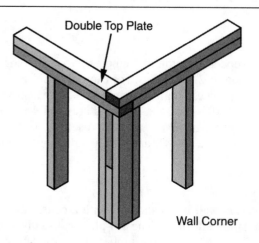

Openings in the wall for doors or windows must be reinforced to pick up the missing support for the vertical load. This process is done with 2" × 8"s, 2" × 10"s, or 2" × 12"s, known as headers, or lintels, erected over the top of the opening. Headers should form a solid wood bridge over the opening and extend to the bottom of the top plate. They actually support the ceiling and the roof over the door and window openings.

The type of framing described above is known as **platform construction** or framing, *because the framing of the structure rests on a subfloor platform.* Platform framing is the most common type of framing used in residential construction.

An alternative to platform framing is balloon framing. This method uses a single system of wall studs that runs from the foundation through the first and second floors to the ceiling support. This method is rarely used in residential construction.

A third type of framing is post-and-beam framing. These members are much larger than ordinary studs and may be 4" or 6" square. The larger posts can be placed several feet apart instead of 16" or 24" on center. Like balloon framing, this type of framing is seldom used in residential construction. Figure 6.4 shows the three types of framing.

FIGURE 6.4   Three types of frames.

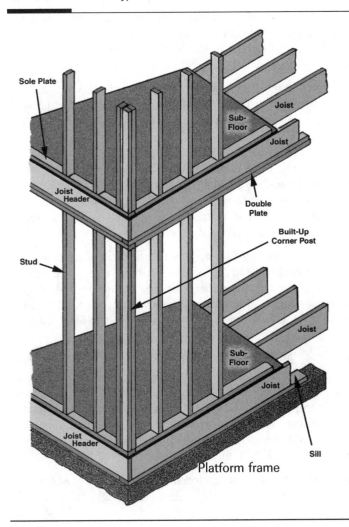

Platform frame

Balloon frame

Post-and-beam frame

Ceiling Framing and Roof

The ceiling joists rest on the top plate of the wall. These joists should be placed directly over the vertical studs for maximum bearing strength. The joists span the structure between the outer walls. In traditional framing, these joists are usually 2" × 8"s, and the inner walls are important in helping to bear the load of the roof. This is different in the contemporary use of roof truss systems, in which the truss carries the load-bearing function to the outer walls. This feature provides freedom of placement of the inner walls. Since a roof truss is made up of a number of smaller members (usually 2" × 4"s), the attic space is almost completely lost.

The ridge beam is the highest part of the framing and forms the apex, or top line, of the roof. **Rafters** *are the long wooden members that are fastened to the ends of the ceiling joists and form the gables of the roof.* Rafters are usually 2" × 6"s or 2" × 8"s. The rafters are fastened to the ridge at the peak of the gable. Characteristics to look for in roof identification include the **pitch.** *The pitch is the slope of the roof.* Construction style and customized forms are other identifying factors.

The roof should extend at least 6" beyond the exterior of the structure. Common construction practices use a 12" overhang on the front and rear, with a 6" overhang on the side. These overhangs, which are part of a sloped roof, are known as the **eaves.** *The eaves are the lowest part of the roof, which project beyond the walls of the structure.* The larger the overhang, the more protection exists from sun and rain for the exterior walls, windows, and doors. It is generally recommended that flashing strips be installed near the edge of the eave and other corners of the roof such as around the base of the chimney. Mostly used in colder climates such as New York, **flashing** *is a metallic material that is used in certain areas of the roof and walls to prevent water from seeping into the structure.*

The overhang is made up of three components: the soffit, the fascia, and the frieze board. The soffit is the area under the roof extension. This is made of wood, aluminum, or vinyl (depending upon the type of siding). The area of material facing the outer edge of the soffit is called the fascia. The fascia is typically a 1" × 6" or a 1" × 8" board and is perpendicular to the soffit. If guttering is installed on the roof, it is fastened to the fascia. The third component of the overhang is the frieze board. This is a wooden member (usually a 2" × 4", 2" × 6", or 2" × 8") that is fastened directly under the soffit, against the top of the wall. The purpose of the frieze board is both decorative and functional. The frieze board prevents wind and moisture from penetrating the junction of the soffit and sheathing.

Once the structural skeleton of the roof system is in place, it is covered with either plywood or particle-board decking. On top of this, roofing paper is applied to aid in weatherproofing. On top of the roofing paper, shingles are applied. Most construction utilizes the fiberglass shingle, but tile and wood shingles are also used. Just as in the crawl space below the house, proper ventilation of the attic space is important.

Once all framing members are in place, including the roof rafters, a plywood covering called **sheathing** *is placed over the exterior framing members.* A final covering is placed over the sheathing, which is generally brick or siding in New York. *Siding* can be a metal, such as aluminum, or wood, or vinyl. Often a combination of materials including fieldstone, brick, siding, or other materials is used. Some communities or subdivisions have regulations as to the outside materials of structures. Licensees working with new construction should be aware of any regulations.

For the interior walls of the structure, a material known as *sheetrock, wallboard, or plasterboard* may be used, and special sheathing materials are also used for insulation.

Fill in the parts of the house as best as you can, and refer to the diagram (Figure 6.1) to check your answers.

The basic parts (structure) of a house.

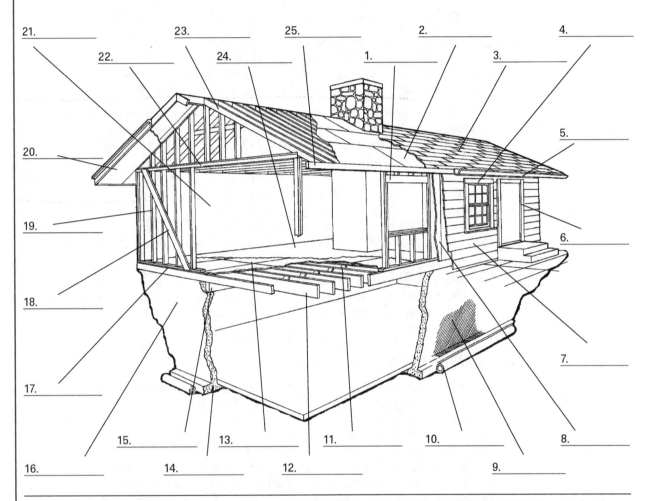

21. _____   23. _____   25. _____   2. _____   4. _____

22. _____   24. _____   1. _____   3. _____

20. _____   5. _____

19. _____

6. _____

18. _____

17. _____   7. _____

15. _____   13. _____   11. _____   10. _____   8. _____

16. _____   14. _____   12. _____   9. _____

Source: From *The Home Inspection Book: A Guide for Professionals*, by Marcia Darvin Spada. © 2002. Reprinted with permission of South-Western Publishing.

Electrical Systems

The proper design, scope, and layout of electrical outlets and components ensures that the system is adequate to handle present and future requirements. A voltage service of 120/240 volts is standard; less voltage does not meet the requirements of residential property. Most residential service is a minimum of 100 amps but new construction generally has 150- to 200-amp service. The electrical distribution panel should be located in a utility room, basement, or garage for ease of access to reset circuit breakers and to perform maintenance. The home should be wired with sufficient electrical wall outlets. Utility areas such as garages and bathrooms require the installation of dedicated circuit breakers to prevent accidental electrical shock.

Volt is the pressure
Amp is the current

Electrical power is brought to the house through outside cables and is then delivered through a series of conductors to the house wiring system. Two types of services exist: some houses are located in areas that have aboveground cables; others have underground or buried cables. Aboveground cables that come from the nearest pole connecting to the service entrance conductors of the house or building, are called the service drop. Underground wiring connecting the house is called the service lateral.

Voltage and Amperage

Voltage is the electrical pressure that pushes through the wires. Voltage is very similar to water pressure; it is the push. Although 120 volts are standard voltage for lighting and small-appliance loads, 240-volt usage is needed for heavy residential and commercial applications. **Amperage** *is the amount of current or electricity flowing through the wire.*

Electrical capacity requirements are determined when a house is built and are normally delineated in watts or kilowatts. *Amperage required for different electrical usage is calculated in* **watts** *or kilowatts.* House electrical circuits are installed according to these kilowatt requirements. If the wire size or service is not strong enough for the electrical needs of the house, the circuit will overheat, causing fuses to melt or circuit breakers to trip and therefore interrupt electrical service. A **fuse** *is a device that will melt and open the circuit, causing electrical power to stop when overheating occurs.* Melted fuses must be replaced with new ones. After melting, they are no longer usable. Fuses also can be mishandled and therefore expose individuals to high voltages.

Circuit breakers are more convenient and safer than fuses. *Circuit breakers will trip; that is, they will switch off the electrical power for a given circuit if the current increases beyond the capacity of the system.* They do not need to be replaced every time the system overloads. Houses built since about 1960 usually have circuit breakers rather than fuses.

Identifying Amperage

The *main panel board* or *distribution panel* may have an amperage rating written on it; the rating may be the same as or larger than the actual service. The distribution panel is where circuit breakers or fuses are located. The only sure indicator of service size is found on the service entrance cables. Therefore, the size of the electrical service in a house cannot necessarily be identified by the number of fuses or circuit breakers on the distribution panel. Individual branch circuits can be anywhere from 15 to 50 amps. Each circuit breaker or fuse must be identified as to its ampere rating, that is, the amount of amperage it can carry, as specified in the National Electric Code (discussed later). Certain sizes of conductors (wires) must have the proper size fuse or circuit breaker to carry the electrical current.

GFCI's (Ground Fault Circuit Interrupters)

GFCI's are highly sensitive circuit breakers that sense extremely small current leakages across a circuit and are used to protect against electrocution hazard. They are generally located where water may be present such as bathrooms, kitchens, basements, garages, outdoor receptacles, and swimming pools. The National Electric Code specifies where these devices should be used.

CONSTRUCTION STANDARDS

A developer or builder must comply with all applicable regulations before beginning land development or construction. Figure 6.5 summarizes laws, regulations, and agencies affecting the construction process.

FIGURE 6.5   Summary of agencies, laws, and codes that affect the construction industry.

Agency, law, or code	Federal/National	NY State	Purpose
Department of Housing and Urban Development	✓		Administers federal guidelines and laws related to and housing
Interstate Land Sales Full Disclosure Act	✓		Regulates sale of unimproved lots across state lines
National Electric Code	✓		Nationally accepted guidelines for electrical installations
Americans with Disabilities Act	✓		Provides guidelines for construction of public accommodations, commercial space, and new multifamily housing
Environmental Protection Agency	✓		Oversees federal regulatory legislation
National Environmental Policy Act	✓		Requires the filing of an environmental impact statement by government agencies which must approve land use projects
Comprehensive Environmental Response, Compensation, and Liability Act	✓		Provides solutions to environmental problems created by uncontrolled disposal of wastes
Superfund Amendments and Reauthorization Act	✓		Imposes stringent clean-up standards and expands the definition of legal liability
Clean Air Act	✓		Regulates air pollution. A developer must obtain a permit to construct property in a clean-air area
Safe Drinking Water Act	✓		Provides drinking water regulations and standards for states
Residential Lead-Based Paint Hazard Reduction Act	✓		Mandates seller or agent disclosure and assessment of lead paint in structures built before 1978
Article 9-A of New York Real Property Law		✓	Protects residents of New York in the sale of vacant subdivided lands sold on the installment plan within and outside New York
New York Environmental Conservation Law		✓	Sets policy and coordinates functions of state and local government bodies to preserve and protect environment
New York State Environmental Quality Review Act		✓	Requires the filing of an environmental impact statement by government agencies that must approve land-use projects
New York State Uniform Fire Prevention and Building Code		✓	Provides minimum standards for construction in New York. Includes new construction, renovation, and additions
New York Energy Code		✓	Sets minimum requirements for energy-efficient design for all structures in New York
New York Human Rights Law		✓	Provides that multiple dwellings must be constructed to allow accessibility for persons with disabilities
New York General Business Law–Warranties on Sales of New Homes		✓	Provides warranties against defects in new construction
New York General Business Law–Home Improvement Contract Provisions		✓	Provides that contractors engaging in home improvement contracts exceeding $5,000 deposit payments received prior to completion in an escrow account
New York Sanitary Code		✓	Lays out specific maximum contaminant levels and standards for water supply
New York Department of Health		✓	Oversees installation of individual wastewater treatment systems and private water supply systems in subdivisions covered under the law
New York State Department of Environmental Conservation		✓	Oversees much of environmental protection law in New York

Federal Standards, Laws, and Regulations

Homes that are built with any financing aid from a federal program, such as an *FHA-insured* or a *VA-guaranteed loan,* must be approved in advance and inspected by the appropriate agency as construction proceeds. (This is in addition to inspections by the local building official.) If this approval is not obtained in advance, the home must be at least one year old to obtain approval for these loan programs. HUD and VA will accept a 10-year homeowner's warranty such as a Home Owners Warranty (HOW) or Residential Warranty Corporation (RWC) warranty in lieu of advance approval and supervision by HUD or VA.

HUD publishes a handbook entitled "Minimum Property Standards for Housing," or MPS, which contains technical construction guidelines for housing and other programs administered by HUD.

Other federal laws, agencies, and regulations include the following:

■ *Interstate Land Sales Full Disclosure Act.* This act, administered by HUD, regulates interstate (across state lines) sale of unimproved lots. Its purpose is to prevent fraudulent marketing schemes that may transpire when land is sold sight-unseen. Before offering lots for sale by mail or phone, a developer must register subdivisions of 100 or more non-exempt lots with HUD. The purchaser must be provided with a disclosure document called a Property Report before signing a contract. The act does provide for several exemptions, such as subdivisions consisting of fewer than 25 lots, and it includes certain penalties for violation.

■ *National Electric Code.* This code offers minimal guidelines and standards for electrical installation. It is written and updated by the National Fire Protection Association. Local building codes may have more restrictive guidelines. In addition, organizations such as the New York Board of Fire Underwriters may be hired by municipalities to inspect the completed installation to make sure that it conforms to the code.

■ *Americans with Disabilities Act.* Under this act, individuals with disabilities cannot be denied access to public transportation, to any commercial facility, or to public accommodation. Individuals with AIDS, alcoholism, or mental illness are included in the category of people with a mental or physical disability. To comply with this law, these buildings are to be designed, constructed, and altered to meet accessibility standards if readily achievable. "Readily achievable" means accomplishable and able to be carried out without much difficulty or expense. Public accommodations must remove structural, architectural, and communication barriers in existing facilities if the removal is readily achievable. Examples might include adding ramps, lowering telephones, widening doors, and installing grab bars in toilet stalls. Commercial facilities are not required to remove the barriers in existing facilities. In the construction of new public accommodations and commercial facilities, all areas must be readily accessible and usable by individuals with disabilities. The Act also requires new multifamily housing with at least four units to have easy access for disabled and elderly persons. The Act is enforced by the U.S. Attorney General. Penalties for violation include injunctions against operation of a business, a fine of up to $50,000 for the first offense, and $100,000 for subsequent offenses.

One of the most regulated aspects of construction on the federal level has to do with the environment. Most of the federal regulatory environmental legislation is overseen by the Environmental Protection Agency (EPA).

■ *The National Environmental Policy Act of 1969.* This act requires the filing of an environmental impact statement with the appropriate state or local agency prior to changing or initiating a land use or development to ensure that the use will not adversely affect the environment. Typical areas regulated by the act include air, noise, and water pollution, as well as chemical and solid waste disposal.

- *Comprehensive Environmental Response, Compensation, and Liability Act (CER-CLA) of 1980.* This act was created to provide solutions to environmental problems created by uncontrolled disposal of wastes. Under CERCLA, a program was designed to identify sites containing hazardous substances, ensure that those sites were cleaned up by the parties responsible or by the government, and establish a procedure to seek reimbursement for clean-up from the responsible party.

- *In 1986 CERCLA was amended by the Superfund Amendments and Reauthorization Act (SARA).* The amendment imposed stringent clean-up standards and expanded the definition of persons liable for clean-up costs. Under CERCLA and SARA, every land owner is potentially affected. New York requires full disclosure, prior to title transfer by deed, if real estate is listed by a federal or state agency as contaminated by a hazardous substance.

- *The Clean Air Act of 1990.* This act gives the EPA the power to regulate air pollution, identify air pollution substances, and mandate states to implement protective measures for public health and welfare. Under this act, the EPA identified national ambient air quality standards (NAAQs). The act requires the states to designate regions that do or do not meet NAAQs. Clean air regions cannot be deteriorated and are divided into classes that allow varying levels of pollution. A developer must obtain a permit to construct property in a clean air area.

- *Safe Drinking Water Act of 1974.* This act is the guideline for New York's drinking water regulations. The New York Department of Health (NYSDOH) is the regulatory agency that oversees the safety of drinking water (discussed later).

- *Residential Lead-Based Paint Hazard Reduction Act of 1992.* This act (discussed more fully later in the chapter) sets forth the procedures to be followed in disclosing the presence of lead-based paint for sales of pre-1978 residential properties.

New York Standards, Laws, and Regulations

Federal regulatory legislation as discussed above must be followed by New York, and much of the legislation serves as a guideline for New York's laws. Laws in New York that affect construction are discussed below.

New York State Article 9-A of the Real Property Law. This law is regulated by DOS and is designed to protect the residents of New York in the purchase or lease of vacant subdivided lands sold on the installment plan. The *installment plan* (or contract for deed) allows the seller to hold title to the property over a specified period of time until the purchaser has made full payment for the property. Title is then conveyed to the purchaser. The land can be located either in New York or in another state. The law, when applicable, covers a sale made by a salesperson, broker, owner, or any other individual empowered to sell the land. To comply with Article 9-A, certain documentation describing the land to be sold and a filing fee must be filed with the New York Department of State. All advertising, before publication, must be submitted for DOS approval. If the subdivision is sold before the offering plan is approved, the offeror is guilty of a felony. If the offering statement is violated after the subdivision is approved, the offeror is guilty of a misdemeanor.

The New York State Environmental Conservation Law. The Environmental Conservation Law of 1972 and its subsequent amendments provide the foundation for New York's commitment to preserving the environment. This law sets policy and provides for the coordination of functions of the state with other government bodies and for cooperation with public and private entities.

The New York State Uniform Fire Prevention and Building Code. This code provides minimum standards for all types of buildings in New York, including residential and commercial structures. If a local building code is more restrictive than the state code, then the more restrictive regulations would apply. If a municipality does not have a specific code, then the New York code would be followed. The code addresses construction, materials, safety, and sanitary standards for a building. It also includes standards for the "condition, occupancy, maintenance, rehabilitation and renewal of existing buildings."

Carbon Monoxide Detectors. The Uniform Fire Prevention and Building Code was amended (2003) to establish standards for the installation and maintenance of carbon monoxide detectors. Regulations require that at least one functioning carbon monoxide detector be installed near the bedrooms in all one- and two-family properties including condos and co-ops that are constructed or offered for sale.

The New York Energy Code. The Energy Code sets minimum requirements for the design of new buildings and renovations or additions to existing buildings. The code regulates building envelopes, hot water, electrical, lighting, and HVAC (heating, ventilation, and air conditioning) systems equipment for efficient use of energy. The *building envelope* is the materials of a building that enclose the interior and through which heating, cooling, or fresh air passes.

The New York Energy Code mandates minimum *R-values* for insulation in various parts of a residential structure and designates where insulation must be installed. Insulation is placed wherever the interior walls, ceilings, or floors are exposed to exterior temperatures such as roofs, ceilings, floors, foundation walls and slab edges. *The R-value is how various types of insulation are rated.* The code also regulates glazing and caulking around windows and skylights and entrance doors. The required performance of the insulation depends on the type of heating system. Table 6.1 indicates the minimum R-value of insulation, glazing, and doors according to the Energy Code.

Local energy codes may be more restrictive than the statewide code. Historic buildings are exempt from the Code.

New York State Human Rights Law. Article 15 of the Executive Law, known as the New York Human Rights Law, provides that multifamily dwellings, or *multiple dwellings* (residences that contain three or more families) that were first occupied after March 13, 1991, must allow accessibility for persons with disabilities. All public use and common areas must be readily accessible to individuals with disabilities, and all doors that allow passage into and throughout the premises must be wide enough to allow an individual in a wheelchair to pass through. The dwelling must contain an accessible route into and throughout the space and electrical outlets, light switches, thermostats, and other controls must be accessible. The bathrooms must be designed so that grab bars can be installed. Kitchens and bathrooms must be designed so that individuals may maneuver with a wheelchair. The design and construction of the mul-

TABLE 6.1 The R-value of insulation, glazing, and doors.	NON-ELECTRIC COMFORT HEATING		ELECTRIC COMFORT HEATING	
Envelope Component	5,000–6,000 Degree Days	7,000–9,000 Degree Days	5,000–6,000 Degree Days	7,000–9,000 Degree Days
Exterior Wall	R-18	R-18	R-23	R-23
Roof/Ceiling	R-19	R-24	R-26	R-33
Floor	R-19	R-19	R-19	R-24
Foundation Wall	R-10	R-10	R-10	R-10
Slab-Edge Insulation	R-10	R-10	R-10	R-10
Glazing	R-1.7	R-1.7	R-2.6	R-2.6
Entrance Doors	R-2.5	R-2.5	R-2.5	R-2.5

Source: New York State Energy Code.

tiple dwelling must follow accessibility requirements mandated by the New York State Uniform Fire Prevention and Building Code.

Warranties on sales of new homes. According to Article 36-B of the New York General Business Law, implied in all contracts of sale for new housing is a one-year builder's warranty against defects in construction; a two-year warranty for all plumbing, electrical, heating and air conditioning systems; and a 6-year warranty covering material defects.

Home improvement contracts. The New York General Business Law (Article 36-A) also provides that home improvement contractors who enter into contracts exceeding $5,000 must deposit all payments received prior to completion into an escrow account. The contractor also has the option of providing a bond or letter of credit guaranteeing the payment. If a payment schedule is arranged according to a specified amount of work completed, the contract must provide a payment schedule indicating the amount of payment due and the corresponding work completed, including materials. An owner may cancel a home improvement contract, through a written notice to the contractor, up to three business days after the contract was signed. The cancellation policy can be forfeited if an owner has initiated the contract for an emergency repair and furnishes the contractor with a written statement waiving the right to the three-day cancellation.

If an owner enters into a contract because of fraudulent representation, the owner may sue the contractor, and if the court determines in the owner's favor, the owner may recover a penalty of $500 (plus attorney's fees) and other damages as determined by the court. (If the owners do not prevail, the contractor may be awarded attorney's fees.) Contractors who violate the deposit provisions of this law may be fined up to $250 or 5 percent of the contract price not to exceed $2,500.

Water supply and wastewater treatment. New York also has specific laws and regulations that govern municipal drinking water, well water, and wastewater treatment, which are regulated by NYSDOH. The New York Sanitary Code lays out specific maximum contaminant levels and standards, establishes design criteria for systems, requires licensing of operators, and enforces the code to make sure the water supply meets federal requirements. Appendix 75-A of the New York Public Health Law covers all guidelines for on-site individual wastewater treatment systems. Some of the important guidelines regulating the site of wastewater treatment systems include:

1. If individual wastewater systems overlay a drinking water aquifer, the local health departments may establish population density limits and minimum lot sizes.
2. There must be four feet of usable soil available above rock for the installation of the absorption field (defined later).
3. Soils with rapid percolation rates must be blended with other less permeable soils to slow down the infiltration rate. **Percolation** *is the movement of water through soil.*
4. Wastewater systems must be separated from buildings, property lines, wells, and waterways according to specified minimum distances (see Table 6.2). For example, a septic tank must be at least 50 feet from a well and the absorption field must be at least 100 feet from the well. These minimum distances can be changed only if plans are submitted by a design professional or an engineer and if approved by the local health department.
5. An additional usable area of 50 percent of the size of the system must be set aside for future replacement or expansion of the system whenever possible.

Prior to construction, an environmental assessment must determine that the development of the site with the system is consistent with the overall development of the area and will not cause adverse environmental effects.

TABLE 6.2 Separation distances from wastewater system components.

SYSTEM COMPONENTS	TO WELL OR SUCTION LINE	TO STREAM, LAKE, WATERCOURSE, OR WETLAND	TO DWELLING	TO PROPERTY LINE
House sewer (watertight joints)	25' if cast iron pipe, 50' otherwise	25'	10'	10'
Septic tank	50'	50'	10'	10'
Effluent line to distribution box	50'	50'	10'	10'
Distribution box	100'	100'	20'	10'
Absorption field	100'	100'	20'	10'
Seepage pit	150'	100'	20'	10'
Dry well (roof and footing)	50'	25'	20'	10'
Raised or mound system	100'	100'	20'	10'
Evapotranspiration-absorption system	100'	50'	20'	10'
Composter	50'	50'	20'	10'

Source: New York State Department of Health.

In most rural and some suburban residential areas, individual household wastewater treatment systems are used to dispose of household wastes. A typical household wastewater treatment system consists of a house sewer, septic tank, distribution box, and an absorption field or seepage pit. This is known as a septic system (see Figure 6.6).

In a septic system, the house sewer is the pipeline connecting the house to the drain and septic tank. Untreated liquid household water will clog the absorption field if not properly treated; therefore the septic tank provides this needed treatment. The distribution box distributes the flow from the septic tank evenly to the absorption field or seepage pits. The absorption field is a system of narrow trenches partially filled with a bed of washed gravel into which perforated joint pipe is placed. The discharge from the septic tank is distributed through these pipes into the trenches and surrounding soil. The seepage pit is a covered pit with a perforated or open-jointed lining through which the discharge from the septic tank infiltrates the surrounding soil. According to health department regulations, if soil and site conditions are adequate for absorption trenches, seepage pits cannot be used.

House sewer construction, including materials, must comply with the New York State Uniform Fire Prevention and Building Code and New York sanitary regulations. With houses that are part of a municipal wastewater system, the wastewater drains through the house drainage system into a house sewer. The house sewer extends from the house drain and connects to the municipal main sewer system.

Local departments of health are arms of the NYSDOH. Local health department regulations can be more restrictive than the state code. The state or local health department reviews and approves the water supply and individual wastewater treatment facilities within covered residential subdivisions. Before a building permit is issued, the health department has to approve the source of water and the individual wastewater

FIGURE 6.6
A house septic system.

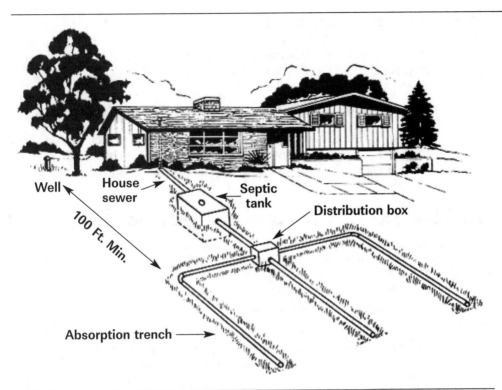

Well

House
sewer

Septic
tank

100 Ft. Min.

Distribution box

Absorption trench

Source: New York State Department of Health.

treatment system for the subdivision. Subdivisions covered under the Public Health Law may not be built until an approved realty subdivision map has been filed with the city or county department of health.

Subdivision and individual lot approval. According to the public health law, a subdivision falls under the jurisdiction of NYSDOH if it has five or more lots that are leased or sold for residential building. The residential lot is defined as a parcel of land five acres or less. This definition applies to residential subdivision lots that are sold or offered for sale within any three-year period. In Suffolk County, this law also applies to commercial or industrial building lots.

Before a building permit is issued, the water supply and wastewater treatment systems must be approved by the local or state health department. In New York, realty subdivision maps cannot be filed in the county clerk's office without health department approval. The map must show the methods for obtaining and furnishing adequate and satisfactory water supply and wastewater treatment facilities for each proposed lot. Proposed Suffolk County projects must also be filed with the County Department of Environmental Control. The owner of one parcel of land in an unapproved subdivision must also have plans for water supply and wastewater treatment facilities approved by NYSDOH.

If land does not fall within the above definition of subdivision or if a lot is not in a subdivision, then approval by the state health department is not required. However, local zoning ordinances, building codes, and/or local county health department regulations may apply. The New York State Department of Environmental Conservation (NYSDEC) retains responsibility for the review, approval, and regulation of plans for public (municipal) and community wastewater treatment facilities.

Private water supply. Community wells are also regulated in New York. Community wells are two or more wells that may serve several different residences. If a community well serves 25 people or it has more than five service connections (five homes, for example), it is regulated by NYSDOH and NYSDEC.

New York State Department of Environmental Conservation (NYSDEC)

This regulatory agency oversees much of the environmental protection law in New York State. The goal of NYSDEC is to prevent the deterioration of the natural and physical environment that constitutes a large sector of publicly owned land in New York.

County and Local Standards, Laws, and Regulations *For land use*

Cities, counties, and other local governing units may impose land use regulations and building codes. These laws may not oppose federal and state laws but may be more restrictive. Local laws also may cover issues that are generic to the locality and are enforced by local governmental agencies, including planning boards/commissions and local building code departments. The local court system decides any relevant legal matters.

Although New York has control over certain public lands and open spaces, planning and zoning are the province of local governments and their respective planning boards. Zoning, subdivision development, budgeting, site-plan reviews, and even building codes are set by the local governments.

DUE DILIGENCE *—> Review*

The Superfund Amendment to CERCLA imposes liabilities to owners whose property is environmentally contaminated. If the property is transferred, this liability is passed on to the new owners. Liability may include the cost of cleaning up the property. These problems may be detected by building inspectors and other experts who investigate the property. This *legal exposure* may cost a new purchaser large sums of money for clean-up, and even then the property may be found unusable for its intended purpose. As a result, in the sale of large tracts of land or other types of *commercial property, lenders, purchasers, and tenants* often conduct **due diligence** *reviews of the property that are written up and evaluated by all interested parties to the transaction.*

These assessments or audits can be conducted by a private engineer or consultant. The assessments may go through four phases. The phases are not necessarily uniform and may depend on what party (lender, purchaser, tenant) initiates the assessment. Phase I is the *investigative phase,* when the due diligence work takes place. Not only are tests done to the property but a review of records pertaining to the history of the property also is made. Properties surrounding the subject property also may be examined. For example, if there are transformers on the property, they will be checked for leakage of polychlorinated biphenyls (PCBs). Responsibility for the transformer is determined and the owner contacted to participate in remediation activities.

If the investigation shows that testing should be done, Phase II, the *testing phase,* is initiated. The appropriate party or agency would go to the property to determine if there was a problem. If testing does not show any significant problems, the assessment would end. However, if a problem is ascertained, Phase III is initiated, in which coordinated clean-up efforts take place. Clean-up activity may involve a number of different parties including state, federal, and private organizations, depending on the nature of the problem and where the responsibility lies. Phase IV, the *management phase,* would include periodic monitoring by responsible parties to check the site and to remediate any future problems.

OTHER LAND USE CONTROLS RELATED TO CONSTRUCTION

Preparations for property development and construction must conform with all governmental requirements. These include compliance with zoning laws, filing a site plan and building specifications, obtaining a building permit before construction and a certificate of occupancy (CO) upon completion. Environmental concerns having to do with the site of the property must also be studied and evaluated.

Building Departments

Building departments enforce the building code. Some have jurisdiction over large cities such as New York City; other departments oversee smaller municipalities. Their role is to protect the public by ensuring that code restrictions are adhered to and that work is performed by licensed and insured contractors. For example, the Department of Buildings in New York City oversees building construction, alteration and the enforcement of building and electrical codes, the State Multiple Dwelling Law, and energy, safety, and labor laws related to construction. The approval, permission, and inspection of construction work, plumbing, elevators, electrical wiring, boilers, and licensing of trades people falls under its jurisdiction. The department inspects buildings under construction for compliance with public safety regulations and oversees more than 800,000 buildings.

Building Permits

Building codes provide another form of land use control to protect the public. **Building codes** *require that a property owner obtain a* **building permit** *from the appropriate local government authority before constructing or renovating a commercial building or residential property.* While construction is in progress, local government inspectors perform frequent assessments to make certain that code requirements are being met. *After a satisfactory final inspection, a* **certificate of occupancy (CO)** *is issued, permitting occupation of the structure by tenants or the owner.* To protect the new purchaser or tenant, inspection is required to reveal any deficiencies in the structure requiring correction before the city will issue a certificate of occupancy.

Site Plan

In New York, local planning boards have the statutory authority to review site plans. The review of the site plan allows the planning board to evaluate the proposal's physical, social, and economic effects on the community. A site plan may be for either residential or commercial development. Other governmental agencies are involved in the review.

Specifications

To comply with building codes, contractors or developers must file plans and specifications with the appropriate governmental body, usually the local building department and/or planning board. The *building plan, also known as a* **blueprint,** *is a detailed architectural rendering of the structure.* The plans for the mechanical systems also may be included. In New York blueprints must be stamped by a licensed *architect* or *engineer.* The plan includes all measurements as well as a layout of the rooms, the location of doorways, windows, bathroom fixtures, and major kitchen appliances. It also includes renderings of the outside appearance and dimensions of the structure including front, back, and side elevations. This blueprint provides the "map" that the builder and his subcontractors will follow.

Building specifications are *written narratives that explain the building plan.* The specifications may include the materials used in the construction; an explanation of the various systems in the structure (heating, air conditioning, and plumbing); any particular design features not entirely visible in the plan; and landscaping plans, including existing vegetation that will remain. Mechanical and structural engineers and soil experts may be involved in the design.

PUBLIC LAND USE CONTROL: ZONING ORDINANCE AND LAND USE REGULATIONS

The need for land use controls has increased along with increasing population density. Abuse by even one property owner in the use of land can have a substantial adverse effect on the rights of other property owners and cause severe depreciation of their properties. Zoning ordinances are a form of *public land use control* that enable the local authority to work with people living and working in the community.

Types of Zoning
Mixed Uses and Cluster Zoning

A developer may wish to create a project that goes beyond the scope of residential housing alone. *Cluster zoning* is an example of multiuse zoning, in which a number of residential uses are allowed in one zone. It allows a cluster development in which single-family houses, town homes, apartments, or other combinations of housing are placed close together in exchange for leaving certain parts of the development open for the enjoyment of the community. The open space might be used for a swimming pool or bike paths. (See Figure 6.7)

Exclusive-Use Zoning

Zoning ordinances may provide for either exclusive-use zoning or cumulative-use zoning. In **exclusive-use zoning,** *property may be used only as designated for that specific zone.* For example, if the zone is commercial, residential uses are not permitted. In

---

FIGURE 6.7
Cluster zoning.

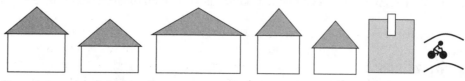

Properties are placed close together to make room for open space such as a pool and bike path.

contrast, **cumulative zoning** *may permit higher-priority uses that are not designated for that zone.* For instance, if an area is zoned commercial, it could still have residential use. In cumulative zoning, however, uses are placed in an order of priority: residential, commercial, industrial. A use of higher priority may be made in an area where the zoned use has a lower priority.

Nonconforming Use

When zoning is first imposed on an area or when property is rezoned, the zoning authority generally cannot require the property owners to discontinue a current use that does not now conform to the new zoning ordinance. A *nonconforming use* occurs when a pre-existing use in a zoned area is different from that specified by the zoning code. This is called a preexisting nonconforming use or a use that is "grandfathered" in.

Spot Zoning

Subdivisions must be developed in areas that are zoned for their intended use and must blend in well with the surrounding community. With **spot zoning,** *a specific property within a zoned area is rezoned to permit a use different from the zoning requirements for that zoned area.* Spot zoning is illegal in New York. Property owners may try to rezone their land from a residential to a commercial or an industrial use because this type of land is often more valuable. Illegal spot zoning has taken place if the rezoning of a property is solely for the benefit of the property owner without a corresponding benefit to the entire neighborhood or if the value of neighborhood properties would decrease as a result of the rezoning. Illegal spot zoning could occur if a property owner is allowed to build a manufacturing plant in a residential zone.

Historic Preservation

In New York, the Historic Preservation Field Service Bureau of the New York State Office of Parks, Recreation and Historic Preservation (OPRHP) coordinates the certified local government program, which offers professional guidance to a community's commitment to historic preservation. Items of historic importance include historic buildings, sites, and neighborhoods. A "historic resource survey" is the principal tool for identifying historic properties. By defining the location and importance of historic resources, a survey enables planners to make decisions about what properties should be protected and where development should be directed. If a proposed development is in or near a place of historic importance, the developer would have to cooperate with the preservation requirements of that particular local governing body.

Transfer of development rights. *Transfer of development rights* is used most frequently in New York City. Inherent in a parcel of land are certain development rights. These development rights are not fully exercised with historic properties, for example, because these properties must be preserved. Therefore, the historic property can sell these rights to a developer, who, for instance, wishes to erect a high-rise office or an apartment building, and whose development rights are not sufficient for the square footage desired for the structure. The developer can buy the development rights from the historic property (that cannot use them); the historic property then realizes income from the sale of these rights. These development rights can also be transferred from other "underbuilt" properties.

| **You Should Know** | **Eminent domain and regulatory taking** |

The right or power of **eminent domain** is *the power of the government or its agencies to take private property for public use.* The actual *taking of property under the power of eminent domain* is called **condemnation.** In New York, the condemning authority may be the state itself, its authorized agencies and departments, municipalities, school districts, public utilities, railroads, and the federal government. The right of eminent domain can be used only if (a) the property condemned is for the use and benefit of the general public, and (b) the property owner is paid the fair market value of the property lost through condemnation. Property owners have the right to trial if they are not satisfied with the compensation.

A **regulatory taking** first was defined by a lawsuit decided by the New York Court of Appeals in 1989, *Seawall Associates v. City of New York* (542 N.E.2d 1059 74 N.Y.2d 92). The court found that *the regulation of the use of private property constitutes a taking if it deprives the owner of all economically viable uses of the property and therefore the property owner can no longer obtain a reasonable return on his investment.*

In 1992, in a landmark decision by the U.S. Supreme Court, *Lucas v. South Carolina Coastal Council* (120 L. Ed. 2d 798, 1992), the Court found that a regulation allowing a taking under eminent domain is unconstitutional if it prohibits the building of any habitable or productive improvement on the owner's land and eliminates all economically beneficial use of the land.

It is important to understand the difference between **police power** and the power of eminent domain. A requirement for an eminent domain taking always implies just compensation to the affected property owner. A *government's right under police power is to decide and legislate matters related to real property for the public benefit.* It does not imply compensation to the property owner. This fact forms the basis for many lawsuits in New York and elsewhere.

BUILDING INSPECTIONS AND DISCLOSURE LAWS
Building Inspections by Governmental Units

Once a proposed construction project receives a building permit, the local building department makes periodic on-site inspections of the construction site to make sure that the structure and site are in compliance with local building codes. Inspections of plumbing, electrical, heating, and cooling systems by the local building inspector must be made before any of these systems can be covered with insulation and wallboard. Other local and state agencies may inspect the property during the building process.

Building inspections are for the protection of the new purchaser as well as for the safety and welfare of the community. Any violations are written up and documented. One example of a serious code violation in New York City is an illegal conversion—the creation of a housing unit(s) without first receiving the approval of, and permits from, the New York City Department of Buildings. Often, it involves the alteration or modification of an existing one- or two-family home by adding an apartment in the basement or attic. Sometimes, an illegal rooming house has been created in a building that was intended to be a one-family house. Illegal conversions reduce the quality of life in neighborhoods by enabling more people to live in an area than was originally intended. Unplanned growth causes a severe strain on local public services.

Prior to occupancy by a new owner or tenant, some municipalities require an inspection even though the structure is not new or has not been renovated. After approval, a new certificate of occupancy is issued.

Building Inspection for Buyers

Prior to transfer of title, and generally written into the contract of sale, contingency agreements are made that render the contract subject to certain structural, environmental, and pest infestation inspections. These inspections are arranged by the prospective purchasers and recommended so that the buyer does not confront unexpected and often costly problems with the property after title transfer. The buyer may hire professionals who specialize in a variety of areas. Professional inspectors may include a licensed engineer, land surveyor, geologist, wood-destroying insect control expert, contractor, or other home inspection expert.

If certain problems are detected by the inspection process, it is the responsibility of the owner to correct these problems prior to title transfer. Depending on the wording of the contract, if specific problems are uncovered, the purchaser may have the right to rescind the contract. Because a property is transferred "as is," it is extremely important that the purchaser obtain a thorough inspection of the property. If problems turn up *after* transfer of title that the purchaser feels should have been disclosed, the purchaser may sue the sellers; but, depending on the circumstances and the wording of the contract, the lawsuit may not prevail in court.

Disclosure Laws and Regulations
The Importance of Investigations Prior to Listing Properties

Typical problems with a property may include wet and flooding basements, foundation cracks, mechanical malfunctioning, leaky roofs, and the like. According to New York law and regulations, "It is not the duty of the broker to verify all representation made by the owner; nonetheless, if the broker knows or has reason to know that the owner has made misrepresentations, or has failed to disclose material defects, then a broker is under a duty not to perpetuate such misrepresentations."

A **defect** in a property is any condition that would:

1. have a material adverse effect on the value of the property
2. materially and adversely impair the health or safety of the future of the occupants
3. significantly shorten or adversely affect the expected normal life of the premises if not repaired, removed, or replaced

Principals must completely disclose information that has a bearing on the subject of the agency agreement. The seller's duty to disclose to the broker any and all hidden defects known by the seller also runs to any buyer brokers, prospective buyers, and subagents of the listing broker.

Mandatory Seller Property Condition Disclosure

Under a new law, real estate licensees must inform their client-sellers of the obligation to provide a signed statement disclosing information regarding the condition and status of their residential one- to four-unit property. The Property Condition Disclosure Act, (Article 14 of the Real Property Law), requires that the disclosure statement (Figure 6.8) be provided to the buyer or buyer's agent prior to the seller's acceptance of the purchase offer. The statement includes 48 questions related to the property's condition, patent and latent defects, structure, and status with respect to occupancy and its location in a flood plain. Failure to provide the form to a buyer before the buyer signs the contract results in a $500 credit from the seller to the buyer at the closing.

FIGURE 6.8   Seller disclosure form.

NYS Department of State
Division of Licensing Services
84 Holland Avenue
Albany, NY 12208-3490
(518) 474-4429
www.dos.state.ny.us

Property Condition Disclosure Statement

Name of Seller or Sellers: _____

Property Address: _____

_____

_____

General Instructions:

The Property Condition Disclosure Act requires the seller of residential real property to cause this disclosure statement or a copy thereof to be delivered to a buyer or buyer's agent prior to the signing by the buyer of a binding contract of sale.

Purpose of Statement:

This is a statement of certain conditions and information concerning the property known to the seller. This Disclosure Statement is not a warranty of any kind by the seller or by any agent representing the seller in this transaction. It is not a substitute for any inspections or tests and the buyer is encouraged to obtain his or her own independent professional inspections and environmental tests and also is encouraged to check public records pertaining to the property.

A knowingly false or incomplete statement by the seller on this form may subject the seller to claims by the buyer prior to or after the transfer of title. In the event a seller fails to perform the duty prescribed in this article to deliver a Disclosure Statement prior to the signing by the buyer of a binding contract of sale, the buyer shall receive upon the transfer of title a credit of $500 against the agreed upon purchase price of the residential real property.

"Residential real property" means real property improved by a one to four family dwelling used or occupied, or intended to be used or occupied, wholly or partly, as the home or residence of one or more persons, but shall not refer to (a) unimproved real property upon which such dwellings are to be constructed or (b) condominium units or cooperative apartments or (c) property on a homeowners' association that is not owned in fee simple by the seller.

Instructions to the Seller:

   a. Answer all questions based upon your actual knowledge.
   b. Attach additional pages with your signature if additional space is required.
   c. Complete this form yourself.
   d. If some items do not apply to your property, check "NA" (Non-applicable). If you do not know the answer check "Unkn" (Unknown).

Seller's Statement:

The seller makes the following representations to the buyer based upon the seller's actual knowledge at the time of signing this document. The seller authorizes his or her agent, if any, to provide a copy of this statement to a prospective buyer of the residential real property. The following are representations made by the seller and are not the representations of the seller's agent.

GENERAL INFORMATION

1. How long have you owned the property? . . . . _____

2. How long have you occupied the property? . . . . _____

3. What is the age of the structure or structures? . . . . _____
   Note to buyer – If the structure was built before 1978 you are encouraged to investigate for the presence of lead based paint..

4. Does anybody other than yourself have a lease, easement or any other right to use or occupy any part of your property other than those stated in documents available in the public record, such as rights to use a road or path or cut trees or crops? . . . . ☐ Yes ☐ No ☐ Unkn ☐ NA

5. Does anybody else claim to own any part of your property? *If Yes, explain below* . . . . ☐ Yes ☐ No ☐ Unkn ☐ NA

_____

_____

Source: New York Department of State.

Residential lead-based paint disclosure   `You Should Know`

The Residential Lead-based Paint Hazard Reduction Act of 1992 sets forth the procedures to be followed in disclosing the presence of lead-based paint for sales of properties built prior to 1978. In 1996, HUD and the EPA released rules to implement Section 1018 of the 1992 act. According to this law, a real estate licensee will generally not be held liable for failure to disclose to a prospective purchaser the presence of lead-based paint if the hazard was known by the landlord or seller but not disclosed to the licensee. Licensees who act on behalf of a purchaser or lessee and are paid exclusively by the purchaser or lessee are not required to comply. However, a selling agent who is working with a buyer would be required to comply with the requirement for placing a clause in the contract to give the buyer 10 days to inspect the property (if the selling agent is preparing the contract).

Penalties for noncompliance include the payment of up to three times the amount of damage incurred by a purchaser or lessee, up to a $10,000 fine, and criminal penalties for repeat offenders. The Act applies to what is known as *target properties*. In addition to sole owners of single family residential property, the Act defines sellers of target housing to include partnerships, individuals, or entities that transfer shares in cooperative apartments, and individuals or entities that transfer leasehold interests. In the transfer of individual cooperative apartments both the tenant–shareholder and the cooperative corporation would be required to comply. Certain types of residential housing are exempt, such as senior citizen housing.

About disclosure requirements   `You Should Know`

Under the Residential Lead-based Paint Hazard Reduction Act:

- Sellers, lessors, or their agents must disclose the presence of known lead-based paint and/or lead-based paint hazards.
- Sellers, lessors, or their agents must distribute a lead hazard pamphlet and disclose any known information to the buyers or their agent concerning lead paint. EPA and HUD have a prepared pamphlet that may be distributed (see Figure 6.9). In many cases, these pamphlets are distributed through local boards of REALTORS®.
- Sellers and lessors must provide purchasers and lessees with copies of any available records or reports pertaining to the presence of lead-based paint and/or lead-based paint hazards.
- There is a mutually agreeable 10-day period for a lead-based paint assessment before a purchaser becomes obligated under the contract. (See Figure 6.10, Lead-based Paint Testing Contingency Form.) During this time, the purchaser may conduct a risk assessment or inspection for the presence of lead-based paint or lead-based paint hazards. The purchaser, however, may agree to waive the assessment.
- Sales and lease contracts must include specific disclosure and acknowledgment language. (See Figure 6.11, Disclosure Form for Lead-based Paint.)

FIGURE 6.9   EPA/HUD lead-based paint pamphlet.

Protect Your Family From Lead in Your Home

EPA
United States
Environmental Protection
Agency

United States Consumer
Product Safety Commission

U.S. EPA Washington DC 20460
U.S. CPSC Washington DC 20207

EPA747-K-94-001
May 1995

Are You Planning To Buy, Rent, or Renovate a Home Built Before 1978?

Many houses and apartments built before 1978 have paint that contains lead (called lead-based paint). Lead from paint, chips, and dust can pose serious health hazards if not taken care of properly.

By 1996, federal law will require that individuals receive certain information before renting, buying, or renovating pre-1978 housing:

LANDLORDS will have to disclose known information on lead-based paint hazards before leases take effect. Leases will include a federal form about lead-based paint.

SELLERS will have to disclose known information on lead-based paint hazards before selling a house. Sales contracts will include a federal form about lead-based paint in the building. Buyers will have up to 10 days to check for lead hazards.

RENOVATORS will have to give you this pamphlet before starting work.

IF YOU WANT MORE INFORMATION on these requirements, call the National Lead Information Clearinghouse at **1-800-424-LEAD**.

This document is in the public domain. It may be reproduced by an individual or organization without permission. Information provided in this booklet is based upon current scientific and technical understanding of the issues presented and is reflective of the jurisdictional boundaries established by the statutes governing the co-authoring agencies. Following the advice given will not necessarily provide complete protection in all situations or against all health hazards that can be caused by lead exposure.

REORDER CAT. No. 3140
Blumberg Excelsior
NYC 10013

Source: U. S. Environmental Protection Agency. U. S. Consumer Products Safety Commission.

PUTTING IT TO WORK   Real estate licensees must inform prospective purchasers of any material defect of which they have knowledge. With this in mind, respond to the following question.* Check your response using the model in the Answer Key at the end of the chapter.

What is the responsibility of the real estate broker for the quality of property that changes hands through the broker's efforts, for instance, a new home with a bad paint job, poor plumbing, and so on?

---

*Source: James A. Ader, "Real Estate Spotlight." Copyright © *The Albany Times Union.* Reprinted with permission.

FIGURE 6.10   Lead-Based Paint Testing Contingency form.

Addendum # _____   **LEAD-BASED PAINT TESTING CONTINGENCY**

THIS IS A LEGALLY-BINDING CONTRACT. IF NOT UNDERSTOOD, WE RECOMMEND CONSULTING AN ATTORNEY BEFORE SIGNING.

ADDENDUM TO CONTRACT FOR PURCHASE AND SALE
OF REAL ESTATE BETWEEN

_____ (Purchaser)

and

_____ (Seller)

Regarding the property located at: _____

This contract is contingent upon a risk assessment or inspection of the property for the presence of lead-based paint and/or lead-based paint hazards' at the Purchaser's expense until 9:00 P.M. on the tenth calendar day after ratification or until _____ .
This contingency will terminate at the above predetermined deadline unless the Purchaser (or Purchaser's agent) delivers to the Seller (or Seller's agent) a written contract addendum listing the specific existing deficiencies and corrections needed, together with a copy of the inspection and/or risk assessment report. The Seller may, at the Seller's option, within _____ days after Delivery of the addendum, elect in writing whether to correct the condition(s) prior to settlement. If the Seller will correct the condition, the Seller shall furnish the Purchaser with certification from a risk assessor or inspector demonstrating that the condition has been remedied before the date of the settlement. If the Seller does not elect to make the repairs, or if the Seller makes a counter-offer, the Purchaser shall have _____ days to respond to the counter-offer or remove this contingency and take the property in ''as-is'' condition or this contract shall become void. The Purchaser may remove this contingency at any time without cause.

'Intact lead-based paint that is in good condition is not necessarily a hazard. See EPA pamphlet *Protect Your Family From Lead in Your Home* **for more information.**

_____   _____   _____   _____
Purchaser   Date   Seller   Date

_____   _____   _____   _____
Purchaser   Date   Seller   Date

6/21/96
Capital Region Multiple Listing Service, Inc.

FIGURE 6.11 Lead-based paint disclosure.

DISCLOSURE OF INFORMATION AND ACKNOWLEDGMENT
LEAD-BASED PAINT AND/OR LEAD-BASED PAINT HAZARDS

Lead Warning Statement

Every purchaser of any interest in residential real property on which a residential dwelling was built prior to 1978 is notified that such property may present exposure to lead from lead-based paint that may place young children at risk of developing lead poisoning. Lead poisoning in young children may produce permanent neurological damage, including learning disabilities, reduced intelligence quotient, behavioral problems, and impaired memory. Lead poisoning also poses a particular risk to pregnant women. The seller of any interest in residential real property is required to provide the buyer with any information on lead-based paint hazards from risk assessments or inspections in the seller's possession and notify the buyer of any known lead-based paint hazards. A risk assessment or inspection for possible lead-based paint hazards is recommended prior to purchase.

Seller's Disclosure *(initial)*

_____ (a) Presence of lead-based paint and/or lead-based paint hazards *(check one below)*:

  ☐ Known lead-based paint and/or lead-based paint hazards are present in the housing *(explain)*:

  _____

  _____

  ☐ Seller has no knowledge of lead-based paint and/or lead-based paint hazards in the housing.

_____ (b) Records and Reports available to the seller *(check one below)*:

  ☐ Seller has provided the purchaser with all available records and reports pertaining to lead-based paint and/or lead-based hazards in the housing *(list documents below)*:

  _____

  _____

  ☐ Seller has no reports or records pertaining to lead-based paint and/or lead-based paint hazards in the housing.

Purchaser's Acknowledgment *(initial)*

_____ (c) Purchaser has received copies of all information listed above.

_____ (d) Purchaser has received the pamphlet *Protect Your Family From Lead in Your Home.*

_____ (e) Purchaser has *(check one below)*:

  ☐ Received a 10-day opportunity (or mutually agreed-upon period) to conduct a risk assessment or inspection of the presence of lead-based paint or lead-based paint hazards; or

  ☐ Waived the opportunity to conduct a risk assessment or inspection for the presence of lead-based paint and/or lead-based paint hazards.

Agent's Acknowledgment *(initial)*

_____ (f) Agent has informed the seller of the seller's obligations under 42 U.S.C. 4852 d and is aware of his/her responsibility to ensure compliance.

Certification of Accuracy

The following parties have reviewed the information above and certify, to the best of their knowledge, that the information they have provided is true and accurate.

Purchaser	Date	Seller	Date
Purchaser	Date	Seller	Date
Agent	Date	Agent	Date

6/21/96
Capital Region Multiple Listing Service, Inc

IMPORTANT POINTS

1. Footings support the foundation wall and, subsequently, the entire weight of the structure. The height of the foundation wall determines if the house has a crawl space or full basement.

2. The floor system starts with the sill plate nailed to the foundation system. Wood joists support the subfloor material.

3. Wall framing is almost exclusively 2" × 4" studs placed 16" on center. The most common wall-framing system is the platform method. Alternative methods are balloon or post-and-beam framing.

4. The roof structural skeleton is usually built with 2" × 8" ceiling joists and 2" × 6" or 2" × 8" rafters.

5. Electrical power is brought to the house through outside cables and delivered through a series of conductors to the house wiring system. Amperage is the amount of current flowing through the wire. Amperage required for different electrical uses is calculated in watts or kilowatts.

6. Construction standards at all levels of government directly impact the transfer, development, and proposed improvements to land.

7. Homes that are built with any program of federal financing such as FHA-insured and VA-guaranteed loans must be approved in advance and inspected by the appropriate agency as construction proceeds.

8. The Interstate Land Sales Full Disclosure Act, regulated by HUD, covers the sale of unimproved lots in interstate commerce to prevent fraudulent schemes in selling land sight-unseen.

9. Federal laws concerning the environment include the Clean Air Act, the Safe Drinking Water Act, and the National Environmental Policy Act.

10. New York laws affecting construction include Article 9-A of the Real Property Law, which addresses the sale of vacant subdivided land in New York and outside of New York when sold on the installment plan.

11. The regulatory agency in New York that oversees much of the environmental conservation law in New York is the New York State Department of Environmental Conservation.

12. The R-value refers to how various types of insulations are rated.

13. The New York State Department of Health has specific laws and regulations governing municipal drinking water, private water distribution systems, and on-site wastewater treatment systems.

14. Cities, counties, and other local governing units may impose land use regulations and building codes.

15. Due diligence inspections and reviews of property are conducted because liability for problems with property may become the responsibility of the new owner upon transfer of title.

16. Preparations for property development and construction must conform with zoning laws. Planning boards require a site plan and building specifications before development can commence. A building permit must be obtained prior to construction and a certificate of occupancy must be obtained before individuals may reside in the property.

17. Cluster development provides for PUDs, which create a neighborhood of zoned cluster housing and supporting business establishments. Other types of zoning include exclusive-use, nonconforming use, and spot zoning.

18. Eminent domain is the government's power to take land for public use when it is used for the public benefit.

19. Building inspections are conducted by governmental units to ensure that the structures meet the specifications of the building code.

20. Contingency agreements in contracts for purchase and sale render them contingent upon certain structural, environmental, and pest-infestation inspections.

21. It is not the duty of the broker to verify all representations by the owner; however, if the broker knows or has reason to know that the owner has failed to disclose a material defect, then a broker must disclose the information.

22. Brokers also must disclose any material defects of which they have knowledge to a prospective purchaser. Liability may be imposed upon the agent for concealing defects or failing to disclose the existence of defects.

23. Under a new law, real estate licensees must inform sellers that a disclosure statement be provided to the buyer or buyer's agent prior to the seller's acceptance of the purchase offer.

24. The Residential Lead-based Hazard Reduction Act of 1992 requires sellers or their agents to disclose the presence of lead-based paint, allow a mutually agreeable 10-day period for inspection, and provide a prescribed pamphlet outlining the dangers of lead-based paint. The Act applies to pre-1978 residential properties only.

SECTION REVIEW   How Would You Respond?

Analyze the following situations and decide how the individuals should handle them based on what you have learned. Check your responses using the Answer Key at the end of the section.

1. The Bindles sign a contract for purchase and sale for a home from the owners, the Wheatfields. The Wheatfields sign the contract offer. However, one week after the signing of the contract, the Bindles inform their real estate agent that they feel there should have been a contingency in the contract making the sale subject to a satisfactory inspection of the house to be performed by Bob Bindle's father, who is a contractor. What obligations do the Wheatfields have concerning this request?

_____

_____

_____

_____

2. Before signing the listing contract, the sellers, Bunny and Chauncy Snodgrass, tell their agent, Eugene, that the reason they are selling is because Chauncy has lost his job and they cannot afford the upkeep on the property. The roof has been leaking, but they cannot afford to repair it. They tell Eugene that they will keep the wet spots on the ceiling patched and painted and, as a condition of the listing, he cannot divulge the problem to prospective purchasers. If a purchaser finds out after title transfer, they assure Eugene that they will assume full legal liability. What should Eugene do, and what would be the extent, if any, of Eugene's liability?

_____

_____

_____

_____

KEY TERM REVIEW

Fill in the term that best completes the sentence and then check the Answer Key at the end of the section.

1. The most important foundation building block is the _____. The _____ determines whether the structure will have a full basement or a crawl space.

2. The slope of the roof is known as the _____. A metallic material that is used on the roof to prevent water seepage is known as _____.

3. A plywood covering placed over the exterior framing members is known as _____.

4. The amount of electricity flowing through a wire is known as the _____. A device that will melt and cause electrical power to stop when overheating occurs is known as a _____.

5. After a satisfactory final inspection, a(n) _____ is issued, permitting occupation of the structure by tenants or the owner.

6. A condition in a property that would have a material adverse effect on its value is known as a(n) _____.

7. Building codes require that a property owner obtain a(n) _____ from the appropriate local government authority before constructing or renovating a structure.

8. If an environmentally contaminated property is transferred, this liability is passed on to the new owners. Therefore, in the sale of large tracts of land or other types of property, purchasers have _____ assessments of the property.

9. Illegal _____ could occur if a property owner is allowed to build a manufacturing plant in a residential zone.

10. Mandatory seller _____ reduces the incidence of complaints, adverse renegotiations, and litigation after closing.

MULTIPLE CHOICE

Circle the letter that best answers the question and then check the Answer Key at the end of the section.

1. Which of the following is NOT a federal standard for construction?
   A. environmental legislation
   B. interstate land sales
   C. guidelines and standards for electrical installation
   D. the sale of vacant subdivided land on the installment plan

2. The federal law that requires the filing of an environmental impact statement with the appropriate state or local agency prior to changing or initiating a land use or development is the:
   A. Environmental Conservation Law
   B. National Environmental Policy Act
   C. Superfund Amendments and Reauthorization Act
   D. Comprehensive Environmental Response, Compensation, and Liability Act

3. Which of the following regarding Article 9-A of the New York Real Property Law is FALSE? It:
   A. addresses the sale of subdivided lands in and outside of New York only when sold on the installment plan
   B. addresses the sale of all vacant subdivided lands in and outside of New York no matter what the terms of sale
   C. requires real property transfers covered by the law to file documentation with the New York Department of State
   D. is a misdemeanor if violated

4. Which of the following water-related regulations is NOT covered by the New York Sanitary Code?

   A. setting specific maximum contaminant levels and standards

   B. establishing design criteria for systems

   C. providing wetland protection guidelines

   D. enforcing the code to make sure the water supply meets federal requirements

5. A subdivision requires approval by the New York State Department of Health (NYSDOH) if it meets all of the following criteria EXCEPT if the:

   A. subdivision has five or more lots that are leased or sold for residential building

   B. residential lot in the subdivision is a parcel of land five acres or less

   C. residential lots are sold or offered for sale within any three-year period

   D. subdivision has five or more lots that are leased or sold for residential and commercial building in all counties of New York

6. Which of the following cannot enforce local building codes?

   A. planning commissions

   B. building departments

   C. public referendums

   D. courts

7. Karen has decided to purchase a factory that produces a cleaning product. There has been some question about the disposal of toxic wastes from the factory. Before purchase, Karen should:

   A. have the property undergo a due diligence review to detect any environmental hazards

   B. ignore the potential problem, because any existing toxic wastes on the property are the problem of the former owners

   C. seek owner financing, because any environmental problems will then go undetected

   D. request that the owners issue her a sworn statement releasing her from legal liability should contamination be found after transfer of title

8. Under the Clean Air Act, the EPA identified:

   A. national ambient air quality standards

   B. safe levels of radon in the home

   C. safe proximity to electromagnetic fields

   D. PCB levels in the nation's waterways

9. The "map" that lays out the dimensions and design of a building is/are the:

   A. site plan

   B. building specifications

   C. blueprint

   D. building permit

10. A certificate of occupancy:

    A. must be obtained before obtaining a building permit

    B. must be obtained after satisfactory approval of the finished structure

    C. is only required for residential construction

    D. is only required for new construction and never for renovation to existing housing

11. A taking under eminent domain:

    A. is subject to approval by the homeowners' association of the subdivision

    B. must include just compensation for the property that is taken

    C. is a right of both public and private entities

    D. need not compensate the owner of the property if the taking is for the public good

12. Which of the following is NOT a reason for sellers to have their property inspected prior to marketing? To:

    A. protect themselves from legal liability after transfer of title

    B. identify areas for improvement prior to showing

    C. rediscover features of their property that would appeal to prospective purchasers

    D. eliminate the need to disclose any material defects that may continue to exist at the time of title transfer

13. An example of a problem on a property that would not be considered a material defect would be which of the following?

    A. a leaky swimming pool

    B. a crack in the foundation

    C. a broken bathroom window

    D. a fireplace chimney that is blocked with soot and dirt

14. A voluntary property condition disclosure form:

   A. does not limit an agent's disclosure obligations for information other than that stated by the seller

   B. should be completed by prospective purchasers of residential property

   C. would increase the amount of complaints and litigation after transfer of title

   D. is not recommended by the New York State Association of REALTORS®

15. Alencia is a buyer agent who represents the Youngs in the purchase of a single-family home. Alencia knows that the heating system in the house does not work. It is summer and no one has mentioned this fact to the Youngs, and they haven't asked. The sellers' agents also know about the heating system. Which of the following parties to the sale should have disclosed this defect to the Youngs?

   A. no one

   B. only the sellers

   C. the sellers and the seller agent

   D. the sellers, the seller agent, and Alencia (the buyer agent)

ANSWER KEY

Putting It to Work

Real estate brokers are not responsible for the quality of workmanship except if they know the quality is so bad that it may constitute a material defect in the property. Even then they would have the responsibility of pointing out only the material defect and would not have financial responsibility for its correction. This would apply to new housing and to resale housing. Brokers are only marketing, on behalf of the seller, the property in an "as is" condition. If the home was purchased new, then there is a legislated builder's warranty that applies. Specifics of what is covered and for what period of time may be obtained from the builder.

In the listing of one- to four-unit residential property, the broker would also have the responsibility of ensuring that the seller property condition disclosure form is completed. This form should be made available to prospective purchasers before they make an offer.

How Would You Respond?

1. The Wheatfields have no legal obligations concerning this request. After there has been a meeting of the minds, any introduction of new contingencies to a contract for purchase and sale must be in writing and be acceptable to all parties to the contract.

2. Under the conditions dictated by the Snodgrasses, Eugene cannot take the listing. His duty as agent requires that he disclose all material defects to a property of which he is aware. It is not up to the Snodgrasses to decide whether or not Eugene would be legally liable for any misrepresentation. In addition, to conceal the defect, the Snodgrasses would have to lie on the seller property condition disclosure form. Should Eugene present this form to prospects knowing it is false, subjects him to liability as well as the sellers.

Key Term Review

1. footing; foundation wall
2. pitch; flashing
3. sheathing
4. amperage; fuse
5. certificate of occupancy
6. defect
7. building permit
8. due diligence
9. spot zoning
10. property condition disclosure

Multiple Choice

1. D
2. B
3. B
4. C
5. D
6. C
7. A
8. A
9. C
10. B
11. B
12. D
13. B
14. A
15. D

SECTION 2	DEVELOPMENT

The development of a residential subdivision is a complex and costly project. However, the results can provide profits to brokers and their clients and a new source of housing and business to the community. This part discusses the procedures pertaining to the acquisition and development of subdivisions and the development and purchase of condominiums and cooperatives.

THE SUBDIVISION

A **subdivision** is *a tract of land divided into lots or plots and is eventually used for building purposes.* Sale of land for subdivisions may include a list of approvals ranging from zoning considerations to environmental impact statements, and many governmental agencies may be involved. Zoning ordinances, subdivision development, and site-plan reviews are set by the local governments through their respective *planning commissions.*

Determination of Use—The Town Board and Zoning Ordinances

The purpose of planning is to provide for the orderly growth of a community that will result in the greatest social and economic benefits to its people. Urban planners first typically develop a master or comprehensive plan to determine the city's make-up by performing a survey of the community's physical and economic assets. In the absence of planning, haphazard development often ensues. Along with the plan, the community agrees on zoning requirements. The proposal is presented by referendum to all property owners. *Municipalities in New York have planning commissions or boards that hold public hearings and have the power to investigate, report, and make recommendations to the appropriate legislative body.* Once the plan is created, **zoning ordinances** are established.

Zoning ordinances consist of two parts: 1) the zoning map, which divides the community into various designated districts, and 2) a text of the zoning ordinance, which sets forth the type of use permitted under each zoning classification, including specific requirements for compliance.

The Planning Board and Subdivision Regulations

New York empowers local government, cities, and counties, through **subdivision regulations,** or ordinances, *to protect purchasers and to control property development within the subdivisions.* Taxpayers in the city or county are thus relieved of an undue tax burden resulting from the demands for services that a new subdivision generates. Subdivision ordinances usually address the following requirements:

1. Streets must be of a specified width, be curbed, have storm drains, and not exceed certain maximum grade specifications.
2. Lots may not be smaller than a specified minimum size.
3. Dwellings in specified areas must be for single-family occupancy only. Specific areas may be set aside for multifamily dwellings.
4. Utilities, including water, sewer, electric, and telephone, must be available to each lot, or plans must include easements to provide utilities later.
5. All houses must be placed on lots to meet specified minimum standards for setbacks from the front property line, as well as from interior property lines.
6. Drainage must be adequate to avoid damage from runoff caused by rainfall.

After adopting a subdivision ordinance, *subdividers* must obtain approval from the appropriate officials before subdividing and selling lots. Compliance with most subdivision ordinances requires the platting of land into lots. Then the *subdivision plat* is recorded on the public record in a *plat book* or other recording method with the county clerk, and development can begin. Until the subdivision plat is approved and recorded, a subdivision reference may not be used in a legal description. Once approved, this type of lot, block, and subdivision description is acceptable.

Wetland Regulations

Wetlands are *transition areas between uplands and aquatic habitats. They are called marshes, swamps, bogs, wet meadows, or flats.* Wetlands are protected areas because they provide flood and storm water control, surface and ground-water protection, erosion control, pollution treatment, a place for fish and wildlife habitats, open space, and natural beauty. In New York, wetlands are protected under *Article 24 of the Environmental Conservation Law, also known as the Freshwater Wetlands Act.*

The agency that oversees wetland protection is the Department of Environmental Conservation (NYSDEC). Wetlands protected under the act must be larger than 12.4 acres and may also include any smaller wetlands of unusual appearance. An adjacent area of 100 feet is also protected, to provide a buffer zone.

The act requires NYSDEC to map all protected wetlands. Certain activities are specifically exempt from regulation and do not require a permit. Other activities require either a permit or a letter of permission. The act allows local governments to assume jurisdiction for regulating wetlands once NYSDEC has filed a map for their area. Under the act, activities in wetlands that require a permit are restoring, modifying, or expanding existing structures; draining, except for agriculture; installing docks, piers, or wharves; constructing bulkheads, dikes, and dams; installing utilities; and applying pesticides.

Section 404 of the *Clean Water Act* also requires that anyone interested in depositing dredged or fill matter into "waters of the United States, including wetlands" must receive authorization for such activities. The U.S. Army Corps of Engineers is responsible for administering the Section 404 permit process. Activities under 404 that require a permit are: placing fill material; ditching; constructing levees or dikes; mechanized land clearing; land leveling; most road constructing; and dam building. The appropriate army corps district office must make the final determination of whether an area is a wetland and whether the activity requires a permit.

In New York, approval for regulated activities in wetlands must be obtained from the state (through local government) *and* federal (army corps) programs. Figure 6.12 illustrates a sample joint application for permit in a wetland area. Figure 6.13 diagrams alternative layouts for a house and septic system located near a wetland.

Steep Slopes and Other Environmental Constraints

A **steep slope** is *land with a slope that ranges from 30 percent to 45 percent or more.* Excavation work on this type of property may cause flooding and other problems. Federal, state, and local laws. These laws are enforced by town planning boards must study these issues and their effect on the surrounding property before granting subdivision approval.

What Determines the Value of Land?

The value of land is determined through a number of factors, including the legally permitted uses, the physical nature of the land, and its location.

A consideration in subdivision development is the *topography* of the land, or its physical features and contours. It includes types of soil; the locations of water such

FIGURE 6.12   NYSDEC and Army Corps Joint Application for permit.

JOINT APPLICATION FOR PERMIT

95-19-3 (8/00) pfp

New York State
United States Army Corps of Engineers

Applicable to agencies and permit categories listed in Item 1.   **Please** read all instructions on back.   Attach additional information as needed.   Please print legibly or type.

1. Check permits applied for:

NYS Dept. of Environmental Conservation

Stream Disturbance (Bed and Banks)

Navigable Waters (Excavation and Fill)

Docks, Moorings or Platforms (Construct or Place)

Dams and Impoundment Structures (Construct, Reconstruct or Repair)

Freshwater Wetlands

Tidal Wetlands

Coastal Erosion Control

Wild, Scenic and Recreational Rivers

401 Water Quality Certification

Potable Water Supply

Long Island Wells

Aquatic Vegetation Control

Aquatic Insect Control

Fish Control

NYS Office of General Services
(State Owned Lands Under Water)

Lease, License, Easement or other Real Property Interest

Utility Easement (pipelines, conduits, cables, etc.)

Docks, Moorings or Platforms (Construct or Place)

Adirondack Park Agency

Freshwater Wetlands Permit

Wild, Scenic and Recreational Rivers

Lake George Park Commission

Docks (Construct or Place)

Moorings (Establish)

US Army Corps of Engineers

Section 404 (Waters of the United States)

Section 10 (Rivers and Harbors Act)

Nationwide Permit (s)
Identify Number(s)

For Agency Use Only:
DEC APPLICATION NUMBER

US ARMY CORPS OF ENGINEERS

2. Name of Applicant (Use full name) — **Telephone Number** (daytime)

Mailing Address

Post Office — **State** — **Zip Code**

3. Taxpayer ID (If applicant is not an individual)

4. Applicant is a/an: (check as many as apply)
Owner   Operator   Lessee   Municipality / Governmental Agency

5. If applicant is not the owner, identify owner here - otherwise, you may provide Agent/Contact Person information.
Owner or Agent/Contact Person   Owner   Agent /Contact Person   **Telephone Number** (daytime)

Mailing Address

Post Office — **State** — **Zip Code**

6. Project / Facility Location (mark location on map, see instruction 1a.)
County: Town/City/Village: Tax Map Section/ Block /Lot Number:

Location (including Street or Road) — **Telephone Number** (daytime)

Post Office — **State** — **Zip Code** — **7. Name of Stream or Waterbody** (on or near project site)

8. Name of USGS Quad Map: **Location Coordinates:**
NYTM-E   NYTM-N   4

9. Project Description and Purpose: (Category of Activity e.g. new construction/installation, maintenance or replacement; Type of Structure or Activity e.g. bulkhead, dredging, filling, dam, dock, taking of water; Type of Materials and Quantities; Structure and Work Area Dimensions; Need or Purpose Served)

10. Proposed Use:	**11. Will Project Occupy State Land?**	**12. Proposed Start Date:**	**13. Estimated Completion Date:**
Private Public Commercial	Yes No		

14. Has Work Begun on Project? (If yes, attach explanation of why work was started without permit.) Yes   No | **15. List Previous Permit / Application Numbers and Dates:** (If Any)

16. Will this Project Require Additional Federal, State, or Local Permits?   Yes   No   If Yes, Please List:

17. If applicant is not the owner, both must sign the application

I hereby affirm that information provided on this form and all attachments submitted herewith is true to the best of my knowledge and belief. False statements made herein are punishable as a Class A misdemeanor pursuant to Section 210.45 of the Penal Law. Further, the applicant accepts full responsibility for all damage, direct or indirect, of whatever nature, and by whomever suffered, arising out of the project described herein and agrees to indemnify and save harmless the State from suits, actions, damages and costs of every name and description resulting from said project. In addition, Federal Law, 18 U.S.C., Section 1001 provides for a fine of not more than $10,000 or imprisonment for not more than 5 years, or both where an applicant knowingly and willingly falsifies, conceals, or covers up a material fact; or knowingly makes or uses a false, ficticious or fraudulent statement.

Date _____   Signature of Applicant _____   Title _____

Date _____   Signature of Owner _____   Title _____

Source: New York State Department of Environmental Conservation.

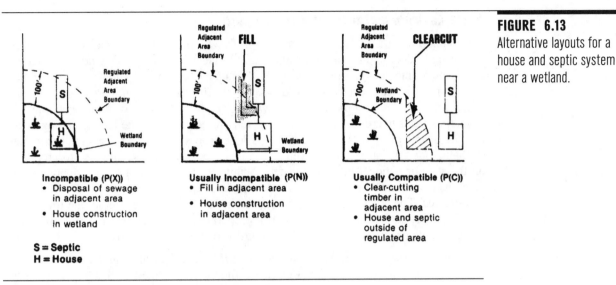

FIGURE 6.13
Alternative layouts for a house and septic system near a wetland.

Source: New York State Department of Environmental Conservation.

as wetlands, springs, or floodplains; and forests and the location of rocks, trees, and other vegetation. These features are relevant to how and where dwellings will be situated, where utilities and pipelines will be located, and how the completed subdivision will look.

A study of the *demographics* of a community, which is its social and economic statistics, helps planners ascertain whether or not the community can support new development. New construction causes *increased use of water, sewers, utilities, schools, roadways, medical services, and police and fire department support. These items make up a community's* infrastructure. The increased burden of population forces the municipality to increase its services. A *developer* may be required to pay *impact fees* to cover the increased cost of at least part of these services.

Planning Board

Local planning boards decide the general layout of a specific municipality—a city, town, or village—and map the zones and uses allowed within each zone. Zoning boards of appeal hear and decide on variances and special-use permits within the municipality.

In New York, the planning board or commission has the statutory authority to review and approve site plans for subdivision development. Site plans must include the proposed subdivision's arrangement, layout, and design. Before approval, town planning boards may request modifications. The plan also must include information about available utilities and implementation of new utility systems, drainage, easements running through the property, zoning surrounding the site, open spaces, configurations of streets and sidewalks, types of structures to be built, environmental considerations as required, and marketing information.

Appointment of Planning Board Members

Planning board members in municipalities with *under one million* people in New York are appointed by the mayor or another appointing authority. The local planning board consists of five to seven members. The term of office is equal in years to the number of members on the planning board; for example, a five-member board would have a term of five years for each member.

State Environmental Quality Review Act

All planning boards in New York must comply with the environmental review process according to the State Environmental Quality Review Act (SEQRA). Under this act, the State Environmental Quality Review (SEQR) is a process that requires all levels of New York state and local government to *assess the environmental significance of actions for which they have discretion to review, approve, fund, or undertake.** For example, if a developer wants to create a subdivision, he requires approval by the local planning board, and the SEQR process is necessary. The SEQR process applies to residential, commercial, and industrial structures as well as to other types of land use and also to properties on the state or national historic registers. Within the assessment process, many government agencies may be involved, as various kinds of environment assessments have to be investigated. The agency that coordinates the investigation, for example, the town planning board, is called the *lead agency.* If a property is simply transferred from owner to owner and its use does not change, the SEQR process does not apply.

The *Environmental Impact Statement (EIS)* describes and analyzes a proposed action that may have a significant effect on the environment. The SEQR process uses the EIS to consider ways to avoid and reduce adverse environmental impacts related to a proposed action and to consider its alternative. The applicant can hire a consultant to write the environmental impact statement. There is a minimum 30-day comment period after which a public hearing can be held. The lead agency reviews all comments. The final environmental impact statement is the culmination of all material relating to the action and becomes the lead agency's final document.

THE ZONING BOARD OF APPEALS

The *zoning board of appeals* has the power to review administrative rulings made by the planning board or other legislative body, grant or deny exceptions and special permits, and process applications for variances. The zoning board of appeals is an administrative agency, but it is only *quasi judicial.* Its decisions are subject to review and change in the state and federal courts. The zoning board does not make policy; it is a local administrative appeal agency that interprets zoning ordinances. The zoning board of appeals perfects and ensures the validity of zoning and safeguards the rights of property owners. It ensures the fair application of zoning regulations and serves as a safety valve for the zoning system. If a property owner wishes an exception to the zoning ordinance, the owner may appeal to the board for a variance or special-use permit. If the request is denied by the zoning board of appeals, the property owner may petition the New York Supreme Court through an Article 78 proceeding. As mentioned in Chapter 1, an Article 78 proceeding is an appeal brought forth because of a ruling by a government agency. Lawsuits involving zoning ordinances are common, and some cases have been brought before the United States Supreme Court.

Appointment of Zoning Board of Appeals

For cities with *under one million* people or cities with *over one million* that may wish to adopt the same terms of appointment as those for the smaller cities, the mayor or city manager or other authority may appoint members to the zoning board of appeals. The board must consist of three to five members, as determined by local law, and the term of membership is equal in years to the number of members on the board.

In cities in New York with more than one million inhabitants, appointments and terms of membership on the planning board and zoning board are made by resolution of the board of estimate and apportionment or other similar governing body.

---

*NYSDEC and the Office of Parks, Recreation and Historic Preservation (OPRHP), "Conserving Open Space in New York . . . the Plan," (January 4, 1993): 4.

Planning Commission in New York City

In New York City, the planning commission and the zoning board are combined and are known as the Board of Standards and Appeals. Zoning applications go through the planning commission and no separate zoning board of appeals exists. A total of 12 members and one chairperson make up the planning commission. Six members and one chairperson are appointed by the mayor. Each borough president appoints one member from each of the five boroughs of New York City, and one member is appointed by the city council.

Variance

A *variance* is a permitted deviation from specific requirements of the zoning ordinance. For example, if an owner's lot is slightly smaller than the minimum lot-size requirement set by zoning ordinances, the owner may be granted a variance by petitioning the appropriate authorities. New York has two types of variances: *use* and *area*. A **use variance** is *permission to use the land for a purpose that under the current zoning restrictions is prohibited.* A use variance must imply that the current zoning ordinance has caused the property owner an unnecessary hardship and should include the following:

1. The property owner is deprived of all economic use or benefit from the property. The property owner must give financial evidence to this effect.
2. The hardship is unique and not universal to the area or neighborhood.
3. The variance will not change the essential character of the neighborhood.
4. The alleged hardship is not self-created.

In the case of a use variance, the zoning board of appeals will grant the minimum variance necessary to address the unnecessary hardship while still protecting the character of the neighborhood and the health, safety, and welfare of the community. An example of a use variance is where the existing zoning allows only one-family homes and a property owner receives a use variance to build a two-family home.

An **area variance** is *permission to use the land not normally allowed by the dimensional or physical requirements of the current zoning ordinance.* An area variance must consider the benefit to the individual property owner weighed against the detriment to the health, safety, and welfare of the neighborhood. The following are considered in granting an area variance:

1. undesirable change or detriment to nearby properties if granted
2. if the benefit sought can be achieved by other feasible means
3. if the requested variance is substantial
4. if it would have an adverse effect or impact on physical or environmental conditions in the neighborhood or district
5. if the difficulty was self-created (even if the difficulty was self-created, it does not preclude granting the variance)

An example of an area variance would be where the existing zoning ordinance mandates that the square footage of a lot for a single-family home has to be 12,000 square feet and a property owner is given an area variance to build a single-family home on a lot that is only 11,850 square feet.

Special-Use Permit

A **special-use permit** is *a permit for a use that is not allowed in the zone without the approval of the planning board or other legislative body.* A special-use permit cannot be granted without a public hearing in which the residents can participate and voice their objections. Unlike a variance request, special-use permits do not require that the property owner demonstrate undue hardship because of the current zoning rules. In New York, a special-use permit can be authorized if the proposed use is in harmony with local zoning ordinances and laws, does not adversely affect the neighborhood, and is beneficial to the community. Figure 6.14 charts the deviations from zoning ordinances and Figure 6.15 illustrates zoning issues.

You Should Know

The development process

The process of developing a subdivision goes through carefully planned stages. They include:

- A market study of the area where the proposed subdivision will be to determine the salability of the proposed project. This would include a *feasibility study*. Factors reviewed are the cost of site development (including environmental factors), available financing, costs of financing (including prevailing interest rates), tax considerations, rates of return on similar type investments, and the benefit to the community and its acceptance of the project. Feasibility studies include demographic information ranging from average income to traffic patterns.

- Application to local and state agencies for necessary approvals. This process includes an environmental review of the site.

- The final marketing of the subdivision. Many developers prepare the lots and supporting infrastructure but will not build the entire subdivision all at once. The project is often divided into *phases* of building that take place over a number of years. Developers may choose to build several model homes and then wait until buyers prepurchase the home based on a viewing of the site and the model. With this method, the developer does not have to outlay large sums of money for construction, and the purchaser has options not only about the house's location within the subdivision but also about the design of the house's interior and exterior.

- In developing either residential or commercial land, developers often consider the purpose and placement of **outlots** or parcels. *Outlots are parcels of land that are outside of the main area of development.* For example, a strip mall may have stores situated in one row or square. Then, a bank may be located on an outlot by the entrance to or behind the strip mall. Outlot development can and should complement the main area of business and consider parking, height, signage and other zoning restrictions, design of the building, and accessibility.

A real estate broker can be involved in many aspects of the development process, from land acquisition to final marketing of the structures (see Figure 6.16).

FINANCING AND ACQUIRING A SUBDIVISION

An issue of prime importance in acquiring a subdivision is that the developer raise and then structure the necessary funds to complete the project. To realize a profit and safeguard the investment, developers must be sure that enough funds are available to see the project through to completion.

Development Costs

The costs of project development include municipal fees paid to different government agencies and other entities involved in the project. They may include engineers' fees and other professional fees for site investigation as well as hook-up fees to municipal

FIGURE 6.14 Deviations from zoning ordinances.

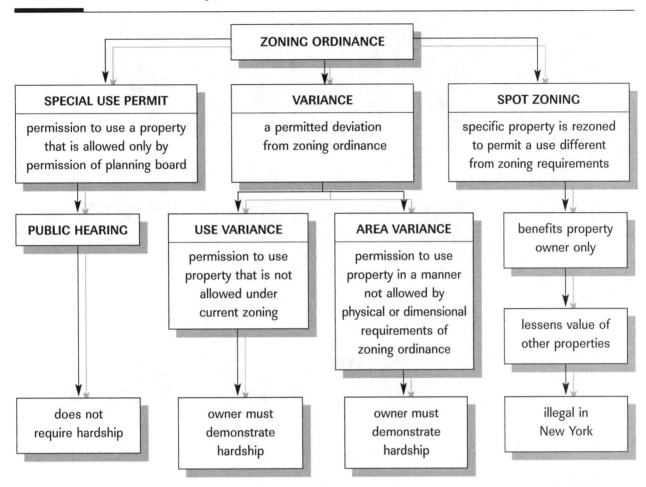

sewer and water systems. The municipality or other agencies may also require the developer to assume all or part of the cost for roads throughout and leading to the subdivision, sidewalks, utility installation, landscaping, and other improvements bordering the project. A developer may need to obtain a **completion bond.** *Also known as a subdivision bond, it ensures the municipality that off-site improvements to the subdivision will be made upon completion of the total project.* In this type of bond, the municipality would be the beneficiary. Developers may also be required to *dedicate* a portion of their land to the municipality for public use.

Mortgages, Construction Loans, and Owner Participation

To obtain financing for a subdivision project, the developer may have to raise funds from a combination of sources. The developer may obtain a construction loan for a percentage of the financing and must participate in raising the remaining funds from other sources, including the developer's personal money, money from investors, or other types of mortgages. (Construction loans are discussed more fully in Chapter 3.) A developer may acquire a *purchase money mortgage.* The security for the mortgage is the *total amount of lots* in the subdivision. The lender may require that this mortgage not be subordinate to any other loans on the project. The mortgage may contain a provision that in order to transfer title to any of the lots, a portion of the mortgage lien must be satisfied. (The purchase money mortgage and the concept of release lot subdivision financing are discussed more fully in Chapter 3.)

FIGURE 6.15
Special use permits, variances, illegal spot zoning, and nonconforming use.

(1) The pizzeria has received a special use permit to operate in an industrial zone.

(2) Dianna Little has obtained a use variance to operate her brokerage out of her garage even though her neighborhood is zoned residential.

(3) The owner has obtained an area variance to add more square footage to his house than is allowable under the zoning ordinance in order to construct a sunroom. He has also been granted a variance to build to within 2 ft. of the lot boundary line (also not allowed under the zoning ordinance).

(4) A commercial zone was written into the zoning ordinance in the middle of a residential neighborhood to accommodate a large factory outlet, probably to increase the tax base. It is the only commercial establishment in the area.

(5) This homeowner owned her house prior to her land being zoned commercial. Her house now sits among many commercial businesses.

(1) SPECIAL USE PERMIT

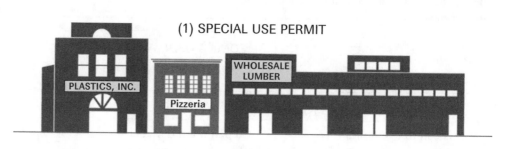

(2) USE VARIANCE

(3) AREA VARIANCE

(4) ILLEGAL SPOT ZONING

(5) NONCONFORMING USE

PRIVATE LAND USE CONTROL: RESTRICTIVE COVENANTS

Developers often place restrictions on the entire subdivision to maintain the quality and consistency of the subdivision. Individual owners have the right to place *private land use controls* on their own real estate. These restrictions may be found on individual deeds or may be restrictions affecting an entire subdivision. *Deed restrictions* take the form of covenants or conditions. These restrictions run with the land (move with the title in any subsequent conveyance). Restrictions that provide for a reversion of title if they are violated are called *conditions*. If a condition is violated, ownership reverts to the grantor.

Restrictive covenants can also be limitations placed on the use of land by the developer of a residential subdivision. The covenants are promises by those who purchase property in the subdivision to limit the use of their property to comply with these requirements. The deeds conveying title to these properties contain references to a recorded plat of the subdivision and references to the recording of the restrictive covenants; or the restrictions may be recited in each deed of conveyance. Restrictions must be reasonable, and they must benefit all property owners.

Covenants may be enforced by the property owner within the subdivision by taking appropriate court action. If property owners do not act to enforce restrictive covenants on a timely basis, the court will not apply the restriction against the violator and it will be terminated. Termination of a covenant in this manner is an application of the *Doctrine of Laches,* which states that if landowners are lax in protecting their rights, they may lose them.

Subdivision developments often have homeowners' associations. Respond to the following question.* Then check your response using the model in the Answer Key at the end of the section.

PUTTING IT TO WORK

   The question is: What are my rights, as a member of the homeowners' association in my development, regarding access to the financial records of the association?

DEVELOPMENT AND PURCHASE OF CONDOMINIUMS AND COOPERATIVES

Condominiums and cooperatives can be newly constructed real estate or converted existing structures; they can be residential or commercial.

Filing Requirements

Special laws and regulations apply to the development and purchase of condominiums and cooperative units in New York. The individual or entity that either constructs or converts a building into a condominium or a cooperative corporation must file a declaration and disclosure statement with the New York attorney general's office. The declaration consists of two parts: The first part includes the scope of the project, a description of the corporate setup and other required information. This review process is called the preliminary prospectus or red herring. At this point, the attorney general can suggest any changes to the project except for the price of shares (in the case of cooperatives). Once the prospectus is approved for filing, it is a "black book," or offering plan, and at this point the condominium or cooperative units may be offered for sale to the public.

---

*Source: James A. Ader, "Real Estate Spotlight." Copyright © The *Albany Times Union*. Reprinted by permission.

FIGURE 6.16 The residential subdivision development process and the real estate broker.

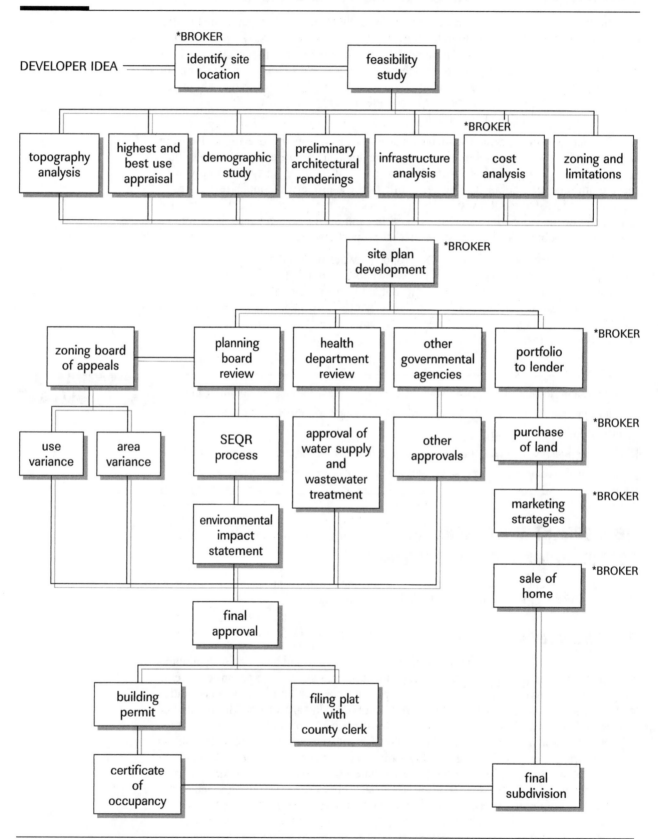

*Note: The real estate broker may be involved in many aspects of the development process. Can you think of other areas not indicated here where you could lawfully lend your expertise?

Elements of a Condominium

Condominium law in New York is contained in the Real Property Law and sets forth the manner in which a condominium is to be created and managed. These include a declaration (master deed); articles of association; and the bylaws that are recorded in the public record in the county where the property is located.

Condominium developments are jointly controlled. Condominium ownership is a combination of ownerships—individual unit plus co-ownership of the common areas available to all owners. The individual unit may be held as a fee in severalty, fee in joint tenancy, fee in common, or fee as tenants by the entireties. Common areas, such as the yard, roof, hallways, elevators, or pool, are owned as tenants in common.

Title to the individual unit may be transferred by deed or by leaving it to an heir by will. Title to the common areas is held as tenancy in common with all other unit owners. The common areas are the responsibility of all unit owners.

Condominium contracts are similar to other fee simple interest real estate contracts except they may contain a right of first refusal clause for the board of managers of a condominium association. This allows the condominium association to have the first opportunity to purchase the condo when it goes up for sale. Therefore, the seller, at the closing, may have to present a waiver of this right issued by the board of managers of the condominium association. The condominium association also, in some instances, inquires as to buyer credentials, bank references, and so on, prior to purchase.

Timeshares

The *timeshare* is a type of ownership of a condominium or other type of ownership in fee that shares the use of the unit with many different owners. This co-ownership is based upon prescribed time intervals. It works by allowing several different individuals to purchase the condominium unit in fee and then divide the use by weeks or months. Each owner of the unit purchases the exclusive right to use the unit for a specified period of time. Timeshares are commonly used for vacation purposes. Maintenance costs, taxes, and insurance are prorated among the different owners. The percentage of expense is equivalent to the percentage of the year (time) purchased. Exchange programs are also available for some timeshares that allow an owner of a specified time at a property to trade time with the owner of another specified time at a totally different property.

Cooperatives

The same types of structures that house condominiums can also house cooperatives. The types and forms of ownership in a cooperative, however, are vastly different from condominium ownership.

The Cooperative (Proprietary) Lease

In a cooperative, the buildings, land, all real property rights, and interests are owned by a corporation in severalty. The title to the property, as shown on the deed, is in the name of the corporation. A cooperative apartment buyer is purchasing an interest in the corporation; therefore the ownership is not a fee simple interest and the cooperative apartment is not realty, but personalty, or personal property. The shareholders of the corporation are tenants in the building. The only real property interest the shareholders have is a leasehold estate providing the right to possession of an apartment and use of the common areas. Therefore, ownership in a cooperative is really ownership of shares of stock in a corporation plus a long-term *proprietary lease*. There is no tenancy in common ownership in the common areas, even though all tenants can use those areas. The common areas, as all of the building, are owned in fee by the corporation. The board of directors usually interviews all prospective shareholders and may decide to deny a prospective tenant from purchasing an apartment.

An owner in a cooperative does not receive a deed. The owner does not own real estate in the typical sense, although the Internal Revenue Service considers this ownership by recognizing the traditional benefits of home ownership such as mortgage interest and property tax deductions (on a pro rata basis).

Financing the Purchase of a Cooperative

A cooperative apartment corporation is like other corporations, in which the value of the ownership is greater or lesser depending on the number of shares owned. The number of shares assigned to a particular apartment is usually a reflection of the size of the apartment, the location within the building, and certain other features that the dwelling may have, or have access to, such as a terrace, pool, and extra kitchen appliances.

The transaction is somewhat similar to the sale of real property. The seller decides the number of shares that the apartment is worth and the purchaser pays the dollar value of these shares as the purchase price to the seller. The shares and apartment are transferred to the purchaser as well as an assignment of the proprietary lease. As lessees, the shareholders pay no rent but do pay an assessment to cover their portion of the cost of *maintenance*. Maintenance includes the cost of operating the building and upkeep of the common areas, as well as the debt service if the corporation has placed a mortgage against the real estate, and payment of real property taxes.

In considering a loan for a cooperative purchase, the lender must consider not only the loan for the individual shareholder but also look at other indebtedness for which the borrower–shareholder has responsibility. For example, if a $1 million mortgage exists on the building, the cooperative shareholder takes on a pro rata share of that mortgage. Moreover, if the loan-to-value ratio is, for example, 70 percent to 30 percent, part of the 70 percent of the loan might include a portion of the mortgage for the entire building as well as the pro rata share of each of the units.

To finance the purchase of a cooperative, the cooperative purchaser uses both the shares of stock assigned to the apartment as well as the proprietary lease as collateral for the loan. In this sense, the loan is different from a mortgage since the security for it is not real estate, but personalty. This type of loan is known as a collateralized security loan. Some of the purchaser's indebtedness, as explained above, also includes a portion of the mortgage on the entire building. Therefore, if a cooperative purchaser has an obligation of $1,000 per month, $300 may go to the lender for repayment of the collateralized security loan while the remaining $700 goes toward maintenance (defined above) and is paid to the cooperative corporation.

IMPORTANT POINTS

1. A subdivision is a tract of land divided into lots or plots and is eventually used for building purposes. Local planning boards coordinate the site-plan review and approval process.
2. Subdivision regulations protect owners within a subdivision and taxpayers from an undue tax burden resulting from the extra cost of services that a subdivision generates.
3. Wetlands in New York are protected by the Fresh Water Wetlands Act, which allows local governments to assume jurisdiction for regulating wetlands once NYSDEC has filed a map for their area.
4. Under the State Environmental Quality Review Act, all levels of New York state and local government must assess the environmental significance of actions about which they have discretion to review, approve, fund, or undertake.

5. The zoning board of appeals reviews applications for special-use permits and area and use variances. The review is beneficial in that it safeguards the rights of property owners and ensures the fair application of zoning regulations.

6. The development process includes a feasibility study, application to the municipality and other appropriate agencies, an environmental review, and final marketing.

7. To obtain financing for subdivision projects, the developer may have to raise funds through a combination of sources.

8. Developers generally place restrictive covenants on the entire subdivision to maintain quality and consistency.

9. In the development of condominiums and cooperatives, a detailed offering plan describing all aspects of the project must be filed with the office of the New York attorney general.

SECTION REVIEW   How Would You Respond?

Analyze the following situations and decide how the individuals should handle them based on what you have learned. Check your responses using the Answer Key at the end of the section.

1. Ermanno, a developer in Buffalo, New York, is attempting to obtain approval for a subdivision of approximately 30 single-family homes and 60 townhouses. The city tells Ermanno that they will approve the subdivision if he donates three acres of his property for a public park that the city would create. Exactly what is the city asking Ermanno to do? What might be the easiest method by which he could donate this land?

_____

_____

_____

2. Isaac is considering the purchase of a raised ranch in a new subdivision. Isaac feels the house is big enough for everything but his riding lawn mower. He agrees to purchase the house if he can build a large equipment shed in the back yard. As Isaac's real estate agent, what might you suggest Isaac do before he signs a contract of sale?

_____

_____

_____

KEY TERM REVIEW

Fill in the term that best completes the sentence and then check the Answer Key at the end of the section.

1. A(n) _____ is a tract of land divided into lots and is eventually used for building purposes.

2. Once a master plan is created, a _____ is established to set forth requirements for various districts.

3. Marshes, swamps, and other similar land that is protected under New York law as to its use and development are known as _____.

4. A(n) _____ is permission to use land for a purpose not permitted under current zoning. A(n) _____ is permission to use land not normally allowed by the physical or dimensional requirements of the zoning.

5. A developer must obtain a(n) _____, which ensures the municipality that offsite improvements to a subdivision will be made upon completion of the project.

6. Parcels of land located outside the main area of development are known as _____.

MULTIPLE CHOICE

Circle the letter that best answers the question and then check the Answer Key at the end of the section.

1. The development process does NOT include which of the following?
   A. spot zoning
   B. demographic study
   C. feasibility study
   D. highest and best use appraisal

2. Iris wishes to buy the lot next to her house in a residential subdivision to construct a small factory that produces gourmet dog food. The development where she lives is zoned residential. If the zoning board of appeals allows this use, this would be an example of:
   A. nonconforming use
   B. illegal spot zoning
   C. exclusive-use zoning
   D. special-use permit

3. In New York, which of the following is FALSE?
   A. local planning boards may not, under any circumstances, regulate protected wetlands
   B. the Department of Environmental Conservation regulates wetland protection in New York
   C. the U.S. Army Corps of Engineers regulates wetland protection in New York
   D. footage surrounding protected wetlands is also protected

4. Which of the following is NOT a governmental regulation affecting the value of land?
   A. zoning ordinances
   B. building codes
   C. subdivision control ordinances
   D. restrictive covenants in deeds

5. The topography is relevant to the development of the subdivision site because it helps to determine all of the following EXCEPT:
   A. how and where the homes will be placed
   B. where utilities and pipelines will be placed
   C. how the overall completed subdivision will look
   D. zoning requirements

6. In New York, in cities with populations of under one million people, the term of membership of a planning board member is:
   A. one year
   B. two years
   C. dependent on the number of members on the planning board
   D. decided at will by the mayor or other governing official

7. In the development of a residential subdivision, which of the following is true?
   A. it is often best to have a timetable for completing the project
   B. a timetable for project completion would hurt the project financially
   C. the entire subdivision should always be entirely built before putting individual homes on the market
   D. the municipality, and not the developer, always decides the timetable for completion

8. All planning boards in New York must comply with the environmental review process according to the:

    A. Army Corps regulations

    B. State Planning Commission

    C. State Environmental Quality Review Act

    D. Real Property Law

9. To ensure itself that off-site improvements to the subdivision will be made upon completion of the total project, a municipality will generally require which of the following from the developer?

    A. his good word that all will be completed according to agreement

    B. a dedication of off-site property if the project is not completed on time

    C. a completion bond

    D. a power of attorney

10. Deed restrictions that run with the land are:

    A. nonconforming

    B. variances

    C. declarations

    D. covenants

11. Which of the following statements about restrictive covenants in subdivisions is FALSE? They:

    A. must be reasonable

    B. are automatically enforceable with or without action by other property owners

    C. must benefit all property owners

    D. maintain the quality and consistency of the subdivision

12. Restrictive covenants are:

    A. statements of record

    B. public land use controls

    C. variances

    D. private land use controls

13. The purpose of subdivision regulations is to:

    A. protect the taxpayer from cost overrides

    B. protect taxpayers in the municipality from an undue tax burden generated by the subdivision

    C. protect purchasers from buying property sight-unseen

    D. make sure that all structures in the subdivision look alike

14. Article 9-A of the Real Property Law addresses regulations for the sale of vacant subdivided lands sold:

    A. on the installment plan in New York only

    B. through any type of financing in New York only

    C. on the installment plan within and outside of New York

    D. through any type of financing within and outside of New York

15. In the cooperative form of ownership:

    A. ownership is evidenced by shares of stock in a corporation holding title to the building

    B. each owner owns a fee simple interest in the land on which the building is located

    C. all owners pay real property taxes on their individual units

    D. each owner holds a freehold interest in the land

ANSWER KEY

Putting It to Work

The New York attorney general's office must review the bylaws of a proposed home-owners' association to approve its formation. The question of access is not one for which they require every homeowners' association to be the same. Their only requirement is that permission of access to these records is included in the governing document of the association. You will have to look to the bylaws of your own association. Buyers should find out about the operation of their association, if one exists, before purchase.*

How Would You Respond?

1. The city of Buffalo is asking Ermanno to *dedicate* the acreage to the city. Ermanno might easily be able to effect this dedication by simply deeding the acreage to the city. The deed and the plat (map) of the subdivision indicating the dedicated land would be filed in the Erie County clerk's office.

2. It is possible that the subdivision has restrictions on the building of structures on the property. If structures are allowed, there may be limitations as to the size and setback requirements. To check the deed restrictions Isaac can ask the developer (if available); contact the homeowners' association, if there is one; check the plat of the subdivision that is filed with the county clerk; or ask his attorney to locate either the plat or an existing deed on the property. This should be done before Isaac signs a contract of sale.

Key Term Review

1. subdivision
2. zoning ordinance
3. wetlands
4. use variance; area variance
5. completion bond
6. outlots

Multiple Choice

1. A	6. C	11. B
2. B	7. A	12. D
3. A	8. C	13. B
4. D	9. C	14. C
5. D	10. D	15. A

References

1. The NYS Department of Health website: *http://www.doh.state.ny.us* and the NYS Department of Environmental Conservation website: *http://www.dec.state.ny.us* contain useful information.

2. *The NYS Conservationist*, an informative and aesthetically pleasing publication, is available by subscription ($12 per year). Call 1-800-678-6399 or access the NYSDEC website.

Chapter 7

KEY TERMS

abstract of title
accretion
acknowledgment
actual notice
adverse possession
assessment
bundle of rights
chain of title
closing statement
constructive notice
conveyance
credits
debits
dedication
delivery and acceptance
erosion
escheat
executor/executrix
full covenant and warranty deed

habendum clause
intestate
involuntary alienation
lien foreclosure sale
marketable title
proration
quitclaim deed
Real Estate Settlement Procedures Act (RESPA)
reconciliation
survey
tacking
testate
title
title closing
title insurance
title search
voluntary alienation

LEARNING OBJECTIVES   *Classroom hours: 3*

1. Explain the term *title* and list what is being conveyed.
2. Explain the bundle of rights.
3. Describe how title is conveyed during life.
4. Describe how title is conveyed after life.
5. List the various forms of voluntary alienation.
6. List the various forms of involuntary alienation.

Conveyance of Real Property and Title Closing

7. Explain the significance of the closing.

8. Describe the various functions of those individuals attending the closing.

9. Identify preclosing responsibilities.

10. List the numerous potential steps or transactions that take place during the course of a closing.

11. Explain the difference between a cooperative and a condominium closing.

SECTION 1   CONVEYANCE OF REAL PROPERTY

Conveyance of real property involves the transfer of title from one party to another and is the most important element of a real estate transaction. This part covers transfer of title during and after life as well as types of voluntary and involuntary title transfer.

TITLE AND THE BUNDLE OF RIGHTS

Title is *the ownership rights to real property.* Title to real property encompasses items such as the right to lease, grant easements, obtain mortgages, and grant options.

The terms *real estate* and *real property* are often used interchangeably, but they have slightly different meanings. *Real estate* is the land and all improvements made both "on" and "to" the land, whether found in nature or placed there by people. *Real property* is broader; it is real estate plus all legal rights, powers, and privileges inherent in ownership of real estate. These rights are many in number, varied in nature, have value, are usually salable, and affect the value of the underlying real estate (land).

To understand the subtle difference between real estate and real property, visualize real property as a bundle of sticks (Figures 7.1 and 7.2). The sticks in the bundle include the major sticks of land, improvements, fixtures, and fruits of soil, all of which are *tangible.* The bundle also includes *intangible* rights such as air rights, water rights, mineral rights, easements, leases, mortgages, licenses, profits, and so on. This visual concept, referred to as a *bundle of rights,* illustrates that real estate licensees sell more than land and houses. They also can sell any rights to, interests in, and title to real property that affect the value of the real property. Every bundle of sticks (one piece of real

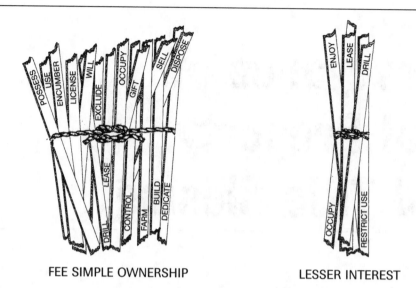

FIGURE 7.1
Real estate ownership as
a bundle of rights.

FEE SIMPLE OWNERSHIP   LESSER INTEREST

property) can be divided in numerous ways. The division referred to here is not that of acres or lots. Instead, it refers to the various rights that can be held in real property.

HOW IS TITLE CONVEYED?

The deed is the document used to convey title legally to real property. Transfer of title to real property is described in law as *alienation*. In a transfer, the property owner is alienated, or separated, from the title. Alienation may be voluntary or involuntary. Transfer may occur during an owner's life or upon the owner's death. Upon an owner's death, a number of determining factors, such as whether the owner died with or without a will, can affect the transfer of real property.

Voluntary transfer of property, either during or after the life of a titleholder, is known as **voluntary alienation.** Voluntary alienation after death is by will or descent. Voluntary alienation, and transfer of title during life, are accomplished by the delivery of a valid deed by the grantor to the grantee while both are alive.

Situations can arise that force a property owner to transfer title against her will. This is known as **involuntary alienation.** Involuntary alienation *may occur during or after the life of an owner. During the life of an owner, title to real property may be transferred by involuntary alienation as a result of a lien foreclosure sale, a creditor filing a petition in bankruptcy, condemnation under the power of eminent domain, and adverse possession. Involuntary alienation after death is escheat.* (See Table 7.1.)

DOCUMENTATION TO CONVEY REAL PROPERTY VOLUNTARILY

Voluntary transfer is the type of alienation that is of major importance to the real estate business. Real property can be conveyed voluntarily by sale, gift, dedication, or grant. *The deed is a form of* **conveyance** *and can be used for these purposes.* Essential elements of a valid deed include the following:

- The deed must be in writing. As required by the Statute of Frauds, every deed must be written. An oral conveyance is ineffective.
- The *grantor,* the one conveying the title, must be legally competent; the individual must have the capacity to contract. This requirement exists for all parties to a valid contract. The grantor must have reached the age of majority, which in New York is

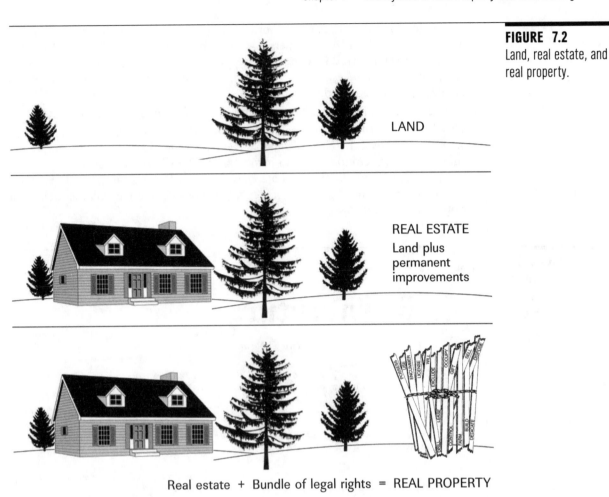

FIGURE 7.2
Land, real estate, and
real property.

LAND

REAL ESTATE
Land plus
permanent
improvements

Real estate + Bundle of legal rights = REAL PROPERTY

18, and must be mentally competent. Also, the grantor must be named with certainty; it must be possible to positively identify the grantor.

■ A *grantee,* the person receiving title, does not need legal capacity; a minor or a mentally incompetent person can receive and hold title to real property. He cannot, however, convey title on his own. To effect a conveyance of title held in the name of an incompetent person, a guardian's deed must be executed by the incompetent individual's guardian as grantor. The conveyance by the guardian may be

TITLE TRANSFER	VOLUNTARY ALIENATION	INVOLUNTARY ALIENATION	BEFORE DEATH	AFTER DEATH
Sale	✓		✓	
Gift	✓		✓	
Dedication	✓		✓	
Grant	✓		✓	
Will	✓			✓
Descent	✓			✓
Lien foreclosure sale		✓	✓	
Bankruptcy		✓	✓	
Eminent domain		✓	✓	
Adverse possession		✓	✓	
Escheat		✓		✓

TABLE 7.1
Summary of title
transfers.

accomplished only with court authority. The grantee must be alive at the time of delivery of the deed. A dead person cannot be a grantee. Within the deed, the grantor may be referred to as *party of the first part* and the grantee referred to as *party of the second part*. In New York, the addresses of the grantor(s) and grantee(s) must be included in the deed.

- The deed must contain an adequate formal *legal description* of the property.
- The *deed must provide evidence that* **consideration** *(something of value, such as money) is present.* In New York, the deed does not have to recite the actual amount of consideration (money) involved. The New York deed states, "One dollar and other good or valuable consideration." This is called *nominal* consideration. Figure 7.3 shows a recital of consideration in conjunction with words showing conveyance.

FIGURE 7.3

A warranty deed showing consideration and words of conveyance.

FORM S 301 – Warranty Deed with Lien Covenant

© NATIONAL LEGAL SUPPLY, INC.
126 Sheridan Ave., Albany, N.Y. 12210

This Indenture

March   *Made the*   28th   *day of*
Two Thousand and   four

Between

Carolyn Butler, residing at 20 Amortization Drive,
City and County of Albany, State of New York

part y   *of the first part, and*

Vanessa Dupree, residing at 5 West Avenue, City and County
of Albany, State of New York

part y   *of the second part,*

Witnesseth *that the part* y   *of the first part, in consideration of*
One and 00/100 ---------------------------- *Dollar*   ($ 1.00   )
lawful money of the United States, and after good and valuable consideration
paid by the party   *of the second part,* do es   *hereby grant and release unto the*
part y   *of the second part,*   her heirs   *and assigns forever, all*

BEGINNING on a stake in the northeast margin of Amortization Drive,
south corner of Lot No. 20 of the subdivision or a portion of the
property of Mortgage Heights Land Company, Inc., and running thence
North 6° 18' East 215.2 feet to a stake; thence North 8° 49' West
241.0 feet to a stake, common corner of Lot Nos. 20 and 19 of said
subdivision; thence with the dividing line between said Lot Nos.
19 and 20, South 87° 50' West 138.5 feet to a stake in the east
margin of a cul-de-sac; thence with the east margin of said
cul-de-sac in a southwesterly direction along a curve with the radius
of 50.0 feet, 61.2 feet to a stake in said margin; thence with the
east margin of a drive leading to Amortization Drive, South 5° 19'
West 132.8 feet to a stake in the point of intersection of said
margin of said drive with Amortization Drive; thence with the
northeast margin of said Amortization Drive, South 51° 17' East
84.7 feet to a stake in said margin; thence still with said margin
of said drive, South 42° 27' East 47.2 feet to a stake in said margin;
thence still said margin of said drive, South 29° 36' East 199.9
feet to the BEGINNING.

Intended to be the same premises as conveyed to the party of the
first part by Consuela Davis by deed dated April 3, 1992 recorded
in the office of the Albany County Clerk on April 10, 1992 in
liber # 240, page 300.

(continued)

FIGURE 7.3
Continued.

Together *with the appurtenances and all the estate and rights of the part* y
of the first part in and to said premises,

To have and to hold *the premises herein granted unto the party*   *of the
second part,*   her heirs   *and assigns forever.*

And *said* party of the first part

                                        covenant s   *as follows:*

First, *That the part* y   *of the second part shall quietly enjoy the said premises;*

Second, *That said* party of the first part

will forever **Warrant** *the title to said premises.*

Third, *That, in Compliance with Sec. 13 of the Lien Law, the grantor*   *will
receive the consideration for this conveyance and will hold the right to receive such
consideration as a trust fund to be applied first for the purpose of paying the cost of
the improvement and will apply the same first to the payment of the cost of the
improvement before using any part of the total of the same for any other purpose.*

In Witness Whereof, *the part* y   *of the first part ha* s   *hereunto set* her
hand   *and seal*   *the day and year first above written.*

IN PRESENCE OF   Carolyn Butler   L.S.

                                                                                  L.S.

                                                                                  L.S.

State of New York   } **ss.**   L.S.
County of Albany

                        On this 28   *day of* March
                        Two Thousand and Four
before me, the subscriber, personally appeared

    Carolyn Butler

to me personally known and known to me to be the same person   *described in and
who executed the within Instrument, and* s he   *acknowledged
to me that*   s he   *executed the same.*

                                    _____
Tax Map No. _____   Notary Public– State of
                                    New York, County of Albany
                                    My Commission Expires 3/30/05
Tax Billing Address _____

Deed

WARRANTY WITH LIEN COVENANT

_____ 19

TO

_____

Dated,

STATE OF NEW YORK

COUNTY OF _____   **SS.**

RECORDED ON THE

____ day of _____ A.D. 19 ____
at ____ o'clock ____ M.
in LIBER ____ of DEEDS
at PAGE ____ and examined

CLERK

The deed must contain *words of conveyance* demonstrating that it is the *grantor's intention to transfer the title to the named grantee.* These words of conveyance appear in the granting clause. In the case of warranty deeds, typical wording is "has given, granted, bargained, sold and conveyed" or "grants and releases."

In addition to the granting clause, the deed sometimes contains a **habendum clause,** *which describes the estate granted and always must be in agreement with the granting clause. This clause begins with the words, "to have and to hold."*

Proper execution of the deed means that it must be signed by each grantor conveying an interest in the property. Only the grantors execute the deed. The grantee does not sign unless he is assuming a mortgage.

For a deed to be eligible for recording, it must have an **acknowledgment.** *A grantor must appear before a public officer, such as a notary public, who is eligible to take an acknowledgment, and state that signing the deed was done voluntarily.* A deed is perfectly valid between grantor and grantee without an acknowledgment. Without the acknowledgment, however, the grantee cannot record the deed and thereby have protection to title against subsequent creditors or purchasers of the same property from the same grantor who records her deed.

To effect a transfer of title by deed, there must be **delivery and acceptance.** *The grantor must deliver a valid deed, and the grantee must accept the deed.*

Property Descriptions

For effective and accurate title transfers, title insurers, abstractors, and attorneys also rely on an *accurate legal description of the land.* The legal description for title transfer must be formal. Informal descriptions, such as street addresses or assessor/tax numbers, are acceptable on listings but not on documents for transferring or encumbering title.

Three acceptable types of property descriptions are discussed below: (a) metes and bounds, (b) description by reference, plat, or lot and block (plat of subdivision), and (c) monuments. The government, or rectangular, survey system of property description is used primarily in the western states, not in New York. It is used generally to transfer large tracts of real property whose shapes are rectangular or square.

Metes and Bounds

New York frequently uses the metes and bounds property description. In the *metes and bounds* description, metes are the distances from point to point and bounds are the directions from one point to another. An example of a metes and bounds description was shown in the deed in Figure 7.3.

A metes and bounds description results from a survey performed by a licensed land surveyor. One of the most important aspects of the metes and bounds description is the selection of the point of beginning. This point should be reasonably easy to locate and well established. After identifying the point of beginning, the surveyor then sights the direction to the next point, or monument. A metes and bounds description always ends at the point of beginning.

Reference, Plat, or Lot and Block (Plat of Subdivision)

A *description by reference, plat, or lot and block,* shown in Figure 7.4, is another valid legal description. Sometimes an attorney incorporates into the deed a description by reference in addition to a metes and bounds description. At other times the description by reference is the only description in the deed. A description by reference to a plat

ALL that certain plot, piece, or parcel of land, with the buildings and improvements thereon erected, situate, lying and being in the Town of East Greenbush, Rensselaer County, State of New York, designated as Lots 4 and 6 on a map entitled "Plat of David Minor 4—Lot Subdivision" Town of East Greenbush, Rensselaer County, New York, made by Evander Grady, Professional Land Surveyor, P.C., dated October 10, 2003, and revised June 10, 2004, and filed in the Rensselaer County Clerk's Office on October 1, 2004, in Drawer 2000 as Map No. 150.

FIGURE 7.4

A description by reference.

may refer to a plat (map) and lot number as part of a recorded subdivision. The former description states the *plat book* and page number in which the plat or map is recorded so that interested parties can look it up and determine the exact location and dimensions of the property. A subdivision plat map is illustrated in Figure 7.5. Property may also be described by reference to section, block, and lot on the tax map or by reference to a prior recorded instrument.

Monument

Description by monument is used in place of the metes and bounds method and is used by surveyors when describing multiple-acre tracts of land that might be quite expensive to survey. The description is drawn from permanent objects such as a stone wall, large trees, or boulders.

Sales

A typical real estate title transfer is simply the sale of a property from seller to purchaser, where the purchaser agrees to a specified price and terms of purchase. Common types of deeds used in New York for this purpose are the full covenant and warranty deed, the quitclaim deed, and the bargain and sale deed.

FIGURE 7.5

A subdivision plat map.

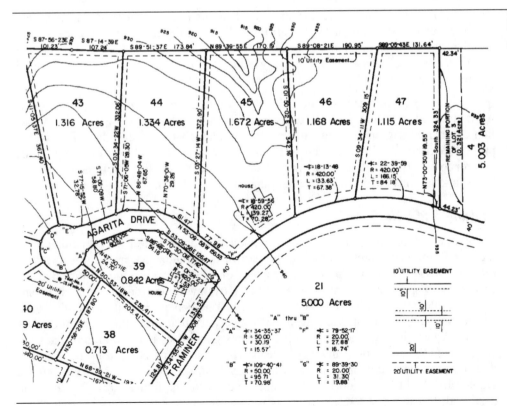

Full Covenant and Warranty Deed

The *full covenant and warranty deed* contains the strongest and broadest form of guarantee of title of any type of deed and therefore provides the greatest protection to the grantee. This deed usually contains six covenants. Exact wording of these covenants may vary:

1. *Covenant of seisin.* Typical wording of this covenant is, "Grantor covenants that he is seised of said premises in fee." This covenant, like the others in the full covenant and warranty deed, is a specific covenant and provides assurance to the grantee that the grantor holds the title that he specified in the deed that he is conveying to the grantee.

2. *Covenant of right to convey.* This covenant, which usually follows the covenant of seisin in the full covenant and warranty deed, typically reads, "and has the right to convey the same in fee simple." By this covenant the grantor provides *an assurance to the grantee that the grantor has legal capacity to convey the title and also has the title to convey.*

3. *Covenant against encumbrances.* This covenant typically states that "said premises are free from encumbrances (with the exceptions above stated, if any)." The grantor assures the grantee that there are *no encumbrances against the title except those set forth in the deed itself.*

4. *Covenant of quiet enjoyment.* This covenant typically reads, "the grantee, his or her heirs and assigns, shall quietly and peaceably have, hold, use, possess, and enjoy the premises." This covenant is an assurance by the grantor to the grantee that the grantee shall have quiet possession and enjoyment of the property being conveyed and will not be disturbed in its use and enjoyment because of a defect in the title.

5. *Covenant for further assurances.* This covenant typically reads, "that the grantor will execute such further assurances as may be reasonable or necessary to perfect the title in the grantee." Under this covenant, the grantor must perform any acts necessary to correct any defect in the title being conveyed and any errors or deficiencies in the deed itself.

6. *Covenant of warranty.* The warranty of title in the full covenant and warranty deed provides that the grantor "will warrant and defend the title to the grantee against the lawful claims of all persons whomsoever." This is the *best form of warranty for protecting the grantee* and contains no limitations as to possible claimants protected against.

Section 13 of the New York lien law, as stated in the lien covenant depicted on the warranty deed in Figure 7.3, addresses the priority of liens. In a warranty deed with lien covenant, the grantor is guaranteeing the grantee that no outstanding liens on the property exist and, if such a lien were to appear, then it would be the duty of the grantor to satisfy that lien. A warranty deed with lien covenant is commonly used in New York and this covenant appears in other forms of deeds.

Bargain and Sale Deed

A *bargain and sale deed* may be with or without covenants of warranty. In either case, there is an implied representation on the part of the grantor that he has a substantial title and possession of the property. Grantees of these deeds should require that the deed contain specific warranties such as the warranty against encumbrances. A bargain and sale deed simply conveys property from one person or entity to another for a consideration. The deed includes words of conveyance together with words of consideration. A bargain and sale deed with covenants guarantees that the grantor "has not encumbered the property in any way" except what is stated in the deed itself. The deed does not deal with any encumbrances that may have been on the property when the grantor acquired title and does not warrant the deed for the future. A bargain and sale deed with the above stated covenants is usually acceptable to lenders because those covenants cover the areas of warranty required by lenders to loan money. A bargain and sale deed *without* covenants offers weaker protection for the grantee and is not acceptable to lenders in New York for mortgage purposes. The bargain and sale deed with covenants is used extensively in the New York City area. Figure 7.6 shows a portion of a sample bargain and sale deed.

Quitclaim Deed

The *quitclaim deed* contains no warranties. It is simply a *deed of release.* It will release or convey to the grantee any interest, including title, that the grantor may have. The grantor, however, does not state in the deed that she has any title or interest in the property and certainly makes no warranties as to the quality of title. Execution of the quitclaim deed by the grantor prevents the grantor from asserting any claim against the title at any time in the future.

Quitclaim deeds may be used to clear a "cloud on a title," which occurs when someone has a possible claim against a title. As long as this possibility exists, the title is clouded and therefore not a good and marketable title. To remove the cloud and create a good and marketable title, the possible claimant executes a quitclaim deed as grantor to the true titleholder as grantee.

Gift

An owner of real property may wish to give title to another without *payment of any funds; therefore, there is no consideration.* A *deed of gift* of real property may be conveyed by either full covenant and warranty deed or quitclaim deed. If using the warranty deed, the grantee cannot enforce the warranties against the grantor; the grantor received no consideration for conveying the title to the grantee, as the conveyance was a gift. A warranty deed, bargain and sale deed, or a quitclaim deed each conveys the property provided the grantor has title to convey.

Dedication

In certain situations, an owner may wish to dedicate or voluntarily give a portion of property to a municipality. The property is given over for public use for parks, roadways, sidewalks, and so on. A developer in the plat of subdivision may set aside a portion of the land for these uses. This practice is called **dedication.** Dedication *occurs when land or an easement to land is given for use to the public by an owner.* A *statutory dedication* occurs when a property owner files a plat that marks or notes on the subdivision plat portions of the property that are dedicated, donated, or granted to the public. A *common-law dedication* involves an act or intention by the party who owns the land to allow use by the public. A common law dedication may be expressed where the appropriation is formally declared or implied by the owner's conduct or other circumstances. An example of an express dedication is when a developer deeds the municipality a parcel of his land to use for a park. This act is a *dedication by deed* and a cession or quitclaim deed may be used for this purpose. An example of an implied dedication is when the public is allowed to have access to a private road. A will may contain a dedication of land to the public domain.

INVOLUNTARY TRANSFER OF TITLE

Eminent Domain, Taking, and Condemnation

The federal government, New York and its agencies, counties, cities, towns, and boroughs have the power of eminent domain and can condemn, or "take" private property for public use (see discussion in Chapter 6, Section 2). Because the property owner cannot prevent the condemnation, the loss of title is involuntary.

FIGURE 7.6

A bargain and sale deed.

T 691

Standard N.Y.B.T.U. Form 8002: Bargain & sale deed,
with covenant against grantor's acts—Ind. or Corp.: single sheet

DATE CODE

JULIUS BLUMBERG, INC., LAW BLANK PUBLISHERS

CONSULT YOUR LAWYER BEFORE SIGNING THIS INSTRUMENT – THIS INSTRUMENT SHOULD BE USED BY LAWYERS ONLY

THIS INDENTURE, made the   day of   , nineteen hundred and

BETWEEN

party of the first part, and

party of the second part,

WITNESSETH, that the party of the first part, in consideration of Ten Dollars and other valuable consideration paid by the party of the second part, does hereby grant and release unto the party of the second part, the heirs or successors and assigns of the party of the second part forever,

ALL that certain plot, piece or parcel of land, with the buildings and improvements thereon erected, situate, lying and being in the

TOGETHER with all right, title and interest, if any, of the party of the first part in and to any streets and roads abutting the above described premises to the center lines thereof; TOGETHER with the appurtenances and all the estate and rights of the party of the first part in and to said premises; TO HAVE AND TO HOLD the premises herein granted unto the party of the second part, the heirs or successors and assigns of the party of the second part forever.

AND the party of the first part covenants that the party of the first part has not done or suffered anything whereby the said premises have been encumbered in any way whatever, except as aforesaid.
AND the party of the first part, in compliance with Section 13 of the Lien Law, covenants that the party of the first part will receive the consideration for this conveyance and will hold the right to receive such consideration as a trust fund to be applied first for the purpose of paying the cost of the improvement and will apply the same first to the payment of the cost of the improvement before using any part of the total of the same for any other purpose. The word "party" shall be construed as if it read "parties" whenever the sense of this indenture so requires.

IN WITNESS WHEREOF, the party of the first part has duly executed this deed the day and year first above written.

IN PRESENCE OF:

Foreclosure

A foreclosure on real property occurs when an owner does not pay a judgment or lien against a property. Example of real property liens may be taxes, mortgage, and mechanic's liens. If, after a prescribed period of time, a lien against a property is not satisfied, the property may be sold at public auction to satisfy the specific or general lien against it.

Results of a Foreclosure

If mortgages remain unpaid, the lender may foreclose. Once the foreclosure is completed, the referee, who is appointed by the court, will offer the property for sale to the highest bidder at an auction. The **lien foreclosure sale** is *without consent of the property owner who incurred the debt resulting in a lien* and is therefore an example of involuntary alienation. Foreclosure sales are ordered by a court or authorized by state law, and title is conveyed to a purchaser at the sale by *judicial deed*. A judicial deed is executed by the official whom the court or state authorizes to conduct the sale and transfer the title. Titles typically are conveyed by a sheriff's deed, a trustee's deed, a commissioner's deed, or a similar document, usually without the participation of the property owner who is losing the title as the result of foreclosure.

If the proceeds of the sale are insufficient to pay the mortgage debt, the lender or other creditor will have a deficiency judgment for the difference against the property owner. (See Chapter 9 that discusses tax lien foreclosures.)

Available Defenses

Real property owners are given the opportunity to satisfy liens against their property prior to foreclosure proceedings. This is known as the *right of redemption*. In a mortgage foreclosure, after default, and up to the time a foreclosure sale is held, the borrower has an equitable right to redeem the property by paying the principal amount of the debt, accrued interest, and lender's costs incurred in initiating the foreclosure. This right is terminated by the foreclosure sale.

Referee's Deed

A referee is an individual empowered by the court to exercise judicial power, such as in the sale and conveyance of real property if decided by court order. A referee may act for a sheriff at a sheriff's sale or act as directed by the court in a bankruptcy or similar case. A referee's deed is then used to convey the real property in question.

Bankruptcy Filing

If a corporate property owner files a reorganization of his debts under Chapter 11 of the United States Code, creditors are prevented from proceeding with any action to foreclose the lien or judgment against the property. If, however, the owner of real estate files a bankruptcy petition under Chapter 7 of the United States Code, title to the real estate is transferred by operation of bankruptcy law to the bankruptcy trustee. Any further conveyance requires the approval and execution of documents by the bankruptcy trustee.

Natural Processes

Property owners may lose or gain portions of their land to the forces of nature. Land and boundaries may be gained, lost, or changed through *accretion* and *avulsion*. The gradual building up of land in a watercourse over time by deposits of silt, sand, and gravel is called **accretion**. Avulsion is the loss of land when a sudden or violent change in a watercourse results in its washing away. Land may also be lost through **erosion,** which is *the wearing away of land by water, wind, or other processes of nature.*

Water Rights

Water rights in real property include percolating water rights, *riparian* water rights, and surface water rights. Percolating water is the water underground that is drawn by wells. Landowners have the inherent right in that land to draw out the percolating water for their own reasonable use. The right of natural drainage is at the heart of surface water rights. No landowner can substantially change the natural drainage of surface water (runoff) in such a manner as to damage neighboring landowners or their property. *Riparian rights belong to the owner of property bordering a flowing body of water. Littoral rights apply to property bordering a stationary body of water, such as a lake or a sea.* Generally, property adjacent to a river or a watercourse affords the landowner the right of access to and use of the water. Actual ownership of the water in a flowing watercourse, however, is complex and depends on numerous factors.

Partition   → *Apple For Not Married person*

The partition of property often occurs when there is more than one owner. A *tenancy in common* is characterized by two or more persons holding title to a property at the same time. The only required unity is that of possession. Each tenant in common holds an undivided interest in the entire property, rather than any specific portion of it. Tenants in common need not have equal interest in the property. For example, one co-tenant may hold one-half interest and two other co-tenants may hold one-quarter each. If no fractional interest of ownership is stated, the ownership interest is assumed to be equal.

A tenant in common may sell his share to anybody without destroying the tenancy relationship and without the permission of the other tenant(s) in common. To do this, a tenant in common may have to bring legal action to have the property *partitioned* so that each tenant may have a specific and divided portion of the property exclusively. If this can be done equitably with a piece of land, each would receive title to a separate tract according to his share of interest. If this cannot physically be done to the land, the court may order the sale of the property and distribute appropriate shares of the proceeds to the tenants in common.

Adverse Possession

A *person other than the owner can claim title to real property,* under **adverse possession,** if the other person makes use of the land under the following conditions:

1. The possession or occupation must be open and well known to others (notorious).
2. Possession of the property must be under color of title or claim of title; that is, the occupant of the property must have some reasonable basis to believe that he is entitled to possession of the property, typically in the form of a defective or quitclaim deed.
3. The possession must be without the permission of the true owner and must be exclusive (not shared with the true owner). Thus, co-owners cannot adversely possess against each other.
4. The possession must be continuous and uninterrupted for a period of 10 years in New York. In a claim of title, possession is based on some type of claim against the land rather than on a written document, as in the case of color of title. Individuals who inherit property and continue the adverse use legally fulfill the continuous use provision of adverse possession.

Moreover, an individual who takes title to the property through inheritance or otherwise, assumes the title subject to the claim of the former adverse possessor. This procedure is known as **tacking,** where the possession of the property is tacked from one person to another. *In order to preserve the adverse possession claim, the possession must be uninterrupted from one individual to another and the individuals must have some kind of interest such as an inheritance.*

The adverse possessor does not automatically acquire title to the property merely by meeting the four requirements. To perfect the claim and obtain title, the claimant must satisfy the court in an action to "quiet title" and fulfill the requirements of Article 15 of the Real Property Action and Proceedings Law, which is the adverse possession statute in New York. If the court is satisfied that statutory requirements have been met, it will award the title to the claimant under adverse possession.

PUTTING IT TO WORK

It is not uncommon for a licensee to market property that has a lien against it. Respond to the following question.* Check your response with the model in the Answer Key at the end of the chapter.

The question is: The property we want to buy has a lien against it. Must we negotiate with the lienholders to buy their part of the property?

CONVEYANCE AFTER DEATH
Voluntarily Through a Will

When someone dies and leaves a valid will or, in the absence of a valid will, has qualified heirs who have been located to receive title to the property, the applicable term is voluntary alienation. If *a person dies and leaves a valid will,* she is said to have died **testate.** An individual who makes a will is called a *testator* if a man and a *testatrix* if a woman. A *person appointed in a will to carry out provisions of the will is called an* **executor** *(man) or* **executrix** *(woman).* A gift of real property by will is a *devise,* and the recipient of the gift of real property by will is the *devisee.* A gift of personal property by will is a *bequest* or *legacy,* and the recipient of the gift of personal property is the *beneficiary* or *legatee.*

Although wills are relatively simple documents, certain absolute requirements must be met or the will may be declared invalid.

Requirements of a Valid Will

A formal or witnessed will is a will signed by the testator or testatrix in front of two witnesses, where he or she declares the writing to be the Last Will and Testament and confirms that it expresses his or her wishes for the disposition of property after death. The testator or testatrix requests the two witnesses to sign the will, acknowledging that the testator or testatrix performed certain required acts and has signed the will.

A holographic will is a will written entirely in the handwriting of the person whose signature it bears. A holographic will does not require witnesses to be valid.

Probate is the *judicial determination of a will's validity* by a court of competent jurisdiction and subsequent supervision over distribution of the estate. The title to any real property is conveyed by the executor of the will on behalf of the estate as per the wishes expressed in the will.

Rights of Those to Whom Real Property Is Devised via the Will

This issue is important because occasions arise when other individuals contest the property or other items devised or bequested in a will. A conveyance of title to real property can be held up until any contests are resolved. The court of jurisdiction in

---

*Source: James A. Ader, "Real Estate Spotlight." Copyright © The *Albany Times Union.* Reprinted by permission.

probate proceedings is the surrogate's court of the county in New York where the decedent had legal residence.

Descent—Intestate

If no valid will exists, a person is said to die **intestate.** The laws of intestacy that in New York fall under the Estates, Powers and Trusts Law, govern the conveyance of real property and the disbursement of other property of the deceased. When a person dies and leaves no valid will, the laws of intestacy determine the order of distribution of property to heirs. The typical order of descent is to spouses, children, parents, brothers and sisters, and then more remote lineal or lateral descendants. **Escheat** *occurs when no one is eligible to receive the property of the decedent as provided by statute. Thus in the absence of heirs, the state takes title to the property of the deceased.* Because the deceased has no control over the transfer of title to the state, an involuntary alienation exists. (This is the only form of involuntary alienation after death except by judicial intervention.)

The person appointed by a court to distribute the property of a person dying intestate, in accordance with provisions of the statute, is called an *administrator* or *administratrix.*

Conveyance via Will Versus a Deed

One of the main differences between the two forms of conveyances is that a person must be dead before a property can be conveyed through a will. When a property is conveyed through a will, New York imposes no real property transfer tax. Also, a deed to the new owner does not necessarily exist. If the new owner wishes to reconvey the property, an executor's deed can be drawn and used for transferring title.

How Is Real Property Conveyed Without a Will?

When a person dies intestate, parties who believe they have a claim to the estate of the deceased generally contact an attorney who petitions surrogate's court with the appropriate legal documents in support of the petitioners' claim. In many cases, opposing parties believe they have a claim to the same property. The surrogate's court judge reviews any supporting documents and makes a ruling based on New York laws. The courts can empower an administrator or administratrix to distribute the property of a person dying intestate.

IMPORTANT POINTS

1. Title means the ownership rights to real property. Title implies a variety of different rights of ownership known as the bundle of rights.
2. Title to real property can be conveyed during or after life and can be conveyed either voluntarily or involuntarily.
3. The deed is the only legal instrument used to convey title to real property during the life of the owner.
4. Examples of voluntary transfer of title during life are through sale, gift, dedication, or grant. Voluntary transfer after death is through a will or New York statutes, as interpreted by the court.
5. Involuntary transfer of title occurs during the life of a property owner as a result of a lien foreclosure, bankruptcy, condemnation, or adverse possession. A form of involuntary transfer after death is escheat.
6. Lien foreclosure sales on real property occur when outstanding debts against the property remain unpaid. Examples of unpaid liens against real property include mortgage liens, tax liens, and mechanic's liens.

7. The processes of nature may increase or decrease the amount of land property owners hold. These processes include accretion, avulsion, and erosion.

8. A legal action to partition real property occurs when property owners own property together as tenants in common and decide to divide their interest in the property.

9. Under adverse possession, a person other than the owner can claim title to real property, on the condition that the possession or occupation must be open and well known to others (notorious).

10. If a person dies intestate (without a will), the laws of intestacy govern the conveyance of real and personal property of the deceased. Probate is the judicial determination of the validity of a will by a court and subsequent supervision over distribution of the estate.

11. A valid will can be formal and witnessed, or in the handwriting of the deceased (holographic will).

12. A gift of real property by will is a devise, and the recipient of the gift of real property is the devisee.

13. Surrogate's court in the county where the deceased had lived is the court of jurisdiction over probate matters.

14. The New York statute that defines the law as to disbursement of property by the deceased is called the New York Estates, Powers and Trusts Law.

How Would You Respond?   SECTION REVIEW

Analyze the following situations and decide how the individuals should handle them based on what you have learned. Check your responses using the Answer Key at the end of the section.

1. Sam's great-grandmother, who recently passed away, left Sam a house on the beach on Carlton Island, by the St. Lawrence River. Sam, who is 17, would like to sell the house immediately to help pay for his college tuition. He has contacted his best friend's mother, Clara, who is a licensed broker, to sell the property for him. What must be done to effect the sale of the property?

_____

_____

_____

_____

2. Megan and Tim are leaving their home in Valatie, New York, where they have lived for 30 years. When they have their property surveyed, they realize that a 20-foot area of their landscaped back yard that had always been bordered by a fence actually is a part of their neighbor's back yard. The neighbor, Bill, notices the surveyor's stakes and realizes what has happened. Bill wants his 20 feet back and threatens to sue Megan and Tim if they don't remove their fence and give him back the land. If a court rules in Megan and Tim's favor, through what operation of law would they prevail? Explain your answer.

_____

_____

_____

_____

Reponse P. 258

KEY TERM REVIEW

Fill in the term that best completes the sentence and then check the Answer Key at the end of the chapter.

1. When an individual willingly transfers title to property, this is known as _____. Unwilling transfer, such as in a deed foreclosure sale, is known as _____.

2. The right of the government to take property for public use in the name of the health, safety, and welfare of its citizens is known as _____. This *taking* is called _____.

3. _____ is the judicial proceeding that determines the validity of the will and the distribution of the estate.

4. A person who dies and leaves a will is said to die _____; if the individual dies and leaves no will, the deceased has died _____.

5. A developer may set aside a portion of the land for common area, parks, sidewalks, and so on. This practice is called _____.

6. A(n) _____ may occur if a property owner defaults on paying the mortgage on his property and the lender institutes legal proceedings to be paid on the money due.

7. If certain conditions are met, a person who openly makes use of the land of another for a specified period of time can claim title to real property under the statutory right of _____.

MULTIPLE CHOICE

Circle the letter that best answers the question and then check the Answer Key at the end of the section.

1. A deed can convey title to which of the following?
   A. condominium
   B. cooperative
   C. yacht
   D. mobile home on leased property

2. Voluntary alienation CANNOT occur in which of the following circumstances?
   A. during life
   B. after life
   C. by a lien foreclosure on the property
   D. by the terms of a decedent's will

3. An example of involuntary alienation is:
   A. adverse possession
   B. deed of gift
   C. dedication
   D. public grant

4. Involuntary alienation CANNOT occur under which of the following conditions?
   A. death of the property owner
   B. through the natural processes of nature
   C. because of a condemnation proceeding against the property
   D. by provisions written into a decedent's will

5. Which of the following is FALSE regarding foreclosure proceedings?
   A. it is a form of involuntary alienation
   B. it may involve the nonpayment of a tax lien, mortgage lien, or mechanic's lien
   C. if a property has several liens against it, property tax liens take priority over all other liens
   D. it is a form of voluntary alienation

6. If tenants in common cannot physically divide their interest in real property:
   A. the property may not be partitioned
   B. the court may order the sale of the property with appropriate shares of the proceeds distributed to the tenants in common
   C. it is of no importance because partition proceedings may occur only upon the death of one of the tenants in common
   D. the property may be partitioned by rewriting the deed description

7. Beatrice's great-aunt Mabel recently passed away and left an unwitnessed holographic will devising her house to Beatrice. Which of the following is true?
   A. any type of unwitnessed will is invalid
   B. the devise of the house in the will is an example of voluntary alienation
   C. the devise of the house in the will is an example of involuntary alienation
   D. Beatrice is not legally entitled to the devise until a thorough search of closer relatives is made, despite the wishes expressed in the will

8. If a person dies and leaves no will but has left personal and/or real property, which of the following does NOT apply? The:
   A. estate will probably undergo probate proceedings in court
   B. real property will escheat to the state immediately upon the person's death
   C. court of jurisdiction is the surrogate's court in the county where the deceased legally lived until time of death
   D. court will appoint an administrator/administratrix to carry out the court orders regarding the estate

9. Which of the following is NOT a type of judicial deed?
   A. sheriff's deed
   B. tax deed
   C. full covenant and warranty deed
   D. executor's deed

10. A deed of gift:
    A. contains no consideration
    B. must be transferred after the death of the grantor
    C. can be used only to convey improved real property
    D. can convey real property only between parties who are related to one another

ANSWER KEY

Putting It to Work

No, you need not negotiate with those lienholders. Instead, you must be sure that the lienholders' claim is satisfied before the title is transferred to you. A lien is a claim against someone's property, which is used to secure a monetary charge or obligation. The lienholders have no rights to the title of the property (unless foreclosure proceedings have been completed) but do have the right to have their financial claim settled out of the sale proceeds. Title will turn up most liens, and satisfactions of liens can be shown as proof that the lien was removed.*

---

*Source: James A. Ader, "Real Estate Spotlight." Copyright © The *Albany Times Union*. Reprinted by permission.

How Would You Respond?

1. Sam is a minor, under the age of 18, so although his great-grandmother's devise was legal, he cannot legally convey the property. Sam's attorney would be able to draw a guardian's deed in which either one of Sam's parents would then be able to convey the property legally for Sam.

2. Megan and Tim may be awarded ownership rights to the 20 feet under adverse possession. The possession was open and notorious; they had reason to believe it was their property; it was held without permission of the true owner; it was also held continuously and without interruption for 30 years, well over the 10-year New York statutory requirement.

Key Term Review

1. voluntary alienation; involuntary alienation
2. eminent domain; condemnation
3. probate
4. testate; intestate
5. dedication
6. lien foreclosure sale
7. adverse possession

Multiple Choice

1. A
2. C
3. A
4. D
5. D
6. B
7. B
8. B
9. C
10. A

| SECTION 2 | TITLE CLOSING |

The title closing is the consummation of the real estate transaction. At the closing, the buyer receives a deed and the seller receives payment for the property. This part covers the various methods of closing, items required at closing, and proration calculations.

WHAT IS A TITLE CLOSING?

At a **title closing,** *the parties and other interested persons meet to review the closing documents, execute the closing documents, pay and receive money, and receive title to real estate.* Those present are buyers, sellers, their attorneys, real estate agents, lender representatives, and possibly title company representatives.

Functions of Those Who Attend the Closing

The buyer attends the closing to pay for and receive clear **title** to the property. *Title is evidence of the right to possess property.* The sellers are present to grant their property to the buyers and receive payment. The real estate agent may be there to collect the commission. The role of the lender's attorneys (if there is a loan) is to examine all documents and make sure that the property for which they are giving a mortgage loan has a clear title. Sometimes representatives of the title company are present to review the documents and, if satisfied, to deliver evidence that the title is insured and answer questions concerning the title. The buyers and sellers may also each be represented by an attorney who examines all documents and works in their respective best interests. Often buyers believe that bank attorneys represent them, but generally they represent the interests of the lending institution.

Title Closing Activities and Recording Acts

At the title closing, the seller is paid the balance of the purchase price, and existing liens against the property are satisfied. The purchaser normally pays the balance of the purchase price through a combination of funds obtained through an acquisition mortgage and the purchaser's own funds.

| The difference between a condominium and cooperative closing | You Should Know |

A condominium transaction is a fee simple transaction just as is the transfer involving any other residential or commercial property. The closing includes a title search, transfer of the property by a deed, and appropriate transfer fees and recordation.

The purchase of a cooperative is very different. Cooperatives are personalty, that is, personal property, and condominiums are real property. In a cooperative purchase, the purchaser becomes a stockholder in a corporation. Upon closing, the purchaser receives stock certificates in her name.

A cooperative purchaser does not obtain a deed but rather a proprietary lease issued by the cooperative corporation. Those present at a cooperative closing include the buyer, the seller, their respective attorneys, the managing agent of the cooperative, and sometimes a member of the board of directors. A financial investigation and search is conducted on the purchaser to discover any judgments or liens against her and also to assess her financial strength.

Before executing the closing documents and disbursing the closing funds, the parties should feel assured that the conditions and contingencies of the purchase agreement have been met. The title to the real estate is transferred upon execution and delivery of the deed. Title insurers, abstractors, and attorneys all rely on recorded documents concerning the property, although not all documents are required to be recorded.

PRELIMINARIES TO CLOSING

Before closing, the involved parties must be sure that all conditions and contingencies of the offer to purchase are met. Some typical items or documents of concern for the closing agent are described below, although not all are applicable at each closing.

Deed and Other Closing Documents

To ensure accurate completion of the closing documents to transfer title and secure debt, the legal names of the parties must be identified prior to closing. *The deed is the instrument used to convey title to real property.*

Survey

In some real estate transfers, the buyer or buyer's lender requires either a full staked survey or a mortgage survey to assure that no encroachments exist. A survey is the process by which a parcel of land is measured. The final **survey** document is *a type of blueprint showing measurements, boundaries, and area of a property.* The cost of the survey is typically the buyer's responsibility.

You Should Know | **Additional documents needed at closing**

Depending on the transaction, any of the following documents also may be involved in closing the real estate transaction:

- bill of sale of personal property
- broker's commission statement
- certificate of occupancy
- closing or settlement statement (HUD Form No. 1)
- deed
- disclosure statement
- estoppel certificate
- fire alarm or smoke detector affidavit
- flood insurance policy
- installment land contract (contract for deed)
- lease
- lien waivers
- mortgage
- mortgage guarantee insurance policy
- note
- option and exercise of option
- original homeowner's policy or hazard insurance policy with proof of payment
- real property transfer report
- sales contract
- seller's and purchaser's proof of identity (i.e., driver's license)
- transfer gains tax affidavit

Recording Acts

Recordation provides protection for the owner's title against all recorded titles. This protection is provided by the theory of **constructive notice:** *all of the world is bound by knowledge of the existence of the conveyance of title if evidence of the conveyance is recorded.* Constructive notice is contrasted with actual notice.

Actual notice *requires that the person in fact knows about the document.* Constructive notice, provided by recording, protects the title for the grantee. This protection is against everyone with a later claim, including other purchasers of the same property from the same grantor. In New York, a deed that is recorded takes precedence over any prior dated unrecorded deed. The recording of a document determines the priority of interests in the property unless a subsequent buyer has actual knowledge of a prior unrecorded transfer.

Title Registration—Torrens System

In addition to the regular method of recording titles, a special form of recording, called the *Torrens System,* is available in some states, but has not been used in New York, except in Suffolk County. Under this method, the titleholder applies to the court to register the property. The court orders the title to be examined by official title examiners, who report the examination results to the court. If the results are satisfactory, the court issues instructions to the Registrar of Titles to record the title and issues certificates of registration of title after giving adequate public notice so that anyone contesting the title has ample opportunity to appear.

The certificate of registration of title contains the type of title the applicant has and sets forth any encumbrances against the title. One certificate is issued to the Registrar of Titles and the other to the titleholder who applied to register the title. The certificate of registration provides conclusive evidence of the validity of the title, and it cannot be contested except in cases of fraud. Title to properties recorded under the Torrens System cannot be obtained by adverse possession.

Marketable Title

Before the title can be transferred, evidence of **marketable title** should be provided. *Marketable title is reasonably free and clear of encumbrances.* (Unmarketable title, however, burdened with many encumbrances, may be saleable.) The purpose of a title examination is to determine the quality of a title. The examination must be made by an attorney or an abstract or title company. Only an attorney can legally give an opinion as to the quality of a title. Marketable title is not perfect title and is not necessarily free of all liens. In the case of a sale with mortgage assumption, the buyer has bargained for and will accept the seller's title with the present mortgage as a lien on the title.

Evidence of marketable title through **title search** *can be provided through a commercially hired search or a personal search of any records that might affect real estate titles.* The records examined through a title search include public records of deeds, mortgages, long-term leases, options, installment land contracts, easements, platted subdivisions, judgments, deaths, marriages, bankruptcy filings, mechanic's liens, zoning ordinances, real property taxes, miscellaneous assessments for improvements, mortgage releases, and lis pendens notices.

Chain of Title

The search of the records will establish a **chain of title** *that must be unbroken for the title to be good and, therefore, marketable.* It involves *tracing the successive conveyances of title* starting with the current deed and going back an appropriate time (typically 40 to 60 years), often researching back to the original title (the last instance of government ownership). The two most-often-used forms of commercial title evidence are abstract of title with attorney opinion and policy of title insurance.

Any missing links in the chain of title create uncertainty as to the path and proof of ownership. If these missing links can be bridged by obtaining proper title-clearing documents, the transaction may occur safely. If not, the sale should not close. Table 7.2 illustrates a broken chain of title.

Abstract of Title with Attorney Opinion

An **abstract of title** is *a condensed history of the title,* setting forth a summary of all links in the chain of title plus any other relevant matters of public record. The abstract contains a legal description of the property and summarizes every related instrument in chronological order. An *abstract continuation* is an update of an abstract of title that sets forth memoranda of new transfers of title. When the abstract is completed, an attorney must examine it to ensure that the chain of title is unbroken and clear. The attorney then gives a written *certificate of title opinion as to what person or entity owns the real estate and the quality of title and exceptions, if any, to clear title.*

Because title insurance binders typically are issued several days or weeks before closing, an update of the abstract or title binder should be obtained prior to closing with an effective date for the date of closing. In addition, the seller may be required to sign a vendor's affidavit, a *document stating that the seller has done nothing since the original title evidence to affect title adversely.*

If title defects are found, the seller is responsible for the cost of curing or removing the defects. Until marketable title is available, closing will not likely be completed.

Title Insurance

A **title insurance** *policy is a contract of insurance that insures the policy owner against financial loss if title to real estate is not good.* Title insurance policies are issued by the same companies that prepare abstracts of title. The company issuing the insurance policy examines the same public records as abstractors do to determine if it will risk insuring the title.

The most common title insurance policy requires the title insurance company to compensate the insured for financial loss up to the face amount of the policy resulting from a title defect (plus cost of litigation or challenge). The policy protects the insured only against title defects existing at the time of transfer of title. If a claim is filed and the title insurance company pays the claim, it may have the right to bring legal action against the grantor for breach of warranties in the deed. The title insurance policy is issued only upon an acceptable abstract or title opinion. A title that is acceptable to the title insurance company is called *insurable title.* The premium for a title insurance policy is a one-time premium, paid at the time the policy is placed in effect.

At or before closing, the title company will require proof of identity for both seller and purchaser such as a driver's license or other official document.

TABLE 7.2	GRANTORS	GRANTEES	DATE OF CONVEYANCE
A broken chain of title. Can you identify the "break" in the chain of title?	Peggy and Frank Delay	Pat and Henry Bird	August 10, 1975
	Pat and Henry Bird	Nancy and John Day	November 15, 1980
	Nancy and John Day	Mary Jo and Bob Ray	April 19, 1995
	George and Tonya Good	Sue and Mike Smith	September 20, 1998
	Sue and Mike Smith	Lois and Art Giles	February 14, 2004

Now that you have read about title insurance, respond to the following question.*   **PUTTING IT TO WORK**
Check your response with the model in the Answer Key.

> *As the date to close on my new home is drawing near, my lender has told me that I need a copy of my insurance policy on the new home to show them satisfactory proof of insurance. My insurance agent says the policy will take some time to issue, but he gave me a binder. The lender says the binder won't do. Must our closing be delayed?*

Location of Closings

The closing typically is held at the office of the lender, attorney for one of the parties, the title company, or at the local county clerk's office.

Structural Inspection

Usually the buyer wants to inspect the premises prior to closing. The inspection most often is performed by a professional inspection company. This is called a *whole-house inspection.* The inspection report indicates any mechanical, electrical, plumbing, design, or construction defects. The buyer pays for this inspection.

Pest Inspection

Often the buyer or the buyer's lender requires proof that no wood-destroying pest, infestation, or damage is present. The purchaser usually pays for this inspection. If infestation exists, the seller has to pay for treating and repairing any damage.

Perc, Soil, and Water-Flow Tests

If the property is connected to a private water supply (discussed in Chapter 6, Part I), the seller is required to provide the results of what is commonly called a *perc test,* an inspection of percolation of the septic system to ensure proper functioning and drainage and to show compliance with local and state health codes. In addition, if the property is for commercial purposes, the seller is responsible for a soil test to ensure the absence of hazardous waste or environmental problems that might not comply with EPA standards. Water-flow tests also may be conducted if the property is not connected to a municipal system.

Role of Licensee Prior to Closing

A broker or salesperson's role prior to closing involves inspecting the property with the purchaser. In addition to the professional inspection, the buyer usually arranges for a final *walk-through* the day of closing, or immediately prior to closing. This is to make sure that no damage has been done since the offer to purchase and that no fixtures have been removed. They are usually accompanied by either the buyer agent (if there is one), or the agent of the seller.

Commission Payment

At the closing, the broker commission is generally paid. Sometimes, all or part of the deposit money is credited toward the broker commission. The broker or agent handling the transaction generally furnishes a commission statement to the participating attorneys. See Figure 7.7. Generally, only one check is cut for the commission, and then the broker who receives the money puts it through his escrow account and disburses portions of the monies due to subagents and cooperating agents.

Homeowner's Insurance

Prior to closing, the buyer customarily provides homeowner's fire and hazard insurance on the real estate being purchased. If the buyer is borrowing money for the purchase, the lender/mortgagee is listed on the policy as an additional insured. The cost of this insurance is the buyer's, and it must be purchased to protect the lender's interest.

Standardized Homeowner's Insurance Policies

Homeowners' policies are identified as HO-1, HO-2, HO-3, HO-4, HO-5, and HO-6. An HO-4 is a tenant's policy, and HO-6 is designed for condominiums and cooperatives. HO-1, HO-2, HO-3, and HO-5 cover owners of single-family dwellings.

Every hazard insurance policy must contain a description of the insured property. The street address usually is adequate, although some insurers require a full legal description.

Specific provisions of the various homeowner's policies are:

- HO-1: *Named perils.* Perils covered are damage or loss from fire at the premises.
- HO-2: *Broad form.* Coverage extends to loss or damage as a result of fire, vandalism, malicious mischief, wind, hail, aircraft, riot, explosion, and smoke.
- HO-3: An *all-risk policy.* It covers loss for damage resulting from anything not specifically excluded from coverage.
- HO-4: *Tenant's broad form.* Its coverage is similar to HO-2's except it applies only to the tenant's contents at the premises.
- HO-5: A *special all-risk policy* offering automatic replacement cost for contents and dwelling.
- HO-6: *Policy similar to a tenant's broad form* but applies to condominium owners and cooperative owners covering their contents. (The structure would be insured by the association.)

The HO-2, -3, -4, -5, and -6 are all package policies that include medical payments coverage and personal liability coverage for negligence.

Real Estate Settlement Procedures Act (RESPA)

Congress enacted the **Real Estate Settlement Procedures Act (RESPA)** in 1974 (revised 1996). The act applies only to residential federally financed or refinanced properties, not to commercial properties or owner-financed loans. It *regulates lending activities of lending institutions in making mortgage loans for housing.* RESPA has the following purposes:

1. to effect specific changes in the settlement process resulting in more effective advance disclosure of settlement costs to homebuyers and sellers
2. to protect borrowers from unnecessarily expensive settlement charges resulting from abusive practices
3. to ensure that borrowers are provided with information on a timely basis about the nature and cost of the settlement process
4. to eliminate referral fees or kickbacks, which increase the cost of settlement services, lenders are permitted to charge only for services actually provided to homebuyers and sellers, and only for the amount that the service actually costs the lender

RESPA Requirements

The act requires:

1. *Good faith estimate.* Within three working days of receiving a completed loan application, the lender is required to provide the borrower with a good faith estimate of the costs likely to be incurred at settlement. Figure 7.7 shows a sample form.

2. *Buyer's guide to settlement costs.* At the time of loan application, the lender must provide the borrower with a booklet entitled *Homebuyer's Guide to Settlement Costs,* which contains the following information:

   a. clear and concise language describing and explaining the nature and purpose of each settlement cost

   b. an explanation and sample of the standard real estate settlement forms required by the act

   c. a description and explanation of the nature and purpose of escrow/impound accounts

   d. an explanation of choices available to borrowers in selecting persons or organizations to provide necessary settlement charges

   e. examples and explanations of unfair practices and unreasonable or unnecessary settlement charges to be avoided

3. *HUD Form No. 1.* When making residential mortgage loans, lenders are required to use a standard settlement form designed to itemize clearly all charges to be paid by borrower and by seller as part of the final settlement. The form (see Figure 7.8), which has become known as HUD Form No. 1, or the HUD 1, must be made available for the borrower's inspection at or before final settlement. This form is not required for assumptions and nonresidential loans.

The difference between the Real Estate Settlement Procedures Act (RESPA) and the Truth-in-Lending Act (TILA)*

You Should Know

	RESPA	TILA
When enacted	1974 (revised 1996)	1969 (revised 1980)
Purpose	Act covers residential federally financed properties and focuses mainly on the *settlement* process (loan and closing fees) of lending institutions in making mortgage loans	Requires *disclosure* by lenders of annual percentage rate, finance charges, amount financed, and total monies to be paid toward mortgage; implemented through Regulation Z, which covers all residential mortgages.
Importance to real estate practitioners	RESPA allows real estate agents to assist homebuyers in selecting and prequalifying for a mortgage	Regulation Z addresses advertisement of credit terms which may not be violated by real estate agents
How to remember the difference	RESPA deals mainly with the cost of the mortgage and calls for a closing statement, HUD Form No. 1, to be made available to purchasers prior to closing	TILA deals mainly with obtaining the mortgage and disclosure of the terms of the loan.

*TILA is discussed more fully in Chapter 3.

FIGURE 7.7   A broker commission agreement.

Real Estate Brokerage
777 Easy Street • New York, New York 10007

Broker Commission Agreement

Address of Subject Property: _____

This Agreement is entered into on _____, 20____ between ABC Real Estate

Brokerage, and _____ Seller(s).

It is agreed by the parties herein that the, _____ , selling broker and _____

_____ , listing broker obtained a ready, willing, and able individual (s) to purchase

the above-named premises according to the terms of the listing agreement between the broker and seller(s) dated

_____ .

It is further agreed that the commission due to the broker(s) is _____ divided as follows:

listing broker $_____ ; selling broker $_____ .

The commission is due to the broker from the proceeds of the sale or by certified check from the seller no later than

the day of title closing and when the deed is delivered to the purchaser(s) pursuant to a contract of sale dated

_____ .

If the deed is not delivered pursuant to the said contract of sale, for any reason, except for the deliberate default of

the seller, no commission is due to the broker(s). Any dispute arising from this Agreement shall be decided by

arbitration according to rules set forth by the American Arbitration Association.

ABC Real Estate Brokerage   Seller

By: _____   _____

                                                                              _____
                                                                              Seller

The brokerage firm generally forwards this agreement to the attorneys for the parties before closing.

A recent federal rule affecting portions of RESPA now allows brokers to assist home buyers in selecting and prequalifying for a mortgage and to charge a reasonable fee for these services. Any fees must be disclosed and agreed to in writing by the buyer. Brokers can even begin the loan application process. In providing these services, brokers typically use computerized loan origination (CLO) systems that list the various loan programs for lending institutions.

Settlement Costs and Helpful Information

FIGURE 7.8
HUD-1 Settlement
Statement Costs Form.

Buying Your Home

Settlement Costs and Helpful Information

June 1997 Disclaimer

HUD-1 Settlement Statement Costs

A. U.S. DEPARTMENT OF HOUSING AND URBAN DEVELOPMENT SETTLEMENT STATEMENT

B. TYPE OF LOAN			6. File Number	7. Loan Number
	1. o FHA	2. o FmHA		
3. o CONV. UNINS.	4. o VA	5. o CONV. INS.	8. Mortgage Insurance Case Number	

C. NOTE: *This form is furnished to give you a statement of actual settlement costs. Amounts paid to and by the settlement agent are shown. Items marked "(p.o.c.)" were paid outside the closing; they are shown here for informational purposes and are not included in the totals.*

D. NAME AND ADDRESS OF BORROWER:	E. NAME AND ADDRESS OF SELLER:	F. NAME AND ADDRESS OF LENDER:
G. PROPERTY LOCATION:	H. SETTLEMENT AGENT: NAME, AND ADDRESS	
	PLACE OF SETTLEMENT:	I. SETTLEMENT DATE:

J. SUMMARY OF BORROWER'S TRANSACTION		K. SUMMARY OF SELLER'S TRANSACTION	
100. GROSS AMOUNT DUE FROM BORROWER:		**400. GROSS AMOUNT DUE TO SELLER:**	
101. Contract sales price		401. Contract sales price	
102. Personal property		402. Personal property	
103. Settlement charges to borrower(line 1400)		403.	
104.		404.	
105.		405.	
Adjustments for items paid by seller in advance		*Adjustments for items paid by seller in advance*	
106. City/town taxes to		406. City/town taxes to	
107. County taxes to		407. County taxes to	
108. Assessments to		408. Assessments to	
109.		409.	
110.		410.	
111.		411.	
112.		412.	
120. GROSS AMOUNT DUE FROM BORROWER		**420. GROSS AMOUNT DUE TO SELLER**	
200. AMOUNTS PAID BY OR IN BEHALF OF BORROWER:		**500. REDUCTIONS IN AMOUNT DUE TO SELLER:**	
201. Deposit of earnest money		501. Excess deposit (see instructions)	
202. Principal amount of new loan(s)		502. Settlement charges to seller (line 1400)	
203. Existing loan(s) taken subject to		503. Existing loan(s) taken subject to	
204.		504. Payoff of first mortgage loan	
205.		505. Payoff of second mortgage loan	
206.		506.	
207.		507.	
208.		508.	
209.		509.	
Adjustments for items unpaid by seller		*Adjustments for items unpaid by seller*	
210. City/town taxes to		510. City/town taxes to	
211. County taxes to		511. County taxes to	
212. Assessments to		512. Assessments to	
213.		513.	
214.		514.	
215.		515.	
216.		516.	
217.		517.	
218.		518.	
219.		519.	
220. TOTAL PAID BY/FOR BORROWER		**520. TOTAL REDUCTION AMOUNT DUE SELLER**	
300. CASH AT SETTLEMENT FROM/TO BORROWER		**600. CASH AT SETTLEMENT TO/FROM SELLER**	
301. Gross amount due from borrower(line 120)		601. Gross amount due to seller (line 420)	
302. Less amounts paid by/for borrower(line 220)		602. Less reductions in amount due seller (line 520)	
303. CASH (_ FROM) (_ TO) BORROWER		**603. CASH (o TO) (o FROM) SELLER**	

(continued)

FIGURE 7.8
Continued.

L. SETTLEMENT CHARGES		
700. **TOTAL SALES/BROKER'S COMMISSION based on price $ @ %=**	PAID FROM BORROWER'S FUNDS AT SETTLEMENT	PAID FROM SELLER'S FUNDS AT SETTLEMENT
Division of Commission (line 700) as follows:		
701. $ to		
702. $ to		
703. Commission paid at Settlement		
704.		
800. **ITEMS PAYABLE IN CONNECTION WITH LOAN**		
801. Loan Origination Fee %		
802. Loan Discount %		
803. Appraisal Fee to		
804. Credit Report to		
805. Lender's Inspection Fee		
806. Mortgage Insurance Application Fee to		
807. Assumption Fee		
808.		
809.		
810.		
811.		
900. **ITEMS REQUIRED BY LENDER TO BE PAID IN ADVANCE**		
901. Interest from to @$ /day		
902. Mortgage Insurance Premium for months to		
903. Hazard Insurance Premium for years to		
904. years to		
905.		
1000. **RESERVES DEPOSITED WITH LENDER**		
1001. Hazard Insurance months @ $ per month		
1002. Mortgage insurance months @ $ per month		
1003. City property taxes months @ $ per month		
1004. County property taxes months @ $ per month		
1005. Annual assessments months @ $ per month		
1006. months @ $ per month		
1007. months @ $ per month		
1008. Aggregate Adjustment months @ $ per month		
1100. **TITLE CHARGES**		
1101. Settlement or closing fee to		
1102. Abstract or title search to		
1103. Title examination to		
1104. Title insurance binder to		
1105. Document preparation to		
1106. Notary fees to		
1107. Attorney's fees to		
(includes above items numbers;)		
1108. Title Insurance to		
(includes above items numbers;)		
1109. Lender's coverage $		
1110. Owner's coverage $		
1111.		
1112.		
1113.		
1200. **GOVERNMENT RECORDING AND TRANSFER CHARGES**		
1201. Recording fees: Deed $; Mortgage $; Releases $		
1202. City/county tax/stamps: Deed $; Mortgage $		
1203. State tax/stamps: Deed $; Mortgage $		
1204.		
1205.		
1300. **ADDITIONAL SETTLEMENT CHARGES**		
1301. Survey to		
1302. Pest inspection to		
1303.		
1304.		
1305.		
1400. **TOTAL SETTLEMENT CHARGES** *(enter on lines 103, Section J and 502, Section K)*		

U.S. Department of Housing and Urban Development
451 7th Street, S.W., Washington, DC 20410
Telephone: (202) 708-1112 TTY: (202) 708-1455

Source: U.S. Department of Housing and Urban Development

Closing Statement

A **closing statement** is a historical document prepared in advance of the closing, and it records what must happen at closing. The statement *sets forth the distribution of monies involved in the transaction*—who will pay a specific amount for each expense and who will receive that amount. A closing statement is prepared by the representatives of the buyer and seller. This could be an attorney, a broker, a lender, a title company, or an escrow agent.

CLOSING COSTS AND ADJUSTMENTS— PREPARATION OF CLOSING STATEMENTS

The first step in preparing the closing statement is to list all items in the transaction. Some of these items involve both the buyer and the seller; other items are of concern only to the buyer, and others are of concern only to the seller. Items included fall into one of two categories: debits or credits. *Items that are owed* are **debits.** Those to be paid by the buyer are called *buyer debits,* and those owed and to be paid by the seller are *seller debits. Monies received* are **credits.** Items representing money to be received by the buyer are called buyer credits. Items representing money to be received by the seller are called *seller credits.*

In the RESPA settlement statement form shown in Figure 7.8, the areas for debits and credits are marked. Although real estate agents usually do not have to complete that form, they should be sufficiently familiar with the format to explain the entries to buyer and seller. For purposes of the examples and practice problems at the end of this chapter, a simplified, basic buyer and seller statement is used.

Some typical debits and credits of buyer and seller are listed in Table 7.3.

Handling Closing Funds

At the closing, the monies the buyer owes are received by the closing agent. The monies owed to the seller are to be disbursed by the closing agent. All other expenses of the sale are paid from the closing proceeds and disbursed by the closing agent. The closing agent basically begins with an empty account, receives money, disburses money, and ends with an empty account.

The money available for disbursement must equal the amount to be disbursed. The closing agent should perform a **reconciliation,** or *a check of the money available and money owed prior to closing.*

Seller's Closing Costs

Title Transfer Taxes (Revenue Stamps)

New York imposes a tax on the conveyance of title to real property, called *real property transfer tax.* New York requires the seller to pay this tax. The amount of tax is based on the consideration the seller receives in selling the property.

The amount of transfer tax charged on the purchase price in New York is $4.00 per $1,000 of the purchase price. New York subtracts the amount of any mortgage being assumed, which is called *old money,* and therefore charges the tax only on the *new money* brought into the transaction above the amount of the assumed loan. In New York, an examination of tax stamps provides only an indication of the new money, an amount below the sales price if a mortgage is assumed. The real estate licensee needs to learn the rate and application of this tax as well as the collection procedures.

New York City real property transfer tax. In addition to the New York State transfer tax for the sale of residential property, New York City imposes an additional

TABLE 7.3 Typical buyer and seller debits and credits.	**BUYER DEBITS**	**SELLER DEBITS**
	Appraisal fee	Balance due to seller at closing (this is a balancing entry only, as seller receives this money)
	Bank attorney and personal attorney fee	
	Broker's fee if a buyer broker agreement exists and the buyer is paying the commission	Broker's fee
		Contract for deed balance
	Credit report	Deed preparation
	Discount points	Delinquent real property taxes
	Hazard or homeowner's insurance	Existing mortgage and accrued interest
	Loan origination fee	Mortgage interest on assumed loan
	Mortgage assumption fee	Mortgage satisfaction fee
	Mortgagee's title insurance	Pest inspection and treatment
	Mortgage insurance	Purchase money mortgage taken back from buyer
	Overpaid (by seller) taxes	
	Prepaid mortgage interest	Soil test (perc test)
	Preparation of loan documents (mortgage and note)	Survey (some counties)
		Transfer tax on transfer of real estate
	Purchase price	Unpaid real property taxes prorated
	Real estate property taxes paid in advance by seller	Unpaid utility bills
	Recording of deed	
	Recording of mortgage documents	
	Survey	

	BUYER CREDITS	**SELLER CREDITS**
	Assumed mortgage and accrued interest on mortgage	Escrow balance on assumed loan
	Balance due from buyer at closing (this is a balancing entry only, as buyer owes this money)	Overpaid insurance premium
		Overpaid real property taxes
		Purchase price
	Contract for deed balance	Sale of personal property
	Earnest money deposit	
	New mortgage money	
	Purchase money mortgage	
	Unpaid real property taxes prorated	

transfer tax of 1 percent of the selling price. If the selling price is over $500,000, the New York City transfer tax is 1.425 percent. For other types of property, the rate is 1.425 percent of the selling price, and if the consideration is more than $500,000, the transfer tax is 2.625 percent.

Broker Commission

In most transfers, the broker commission is a percentage of the selling price of the property. Even if a buyer broker has been involved, he is paid a percentage of the selling broker commission through a cooperative arrangement. The commission, therefore, is generally the responsibility of the seller. Other commission or fee arrangements are possible. (See Chapter 2 for a discussion of broker commissions and fees.)

Attorney Fees

The sellers generally have an attorney represent their interests in the closing and must pay her fee. Attorney fees vary a great deal depending on the scope of the transaction and the amount of work involved. If the buyers are giving the sellers a purchase money mortgage, the buyer generally pays the seller's attorney to prepare the mortgage.

Cost of Recording Documents to Clear Title

Depending on what is required for a particular property, the seller, through his attorney, may have to file a satisfaction of mortgage and/or satisfaction of other judgments. In New York, these documents are usually recorded in the office of the county clerk and the fees for recordation vary according to county. In New York City, these documents are generally recorded in the Register's office.

Existing Liens

Generally, a property cannot transfer unless all existing liens against it have been discharged (paid). The cost of discharging the liens depends on the dollar amount of the lien. For example, if a roofer has not been paid for a $2,000 roof job and has filed a mechanic's lien, then this money together with interest must be paid before the title is transferred.

Condo and Co-op Fees

Cooperatives may have a *flip tax* imposed upon transfer. This is a revenue-producing tax for the cooperative and is paid by the seller. The tax amount is sometimes based on a fixed percentage of the purchase price of the apartment. The flip tax is *not* paid to any government agency but rather to the cooperative corporation.

According to regulations set forth in the Uniform Commercial Code, the buyer of a cooperative must also pay a $25 UCC-1 filing fee and the seller must pay a $25 UCC-3 filing fee.

Condominiums charge special fees called **assessments** payable to the homeowner's or condominium association for maintenance of the common elements. These items may include but are not limited to trash pickup, landscaping, and snow removal. Any outstanding seller obligations must be brought up to date by the seller, and adjustments by both purchaser and seller must be made for services already paid for by the seller but to be used by the purchaser.

Purchaser's Closing Costs

If the buyer is borrowing money from an institutional lender, a mortgagee's title insurance policy also is needed. The buyer usually bears the cost of this title insurance policy. Evidence of marketable title should be provided for transfer. Proof that a marketable title exists can be provided by the update of an abstract of title or by issuance of a title insurance binder. In New York, depending on the county, the buyer or seller may have to pay for the title search. As mentioned earlier, the buyer pays for the structural inspection.

Appraisal and Credit Report Fees

The purchaser is generally charged by the lender for both the appraisal of the property and the credit investigation. This is part of the application process.

Mortgage Recording Tax

In New York, the mortgage recording tax is three-fourths of a percent of the mortgage amount in certain counties. In counties where there is a public transportation system, the amount is 1 percent. In this case, in the sale of one- to six-family residential properties, typically three-fourths of the mortgage recording tax is paid by the purchaser and one-fourth paid by the lender. If there is no outside lender involved in the transaction, then the purchaser must pay the entire mortgage recording tax.

Attorney Fees

The purchasers are responsible for both the payment of the lender's attorney as well as the fees for their own attorney.

Lender Fees

Lender costs and fees may include any or all of the following:

- an escrow account for property taxes (in certain cases, interest must be paid on escrow accounts)
- discount points on a mortgage, if applicable (these are negotiable between seller and buyer at contract)
- a credit check of the prospective purchaser, usually paid before closing (this may be paid for by the purchaser)
- loan origination fees (these are charged by the lender and usually paid for by the buyer)
- a survey of the property (this is negotiable between seller and buyer)

Other Recording Fees

The New York State Office of Real Property Services requires the recordation of a sworn statement of consideration paid signed by both buyer and seller, called a *real property transfer report*. The form is filed with the county clerk and costs $25 to file. A copy of this form is forwarded by the county to the town, city, or village assessors. The filing fee is typically paid by the buyer.

Also required by the New York State Department of Taxation and Finance is the filing of a *transfer gains tax affidavit,* signed and sworn to by the buyer and seller. This form indicates the purchase price of the property. A capital gain is the amount of profit realized by the seller. The form is filed with the county clerk with a $6.00 filing fee typically paid by the seller.

ADJUSTMENTS—PRORATIONS AT CLOSING

The obligation for paying various costs is determined by local custom, New York law, and the type of financing incurred, if any.

Items Adjusted and Prorated

A closing usually involves the *division of expenses and income between buyer and seller.* The items that are usually adjusted and divided include: real estate taxes, fuel, survey, water and sewer charges, rent, security deposits, interest, homeowners' association dues, and insurance. (In many cases, purchasers wish to buy their own insurance.)

This division, called **proration,** *is necessary to ensure fair apportioning of expenses between buyer and seller.* Prorated items are either accrued or prepaid. *Accrued expenses* are costs the seller owes at the day of closing that the buyer will eventually pay. The seller therefore gives the buyer a credit for these items at closing. Typical accrued items to be prorated are: unpaid real estate taxes, rent collected by the seller from the tenant, and interest on the seller's mortgage assumed by the buyer.

Prepaid expenses are costs the seller pays in advance and are not fully used up. At closing, these items are shown as a credit to the seller and a debit to the buyer. Typical prepaid items to be prorated are: prepaid taxes and insurance premiums, rent paid by the seller under lease assigned to the buyer, utilities billed and paid in advance, and heating oil.

Arithmetic of Proration—Rules and Methods

1. Either the buyer or the seller may pay the costs on the day of closing. The calculations presented in this book reflect the seller as the one who will pay the costs on the day of closing. Local practices in certain areas of New York provide that, beginning with the day of closing, all expenses are borne by the purchaser and all income goes to the purchaser.

2. Mortgage interest, taxes, insurance, and like expenses are sometimes prorated according to 360 days per year with 30 for each day. However, lenders, attorneys, and closing agents may also base the prorations on a 365-day year, with the exact amount of days in each month. Mortgage interest generally is paid in arrears, so the parties must understand that the mortgage payment for August will include interest not for August but instead for the month of July. In many areas, taxes are paid in advance. This means the seller will receive reimbursement at closing for the remaining days of the tax year following closing.

3. Accrued real estate taxes that are assessed but not yet due are generally prorated to the day of closing, with the seller having a debit and the buyer a credit for the amount owed as of the day of closing.

4. In prorating rent, the seller usually receives the rent for the day of closing.

5. Personal property taxes may be prorated between buyer and seller, or they may be paid entirely by the seller. In the calculations here, personal property taxes are not prorated.

6. Basically, the computation involves determining a yearly, monthly, or daily charge for the item being prorated. This charge then is multiplied by the number of months or days of the year for which reimbursement or payment is to be made.

Work through the following two exercises in Figure 7.9 and follow how the prorated costs were determined. For a further explanation of closing computations, work through the sample problems and solutions in Chapter 10.

PUTTING IT TO WORK

For practice in working with closing settlement statements, complete Practice Problem 1, New First Mortgage, and 2, Mortgage Assumption, on the following pages. Check your responses with the Answer Key at the end of the chapter.

PUTTING IT TO WORK

FIGURE 7.9

Exercises for determining prorated costs.

Reponse

P 280

EXERCISE 1

Accrued Items: The closing of a property is to be held on October 14. The real estate taxes of $895 for the year have not been paid and are due at the end of the year. What entry will appear on the seller's and buyer's closing statements?

January 1	October 14	December 31

Accrued period of taxes owed by seller at closing:

$ 895 ÷ 12 = $74.58 taxes per month

$74.58 ÷ 30 = $2.49 taxes per day

$ 74.58	plus	2.49		
× 9 full months		× 14 days		
$ 671.22	plus	$34.86	=	$706.08

Thus, the accrued taxes owed by seller at closing are $706.08. This will be a seller debit and a buyer credit at closing.

EXERCISE 2

Prepaid Items: The closing of a sale of a rental is to be held March 10. The seller has received the rent for March in the amount of $500. What entry will appear on the seller's and buyer's closing statements?

March 1	March 10	March 30

$500 ÷ 30 = $16.67 rent per day

$ 16.67

× 20 days not used

$333.40 unused rent

Prepaid period not earned by seller prior to closing and assigned to buyer at closing.

Thus, the prepaid rent credited to the buyer at closing is $333.40. This will be a seller debit and a buyer credit at closing.

Practice Problem 1: New First Mortgage

Use the following information to prepare statements on the provided worksheet. The solution to this practice problem is found at the end of the chapter.

Settlement date: July 18, 20xx

Purchase price: $140,000

Earnest money deposit: $10,000

New insurance premium: $547

New mortgage: 90% of the purchase price; 4 points to be paid by buyer

Annual real property taxes: $1,700 unpaid

Additional property assessment: $1,540 unpaid to be prorated

Seller's existing mortgage: $83,760

Private mortgage insurance: 1% of the loan

Deed preparation: $60

Credit report: $50

Survey: $225

Termite clearance: $650

Loan service charge: 1% of the loan

Mortgagee's title insurance: $385

Recording fees: $12

Broker's commission: 6% of the sales price

Owner's title insurance: $785 (seller pays)

PRACTICE PROBLEM 1 WORKSHEET

Settlement Date:	Summary of Buyer's Transaction		Summary of Seller's Transaction	
	Debit	Credit	Debit	Credit
Totals				

Practice Problem 2: Mortgage Assumption

Use the following information to prepare statements on the provided worksheet. The solution to this practice problem is found at the end of the chapter.

Settlement date: July 10, 20xx

Purchase price: $69,500

Earnest money deposit: $4,500

New insurance policy premium: $278

Annual real property taxes: $900 unpaid

Assumed mortgage balance: $42,000

Mortgage interest rate for July: 9% paid in advance

Mortgage assumption fee: $50

Purchase money second mortgage from buyer to seller: $9,000

Seller's escrow account for taxes and insurance (to be purchased by buyer at closing): $735

Deed preparation: $25

Second mortgage preparation: $30

Recording of deed and second mortgage: $8

Title insurance binder: $320 (seller pays)

Lighting allowance given to buyer by seller for fixtures being removed by seller: $180

Broker's commission: 7 1/2%

PRACTICE PROBLEM 2 WORKSHEET

Settlement Date:	Summary of Buyer's Transaction		Summary of Seller's Transaction	
	Debit	Credit	Debit	Credit
Totals				

IMPORTANT POINTS

1. At a title closing, all interested parties meet to review closing documents and transfer title to real estate. The deed is the document that conveys the title from seller to purchaser (grantor to grantee).

2. Recordation of a deed in the county clerk's office of the county where the property is situated provides protection for the owner's title against subsequent claimants. In New York City, deeds are filed in the Registrar's office.

3. The purpose of a title examination is to determine the quality of a title. The examination must be made by an attorney or a title company. Only an attorney can legally give an opinion as to the quality of the title.

4. A title insurance policy protects the insured against financial loss caused by a title defect.

5. Various types of tests and inspections of the property take place prior to closing. A real estate agent may take a prospective purchaser to a walk-through of the property immediately prior to closing.

6. The Real Estate Settlement Procedures Act (RESPA) regulates activities of lending institutions that take mortgages for housing.

7. The closing statement sets forth the distribution of monies involved in the transaction. Seller closing costs may include New York title transfer taxes, broker commission, attorney fees, costs of document preparation, and the satisfaction of existing liens, if any. Purchaser costs may include a title search and title policy, survey fees, the mortgage recording tax, lender fees, recording fees, and possibly broker commission.

8. In a condominium purchase, the buyer is conveyed title through a deed. In a cooperative purchase, the buyer receives a proprietary lease and shares of stock.

9. Prorations are the division of expenses and income between the purchaser and seller at closing.

SECTION REVIEW

KEY TERM REVIEW

Rep. P 279

Fill in the term that best completes the sentence and then check the Answer Key at the end of the section.

1. A type of notice that requires a person to know about and see a document is _____.

2. A type of blueprint showing measurements, boundaries, and area of a property is called a(n) _____.

3. A federal law that regulates lending institutions in making mortgage loans for housing is the _____.

4. At a closing, monies owed by a buyer or seller are called _____; monies that are to be received by a buyer or seller are called _____.

5. The closing agent should perform a _____, or a check of money available and owed, prior to closing.

6. The tracing of successive conveyances of title starting with the current deed and going back an appropriate amount of time establishes a(n) _____.

MULTIPLE CHOICE

Circle the letter that best answers the question and then check the Answer Key at the end of the section.

1. The title to real estate is transferred upon:
   A. issuance of the title policy
   B. execution and delivery of the deed
   C. obtaining a purchase money mortgage
   D. payment of the broker commission

2. Recordation of a deed provides which kind of notice?
   A. actual
   B. constructive
   C. final
   D. obligatory

3. A condominium purchase is different from a cooperative purchase because:
   A. a board of directors must consent to a condominium purchase, but not a cooperative purchase
   B. a condominium purchase requires the purchaser to obtain financing; cooperatives do not
   C. a cooperative purchase involves the transfer of shares of stock in a corporation, and a condominium purchaser receives a deed
   D. attorneys need not be present at condominium closings, but must always be present at cooperative closings

4. A condensed history of a title is known as a(n):
   A. abstract of title
   B. insurable title
   C. attorney's opinion as to title
   D. marketable title

5. According to RESPA, the lender is required to provide the borrower, within three working days of closing, which of the following?
   A. HUD Form No. 1
   B. Policy HO-1
   C. a final closing statement
   D. good faith estimate of likely closing costs

6. A seller debit at a closing is which of the following?
   A. overpaid taxes
   B. purchase price
   C. credit report
   D. purchase money mortgage taken back from buyer

7. A buyer debit at a closing is which of the following?
   A. earnest money deposit
   B. purchase money mortgage
   C. purchase price
   D. new mortgage money

8. The New York real property transfer tax is typically paid by the:
   A. seller
   B. purchaser
   C. lender
   D. It is not required to be paid in purchases under $500,000

9. The proper entry on the closing statements for a transaction closed on April 15 in which the buyer is purchasing the seller's insurance policy (for which the seller paid an annual premium of $156 on November 30) would be a:
   A. credit to buyer of $58.50
   B. debit to buyer of $58.50
   C. credit to seller of $97.50
   D. debit to seller of $97.50

10. A buyer purchased a rental property and closed the transaction on July 20. The tenant had paid rent for the month of July in the amount of $540 on July 1. The rent should be shown as a:
    A. debit to buyer of $180
    B. debit to seller of $180
    C. credit to buyer of $360
    D. debit to seller of $360

ANSWER KEY

Putting It to Work

Your attorney and insurance agent should try to convince your lender (a mortgage banker) to accept the insurance binder as proof of insurance. Their argument on your behalf can be based on Chapter 445 of the Laws of 1990. Chapter 445 requires lenders to accept a binder as proof of insurance. A binder, issued by the insurance agent, establishes a temporary obligation for the insurer to provide coverage pending issuance of the policy. This legislation was passed to avoid the unnecessary inconvenience and possible costly delays that often result for both the buyer and the seller when a lender requires the policy itself.

Key Term Review

1. actual notice
2. survey
3. Real Estate Settlement Procedures Act
4. debits; credits
5. reconciliation
6. chain of title

Multiple Choice

1. B
2. B
3. C
4. A
5. D
6. D
7. C
8. A
9. C
10. B

Solution to Practice Problem 1: New First Mortgage

Settlement Date: July 18, 20XX	Summary of Buyer's Transaction		Summary of Seller's Transaction	
	Debit	Credit	Debit	Credit
Purchase Price	$140,000.00	$	$	$140,000.00
Earnest Money		10,000.00		
Insurance Premium	547.00			
First Mortgage		126,000.00		
Discount Points	5,040.00			
Real Property Taxes		935.00	935.00	
Assessment		847.00	847.00	
Existing Mortgage			83,760.00	
P.M.I.	1,260.00			
Deed Preparation			60.00	
Credit Report	50.00			
Survey	225.00			
Termite Clearance			650.00	
Loan Origination	1,260.00			
Owner's Title Insurance			785.00	
Mortgagee's Title Insurance	385.00			
Recording Fees	12.00			
Commission Due			8,400.00	
Balance Due from Buyer		10,997.00		
Proceeds Due Seller			44,563.00	
Totals	$148,779.00	$148,779.00	$140,000.00	$140,000.00

Solution to Practice Problem 2: Mortgage Assumption

Settlement Date: July 10, 20XX	Summary of Buyer's Transaction		Summary of Seller's Transaction	
	Debit	Credit	Debit	Credit
Purchase Price	$69,500.00	$	$	$69,500.00
Earnest Money Deposit		4,500.00		
Insurance Premium	278.00			
Prorated Real Property Taxes		475.00	475.00	
Assumed Mortgage		42,000.00	42,000.00	
Mortgage Interest	210.00			210.00
Mortgage Assumption Fee	50.00			
Purchase Money Second Mtg.		9,000.00	9,000.00	
Seller's Escrow Account	735.00			735.00
Cost of Preparing the Deed			25.00	
Cost of Preparing Second Mtg.	30.00			
Cost of Recordings	8.00			
Cost of Title Insurance Binder			320.00	
Light Fixture Allowance		180.00	180.00	
Commission Due			5,212.50	
Balance Due from Buyer		14,656.00		
Proceeds Due Seller			13,232.50	
Totals	$70,811.00	$70,811.00	$70,445.00	$70,445.00

Chapter 8

KEY TERMS

actual eviction

anchor stores

capital expense

capital reserve budget

constructive eviction

corrective maintenance

eviction

fixed expense

lessee

lessor

management agreement

management proposal

operating budget

planned unit development (PUD)

preventive maintenance

property management

property management report

property manager

resident manager

risk management

stabilized budget

tenancy for years

variable expense

LEARNING OBJECTIVES   *Classroom hours: 5*

1. Describe the functions of property management.
2. Discuss the requirements and the elements of a management agreement.
3. List the required skills that an individual must have in order to be a property manager.
4. Discuss the differences in the management of various types of properties.
5. Review the different relationships a property manager must have with the owners, tenants, and employees.
6. Review how an individual can become a property manager.

Real Estate Property Management

A **property manager** *manages properties for owners as an agent.* As an agent, the property manager is a *fiduciary* and therefore owes all the obligations imposed by the law of agency to each owner–principal. This chapter centers on the function, purpose, and skills of property managers, the management agreement, and property management as a career.

TYPES OF LEASEHOLD ESTATES

Property managers deal with different types of rental agreements. It is important to understand the types of lease arrangements. Leasehold (rental) estates exist for less than a lifetime and are created by a contract providing rights and duties to both parties. Leasehold estates provide possession, but not title, to the tenant. Figure 8.1 delineates the differences between freehold and leasehold estates and Figure 8.2 describes various types of leasehold estates.

Tenancy for Years

The key feature of the *estate, tenancy, or leasehold for years is that it exists for only a fixed period of time,* which can be as short as one day. At the end of that time, the estate (rental agreement) terminates automatically without any need for either party to give notice to the other. If any uncertainty exists about the duration of the lease, it is not an estate for years. New York law requires that if this estate lasts for more than one year, the lease must be in writing.

In New York City, a lease establishing a tenancy for a term, but not specifically stating the duration of the term, continues until the first day of October after the possession. If a lease does not have to be recorded and the property is sold with a tenant in possession at the time of sale, the purchaser will have to honor the lease. At the death of either the landlord or the tenant, heirs of the deceased party are bound by the terms of the lease. The lease is considered to be inheritable because the obligations and rights of the lease pass to the estate or heirs of the decedent.

FIGURE 8.1
Freehold and nonfreehold (leasehold) rights in real property.

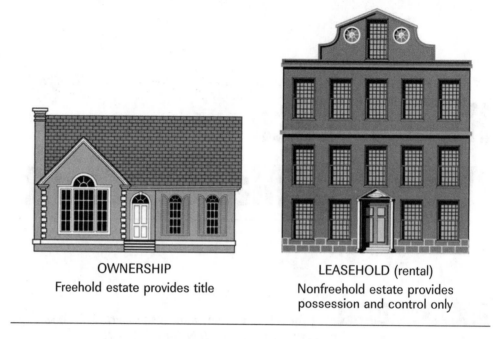

OWNERSHIP
Freehold estate provides title

LEASEHOLD (rental)
Nonfreehold estate provides possession and control only

Periodic Estate (Estate from Year to Year)

The *estate from year to year* is commonly known as a *periodic tenancy.* The period length can be a week, a month, or any other negotiated time period. *The key feature of a periodic lease is that it automatically renews itself for another period at the end of each period unless one party gives notice to the other* at a prescribed time prior to the end of the lease. For example, if the required period is one year and the parties enter the last 30 days of the lease without notifying the other of any change, a new lease is automatically created for another time period equal to the previous one, with the same terms.

In New York, any lease stating that it will be renewed automatically unless the tenants give notice to the owner that they are leaving is not enforceable unless the

FIGURE 8.2
Leasehold (nonfreehold) estates.

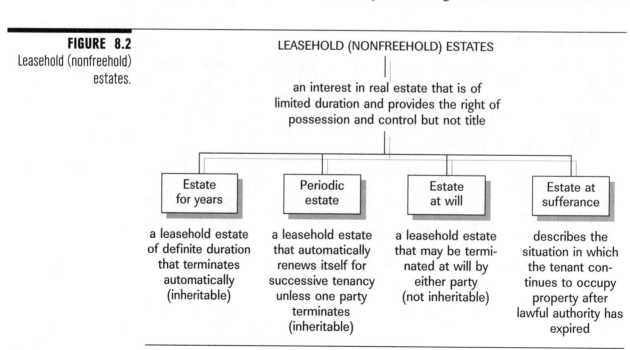

LEASEHOLD (NONFREEHOLD) ESTATES

an interest in real estate that is of limited duration and provides the right of possession and control but not title

Estate for years	Periodic estate	Estate at will	Estate at sufferance
a leasehold estate of definite duration that terminates automatically (inheritable)	a leasehold estate that automatically renews itself for successive tenancy unless one party terminates (inheritable)	a leasehold estate that may be terminated at will by either party (not inheritable)	describes the situation in which the tenant continues to occupy property after lawful authority has expired

landlord gives the tenant written notice at least 15 to 30 days before the renewal reminding the tenant about this provision in the lease. In New York City, a monthly periodic tenancy may be terminated by notice from the owner at least 30 days from the expiration of the term; in areas outside of New York City, the owner's notice must come one month before the expiration of the term. In areas outside of New York City, no notice of termination is required if a definite term for the lease has been set (unless there is a lease clause requiring notice, as explained above). At the death of either the owner or tenant, heirs of the deceased party are bound by terms of the lease, including giving notice if the heirs wish to terminate.

Estate at Will   —> Month to Month

In an *estate at will,* duration of the term is completely unknown at the time the estate is created, because either party *may terminate the lease simply by giving notice to the other party.* In this sense, the estate is open-ended. New York statute requires that notice of termination be given at least 30 days before the date upon which termination is to be effective. The notice must be served personally to the tenant or conspicuously posted on the premises. This type of leasehold is typical in a casual arrangement, such as a family setting in which a parent rents to an adult child. At the death of either the owner or the tenant, this leasehold terminates, unlike the estate for years or the periodic lease.

Estate at Sufferance   —> month to moth) possesion ofter the ltote Finish

An *estate at sufferance* describes *a tenant who is originally in lawful possession of another's property but refuses to leave after his right to possession terminates.* During this period, the occupier is called a *tenant at sufferance.* The term is used to distinguish between the tenant at sufferance who originally was in lawful possession of the property and someone who was on the property illegally from the beginning (trespasser). A tenant who does not leave upon expiration of the lease is termed a holdover tenant. According to real property law in New York, a landlord may remove a holdover tenant by initiating an eviction proceeding. In addition, if an owner accepts rent after the expiration of the term, a month-to-month tenancy is created.

BASICS OF PROPERTY MANAGEMENT

Expert management is generally needed for income property to be a profitable investment. Competent **property management** provides a *comprehensive, orderly program on a continuing basis, analyzing all investment aspects of a property to ensure a financially successful project.* The need for property management has increased in recent years because of the trend toward absentee ownership by investors and larger and more complicated properties that need management. As a result, many brokerage firms have separate staffs of property managers.

What Are the Functions of a Property Manager?

By applying real estate knowledge and expertise, a property manager strives to produce the greatest net return possible for the owner. She is responsible for protecting the owner's investments. The property manager acts as the owner's agent in managing and, typically, renting, leasing, and perhaps selling the property. In New York, if the property manager represents one owner in the performance of these functions, the manager does not require a real estate license. However, if the manager performs these functions for more than one owner, a real estate license is required. Individuals working for a company that provides services for more than one owner are required to hold at least a salesperson license. In addition, individuals who collect rents for more than one owner must be licensed.

A **resident manager** *lives on the premises and is a salaried employee of the owner.* In New York, this person is not required to have a real estate license if employed directly by the owner.

What Types of Properties Are Managed?

Many different types of properties can benefit from real estate management services, including (a) residential property management, which includes apartments, condominiums, townhouses, planned unit developments (PUDs), cooperatives, single-family homes, and vacation property (Figure 8.3); (b) retail or commercial property management, which includes offices, small retail stores, office condominiums, and large shopping malls; (c) industrial property management, including industrial parks and industrial warehouses; and (d) farm property management.

THE MANAGEMENT PROPOSAL AND AGREEMENT

The Management Proposal

One of the first duties of a prospective property manager is to submit to the property owner a **management proposal,** *setting forth the commitments of the manager* if employed by the owner. A typical proposal includes:

1. A complete description of the land and all improvements.
2. A listing of all maintenance required and existing curable obsolescence.
3. Information regarding maintenance records and accounting procedures that the manager will use.
4. Schedules of property inspections and owner conferences.
5. A thorough operating budget, capital improvement budget, and stabilized budget (discussed later).
6. A document citing the management fee.

The Management Agreement

The owner-manager relationship is formalized by a **management agreement.** This contract creates *an agency relationship in which the owner is the principal and the property manager is the agent* for the purposes specified in the agreement. This relationship imposes the same serious fiduciary duty as demanded of listing agents toward their principals in the sale of real property.

Provisions of a typical property management agreement include:

1. Inception date and names of the parties.
2. Property location and description of the premises.
3. Duration of the management agreement.

FIGURE 8.3 Types of residential housing requiring a property manager.	Apartments Condominiums, townhouses, and cooperatives Apartment buildings Mobile home parks Housing for the elderly Planned unit developments (PUDs) Government-assisted housing Some single-family housing and vacation homes

4. Scope of agent's management authority.

5. Manager's covenants that include the method and scope of the manager's reporting system.

6. Manager's fee. The property manager's fee is negotiated between the property owner and the manager. It commonly consists of a base fee and/or a percentage of the rents actually collected.

7. Accounting responsibilities that include handling of security deposits, rents, and expenses. The property manager collects all monies owed to the owner. Any monies collected are held in a trust account for the benefit of the owner. The only monies taken from the account are to be used for expenses in the property management budget. In handling security deposits, the property manager must comply with local laws for collecting and retaining security deposits. New York has specific requirements regarding handling rents, deposits, and expenses. The broker must be scrupulous in maintaining records and avoid commingling and conversion. Security and rental deposits must be kept in a separate account and not commingled with the operating account.

8. Insurance and risk management (discussed below).

9. Owner's covenants, which include owner's responsibility and objectives.

10. Method of termination by either party.

11. Execution of the agreement by owner–principal and agent–manager.

The authority of the manager comes from and must be explicitly set out in the management agreement. The *management agreement creates a general agency* (see Chapter 2) *and as such the manager owes undivided loyalty to the owner–principal.* The management agreement should be in writing. This agreement creates the responsibility for the property manager to realize the highest return on the property while obeying the owner's instructions and the laws of agency and owner-tenant relations.

Insurable Interest

To be eligible for insurance coverage, the insured must have a legitimate financial interest, known as an *insurable interest,* in the property. In the absence of an insurable interest, the policy is void. Examples of people having an insurable interest are buyer and seller in a contract of sale or land contract, the owner, owner of a partial interest, trustee, receiver, life tenant, mortgagor, and mortgagee. The mortgagee usually requires, in the mortgage, that the borrower maintain adequate hazard insurance coverage on the property to satisfy the debt in the case of destruction.

Insurance and Risk Management

The modern term **risk management** *embodies the concern for controlling and limiting risk in property ownership.* Ownership and use of real estate necessarily entails risk, but one must consider the questions: How is the risk to be controlled? or can some risk be transferred by means of an insurance policy? The manager should find a competent insurance agent familiar with the type of property to be insured. Written specifications by the manager to competing agents will ensure comparable quotes for consideration. The insured property is the property being managed. The person or entity insured is the person or entity who owns the property.

Property and Liability Insurance

Most insurance policies in the United States are based on the New York standard fire policy form as revised in 1943. This fire insurance policy indemnifies the insured against loss caused by fire. If the insured wishes to have protection against losses from other hazards, an extended coverage endorsement to the fire policy must be obtained.

Public *liability insurance* covers the risks an owner assumes when the public enters the premises. Payments under this coverage are to pay claims for medical expenses incurred by the person injured on the property as a result of the owner's negligence.

OBLIGATIONS TO THE OWNER

Although renting space, collecting rents, and paying expenses are basic functions of property managers, their functions and responsibilities extend beyond these activities.

Goals for the Property

Both the owner–principal and manager–agent should share the same goal for the property. In essence, the overall goal and the property manager's responsibilities are: (a) to produce the highest possible net operating income from the property, and (b) to maintain and increase the value of the principal's investment. The property manager fulfills these goals by performing the specific activities as outlined in the management proposal.

Maintenance Criteria

One of the most important functions of a property manager is to supervise physical property maintenance. Efficient maintenance requires accurate analysis of the building's needs, coupled with consideration of the costs of any work done. Increasingly in the property management field, to save payroll and other employee costs, individuals and companies are subcontracted by the property manager to perform maintenance duties. Maintenance can include preventive maintenance, corrective maintenance, and construction.

Preventive maintenance requires a *periodic check of mechanical equipment on the premises to minimize excessive wear and tear from improper operation.* An example is changing the air filters in air conditioners and furnaces.

Corrective maintenance is *the work performed to fix a nonfunctioning item* that a tenant has reported. An example is repairing a leaky faucet.

Construction occurs if money has been budgeted for remodeling, interior redecorating, or new capital improvements. Renovation often increases a property's desirability and can lead to increased income. Figure 8.4 illustrates a sample annual maintenance schedule.

Future of the Project

The property manager must continuously evaluate and make appropriate changes in the rental schedule, budgeting, and marketing of the property to ensure the best return on the investment, not only for the present but for the future.

Rental Schedule

When setting rental rates, the property manager must be aware of the owner's goals for return on investment as well as the current market for rental rates. He must consider current rates in like properties. The manager must also consider supply and demand for rental properties and present vacancy rates. Adjustments in rental rates should be made only after a survey and analysis of the factors affecting rental. If a building is 98 percent occupied, the property manager may feel justified in raising the rents, since the laws of supply and demand are working in favor of the property.

FIGURE 8.4

Sample annual maintenance schedule.

ANNUAL MAINTENANCE SCHEDULE

Name and address of property _____

Proposed maintenance schedule as of (date) _____

Type of maintenance	Minimum frequency	Approximate time of year	Special instructions
full inspection repair exterior grounds	2x/yr.	spring/late fall	
full inspection repair roof/gutter	2x/yr.	spring/fall	inspect after severe weather
repair parking lot	2x/yr.	spring/fall	check regularly for potholes
exterior painting/touchup	2x/yr.		
window cleaning	quarterly	seasonal, when possible	check for cracks, breakage, seepage
check all fire safety equipment	1x/mo.		replace if necessary
test and check, clean HVAC system	1x/mo.		
interior painting/touchup			as needed
interior/exterior lighting	1x/wk.		check after severe weather
cleaning exterior common areas	1x/wk.		
snow removal, other hazard removal	daily		as needed
other special maintenance needs			

Note: The property manager must continuously evaluate and modify the maintenance schedule to meet the needs of the property.

Budget

An operating budget, capital reserve budget, and stabilized budget should be established before organizing and structuring rental of a project. The budgets are always subject to adjustments, particularly in the first months of a project. The **operating budget** is *an annual budget and includes only the items of income and expense expected for week-to-week operation.* The **capital reserve budget,** also called a replacement reserve, is *a projected budget over the economic life of the improvements of the property* for variable expenses such as repairs, decorating, remodeling, and capital improvements. A **variable expense** is *one that is not specifically predictable and is subject to the needs of the property at any given time.* The **stabilized budget** is *a forecast of income and expenses as may be reasonably projected over a short term, typically five years.*

The budgeting practices described above are common, expected, and necessary on larger projects. With smaller buildings, however, budgets may be subject to extreme fluctuations as expenses are not always predictable. For example, if three of four air conditioners fail in a single year in a four-plex, this could completely exhaust the typical repair budget.

Analysis of Operating Statement

The operating statement is a method used by property managers to project net operating income for a particular property. Net operating income is the gross income minus the operating expenses.

The apartment complex in Figure 8.5 has a potential gross income of $1,350,000. This is the income that would be produced if every apartment were rented 100 percent of the time at $450 per month for a 12-month period. To expect any rental property to be occupied 100 percent of the time on a continuing basis is unrealistic. Therefore, the potential gross income must be reduced by the vacancy rate and credit loss. This example estimates the vacancy rate at 6 percent. The credit loss may include uncollected rent from defaulting tenants. In the example, the vacancy and credit losses are expected to reduce the potential gross income by $81,000.

This apartment complex has other income generated by vending machines and laundry facilities. This income is projected to be $25,000 per year. Any income added to the rental income yields the effective gross income. The effective gross income in this example is $1,294,000. This is the amount of money the complex may generate in a 12-month period. To arrive at the net income, various expenses must be subtracted from the effective gross income. These expenses are categorized into fixed expenses, operating expenses, and replacement or capital reserve expenses. **Fixed**

FIGURE 8.5

A sample operating statement.

OPERATING STATEMENT

250-unit apartment complex with rent schedule of $450 per month per unit.

Potential Gross Income: 250 × $450 × 12		$ 1,350,000
Less Vacancy and Credit Losses (6%)		(81,000)
Plus Other Income		25,000
Effective Gross Income		$ 1,294,000
Less Expenses		
Fixed Expenses:		
Property Insurance	$ 24,500	
Property Taxes	95,300	
Licenses and Permits	1,200	($ 121,000)
Operating Expenses:		
Maintenance	$ 106,000	
Utilities	103,200	
Supplies	16,000	
Advertising	7,500	
Legal & Accounting	15,000	
Wages & Salaries	90,000	
Property Management	64,700	($ 402,400)
Replacement Reserve:		($ 25,000)
Total Expenses		$ 548,400
Net Operating Income		$ 745,600

expenses *are costs that do not fluctuate with the operating level of the complex.* They will remain the same whether the occupancy rate is 95 percent or 50 percent. These include real property taxes, insurance, licenses, and permits. The fixed expenses in the illustration total $121,000 and are 9.35 percent of the effective gross income.

Operating expenses fluctuate with the operating level or occupancy of the property. As the example shows, maintenance is the major operating expense, totaling $106,000. The property manager's fee also is an operating expense. Property managers typically are paid on a percentage of effective gross income. Total operating expenses of the sample complex are $402,400, or 31.1 percent of the effective gross income.

In the figure, the capital or replacement reserve is $25,000. Net operating income can now be determined by subtracting the expenses from the effective gross income. The annual net operating income in the example is $745,600.

Marketing

The manager's strategy of marketing available rental space is shaped by the present demand for space, newness of the project, and the tenant selection process. In designing and implementing any marketing activity, managers must comply with all federal, state, and local fair housing laws.

Reporting

The property manager should provide a *periodic* (usually monthly) *accounting of all funds received and disbursed,* called a **property management report.** It contains detailed information of all receipts and expenditures for the period covered (plus the year-to-date figures) and relates each item to the operating budget for the period. In addition to reports to the owner, the manager should maintain the necessary records for compliance with local laws on fair housing, security deposits, and trust accounts.

A PROPERTY MANAGER'S SKILLS

To accomplish the goals of the property effectively, the property manager must demonstrate knowledge and skill in diverse areas. A property manager must be able to:

- supervise others; the property manager must have people skills and communicate effectively and productively with the owner, tenants, and individuals employed by the owner or property manager
- understand general accounting principles (GAP) and prepare and interpret monthly and yearly reports
- understand building systems; heating, ventilating, and air conditioning (HVAC); structural engineering; waterproofing; plumbing; electric, gas, oil, water, and security systems; elevators; and other components of a structure (Figure 8.6 illustrates a sample property inspection report)
- handle owner-tenant relations (discussed more fully below)
- lease space and have a knowledge of space planning, area design, and building layout
- competently advertise and market the property
- have knowledge of local building codes, including the minimal requirements of the New York State Uniform Fire Prevention and Building Code, the New York Energy Code, and local codes and regulations governing building operations
- be able to work with union representatives and employees from various trades and professions who perform maintenance on the property

FIGURE 8.6

Sample property/building inspection report.

PROPERTY/BUILDING INSPECTION REPORT

Name and address of property _____

Inspector/Inspection company _____

Date _____ Time _____

	Subject	In need of repair	Type of repair	Regular maintenance repair	No repair or maintenance needed
Exterior grounds	lawn/shrubs				
	sidewalks				
	parking lot				
	roadways				
	signs				
Building exterior	foundation				
	exterior walls				
	windows				
	roof/gutters				
	doors/locks				
	dumpsters				
Building interior	elevators				
	hallways				
	entryway				
	walls/floors				
	stairways				
Mechanical repairs	security system				
	furnace/fuel lines				
	HVAC				
	electrical				
	fire safety equipment				
	plumbing				
	Comments or other repairs:				

Note: Inspection reports vary to address the needs of a specific property.

- understand how to purchase quality goods and materials at the best possible price
- apply an understanding of appraisal, finance, money markets, building depreciation, financial trends, and local market conditions to the overall management of the property
- have a general knowledge of construction
- be aware of any environmental factors and problems that exist either locally or on site and observe local and state laws governing these factors

Owner-Tenant Relations

A lease (Figure 8.7) is a contract in which, for consideration (usually rent), an owner of property transfers to the tenant a property interest, or possession, for a prescribed period of time. *The owner of the property is called the landlord, or* **lessor.** *The tenant placed in possession is called the* **lessee.** The tenant is entitled to quiet enjoyment of the premises, and the owner is expected to receive money plus a reversionary interest in the property; that is, possession of the property will revert to the owner at the end of the lease.

If the property manager is careful in selecting tenants, legal actions for eviction and collection of rents will be minimal. See Figure 8.8, Application for an Apartment Lease, which facilitates the selection process. Effective property managers attempt to resolve any disputes before they initiate a lawsuit. If a lawsuit is necessary, the property manager's file must show compliance with all terms of any lease agreement.

Eviction Remedies

A lease also can be terminated when the owner chooses to evict the tenant if the tenant breaches the lease agreement, for example, by failing to pay rent. It also can occur after the lease agreement expires and the tenant fails or refuses to vacate the premises. *Eviction is a legal action in the court system for removal of the tenant and his belongings and a return of possession of the premises to the owner.* Eviction is different from **actual eviction,** *in which the owner, without the aid or control of the court system, removes the tenant from the premises.* In some cases, the owner requests a owner's lien on the tenant's belongings as security for payment of rent owed. Actual eviction is wrongful use of self-help. Self-help occurs when the owner violates statutory law by physically removing the tenant and the tenant's belongings from the premises or takes action to prevent the tenant from access to the premises.

A lease also can be terminated by the tenant's claim of **constructive eviction** that is mainly limited to residential properties, but can apply to commercial properties. In some cases, the tenant can claim constructive eviction and be relieved of the obligation to pay rent.

A constructive eviction occurs when the tenant is prevented from the quiet enjoyment of the premises. In New York, unless there is an agreement to the contrary and the tenant did not cause the problem, he can leave the leased premises and forfeit his obligations (rental payment) under the lease if the building becomes unlivable. In such cases, through the owner's lack of care, the tenant has been evicted for all practical purposes because enjoyment of the premises is not available. An example is when heat and water are not available to the tenant because of the owner's negligence. To claim constructive eviction, however, the tenant must actually vacate the premises while the conditions that make the premises uninhabitable still exist. The lease is then terminated under the constructive eviction claim. Such cases do not reflect an automatic right that the tenant can assume; they may have to be litigated.

In filing a suit, the property manager must be familiar with local court rules and procedure. Some courts require that the property manager be represented by an attorney. If so, the property manager should consult with legal counsel prior to any court appearance to ensure that any witnesses will attend and that all exhibits for the hearing are available. The property manager need not be an expert in all of the above-mentioned skills but should have access to professionals as needed.

DIFFERENCES BETWEEN THE MARKETS

Residential Property Management

Residential property includes apartments, single-family housing, multifamily housing, condominiums, cooperatives, vacation houses, and mobile home parks. The concerns

FIGURE 8.7 Lease agreement.

T 8018—NLS Lease Agreement, House, Flat or small Apartment Building, 12-78 (formerly T 18 B).

JULIUS BLUMBERG, INC., PUBLISHER, ALBANY, NY

LEASE AGREEMENT

The Landlord and Tenant agree to lease the Premises at the Rent and for the Term stated on these terms:

LANDLORD: TENANT:

Address   Address

Premises: _____

Lease date: _____ 19____	Term_____ beginning _____ 19____ ending _____ 19____	Yearly Rent $_____ Monthly Rent $_____ Security $_____
Broker*		

1. Rent   The tenant must make the rent payment for each month on the 1st day of that month at the landlord's address as set forth above. The landlord need not notify the tenant of tenant's duty to pay the rent, and the rent must be paid in full and no deductions will be allowed from the rent. The first month's rent must be paid at the time of the signing of this Lease by the tenant. If the landlord permits the tenant to pay the rent in installments, said permission is for the tenant's convenience only and if the tenant does not pay said installments when they are due, the landlord may notify the tenant that the tenant may no longer pay the rent in installments.

2. Use   The tenant agrees to use the premises rented to the tenant by the landlord, to live in only and for no other reason. Only a party signing this Lease, spouse and children of that party may use the Premises. If the tenant wishes to use the leased premises for any other reason, the tenant must obtain the written permission of the landlord to do so. The landlord is not required to grant permission to the tenant to use the leased premises for any purpose other than the purpose listed above.

3. Tenant's duty to obey laws and regulations   Tenant must, at tenant's expense, promptly comply with all laws, orders, rules, requests, and directions, of all governmental authorities, landlord's insurers, Board of Fire Underwriters, or similar groups. Notices received by tenant from any authority or group must be promptly delivered to landlord. Tenant may not do anything which may increase landlord's insurance premiums; if tenant does, tenant must pay the increase in premium as added rent.

4. Repairs   The tenant must maintain the apartment and all of the equipment and fixtures in it. The tenant agrees, at tenant's own cost, to make all repairs to the apartment and replacement to the equipment and fixtures in the apartment whenever the need results from the tenant's acts or neglect. If the tenant fails to make a repair or replacement, then the landlord may so do and charge the tenant the cost of said repair or replacement as additional rent, which rent shall be due and payable under the terms and conditions as normal rent is due and payable.

5. Glass, cost of replacement   The tenant agrees to replace, at the tenant's own expense, all glass broken during the term of this lease, regardless of the cause of the breakage. The tenant agrees that all glass in said premises is whole as of the beginning of the term of this lease.

6. Alterations   The tenant agrees not to make any alterations or improvements in the leased premises without the landlord's written permission and any alterations and improvements made by the tenant after obtaining the written permission of the landlord shall be paid at the sole expense of the tenant and will become the property of the landlord and be left behind in the leased premises at the end of the term of this lease. The landlord has the right to demand that the tenant remove the alterations and installations before the end of the term of this lease. That demand shall be by notice, given at least 15 days before the end of the term, and the removals shall be at the sole expense of the tenant. The landlord is not required to do or pay for any of the work involved in the installation or removal of the alterations unless it is so stated in this lease.

7. Assignment and sublease   Tenant must not assign this lease or sublet all or part of the apartment or permit any other person to use the apartment. If tenant does, landlord has the right to cancel the lease as stated in the Tenant's Default section. State law may permit tenant to assign or sublet under certain conditions. Tenant must get landlord's written permission each time tenant wants to assign or sublet. Permission to assign or sublet is good only for that assignment or sublease. Tenant remains bound to the terms of this lease after a permitted assignment or sublease even if landlord accepts rent from the assignee or subtenant. The assignee or subtenant does not become landlord's tenant.

8. Entry by the landlord   The tenant agrees to allow the landlord to enter the leased premises at any reasonable hour to repair, inspect, install or work upon any fixture or equipment in said leased premises and to perform such other work that the landlord may decide is necessary. In addition, tenant agrees to permit landlord and/or landlord's agent, to show the premises to persons wishing to hire or purchase the same, during the reasonable hours of any day during the term of this Lease, tenant will permit the usual notices of "To Let" or "For Sale" to be placed upon conspicuous portions of the walls, doors, or windows of said premises and remain thereon without hindrance or molestation.

9. Fire, accident, defects and damage   Tenant must give landlord prompt notice of fire, accident, damage or dangerous or defective condition. If the apartment can not be used because of fire or other casualty, tenant is not required to pay rent for the time the apartment is unusable. If part of the apartment can not be used, tenant must pay rent for the usable part. Landlord shall have the right to decide which part of the apartment is usable. Landlord need only repair the damaged structural parts of the apartment. Landlord is not required to repair or replace any equipment, fixtures, furnishings or decorations unless originally installed by landlord. Landlord is not responsible for delays due to settling insurance claims, obtaining estimates, labor and supply problems or any other cause not fully under landlord's control.

If the fire or other casualty is caused by an act or neglect of tenant or guest of tenant, or at the time of the fire or casualty tenant is in default in any term of this lease, then all repairs will be made at tenant's expense and tenant must pay the full rent with no adjustment. The cost of the repairs will be added rent.

Landlord has the right to demolish or rebuild the building if there is substantial damage by fire or other casualty. Even if the apartment is not damaged, landlord may cancel this lease within 30 days after the fire or casualty by giving tenant notice of landlord's intention to demolish or rebuild. The lease will end 30 days after landlord's cancellation notice to tenant. Tenant must deliver the apartment to landlord on or before the cancellation date in the notice and pay all rent due to the date of the fire or casualty. If the lease is cancelled landlord is not required to repair the apartment or building.

(continued)

FIGURE 8.7   Continued.

10. Waivers   If the landlord accepts the rent due under this lease or fails to enforce any terms of this lease, said action by the landlord shall not be a waiver of any of the landlord's rights. If a term in this lease is determined to be illegal, than the rest of this lease shall remain in full force and effect and be binding upon both the landlord and the tenant.

11. Tenant's default
   A. Landlord may give 5 days written notice to tenant to correct any of the following defaults:
      1. Failure to pay rent or added rent on time.
      2. Improper assignment of the lease, improper subletting all or part of the premises, or allowing another to use the premises.
      3. Improper conduct by tenant or other occupant of the premises.
      4. Failure to fully perform any other term in the lease.
   B. If tenant fails to correct the defaults in section A within the 5 days, landlord may cancel the lease by giving tenant a written 3 day notice stating the date the term will end. On that date the term and tenant's rights in this lease automatically end and tenant must leave the premises and give landlord the keys. Tenant continues to be responsible for rent, expenses, damages and losses.
   C. If the lease is cancelled, or rent or added rent is not paid on time, or tenant vacates the premises, landlord may in addition to other remedies take any of the following steps:
      1. Enter the premises and remove tenant and any person or property;
      2. Use dispossess, eviction or other lawsuit method to take back the premises.
   D. If the lease is ended or landlord takes back the premises, rent and added rent for the unexpired term becomes due and payable. Landlord may re-rent the premises and anything in it for any term. Landlord may re-rent for a lower rent and give allowances to the new tenant. Tenant shall be responsible for landlord's cost of re-renting. Landlord's cost shall include the cost of repairs, decorations, broker's fees, attorney's fees, advertising and preparation for renting. Tenant shall continue to be responsible for rent, expenses, damages and losses. Any rent received from the re-renting shall be applied to the reduction of money tenant owes. Tenant waives all rights to return to the premises after possession is given to the landlord by a Court.

12. Tenant's additional obligations   Tenant shall keep the grounds and common areas of the leased premises as well as the leased premises themselves neat and clean. Tenant agrees not to use any of the equipment, fixtures or plumbing fixtures in the leased premises for any purpose other than that for which said equipment, fixtures or plumbing fixtures were designed. Any damage resulting from the misuse of such equipment, fixtures and plumbing fixtures shall be paid for by the tenant as additional rent, which additional rent shall be due and payable under the terms and conditions as normal rent is due and payable.

All furniture and other personal belongings, equipment or the like, if any, provided by the landlord and included within the terms of this lease shall be returned to the landlord at the end of this term of this lease or any earlier termination in as good condition as possible taking into account reasonable wear and tear. If the tenant vacates the premises or is dispossessed and fails to remove any of tenant's furniture, clothing or personal belongings, those items shall be considered abandoned by the tenant and the landlord shall be authorized to dispose of those items as the landlord sees fit.

13. Quiet enjoyment   The landlord agrees that if the tenant pays the rent and complies with all of the other terms and conditions of this lease, then the tenant may peaceably and quietly have, hold and enjoy the premises leased hereunder for the term of this lease.

14. Lease, parties upon whom binding   This lease is binding upon the landlord and the tenant and their respective heirs, distributees, executors, administrators, successors and lawful assigns.

15. Utilities and services   Tenant agrees to pay for all utilities and services provided to the leased premises with the following exceptions:

_____

_____

_____

16. Space "as is"   Tenant has inspected the Premises. Tenant states that they are in good order and repair and takes the Premises "as is."

17. Tenant restrictions   No sign, advertisement or illumination shall be placed upon any portion of the exterior, or in the windows of premises and no television aerials shall be installed without written consent of Landlord. Washing machine or driers or water beds are not permitted in the premises. No animal shall be permitted in these premises without the consent in writing of Landlord and Tenant will be responsible for all damages which may be caused by such animal permitted by the Landlord.

18. Security   Tenant has given Security to landlord in the amount stated above. If tenant fully complies with all the terms of this lease, landlord will return the security after the term ends. If tenant does not fully comply with the terms of this lease, landlord may use the security to pay amounts owed by tenant, including damages. If landlord sells the premises, landlord may give the security to the buyer. Tenant will look only to the buyer for the return of the security.

Rider   Additional terms on _____ page(s) initialed at the end by the parties is attached and made a part of this Lease.

Signatures, effective date   The parties have entered into this Lease on the date first above stated. This lease is effective when landlord delivers to tenant a copy signed by all parties.

LANDLORD: **TENANT:**

_____   _____

WITNESS: _____

_____

FIGURE 8.8 Application for an apartment lease.

Blumbergs Law Products

71—Application to lease apartment with deposit receipt and references, plain English, 1979.

© 1979 BY JULIUS BLUMBERG, INC., PUBLISHER, NYC 10013

Application to Lease

Landlord..

Application for apartment............................at...

Applicant(s)...

....Tel. No. (............)..................................
Present address...

Present landlord..

address..

....Tel. No. (............)..................................
Applicant(s) occupation...

Business name...

address..

....Tel. No. (............)..................................
Bank and other references (give telephone numbers) :

....
....
....
....
....
....

Term	Annual Rent $...................
beginning................19........	Monthly Rent $...................
ending ....19........	Security $...................

If there is more than one Applicant the word "Applicant" shall include them.

Rent Only a party signing this Application and the Lease and the spouse and children of that party may live in the Apartment.

Use The Apartment will be rented to be used only as a private residence to live in.

Security The Security shall be given to Landlord at the time Landlord delivers to Applicant a copy of the Lease signed by all parties.

Lease The Lease shall be basically in the same form as the leases for other Apartments in the building. When the Landlord offers the Lease to Applicant, Applicant shall immediately sign and return to Landlord 2 original signed Leases.

Receipt of Payment Applicant has deposited $............................ in payment of the first............................months rent.

....
....
....
....
....
....

Date .... 19........

Applicant's failure, damages If Applicant fails to sign the two leases or fails to pay the Security

1. Applicant may not move into the Apartment and has no rights related to it.

2. Applicant shall be liable for Damages to Landlord in an amount equal to the total Rent for the full Term. The Damages shall be paid in the same manner as the Rent.

3. Landlord may rent the Apartment without notice to Applicant. The period of the rental may be shorter or longer than the Term.

4. Applicant shall pay Landlord all Landlord's renting expenses in addition to the Damages.

5. If Landlord rents the Apartment the Damages shall be reduced by the amount collected as rent by Landlord from the new tenant during the Term.

Failure to give possession Landlord shall not be liable for failure to give Applicant possession of the Apartment on the beginning date of the Term. If for any reason Landlord is unable to give possession, Rent shall then be payable as of the date possession is available. The ending date of the Term shall not change.

Representations All promises made by Landlord or Landlord's agents are in this Application. Landlord will not make any decorations or alterations in the Apartment unless specifically stated in this Application. This Application may not be changed orally.

Landlord relies on the truth of this Application The Landlord is relying on the truth of all Applicant's statements in this Application in deciding whether to rent the Apartment to Applicant.

This is only an Application and Receipt of Deposit. This Application is subject to Landlord's approval. The Apartment is not rented until both parties have signed a Lease and Applicant is given a signed copy.

Signatures

Applicant(s)..

Source: BlumbergExcelsior, Inc. Forms may be purchased from BlumbergExcelsior, Inc. or any of its dealers. Interactive electronic forms may be purchased at *http://www.blumberg.com.* Reproduction prohibited.

of a property manager when selecting tenants for residential properties include credit history of tenants, past landlord references, and employment status. The manager also must be involved with maintenance and repair of the premises and eviction of tenants. The manager has to be aware of the local housing market.

Office Building Management

In the management of office space, property managers must deal with other vacant office space and attempt to keep vacancies at a minimum in a competitive market. Some of the specific skills involved include analyzing demographics to attract tenants to the office building, negotiating leases that will work well for owner and tenant, developing a competitive rent schedule, marketing to certain target professions that will best utilize the office space, and enhancing and rearranging available space to best serve the needs of the tenant.

Retail Property Management

Most retail properties managed by a property manager are in strip malls, neighborhood shopping centers, and regional malls. Regional malls generally contain one or more anchor stores. An **anchor store** *is a well-known commercial retail business, such as a national chain store or regional department store, placed in a shopping center to generate the most customers for all stores in the shopping center.* A manager of these properties must select tenants suitable for each type of center and consider appropriate tenant mix. The manager also must be aware of the desires of retail tenants regarding noncompetition from like tenants, group or common advertising, and common-area maintenance.

Industrial Property Management

Based upon the desired economic growth of many cities and towns, industrial developments and industrial parks are common. They often are handled by a professional manager. Property managers must be aware of the transportation systems, utility services, and other components of the infrastructure available in the area. In addition, they must be knowledgeable about tax rates, tax incentives, available labor force, commercial financing, and community services.

Farm Property Management

Farm property can consist of grain crops, animal production, dairy production, or a combination of these. Besides understanding accounting methods, the property manager must be familiar with crop production, commodity prices, soil types, environmental controls, and soil conservation. As more farms are owned by corporations, a property manager becomes indispensable.

Condominium, Cooperative, Townhouse, and PUD Management

A **planned unit development** *is a neighborhood of cluster housing or other configurations with supporting business establishments.* It may also contain common usage areas such as swimming pools, tennis courts, nature paths, meeting rooms, and other elements. The homeowner's association is generally formed to maintain the aesthetic standards of the PUD and to deal with property improvements to benefit all homeowners.

Although not always involved with leasing or renting, a manager for a *condominium,* townhouse, or PUD homeowners' association or a *cooperative* corporation is involved tremendously in the physical management of the property for owners and occupants. The responsibility begins with budgeting expenses and collecting assessments, and progresses to coordinating common facility maintenance, landscaping, security, and enforcement of the association's or board of directors' regulations.

OPERATION OF A PROPERTY MANAGEMENT OFFICE

Large property management offices may handle a number of different properties for either the same owner or a number of different owners. If a management office works for more than one owner, a real estate broker license is required. The agent or managers employed by the company would require a minimum of a salesperson license.

A property management office must engage actively in acquiring new properties to manage, effectively service existing clients, negotiate management agreements with new clients, distribute the workload efficiently among the employees of the management company, evaluate price-setting policies to compensate employees, and keep a comfortable margin of profit in the company. This profit allows the management office to market themselves and expand services when necessary to meet the changing needs of clients.

PUTTING IT TO WORK   As a licensee, you are in a good position to acquire work as a property manager. The following hypothetical client's question addresses this opportunity.* Check your response using the Answer Key at the end of the chapter.

The client asks: My husband recently passed away and now I have to manage two apartment buildings. This, plus my home, is too big a worry. What do you suggest?

THE MANAGEMENT PROFESSION

Many individuals, either in the real estate profession or other fields, wish to enter the property management profession. Because the profession encompasses a wide area of skills and talents, it attracts a diversity of people.

How Does One Become a Property Manager?

Several approaches are possible to enter a career in property management. For example, an individual may acquire a property for investment purposes, such as an apartment complex, several residential rental properties, or an office building and thus can become a manager. Other individuals make a specific career decision to enter the field. In recent years, many property managers have attended an MBA program, where they have studied asset management. An asset manager is an individual who is knowledgeable about all types of investments including real property and may not have specific real estate expertise. The asset manager may then hire a person with specific property management expertise to oversee the property of the client.

Many property managers come from other areas of the real estate industry such as real estate brokerage, appraisal, investment, and subdivision development. Through their contacts, they may be called upon to manage or assist with a property.

Other individuals interested in the field may choose to obtain an entry-level position with a management company and learn about the business through an apprentice-type arrangement. Continuing education and training are a must for *any* property manager, regardless of background.

Source: James A. Ader, "Real Estate Spotlight." Copyright © The *Albany Times Union.* Reprinted by permission.

Education and certification for property managers   You Should Know

Specialized education courses are available in New York and throughout the country to meet the training needs of either the beginner or experienced property manager. Some of this knowledge may be acquired through courses provided by the Institute of Real Estate Management (IREM), an affiliate of the National Association of REALTORS®. After completing their program, individuals may be eligible for the professional designation of Certified Property Manager (CPM). Three chapters of IREM exist in New York. For further information and a catalogue that lists books and tapes as well as courses given in New York and other parts of the country, call (800) 837-0706 or online: *http://www.irem.org*. The Greater New York chapter of IREM can be reached by calling Sheila W. Still at (212) 944-9445 or online: *http://www.iremnyc.org*. IREM courses are offered at the Real Estate Institute, a division of New York University in Manhattan. The Real Estate Institute offers a certificate program in property management that includes courses that lead to all of the designations discussed below. For further information, write to the Real Estate Institute, 11 West 42d Street, Room 401, New York, NY 10036 or online: *http://www.scps.nyu.edu*. The Associated Builders and Owners of Greater New York (ABO) offers HUD-certified courses leading to ABO's Registered in Apartment Management (RAM) designation. For more information on the RAM designation, call Nicholas LaPorte at (212) 385-4949 or online: *http://www.abogny.com*.

The New York Accredited Realty Manager (NYARM) designation is offered by the New York Association of Realty Managers. This certification is recognized and approved by New York State Division of Housing and Community Renewal (DHCR) and the New York City Department of Housing Preservation and Development (HPD). For information on NYARM certification requirements, call (212) 216-0654 or online: *http://www.nyarm.com*.

The BOMI Institute is an international organization that offers professional education for property managers, facility managers, and building engineers. For further information about the BOMI Institute, call international headquarters at (800) 235-BOMI (2664) or online: *http://www.bomi-edu.org*.

The above designations may require a combination of coursework, examinations, field experience, and fees. NYSAR, colleges, and proprietary schools throughout New York offer basic and advanced level property management courses that can be taken for continuing education credit for the salesperson and broker licenses.

IMPORTANT POINTS

1. Rental of property creates a leasehold estate. Types of leasehold estates include tenancy or estate for years, periodic (year-to-year) estates, estate at will, estate at sufferance.

2. When a property manager enters into a management agreement, a general agency is created. The manager owes a fiduciary (undivided loyalty) responsibility to his principal.

3. In New York, if property management companies or individual property managers work for more than one owner, a real estate license is required. Employees of property management companies or individuals that collect rent for more than one owner must have a minimum of a salesperson's license.

4. Properties that may require management are condominiums, cooperatives, apartments, single-family rental houses, mobile home parks, office buildings, shopping malls, industrial property, and farms.

5. The management agreement is a contract in which a property owner employs a property manager to act as the owner's agent. The management agreement creates a general agency and the manager owes undivided loyalty to the owner–principal.

6. To be eligible for insurance, the applicant must have an insurable interest in the property.

7. Risk management embodies the concern for controlling and limiting risk in property ownership.

8. The overall goals of the property manager are (a) to produce the best possible net operating income from the property, and (b) to maintain and increase the value of the principal's investment.

9. Property managers fulfill their basic responsibilities by formulating a management plan; handling rentals, tenant relations, and employees; overseeing the budget; paying bills; and supervising maintenance.

10. The property manager must continuously evaluate rents, budgets, and markets to ensure the best future return on the investment.

11. The property management report is a periodic accounting provided by a property manager to the property owner.

12. The property manager must be skilled in a diverse number of areas, including accounting, budgeting, construction and building systems, and owner-tenant relations. Real estate–related knowledge is also essential.

13. Eviction is a legal action for removal of the tenant and his belongings from the premises. Actual eviction occurs when an owner removes a tenant without the aid of the court system. A tenant can claim constructive eviction when the tenant is prevented from the quiet enjoyment of the premises such as in the absences of heat or electricity.

14. Many individuals from diverse backgrounds are attracted to the property management profession. Formal education and training are available through various institutions, and different types of designations may be awarded to individuals demonstrating competence through education and field activity.

CHAPTER REVIEW   How Would You Respond?

Licensees often enter the field of property management. Analyze the following situations and decide how the individuals would handle them in accordance with license law and regulations. Check your responses using the Answer Key at the end of the section.

1. Aviva is a rental agent for Vanderbilt Apartments in Cooperstown, New York. Aviva's job is to show apartments, sign up tenants, and collect rents. Because of her competent work, she has been approached by four other apartment owners to do similar work for them. She would likely collect rents for several different owners. Will Aviva need to obtain a license if she decides to do this? If so, what level of licensure would she need?

_____

_____

_____

2. Steve is a broker who specializes in leasing office space. He has been approached by the owner of a 500,000-square-foot office building to manage the entire property. Because of his leasing experience, Steve feels equal to the task. What are the most important steps Steve must take in negotiating this position? Does Steve require any additional licensure or designations?

_____

_____

_____

3. Daryl has been a broker and a property manager for the past 16 months for an industrial park in Long Island, New York. Soon after Daryl took on the management position, two major tenants moved out, leaving 50,000 square feet of space vacant. Daryl has been unable to rent out this space and does not know what to do. Recently, he has been approached by a furniture distributor who wishes to buy the entire complex. First, what steps could Daryl have taken to market the vacant space? Second, can Daryl represent the owner as a real estate broker should the owner wish to negotiate for the sale of the industrial park?

_____

_____

_____

KEY TERM REVIEW

Fill in the term that best completes the sentence and then check the Answer Key at the end of the chapter.

1. The _management agreement_ is a contract that creates an agency relationship between an owner–principal and a property manager–agent.
2. A(n) _Resident_ is a person living on the premises who is a salaried employee of the owner.
3. The concept of _Risk management_ implies that properties must be covered by appropriate insurance policies.
4. _prevent Maintenance_ requires a periodic check of mechanical equipment on the premises; and _Corrective mainten_ is the work performed to fix a nonfunctioning item.
5. The projected annual budget that includes only the items of income and expense expected for week to week operation is the _operating budget_
6. The projected budget over the economic life of the improvements of the property for expenses such as remodeling is the _capital Reserve budget_
7. The periodic accounting of all funds received and disbursed is included in the _property management report_
8. A forecast of income and expenses as may be reasonably projected over typically five years is known as a(n) _Stabalize budget_
9. The commitment, in writing, of the property manager if employed by an owner, is known as the _management proposal_

MULTIPLE CHOICE

Circle the letter that best answers the question and then check the Answer Key at the end of the chapter.

1. Which of the following statements about property management is FALSE?
   A. property management is a specialized field within the real estate industry
   B. a property manager acts as an agent of the property owner
   C. the terms *property manager* and *resident manager* always have the same meaning
   D. a property manager is a fiduciary

2. Public liability insurance covers:
   A. manager's employees' health care costs
   B. risks an owner assumes when the public leases the premises
   C. flood damage
   D. title insurance

3. When a building occupancy reaches 98 percent, this tends to indicate that:

   A. rents should be lowered

   B. rents could be raised

   C. management is ineffective

   D. the building needs remodeling

4. Telly Able works solely for the Heritage Apartment complex in Albany, New York, as a rental agent. Which of the following is true?

   A. Telly must obtain a broker license

   B. Telly must obtain a salesperson license

   C. Telly need not obtain any type of real estate license

   D. only owners can collect the rent in apartment complexes they own

5. Which of the following is NOT a function of the property manager?

   A. renting the property

   B. leasing the property

   C. selling the property

   D. preparing the deed to the property

6. The management agreement creates a:

   A. special agency

   B. general agency

   C. sole proprietorship

   D. power of attorney

7. Risk management has to do with:

   A. controlling and limiting risk through appropriate insurance

   B. limiting financial risk through the operating budget

   C. preventive maintenance

   D. clearing the parking lot soon after a snowstorm to avoid traffic accidents

8. One of the most important *overall* goals of the property manager is to:

   A. cure functional obsolescence

   B. produce the highest possible net operating income from the property

   C. obtain liability insurance

   D. prosecute tenants who are delinquent in their monthly rental payments

9. Which of the following is NOT included in a management proposal?

   A. complete description of the property

   B. listing of all maintenance required

   C. credit history of all tenants occupying the property

   D. document citing the management fee

10. A manager's market strategy of marketing available rental space is shaped by all of the following EXCEPT the:

    A. racial composition of the surrounding community

    B. present demand for space

    C. newness of the project

    D. tenant selection process

11. Which of the following is NOT grounds for a lawsuit against a tenant?

    A. property manager's file showing the tenant's compliance with all terms of the lease agreement

    B. property manager's file showing the manager's compliance with all terms of the lease

    C. property manager's familiarity with local court rules and procedure

    D. property manager's proof of having consulted with legal counsel to ascertain whether attorney representation is necessary or desirable

12. One of the biggest problems in office building management is:

    A. dealing with faulty wiring systems

    B. handling a long waiting list of prospective tenants

    C. keeping an anchor store from moving

    D. attempting to keep vacancies at a minimum in a competitive market

13. One of the most important tasks of a property manager in managing a cooperative or condominium is:

    A. allocating shares of stock for each apartment

    B. physical management of the property

    C. evaluating the utility services available in the community

    D. evaluating tax incentives to attract tenants

14. A designation from a college, an institute, or an association:

    A. is mandatory to become a property manager in New York

    B. may be obtained instead of a real estate license if the manager wishes to work for more than one owner

    C. represents accomplishment in both education and work activity in the property management field

    D. is necessary if one wishes a position in commercial management

15. Kathy wishes to become a property manager but has no prior experience in the field. Kathy should:

    A. give up on the idea completely

    B. investigate possible apprentice-type positions as an introduction to the business

    C. obtain a real estate salesperson license before doing anything else

    D. apply for a job as a property manager at a local shopping center

ANSWER KEY

Putting It to Work

Quite frequently, people in your position feel the need to sell real estate holdings to rid themselves of management concerns. Unfortunately, impulse sales generally are often well below market value. Many experts recommend a one-year waiting period to ensure that decisions are not clouded by the emotions of the moment. For the immediate future, your investment property most likely will run itself, or with the help of family or friends. If not, consider employing a licensee with property management experience.*

How Would You Respond?

1. If Aviva works for a number of individuals or companies as a rental agent, she would need to obtain at least a salesperson license that in New York includes broker sponsorship.

2. So that the owner can evaluate Steve's management potential, Steve should submit a management proposal. The proposal should include, but is not limited to, a description of the property, the scope of Steve's duties, and a statement as to the management fee. After the proposal is accepted, Steve should enter into a written management agreement. The agreement should detail the duration of the contract as well as items in the management proposal and provide for a method of termination. Steve does not need further licensure or a designation, but may explore educational and designation options.

3. Daryl should study the transportation, utility services, and other appropriate infrastructure benefits and demonstrate their usefulness to prospective tenants. He should have knowledge of tax rates and incentives, the labor force, and commercial financing. He must be able to present a complete package of benefits to prospective tenants. To communicate the industrial park's vacancies, he should create a report detailing these benefits and contact businesses that might need this type of space. Should an owner decide to sell, Daryl may negotiate on behalf of the owner but must disclose and document the nature and scope of his agency relationship with the owner (according to New York law) in all negotiations with any prospective purchasers.

Key Term Review

1. management agreement
2. resident manager
3. risk management
4. preventive maintenance; corrective maintenance
5. operating budget
6. capital reserve budget
7. property management report
8. stabilized budget
9. management proposal

Multiple Choice

1. C
2. B
3. B
4. C
5. D
6. B
7. A
8. B
9. C
10. A
11. A
12. D
13. B
14. C
15. B

Chapter 9

LEARNING OBJECTIVES   *Classroom hours: 2*

1. Explain the difference between tax assessment and tax appraisal of real property.
2. Describe the process of taxation.
3. Explain how taxes are computed.
4. Explain how an owner of real property may appeal an assessment.
5. Explain the equalization rate and how it is determined.

Taxes and Assessments

IN THIS CHAPTER Even if there is no mortgage, taxes must be paid continuously throughout the term of property ownership. As a result, purchasers are extremely interested in the nature of the assessment process, the tax rate, and the resulting tax amount levied on properties they wish to purchase.

PROPERTY TAXES AND ASSESSMENTS

Property is taxed on an **ad valorem** *basis—that is, according to value. In New York, the real property tax is based on the fair market value of real property.* **Assessing units** *such as counties, cities, towns, villages, school districts, and special districts raise money through real property taxes.* Special districts include, for example, a volunteer fire department. These taxes pay for the infrastructure of the community as well as other services.

What Determines the Amount of the Property Tax Bill?

A tax bill is determined by two items: first, the property's taxable assessment; and second, the tax rates of the taxing jurisdiction in which the property is located. *A property's* **assessment** *is a percentage of its market value.* The market value is the amount for which a property would sell under normal conditions. The **tax rate** is determined by the amount of the tax levy. *The rate must be sufficient to provide the amount of revenue required to accomplish the budgetary requirements of the local governmental unit.* It is the amount of the tax levy that is raised through property tax. The graph in Figure 9.1 illustrates the percentages of funds that make up a typical town budget.

What Property Is Subject to Assessment?

All real property is subject to assessment, including houses; gas stations; office buildings; vacant land; motels; shopping centers; salable natural resources such as oil, gas, and timberland; farms; apartment buildings; factories; restaurants; and, in most instances, mobile homes.

FIGURE 9.1
A sample town budget.

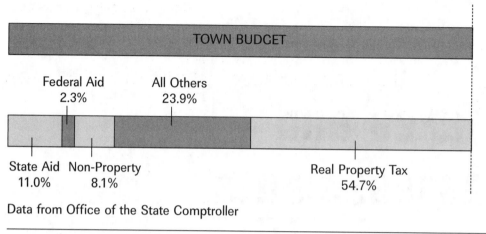

Data from Office of the State Comptroller

Source: New York State Office of Real Property Services.

What Assessable Property Is Subject to Taxation?

Though all real property in an assessing unit is assessed, *not all of it is taxable.* **Tax exemptions** *are set by state law, and in some cases municipalities are authorized by law to determine whether exemptions will be granted and what their amounts will be.* Exemptions are either *full exemptions* or *partial exemptions.* Properties owned by religious organizations and government-owned property are completely exempt. Other exemptions may include farms or nonprofit educational and charitable organizations. Lesser-known exemptions may exist for water and wastewater treatment facilities, business and industrial development, solar and wind energy, and specific types of housing. Certain groups of people such as *senior citizens* and *veterans* in New York may be partially exempt.

Senior Citizen Exemption

New York law gives local governments and public school districts the option of granting a reduction on the amount of property taxes paid by qualifying senior citizens. This is accomplished by reducing the assessed value of residential property owned by seniors by 50 percent. To qualify, seniors must be 65 or older and must show that they have owned the property for at least 12 consecutive months prior to the date of filing the application (unless the owner received a senior citizen exemption for her previous residence, in which case the 12-month requirement is considered satisfied). For the 50 percent exemption, the law allows each assessing unit to set the maximum income limit at any figure between $3,000 and $21,500. Localities have the further option of granting an exemption of less than 50% to senior citizens whose incomes exceed the local income limit by less than $1,000 in three income ranges or $900 in six other income ranges.

Veterans' Exemptions

The tax law provides a partial exemption to veterans if the veteran's property has been purchased with a veterans' pension, bonus, or insurance monies, which are referred to as *eligible funds.* Another exemption, known as the *alternative veterans' exemption,* is available only for residential property of veterans who served during wartime. This provides a tax exemption of 15 percent of assessed value to veterans who served during wartime and an additional 10 percent to those who served in a combat zone. Each

---

The new school tax exemption   You Should Know

A School Tax Relief (STAR) program provides a partial exemption from school property taxes for owner-occupied primary residences including one- to three-family homes, condominiums, and cooperatives. The **Basic STAR** exemption is available for owner-occupied, primary residences regardless of the owners' age or income. Basic STAR works by exempting the first $30,000 of the full value of a home from school taxes.

The **Enhanced STAR** exemption is available for the primary residences of senior citizens (age 65 and older) with yearly household incomes not exceeding the statewide standard (maximum.) For 2003 assessment rolls, the applicants' 2001 income, based on their 2001 income tax return, may not exceed $62,100. A cost of living adjustment will be made to the STAR income standard again for 2004 assessment rolls and annually thereafter.

For qualifying senior citizens, the Enhanced STAR program works by exempting the first $50,000 of the full value of their home from school property taxes. For property owned by a husband and wife, or by siblings, only one of them must be at least 65 years of age to qualify for the Enhanced exemption. Their combined annual income, however, must not exceed the STAR income standard.

---

municipality in New York was given the option of not granting this alternative exemption. Residents must check to see if the alternative exemption is available in their municipality. The eligible funds exemption generally carries a maximum $5,000 deduction of a property's assessed value. It applies to general municipal taxes but not to school districts or special district levies. Exemptions are not automatically provided. An application must be filed with the local assessing unit.

ASSESSMENTS

Municipal and school budgets determine the amount of money that must be raised through taxes. Assessments determine how that *total tax is shared among property owners.*

Assessments are determined by the **assessor,** *an elected or appointed local official or officials who have the legal authority to estimate independently the value of real property in an assessing unit.* Some municipalities have a single appointed assessor, and some have a board of elected assessors. Assessing units follow municipal boundaries: county, city, town, or village. All cities and towns in New York are assessing units and have assessors, except for Nassau and Tompkins Counties, which have county assessing. Villages in New York are also assessing units, but have the option of ceasing to be assessing units and levying their taxes on the village portion of the town roll. School districts and special districts use assessment rolls prepared by the various assessing units as the basis for collecting taxes.

Deadlines for Real Property Assessment

Important dates in the tax cycle may differ throughout New York. Some counties have their own tax acts, and cities operate under charters that allow them to set their own dates. New York City also operates under its own schedule. The following dates apply to towns and villages in New York. *March 1 in towns and January 1 in villages are known as* **taxable status dates.** Real property is assessed with respect to its condition on those dates. For example, if a homeowner installs central air conditioning on March 2 (in a town) or January 2 (in a village), its contribution to market value will not be reflected on the assessment roll (and therefore the tax bill) until the following year. Normally, the taxable status date is the last day on which exemption applications may be filed.

On May 1, in most towns and in Tompkins County, and February 1 in villages, a tentative assessment roll must be filed by the assessor and made available for public inspection. Again, schedules vary in cities, some villages, and in Erie, Nassau, Suffolk, and Westchester Counties. Figure 9.2 illustrates the important events in the annual real property assessment tax cycle. The **assessment roll** is *usually in section, block/lot order and contains a list of all real property in the jurisdiction with annual information about each parcel including its assessed value and exempt status.* After this date, the assessor may not make any changes to the roll. The changes can be made only by a board of assessment review (discussed later).

Making Assessments

Assessment of property for tax purposes involves first establishing the market value of each parcel of land to be taxed within the taxing unit, such as a city, town, or county. Market value is what a willing buyer will pay a willing seller for a property. Market value is determined by an appraisal of the property. Property values must be reasonably uniform to provide equal taxation of property owners. Reassessment of property for tax purposes occurs on a regular basis established by statutes and by when improvements are made to the real estate.

Assessing Units and Uniform Percentage

The New York Real Property Tax Law requires the use of "uniform percentage" as the basis for assessing. This means that all taxable properties in a city, town or village must be assessed at market value or all at the same uniform percentage of market value each year. That percentage of market or full value at which properties are assessed within a community is called the Level of Assessment (LOA). For example, an LOA of 50 percent would indicate that assessments are at half of the market value; whereas, an LOA of 100 percent represents a community that is assessing at full value. Table 9.1 indicates the different assessed values of a property whose market value is $100,000.

	PERCENTAGE OF VALUE	ASSESSED VALUE
TABLE 9.1 Market value of property = $100,000	5%	$5,000
	15%	$15,000
	50%	$50,000
	100%	$100,000

You Should Know   **The difference between tax assessment and tax appraisal**

A tax appraisal of an individual property is the same as an appraisal for other purposes, such as a valuation for mortgage purposes. A tax assessment, however, takes the market value obtained from the appraisal and applies a uniform percentage, which then reflects only a portion of the value.

Therefore, no matter what LOA the municipality uses, all of the assessments in the community are required to be at a "uniform percentage of value." If a town chooses to assess at 40% of market value, then all of the properties in the town should be assessed at 40%. (Only New York City and Nassau County are authorized by New York law to assess each of four specific classes of property at different levels.)

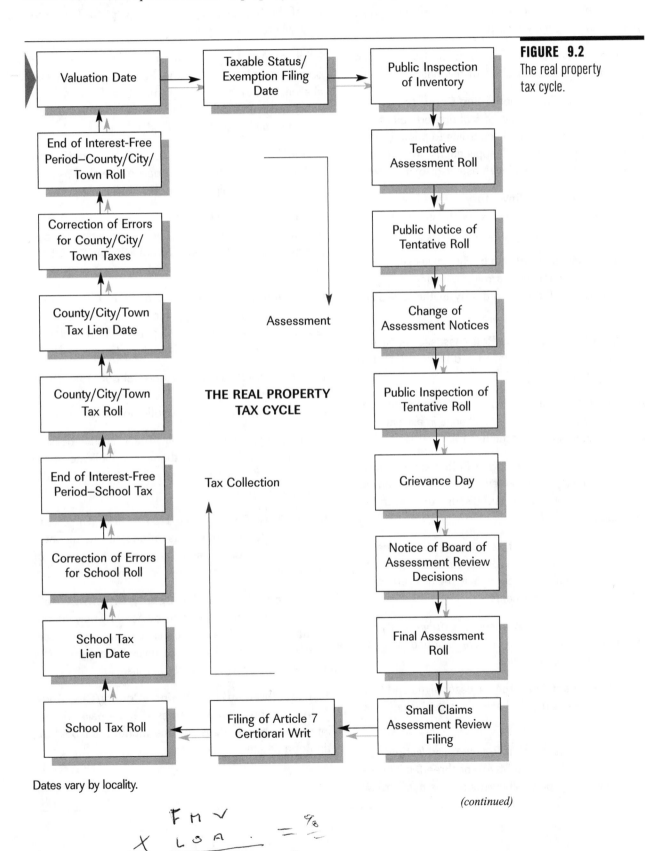

FIGURE 9.2
The real property tax cycle.

THE REAL PROPERTY TAX CYCLE

Dates vary by locality.

(continued)

FMV
X LOA   = %

ASSessment value

FIGURE 9.2 Continued.

The Real Property Tax Cycle

The following identifies and explains important events in the annual real property assessment tax cycle. Specific dates vary by locality.

Valuation Date: Real property price level for the assessment cycle is frozen as of this date.

Taxable Status Exemption/Filing Date: The ownership and physical condition of real property as of this date are assessed (valued) according to price fixed as of the valuation date. All applications for property exemptions must be filed with assessor by this date.

Public Inspection of 'Inventory': Period of time in which property owners can review the information on file for their property.

Tentative Assessment Roll: The assessor completes, certifies, and files a roll containing proposed assessed values for each property in the assessing unit.

Public Notice of Tentative Roll: Assessor publishes and posts notice of completion and filing of tentative assessment roll.

Change of Assessment Notices: Notices are sent to property owners who have a change in assessment or taxable status on the tentative roll.

Public Inspection of Tentative Roll: Period of time in which property owners may examine the assessed values on the tentative roll and discuss them with the assessor.

Grievance Day: Board of assessment review meets to hear assessment complaints. *Last day* property owners may file a formal complaint seeking reduction in their tentative assessments.

Notice of Board of Assessment Review (BAR) Decisions: Property owners are notified of the results of the review by the Bar.

Final Assessment Roll: The assessor signs and files a roll that contains the final assessments, including all changes.

Small Claims Assessment Review: The *last date* by which an owner of a one-, two-, or three-family residence may apply for small claims assessment review

of the Bar determination. This is 30 days after the filing of the final assessment roll, except for New York City, where it is October 25.

Filing of Article 7 'Certiorari Writ': A legal action pursuant to Article 7 of the Real Property Tax Law challenging an assessment must be filed in state supreme court no later than 30 days after the date the final assessment roll is filed.

School Tax Roll: The assessor delivers to the school authorities a duplicate of the part of the final assessment roll that applies to the school district.

School 'Tax Lien' Date: The date school authorities attach to the school tax roll an authorization for collection of taxes. Tax collector publishes notice of tax collection.

Correction of Errors for School Roll: The last date for a property owner to apply to the county director of real property tax services for correction of a clerical error or unlawful entry on the school tax roll.

End of Interest-Free Period—School Tax: Taxes may be paid without interest or penalty fees for one month after publication of a notice of collection.

County/City/Town Tax Roll: The assessor delivers to the county/city/town authorities a duplicate of the part of the final assessment roll that applies to the county/city/town.

County/City/Town Tax Lien Date: The date county/city/town authorities attach to the county/city/town tax roll an authorization for collection of taxes. Tax collector publishes notice of tax collection.

Correction of Errors for County/City/Town Roll: The last date for a property owner to apply to the county director of real property tax services for correction of a clerical error or unlawful entry on the county, city, town, or school tax rolls.

End of Interest-Free Period—County/City/Town Taxes: County/city/town taxes may be paid without interest or penalty fees for one month after publication of a notice of collection.

Approved Assessing Units and Classification of Homestead and Nonhomestead Properties

An **approved assessing unit** is one that *has completed a property reevaluation and has been certified by the New York State Office of Real Property Services.* Local assessing bodies can tell property-tax payers how properties in their community have been classified. Approved assessing units may elect to establish separate *tax rates* (discussed later) for homestead and nonhomestead real property. The **homestead** class includes:

- one-, two-, or three-family residential parcels
- residential condominiums
- mixed-use parcels if they are used primarily for residential purposes
- mobile homes and trailers, only if they are owner-occupied and separately assessed
- all vacant land parcels not exceeding 10 acres that are located in an assessing unit with a zoning law, provided that such parcels are located in a zone that does not allow a residential use other than for one-, two-, or three-family residential properties
- farm dwellings
- land used for agricultural production and farm buildings and structures on this land

The **nonhomestead** *class includes all other real property, that is, commercial, industrial, special franchise, and utility property, and some vacant land.*

In most jurisdictions, all properties, regardless of classification or type must be assessed at a uniform percentage. In New York City and Nassau County, however, different classes of property—residential, vacant land, commercial, industrial, and so on, are assessed at different percentages of market value. However, all property *within* a certain class, such as one-, two-, and three-family homes, must be assessed at the same uniform percentage.

Assessment Standards—Evidence

The market value standard is the only true and impartial theory for setting assessments. Even though New York law allows for maintaining assessments at a uniform percentage of full value, the current market value of each property must still be determined in order to apply the uniform percentage in setting the assessment. The most recent purchase price of a property, for example, would not work as a standard for setting assessments. For example, two identical houses built in 1975 sold for $100,000. If one of the houses remained under the same ownership, its assessment today would be based on $100,000. If the other sold last year for $200,000, its assessment would be based on $200,000. Therefore, the new homeowner would be paying twice as much in property taxes as the other homeowner.

PROTESTING ASSESSMENTS

Taxpayers have the right to look at the assessment of their property, compare it with other properties on the assessment roll, and if a property owner believes the assessment is wrong, *the owner may file a written complaint, called a* **grievance,** with the local board of assessment review.

When May Complaints Be Filed?

Property owners in New York may meet with their local assessors to discuss their property assessment at any time in an informal meeting. Each year, however, on May 1 in towns, and on February 1 in villages, and on other dates in cities throughout New York, the tentative assessment roll is made available for public inspection. If a property owner wishes to protest his assessment, he must file a standard complaint form with the board of assessment review for his municipality. Complaint forms (RP-524) may be obtained at the assessor's office, the real property tax service agency of the county, or the New York State Office of Real Property Services website: *http://www.orps.state.ny.us*. The completed complaint must be mailed or delivered to the board of assessment review on or before "Grievance Day," which is usually held on the fourth Tuesday in May for towns, and the third Tuesday in February for villages.

To Whom Must the Protest Be Directed?

Grievances are heard by the **board of assessment review.** *The board consists of three to five members appointed by the governing body of the municipality.* The board does not include the assessor or any of the assessor's staff. Property owners who file a protest may appear in person before the board, assign an agent to appear on their behalf, such as an attorney, or not appear at all. The complaint will still be considered.

Grounds for Protest

Complainants must make a case that the assessor or assessing body is wrong and must name a specific figure that they believe is the accurate assessment. There is a presumption under the law that the assessor is correct. The burden of proof is on the complainant to prove the assessor incorrect. The four grounds for review in New York are: unequal assessment, excessive assessment, unlawful assessment, and misclassification.

Unequal Assessment

As previously discussed, New York law requires that assessments must be made at a uniform percentage of value. A complainant may believe that her property is assessed at a higher percentage of value than the average of all other properties on the same assessment roll. For example, if a property owner proves that the value of her property is $100,000, an assessment of $75,000 would mean that it is assessed at 75 percent of its value. If the property owner proves that all other property on the average is assessed at 50 percent, the owner may claim a reduction of her assessment to $50,000. To demonstrate that the property is unequally assessed, the value of the property must first be established. Examples of information to be provided in defense of a protester's complaint are:

- purchase price of the property, if recent
- offering price of the property if recently offered for sale
- professional appraisal of the property
- rental information if property is rented
- income and expense information if property is commercial, industrial, or rented
- purchase price of comparable property recently sold including information describing each comparable property and a comparison with the protested property
- cost of construction if recently built

Excessive Assessment

If property owners believe that the assessed value of the property is greater than the full value of the property, they may claim excessive assessment. This category also includes complaints that a portion of a partial exemption was denied.

Unlawful Assessment

This category includes properties that under law are fully exempt from real property taxation. If a property is located outside the boundaries of the city, town, village, school district, or special district indicated on the assessment roll, the assessment is unlawful. Other unlawful assessments include property entered on the assessment roll by someone other than the assessing unit and inaccurate identification of a property.

Misclassification—Homestead and Nonhomestead Classes

This protest can be used only in approved assessing units that have adopted homestead and nonhomestead classes, as discussed earlier. The two possible types of claims of misclassification are: (1) the parcel has been designated in the wrong class on the assessment roll, or (2) the allocation of the parcel's total assessed value between the homestead and the nonhomestead part is incorrect. For example, a 100-acre parcel is assessed for $100,000. The assessor allocates $50,000 of that amount to the residence and its surrounding 10 acres. The other $50,000 is allocated to the remaining 90 acres. The protester may believe that the $100,000 total assessment is correct but believes that the residence and 10 acres are worth more than one-half of that total, for example, $67,000. The question of allocation will become significant because of the different tax rates assigned for the homestead and nonhomestead classes. In these cases, the protester can claim that the property is misclassified and require that the assessed value be allocated equally between the residence and surrounding 10 acres and the remaining 90 acres.

Who Makes the Protest?

The complainant (property owner) may make the protest on his behalf or have someone, such as an attorney, represent him. The decision of the board of assessment review appears on the final assessment roll, which is published for towns on July 1 and villages on April 1.

Small Claims Assessment Review

If homeowners who protest their assessments still are dissatisfied with the decision of the board of assessment review, they have the option of a further review either in state supreme court or before specially appointed small claims hearing officers. The supreme court form of review is expensive and costly for most homeowners. *A judicial review of the case in state supreme court is called a* **tax certiorari proceeding.** The small claims assessment review process is generally the next step.

Who Is Eligible to File?

Individuals who own and live in a one-, two-, or three-family home used for residential purposes may file. Complainants may not request a reduction greater than that already sought from the board of assessment review. Among those *not* eligible to file are: owners of cooperatives; apartment renters; and condominium owners, *except* for those who own condominiums in Class One special assessing units, which include Nassau and New York City and those designated in the homestead class as "approved assessing units." Also not eligible are owners of buildings not used for residential purposes and owners of vacant land other than the exceptions noted above, farm buildings, and commercial property. Small claims assessment review petitions are available through the offices of the county clerk. The fee for filing is $25. The petition must be filed within 30 days of the last date allowed for filing a final assessment roll for the assessing unit where the property is located. After the petition is filed, the assessment review clerk in state supreme court will assign a hearing officer to decide the case. The hearing is held within 45 days of the final date for filing the petitions. The only recourse for the taxpayer if he is dissatisfied with the decision of the small claims hearing officer is to commence an Article 78 proceeding, which is a type of appeal process according to the New York Civil Practice Law and Rules for administrative decisions.

TAX RATE FIXATION

Budgeting and Setting the Tax Rate

Each taxing unit of government—counties, cities, towns, villages, schools, and special districts—adopts an annual budget. The proposed expenditures are determined and the revenues from various sources such as state and federal aid are estimated. *The difference between the two represents the amount that the municipality must raise by taxes on real property.* This is the **tax levy.** That amount divided by the taxable assessed and nonexempt value of all the real property within that jurisdiction produces the tax rate for that year. *The tax rate is therefore set by the municipality to meet the needs of budgetary requirements.* The formula for the tax rate is:

Rate = Tax dollars required
     Taxable assessed value

The tax rate is usually expressed in terms of a certain number of tax dollars per $1,000 of assessed value, for example, $40 for each $1,000 of assessed value. If a town levy is $2 million and the entire town has a taxable assessed value (the sum of the assessment of all taxable properties) of $40 million, the tax rate would be $50 for each $1,000 of taxable assessed value.

$2 million/$40 million = 0.050 × $1,000 = $50

Different localities use different tax rates—for example, dollars per hundred or thousand, mills, or percentages. The tax rate is stated in dollars or mills (one-tenth of a cent). Find out what the standard is in your area.

Multiple Tax Districts

In New York, with some exceptions, all types of property *within* the municipality will pay taxes using the same tax rate. *Only differences in assessed value account for differences in tax bills among properties.* The exceptions to the single rate tax system are "special assessing units" in New York City and Nassau County, which use four classified tax rates depending on the type of property, and some approved assessing units that use two tax rates.

Determination of the Property Tax Bill

The annual property tax bill is calculated by multiplying the assessed value by the tax rate. The formula for calculating property tax is:

Assessed value × tax rate = annual taxes

For example, a house valued at $100,000 is assessed at a uniform percentage rate of 15 percent. Therefore the assessed value is $15,000.

The tax rate for the municipality is $50 per $1,000 of assessed value. To obtain the property tax bill, you must first divide the assessment of $15,000 by $1,000 to obtain

$15 (because the tax rate is based on each $1,000 of assessed value). Then multiply the $15 by the tax rate to obtain the tax bill of $750.

$15,000/$1,000 = $15 × $50 = $750 (tax bill)

Tax Share Preservation

Tax rates sometimes cannot be set until the tax levy is apportioned, or divided, among various municipalities. **Apportionment** *occurs if parts of a school district, or special district, exist in more than one city or town. Taxes are apportioned so that the districts in the different municipalities all pay their fair share of the district tax levy.* The county tax levy also is apportioned among the towns and cities in the county so that cities and towns will pay their fair share of the county tax levy. In New York City, Nassau County, and other municipalities, the tax levy is apportioned among various classes of real property.

The Equalization Rate

Because the law does not specify any particular percentage for assessment purposes, homes in one town may be assessed at 5 percent of value while those in a neighboring town may be assessed at 50 percent of value. Therefore in two neighboring towns, homes that have identical market values will have greatly different assessed values. This can be a problem when a taxing jurisdiction such as a county or a school district contains more than one assessing jurisdiction (several cities or towns). Some common denominator must be used to apportion taxes fairly. To remedy this problem, the New York Office of Real Property Services (NYSORPS) has developed an equalization rate to determine at what percent of market value different municipalities are assessing. The rate is the result of the appraisal of all types of properties in every city, town, and village, and the comparison of these appraised market values with assessed values. The ratio of assessed value to market value is the equalization rate. The equalization rate represents the average percentage of market value at which assessment in a municipality is set at a given point in time. If, for example, a municipality has an equalization rate of 10, it means that NYSORPS found that assessments were on the average at 10 percent of the market values established for the survey. Valuation dates used in New York State surveys are usually a few years behind current market value.

Equalization rates and the data on which they are based are used for many purposes, including setting municipal tax and debt limits; apportioning school taxes, when school districts are located in more than one city or town; establishing county taxes among member municipalities; and distributing many forms of assessments on specialized types of properties.

SPECIAL IMPROVEMENT ASSESSMENTS

At times, taxing units levy special assessments in addition to real property taxes to collect payment for a share of the cost of improvements made to areas nearby or adjoining the property. These assessments can be levied against property only if the property benefits from the improvement. Examples are assessments for streets, sidewalks, sewers, rural drainage ditches, and other public improvements. The **special assessment** is *a specific lien against the property until paid.* If the lien is not paid, the taxing unit may execute on the lien, forcing a sale of the property for payment of the assessments. These assessments may be calculated on an ad valorem basis or an alternative method, such as length of road frontage or percentage of cost.

Though special assessments resemble property taxes in that they are collected and often calculated in the same way, they are different. Special assessments can represent a major drawback for a property owner because the IRS will not allow special assessments to be deducted, whereas property taxes are tax deductible.

ENFORCEMENT

If a taxpayer is delinquent in paying property taxes, the taxing jurisdiction initiates a **tax lien** *against the property.* Like other types of liens, a property tax lien creates an encumbrance against the property. However, a property tax lien takes first priority over all other liens so that when and if a transfer of title takes place, any tax lien against the property must be paid first.

Foreclosure and In Rem Tax Sale

An **in rem legal proceeding** *occurs when an action is brought against the real property directly and not against an individual and his personal property.* The following sections describe examples of in rem tax sales.

Administrative Tax Sale

In New York, the taxing district can *foreclose* on the property and hold an administrative tax sale—sell the property to collect the taxes owed. When a real property tax remains unpaid for a specified time according to local statutes, a list of delinquent properties is published, and a notice of tax sale is sent to the owner of the property. On the date specified on the notice, the property is sold, and the purchaser also assumes any interest and penalties against the property. The purchaser at a tax sale receives a certificate of sale, which is an assignment of the tax lien. If the owner does not redeem the taxes by paying the purchaser in a prescribed period of time, the purchaser then receives a deed from the county clerk and may record the deed or foreclose on the lien.

The original theory behind this procedure is that the owner could come forth and pay his back taxes before the foreclosure sale. This method is seldom used in New York because owners have not always protected their property by paying their back taxes.

Foreclosure of a Tax Lien by an Action In Rem

A situation may occur when a tax district holds a tax lien for more than four years (local statutes may reduce this time period). In New York, with proper notice to the property owner, and publication of the delinquent property, the tax lien is sold to the taxing district, and the enforcing officer executes a deed to the taxing district. As with any other deed, the deed is executed, delivered, and recorded. The proceeding is officially concluded two years after the recorded date of the deed. The taxing district may then sell and deed the property over to a purchaser. The time frame for foreclosure of a tax lien may vary according to local tax districts. This procedure is the most popular method because it is inexpensive and timely.

Personal Liability

The New York Real Property Law imposes personal liability for property taxes against the owner. However, after the local taxing unit transfers the tax liability to the county in the form of a tax sales certificate, this personal liability is extinguished. This transfer from the local unit to the county must be effected within a maximum of 90 days of the time the tax is due to the local authority. Therefore, the property owner is seldom personally liable for property taxes.

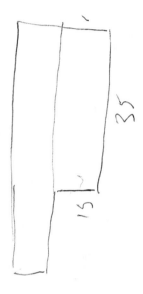

1. *Calculation of Ad Valorem Taxes.* Real estate brokers should understand how taxes are calculated so that if the market value of a property increases, predictions can be made as to future tax obligations. Turn to Chapter 10, Real Estate Math, and work through the sample problems and solutions in the section on ad valorem taxes. Also complete the practice problems in the multiple-choice section of that chapter.

2. Although notices are sent out by the taxing authority, it is ultimately the responsibility of the property owner to pay tax bills on time. Respond to the following question. Compare your response with the model in the Answer Key at the end of the chapter.

   The question is: I just received my property tax bill indicating that I am late with payment and that I must pay a late fee. I never received the first notice, so how can they charge a late fee?*

   *Source: James A. Ader, "Real Estate Spotlight." Copyright © *The Albany Times Union.* Reprinted with permission.

IMPORTANT POINTS

1. In New York, property is taxed on an ad valorem basis, that is, according to the market value of the property.

2. A tax bill is determined by a formula that includes two items: the property's assessment and the tax rate of the taxing jurisdiction.

3. A property's assessment is a percentage of its market value and, in most areas outside of New York City and Nassau County, must be a uniform percentage of the property's market value throughout the taxing jurisdiction.

4. All property is subject to assessment; however, not all property is taxed. Property tax exemptions may be full or partial.

5. An approved assessing unit is a taxing jurisdiction that has completed a property reevaluation and has been certified by the New York State Office of Real Property Services.

6. The assessment roll that describes all properties and their assessed value is published each year. Taxpayers who disagree with their assessment may file a complaint called a grievance.

7. If taxpayers are still dissatisfied with the decision of the board of assessment review, they may either file a complaint with the New York Supreme Court, called a tax certiorari proceeding, or be heard by specially appointed small claims hearing officers.

8. The tax rate must be sufficient to provide the amount of revenue to accomplish the budgetary requirements of the local governmental unit.

9. The equalization rate represents the average percentage of market value at which assessments in a municipality are set at a given point in time.

10. If a property owner is delinquent in paying property taxes, his taxing jurisdiction may impose a lien against the property.

CHAPTER REVIEW

KEY TERM REVIEW

Fill in the term that best completes the sentence and then check the Answer Key at the end of the chapter.

1. A(n) _____ legal proceeding means that an action is brought against the real property directly and not against an individual and his personal property.

2. If a property owner believes the assessment is wrong, the owner may file a written complaint, called a(n) _____, with the local board of assessment review.

3. A property's _____ is a percentage of its market value.

4. A judicial review of a decision of a local taxing unit in Supreme Court is called a(n) _____.

5. If a taxpayer is delinquent in paying property taxes, his taxing jurisdiction may initiate a(n) _____ against the property.

6. When taxes are levied against property only if the property is specifically benefited by the improvement, such as the construction of a sidewalk, it is called a(n) _____.

MULTIPLE CHOICE

Circle the letter that best answers the question and then check the Answer Key at the end of the chapter.

1. A property tax bill is determined by:
   A. a property's assessed value only
   B. a property's full value only
   C. a combination of the tax rate and the property's assessed value
   D. the tax rate only

2. The property tax rate is determined by:
   A. the amount of the tax levy
   B. New York law
   C. the amount needed by the school district and special districts only
   D. the amount voted on by citizen referendum

3. A property whose market value is $150,000 in a community where the uniform percentage for assessment is 70 percent will have an assessed value of:
   A. $70,000
   B. $105,000
   C. $115,000
   D. $125,000

4. Which of the following does NOT belong to the homestead class of properties?
   A. residential condominiums
   B. three-family residential dwellings
   C. industrial parks
   D. residentially zoned vacant land

5. Approved assessing units may:
   A. elect not to assess any properties in their jurisdictions
   B. establish separate tax rates for homestead and nonhomestead properties
   C. elect not to establish uniform percentages within a particular property classification
   D. receive total state aid and not have to depend on local property taxes

6. If property owners believe their assessment is inaccurate, they:
   A. must simply accept this as a matter of law
   B. must first file a summons and complaint against the taxing jurisdiction in Supreme Court
   C. may file a complaint, called a grievance, with the local assessment board of review
   D. must wait until they transfer title to their property for a reassessment to occur

7. An excessive assessment may mean that:
   A. the assessed value of a property is greater than its full value
   B. the assessed value of a property is less than its full value
   C. too many properties in the assessing unit were assessed
   D. the uniform percentage applied to the assessment of the property was too low in comparison with other similar properties

8. The tax rate is:
   A. set by New York law and is uniform throughout the state
   B. set by the individual municipality to meet its budgetary needs
   C. is not needed in municipalities where all classes of properties are assessed at a uniform percentage
   D. is the same amount as the tax levy

9. The annual property tax bill is calculated by:
   A. multiplying the assessed value by the tax rate
   B. dividing the assessed value by the tax rate
   C. dividing the total budget by the tax rate
   D. multiplying the total budget by the tax rate

10. Which of the following is FALSE regarding the equalization rate? It:
    A. is computed by the New York Office of Real Property Services
    B. is used in the setting of municipal tax and debt limits
    C. represents the average percentage of market value at which assessments in a municipality are set at a given point in time
    D. is computed by considering the appraisal of residential properties only in a given municipality

ANSWER KEY

Putting It to Work

Even though taxing authorities routinely mail copies of their tax bills to remind property owners how much is due and when, failure to receive such notice does not relieve taxpayers of the responsibility to make payment in a timely manner. Property owners must be aware of tax due dates and must be sure they make payments on time, regardless of whether they receive a bill.*

Key Term Review

1. in rem
2. grievance
3. assessment
4. tax certiorari proceeding
5. tax lien
6. special assessment

Multiple Choice

1. C	4. C	7. A	10. D
2. A	5. B	8. B	
3. B	6. C	9. A	

---

*Source: James A. Ader, "Real Estate Spotlight," Copyright © *The Albany Times Union.* Reprinted with permission.

Chapter 10

Real Estate Math

IN THIS CHAPTER Real estate licensees need an understanding of arithmetic fundamentals. Using these fundamentals, you need to master certain mathematical calculations related to real estate. Some people have difficulty with math. The practice exercises in this chapter, coupled with on-the-job experience, will reinforce understanding. The multiple choice questions designate specific chapters that correspond with the questions.

GENERAL PRACTICE IN REAL ESTATE MATHEMATICS

Percentages

In the real estate business, many calculations involve percentages. For example, a real estate broker commission is often a percentage of the sales price. A percentage is a number that has been divided by 100. To use a percentage, you must change the percentage to its decimal equivalent. The rule for changing a percentage to a decimal is to remove the percent sign and move the decimal point two places to the left (or divide the percentage by 100). Examples of converting a percentage to a decimal are:

$$98\% = 0.98 \qquad 1\tfrac{1}{2}\% = 1.5\% = 0.015$$
$$1.42\% = 0.0142 \qquad 1\tfrac{1}{4}\% = 1.25\% = 0.0125$$
$$0.092\% = 0.00092 \qquad \tfrac{3}{4}\% = 0.75\% = 0.0075$$

To change a decimal or a fraction to a percentage, simply reverse the procedure. Move the decimal point two places to the right and add the percent sign (or multiply by 100). Some examples of this operation are:

$$1.00 = 100\% \qquad \tfrac{1}{2} = 1 \div 2 = 0.5 = 50\%$$
$$0.90 = 90\% \qquad \tfrac{3}{8} = 3 \div 8 = 0.375 = 37.5\%$$
$$0.0075 = 0.75\% \qquad \tfrac{2}{3} = 2 \div 3 = 0.667 = 66.7\%$$

Formulas

Almost every problem in a real estate transaction uses the format of something × something = something else. In mathematics language, factor × factor = product. Calculating a real estate commission is a classic example:

sales price paid $\times$ percentage of commission $=$ commission
$80,000 $\times$ 7% $=$ $5,600

   In most real estate problems, two of the three numbers are provided. Calculations to find the third number are required. If the number missing is the product, the calculation or function is to multiply the two factors. If the number missing is one of the factors, the calculation or function is to divide the product by the given factor.

Solving for product:	Answers:
43,500 $\times$ 10.5% = _____	(43,500 $\times$ 0.105 = 4,567.50)
100,000 $\times$ 4% = _____	(100,000 $\times$ 0.04 = 4,000)
51.5 $\times$ 125 = _____	(6,437.50)

Solving for factor:	Answers:
43,500 $\times$ _____ = 4,567.50	(4,567.50 $\div$ 43,500 = 0.105 = 10.5%)
_____ $\times$ 4% = 4,000.00	(4,000.00 $\div$ 0.04 = 100,000)
51.5 $\times$ _____ = 6,437.50	(6,437.50 $\div$ 51.5 = 125)

Commission Problems

Problems involving commissions are readily solved by the formula:

   sales price $\times$ rate of commission $=$ total commission

Sales

1. A real estate broker sells a property for $90,000. Her rate of commission is 7%. What is the amount of commission in dollars?

   Solution: sales price $\times$ rate $=$ commission
                    $90,000 $\times$ 0.07 = _____
                    product missing: multiply

   Answer: $6,300 commission

2. A real estate broker earns a commission of $6,000 in the sale of a residential property. His rate of commission is 6%. What is the selling price?

   Solution: sales price $\times$ rate $=$ commission
                    _____ $\times$ 0.06 = $6,000
                    factor missing: divide $6,000 by 0.06 = _____

   Answer: $100,000 sales price

3. A real estate broker earns a commission of $3,000 in the sale of property for $50,000. What is her rate of commission?

   Solution: sales price $\times$ rate $=$ commission
                    $50,000 $\times$ _____ = $3,000
                    factor missing: divide $3,000 by $50,000 and convert to percentage

   Answer: 6% rate

Rentals

4. A real estate salesperson is the property manager for the owner of a local shopping center. The center has five units, each renting for $24,000 per year. The center has an annual vacancy factor of 4.5%. The commission for rental of the units is 9% of the gross rental income. What is the commission for the year?

Solution: gross rental $\times$ rate   =   commission
gross rental   = $24,000 $\times$ 5 minus the vacancy factor
vacancy factor = $120,000 $\times$ 0.045 = $5,400
$120,000   − $5,400   = $114,600
$114,600 $\times$ 0.09   =   _____
product missing: multiply

Answer: $10,314 commission

Splits

5. A real estate salesperson sells a property for $250,000. The commission on this sale to the real estate firm with whom the salesperson is associated is 7%. The salesperson receives 60% of the total commission paid to the real estate firm. What is the firm's share of the commission in dollars?

   Solution: sales price $\times$ rate   =   commission
   $250,000 $\times$ 0.07 =   _____
   product missing: multiply
   $250,000 $\times$ 0.07 = $17,500
   100%   −   60%   =   40% is the firm's share
   $17,500 $\times$ 0.40 = $7,000

   Answer: $7,000 firm's share of commission

6. A broker's commission is 10% of the first $50,000 of sales price of a property and 8% of the amount of sales price over $50,000. The broker receives a total commission of $7,000. What is the total selling price of the property?

   Solution:

   Step 1:   sales price $\times$ rate   =   commission
   $50,000 $\times$ 0.10 =   _____
   product missing: multiply
   $50,000 $\times$ 0.10 = $5,000 commission on first $50,000 of sales
     price

   Step 2:   total commission − commission on first $50,000 = commission
   on amount over $50,000
   $7,000   − $5,000 = $2,000 commission on selling price over
     $50,000

   Step 3:   sales price $\times$ rate   =   commission
   _____ $\times$ 0.08 = $2,000
   factor missing: divide
   $2,000 $\div$ 0.08 = $25,000

   Step 4: $50,000   + $25,000 = $75,000

   Answer: $75,000 total selling price

Estimating Net to Seller

The formula used to estimate the net dollars to the seller is:

   sales price $\times$ percent to seller = net dollars to seller

   The percent to the seller is 100% minus the rate of commission paid to the real estate agent.

7. A seller advises a broker that she expects to net $80,000 from the sale of her property after the broker commission of 7% is deducted from proceeds of the sale. For what price must the property be sold?

Solution: 100%   = gross sales price
100%   − 7% = 93%
93%   = net to owner
$80,000 = 0.93 × sales price
factor missing: divide
$80,000 ÷ 0.93 = _____

Answer: $86,022 sales price (rounded)

Estimating Partial Sales of Land

8. A subdivision contains 400 lots. If a broker has sold 25% of the lots and his sales staff has sold 50% of the remaining lots, how many lots are still unsold?

Solution: 0.25   ×   400   = 100 sold by broker
400   −   100   = 300
300   ×   0.50   = 150 sold by sales force
400   −   250 sold = 150 unsold

Answer: 150 lots still unsold

AREA CALCULATIONS

It is often necessary to determine the size of an area in square feet, cubic feet, and number of acres. In taking a listing, the broker should determine the number of square feet of heated area in the house. To establish the lot size, the number of square feet should be determined so it may be translated into acreage, if desired. Table 10.1 provides a list of measures and formulas.

The area of a rectangle or square is determined by simply multiplying the length times the width. In a square, the length and width are the same. The area of a triangle is calculated by multiplying one-half times the base of the triangle times the height of the triangle.

Formula for rectangle: area = length × width or $A = L \times W$

Formula for square: area = side × side or $A = S \times S$

Formula for triangle: area = 0.5 × base × height

Acreage

1. An acre of land has a width of 330 feet. If this acre of land is rectangular in shape, what is its length? An **acre** *contains 43,560 square feet.*

Solution: A   =   L   × W
43,560 = _____ × 330
factor missing: divide
43,560 ÷ 330   = _____

Answer: 132' long lot

2. If a parcel of land contains 32,670 square feet, what percent of an acre is it?

TABLE 10.1

Measures and formulas.

LINEAR MEASURE
12 inches = 1 ft
39.37 inches = 1 meter (metric system)
3 ft = 1 yd
16½ ft = 1 rod, 1 perch, or 1 pole
66 ft = 1 chain
5,280 ft = 1 mile

SQUARE MEASURE
144 sq inches = 1 sq ft
9 sq ft = 1 sq yd
30¼ sq yd = 1 sq rod
160 sq rods = 1 acre
2.47 acres = 1 hectare or 10,000
  square meters (metric system)
43,560 sq ft = 1 acre
640 acres = 1 sq mile
1 sq mile = 1 section
36 sections = 1 township

FORMULAS
1 side × 1 side = area of a square
width × depth = area of a rectangle
½ base × height = area of a triangle
½ height × (base$_1$ + base$_2$) = area of a trapezoid
½ × sum of the bases = distance between the other two sides at the mid-point of
                                   the height of a trapezoid
length × width × depth = volume (cubic measure) of a cube or a rectangular solid

CUBIC MEASURE
1,728 cubic inches = 1 cubic foot
27 cubic feet = 1 cubic yard
144 cubic inches = 1 board foot
          (12" × 12" × 1")

CIRCULAR MEASURE
360 degrees = circle
60 minutes = 1 degree
60 seconds = 1 minute

TAX VALUATION
Per $100 of Assessed Value (AV): Divide the
  AV by 100, then multiply by tax rate.
$$\frac{\text{assessed value}}{100} \times \text{tax rate}$$

Per Mill: Divide the AV by 1000,
  then multiply by tax rate.
$$\frac{\text{assessed value}}{1000} \times \text{tax rate}$$

Solution: 32,670 square feet is what percent of an acre?
32,670 = _____% × 43,560
factor missing: divide and convert decimal to percent
32,670 ÷ 43,560 = 0.75

Answer: 75% of an acre

Square Footage

3. A rectangular lot measures 185 feet by 90 feet. How many square feet does this lot contain?

   Solution: A   = L   × W
                   _____ = 185 × 90

   Answer: 16,650 sq ft

4. A room measures 15 feet by 21 feet. Prospective buyers want to purchase wall-to-wall carpeting and need to calculate the exact amount of carpeting required.

   Solution: Carpeting is sold by the square yard, so we need to convert square feet to square yards. The number of square feet per square yard is

$3 \times 3 = 9$ square feet per square yard. Therefore, to convert size in square feet to size in square yards, we need to divide by 9.

Area $\times$ 15 $\times$ 21 = 315 sq ft

sq yd = 315 $\div$ 9 = _____

Answer: 35 sq yd of carpeting

5. A new driveway, 115 feet by 20 feet, will be paved. The paving cost is $0.65 per square foot. What will be the minimum cost for paving?

Solution:

Step 1:   A = L $\times$ W

           A = 115 $\times$ 20

           A = 2,300 sq ft

Step 2:   cost = 2,300 $\times$ $0.65

Answer: $1,495

6. A house measures 28 feet wide by 52 feet long and sells for $64,000. What is the price per square foot?

Solution:

Step 1:   calculate the area

           A = 28 $\times$ 52 = 1,456 sq ft

Step 2:   divide the sales price by the area

           $64,000 $\div$ 1,456 = _____

Answer: $43.96 per sq ft

PRORATIONS AT CLOSING

Prorations at closing involve the division between seller and buyer of annual real property taxes, rents, homeowners' association dues, and other items that may have been paid or must be paid. Proration is the process of dividing something into respective shares.

In prorating calculations, the best method is first to draw a time line with the beginning, ending, and date of proration, then decide which part of the time line you need to use. In calculating prorations for closing statements, the amount is figured to the day of closing. Therefore, in problems that require calculating a daily rate, the monthly rate is divided by the number of days in the month.

An alternative approach to proration is to reduce all costs to a daily basis. Assuming 30 days in every month and 12 months per year, we can assume 360 days per year for our purposes (and most standard exams). One other rule to remember in prorating various costs for closing statements is that the day of closing is charged to the seller. In the "real world," be sure to check with an attorney about local customs regarding prorations.

1. In preparing a statement for a closing to be held August 14, a real estate broker determines that the annual real property taxes in the amount of $360 have not been paid. What will the broker put in the buyer's statement as the entry for real property taxes?

Solution: $360   ÷ 12   = $30/mo

$30/mo ÷ 30 days = $1/day

7 mos × $30   = $210

$210   + $14   = $224

Answer: $224 buyer credit (this is the seller's share of the real property taxes to cover the 7 months and 14 days of the tax year during which he owned the property).

2. A sale is closed on September 15. The buyer is assuming the seller's mortgage, which has an outstanding balance of $32,000 as of the date of closing. The annual interest rate is 8%, and the interest is paid in arrears. What is the interest proration on the closing statements the broker prepares?

Solution: $32,000 × 0.08   = $2,560 annual interest

$2,560 ÷ 12   = $213.33 interest for September (rounded)

½ × $213.33 = $106.67 interest of ½ mo

or

$2,560 ÷ 24   = $106.67 interest for ½ mo

Answer: $106.67 buyer credit

$106.67 seller debit

Because the interest is paid in arrears, the buyer is required to pay the interest for the full month of September when making the scheduled monthly payment on October 1. Therefore, the buyer is credited with the seller's share of a half-month's interest for September in the amount of $106.67. The entry in the seller's closing statement is a debit in this amount.

FINANCIAL CALCULATIONS

Typical calculations pertaining to real estate finance include annual interest, debt service on a loan, loan origination fees, loan-to-value ratios in qualifying for, and amortization of a loan.

Annual interest on a loan is calculated by multiplying the rate of interest as a percentage times the loan balance (also known as the principal balance). The number resulting from the calculation is the annual interest. The annual interest calculation also may be used in amortizing a loan on a monthly basis. The annual interest is divided by 12 (number of months in a year) to determine the monthly interest. The monthly interest then is subtracted from the monthly loan payment to determine what amount of the monthly payment paid applies to reduce the loan principal.

Debt service is the annual amount paid to retire or reduce a loan or mortgage balance. The annual debt service on a mortgage is the monthly mortgage payment times 12 (number of months in a year). Lending institutions use loan-to-value ratios to determine the maximum loan to be issued on a given parcel of real estate. The loan-to-value ratio also can be stated as a percentage of the value of the real estate; in fact, the ratio is much more commonly expressed as a percentage. Some lending institutions lend up to only 90% of the appraised value of the property (a 9:10 ratio). If a lending institution approved a loan of 100% of the value, the loan-to-value ratio would be 1:1. If a lending institution approved a loan that was only 70% of the value, the loan-to-value ratio would be 7:10.

Simple Interest

Interest calculations use the formula:

loan balance $\times$ rate of interest = annual interest

1. A loan of $15,000 is repaid in full, one year after the loan is made. If the interest rate on the loan is 12.5%, what amount of interest is owed?

   Solution: loan $\times$ rate   = annual interest

   $15,000 $\times$ 0.125   = _____

   product missing: multiply

   Answer: $1,875 interest

Principal and Interest

2. On October 1, a mortgagor makes a $300 payment on her mortgage, which is at the rate of 10%. Of the $300 total payment for principal and interest, the mortgagee allocates $200 to the payment of interest. What is the principal balance due on the mortgage on the date of the payment?

   Solution: $200 $\times$ 12 mo = $2,400 annual interest income

   principal $\times$ rate   = annual interest

   _____ $\times$ 10%   = $2,400

   factor missing: divide

   $2,400 $\times$ 0.10   = _____

   Answer: $24,000 mortgage balance on date of payment

3. If an outstanding mortgage balance is $16,363.64 on the payment date and the amount of the payment applied to interest is $150, what is the rate of interest charged on the loan?

   Solution: $150 $\times$ 12 mo = $1,800 annual interest

   principal $\times$ rate   = annual interest

   $16,363.64 $\times$ _____   = $1,800

   factor missing: divide and convert to percentage

   $1,800 $\times$ $16,363.64   = _____

   Answer: 11% interest rate (rounded)

Debt Service

4. The monthly amortized mortgage payment Belinda owes is $1,450. What is her annual debt service on this loan?

   Solution: debt service is monthly payment $\times$ 12

   $1,450 $\times$ 12 = _____

   Answer: $17,400 annual debt service

5. A commercial loan of $50,000 at 11% interest requires monthly payments of principal and interest of $516.10 to fully amortize the loan for a term of 20 years. If the loan is paid over the 20-year term, how much interest does the borrower pay?

   Solution: 20 years $\times$ 12 mo payments = 240 payments

   240        $\times$ $516.10   = $123,864 total amount paid

   total amount paid $-$ principal borrowed = interest

   $123,864 $-$ $50,000   = _____

Answer: $73,864 interest paid

Fees and Points

The typical fees for real estate mortgages are loan origination fee, points, discount points, interest escrows, and tax escrows. The amount of the fees and escrows often depends upon the loan amount or assessed annual taxes. The formula for calculating the dollar amount owed in points on a loan is:

loan × number of points (percentage) = dollars in points

6. A house sells for $60,000. The buyer obtains an 80% loan. If the bank charges 3 points at closing, how much in points must the buyer pay?

    Solution: loan   × number of points (%) = dollars paid

                     ($60,000 × 0.80) × 0.03   = _____

                     $48,000   × 0.03   = _____

                     product missing: multiply

    Answer: $1,440 points payment

7. Kim and Glenn borrow $64,000. If they pay $4,480 for points at closing, how many points are charged?

    Solution: loan   × number of points (%) = dollars paid

                     $64,000 × _____   = $4,480

                     factor missing: divide

    Answer: 7 points

8. Horatio and Marge borrow $55,000 at 6% interest for 30 years. The bank requires 2 months' interest to be placed in escrow and a 1% loan origination fee to be paid at closing. What is the amount of interest to be escrowed? What is the amount charged for the loan origination fee?

    Step 1:   interest escrow

    Solution: $55,000 ×   0.06 = $3,300 annual interest

                     $3,300   ÷   12   = $275 monthly interest

                     $275   × 2   = _____

    Answer: $550 interest escrow

    Step 2:   loan origination fee

    Solution: $55,000 ×   0.01   = _____

    Answer: $550 loan origination fee

Loan-to-Value Ratios

9. In problem 8 above, the appraised value of the home purchased is $68,750. What is the loan-to-value ratio?

    Solution: loan   ÷ value   = ratio

                     $55,000 ÷ $68,750 = 0.80

                     0.80   = 80:100

    Answer: 80% loan-to-value ratio

10. The Blacks apply for a loan. The purchase price of the home is $80,000. The bank authorizes a loan-to-value ratio of 90%. What is the amount of loan authorized?

Solution: $80,000 × 90% = loan

Answer: $72,000 loan

Qualifying for a Loan

Typically, for a borrower to qualify for a loan, the ratios of the borrower's housing and total debts to income must meet the lender's requirements. The typical housing debt-to-income ratio for conventional loans is 25–28%. The typical total debt-to-income ratio for conventional loans is 33–36%. The 25–28% means that for the borrower to qualify, PITI (principal, interest, taxes, insurance) must not be more than 25–28% of the borrower's monthly gross income. The 33–36% means that for the borrower to qualify, the total monthly expenses (including housing expense) must not be more than 33–36% of the borrower's monthly gross income.

11. Dick and Jane have a combined total monthly income of $2,500. If the lender requires a debt-to-income ratio of 25:33 for housing and total expenses, what is the maximum house payment they will qualify for? What is the maximum total monthly expenses besides PITI that will be allowed?

Solution:

Step 1: housing: $2,500 × 0.25 = $625
Step 2: total expenses: $2,500 × 0.33 = $825
$825 − $625 = _____

Answer: $200 other than PITI

REAL ESTATE INVESTMENT

Analysis of Income, Rate, and Value

Income is defined as *the amount of money one receives.* The most common application of income are commission, rents, or other moneys in your pocket. Although income can be received on a monthly basis, for purposes of this section, all monthly income must be converted to annual income. To do that, simply multiply the amount by 12 if it is not already converted to the annual figure. **Gross income** is *income received without subtracting expenses.* **Net operating income** is *gross income less operating expenses.*

Rate is defined as *a percentage.* The most common application of rate will be an interest rate, a capitalization rate, or a commission rate. Once again, remember that rate is always calculated on an annual percentage.

Value is defined as *the total amount of worth or cost of the unit.* The most common applications of value will be the principal balance of a mortgage and the sale price of a house.

In calculating either income, rate, or value, you must know two of the three variables to solve for the third. For example, if the sale price of a home is $400,000 (the value), and the commission rate is 6% (the rate), what is the income? To solve this, one could simply multiply $400,000 by 6% and get the answer. This is a fairly simple application, but it can be achieved in the same way using IRV.

To calculate IRV, use the table on the following page.

The net monthly income of a five-unit apartment building is $2,250. The capitalization rate the lender uses is 7%. Use the IRV formula to find the value of the building.

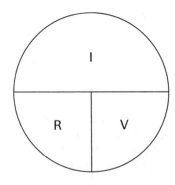

I	=	Income
R	=	Rate
V	=	Value or Sales Price
I ÷ R	=	V
R × V	=	I
I ÷ V	=	R

To solve for this, using IRV, you would multiply the income by 12 (to bring it to an annual figure) and divide by the rate: $2,250 × 12 = $27,000 ÷ .07 = $385,714.

Profit/Loss on Sale of Real Estate

Profit or loss is always based upon the amount of money invested in the property.

The formula for profit is:

investment × percent of profit = dollars in profit

The formula for loss is:

investment × percent of loss = dollars lost

1. Richard buys a house for investment purposes for $175,000. He sells it six months later for $200,000 with no expenditures for fix-up or repair. What is Richard's percentage of profit?

   Solution: investment × percentage of profit = dollars in profit
   $175,000   × _____ = $25,000
   factor missing: divide and convert decimal to percentage
   $25,000   ÷ $175,000 = _____

   Answer: 14% for the year; 7% for the six months

2. Rhonda purchases some land in 2000 for $35,000. She puts up a fence in 2002 costing her $15,500. In 2004 she sells the property for $46,000. What is her percentage of loss?

   Solution: investment × percentage lost = dollars in loss
   $50,500   × _____ = $4,500
   factor missing: divide and convert decimal to percentage
   $4,500   ÷ $50,500 = _____

   Answer: 8.91%, rounded to 9%

3. An owner purchases his home at 8% below market value. He then sells the property for the full market value. What is the rate of profit?

   Solution: market value   × 100%
   100%   × 8%   = 92% purchase price
   8%   × 92% = rate of profit
   0.08   × 0.92 = _____

Answer: 8.7% profit

INCOME TAX CALCULATIONS

Deductions

4. Sanford has owned his home for 12 years. His annual real property taxes are $360, annual homeowners' insurance is $270, annual principal payment on his mortgage is $13,000, and annual interest payment on his mortgage is $15,500. What is the total deduction allowed against his income for income tax purposes?

    Solution: Only mortgage interest and property taxes are deductible when dealing with the principal residence. Total deductions are the sum of mortgage interest and taxes.

    Answer: $15,860

Basis

5. Sue and John purchased their home 15 years ago for $32,500. During their ownership, they made capital improvements totaling $19,400. They sold the home for $72,900. What amount of gain did they make on the sale?

    Solution: basis   = purchase price   = improvements
                     $32,500   + $19,400   = $51,900 basis
                     sales price   − basis   = gain
                     $72,900   − $51,900   = _____

    Answer: $21,000

6. In problem 5, above, if the Swifts purchase another home costing $90,000 and choose to defer reporting the gain, what is the basis in the new home?

    Solution: purchase price   − any deferred gain   = basis
                     $90,000   − $21,000   = _____

    Answer: $69,000 is basis in new home

AD VALOREM PROPERTY TAXES

Assessed value is the value established by a tax assessor. The assessed value usually is a percentage of the estimated market value of the property and may be up to 100% of market value. The amount of tax is calculated by multiplying the assessed value by the tax rate, which is expressed either in dollars per $100 of assessed value or in mills (one mill is one-tenth of a cent) per $1,000 of assessed value. The tax rate is determined by the amount of the tax levy. The rate must be sufficient to provide the revenue required to accomplish the budgetary requirements of the local government unit. The formula for calculating property tax is:

assessed value $\times$ tax rate = annual taxes

1. If the assessed value of the property is $80,000 and the tax value is 100% of the assessed value, what is the annual tax if the rate is $1.50 per $100?

    Solution: assessed value $\times$ tax rate   = annual taxes
                     $80,000 $\times$ $\dfrac{\$1.50}{100}$ = _____

                     product missing: multiply
                     $80,000 $\times$ 0.0150   = $1,200

Answer: $1,200 annual taxes

2. A property sells at the assessed value. The annual real property tax is $588.80 at a tax rate of $1.15 per $100 of tax value. The property is taxed at 80% of assessed value. What is the selling price?

   Solution: assessed value   × tax rate = annual taxes

   $$\underline{\hspace{3cm}} \times \frac{\$1.15}{100} = \$588.80$$

   factor missing: divide
   $588.80   ÷ 0.0115 = $51,200 assessed value
   assessed value is 80% of selling price
   $51,200   =   0.80   × _____
   factor missing: divide
   $51,200   ÷   0.80   = selling price

   Answer: $64,000 selling price

3. If the assessed value of property is $68,000 and the annual tax paid is $850, what is the tax rate?

   Solution: assessed value × tax rate   =   annual taxes
   $68,000   × _____ = $850
   factor missing: divide, then convert to per $100 of value
   $850   ÷ $68,000 = $1.25

   Answer: $1.25 tax rate per $100 of tax value

4. If the market value is $70,000, the tax rate is 120 mills, and the assessment is 80%, what is the semiannual tax bill? (To calculate mills, divide by 1,000.)

   Solution: assessed value = 0.80 × $70,000
   assessed value = $56,000
   assessed value × tax rate   = annual taxes
   $56,000   × 120 mills   = _____
   annual tax bill = $6,720
   semiannual tax bill = $6,720 ÷ 2

   Answer: $3,360 semiannual tax bill

5. The real property tax revenue required by a small hamlet is $140,800. The assessed valuation of the taxable property is $12,800,000. The tax value is 100% of the assessed value. What must the tax rate be per $100 of assessed valuation to generate the necessary revenue?

   Solution: assessed value × tax rate   = annual taxes
   $12,800,000   × _____   = $140,800
   factor missing: divide and convert to per $100 of value
   $140,800   ÷ $12,800,000   = $0.011 (rate per $1.00)
   $0.011   × 100   = $1.10 per $100

   Answer: $1.10 tax rate per $100 of assessed value

APPRAISAL

Typical mathematical calculations involved in real estate appraisal include depreciation on improvements, comparison of properties based upon gross income, and the capitalization rate (rate of return an investor can achieve on a property based upon the present annual net income).

Depreciation

Depreciation is a loss in value from any cause. The two examples of depreciation that follow represent the types of depreciation problems a real estate student or practitioner may encounter. In the first problem, the present value of a building is given and the requirement is to calculate the original value. The second problem provides the original value to be used in arriving at the present depreciated value.

Depreciation problems use the formula:

original value × % of value NOT lost = present value

1. The value of a 6-year-old building is estimated to be $450,000. What was the value when new if the building depreciated 2% per year?

   Solution: 6 yrs.   × 2%   = 12% depreciation

   100% (new value) − 12%   = 88% of value not lost

   original value × % not lost = present value

   _____   × 88%   = $450,000

   factor missing: divide

   $450,000   ÷ 0.88   = _____

   Answer: $511,364 (rounded) value when new

2. A 14-year-old building has a total economic life of 40 years. If the original value of the building was $75,000, what is the present depreciated value?

   Solution: 100%   ÷ 40 yrs.   = yearly depreciation rate

   $1.00   ÷ 40   = 0.025, or 2.5% year depreciation

   14 yrs   × 2.5%   = 35% depreciation to date

   100%   − 35%   = 65% not lost

   original cost   × % not lost = remaining dollar value

   $75,000   × 0.65   = _____

   product missing: multiply

   $75,000   × 0.65   = _____

   Answer: present depreciated value is $48,750

Capitalization

The *capitalization rate* is the percentage of the investment the owner will receive back each year from the net income from the property. This rate is based upon the dollars invested and the annual net income from the property.

3. In appraising a small produce store, the appraiser establishes that the center produces an annual net income of $97,500. The appraiser determines the capitalization rate to be 13%. What should be the appraiser's estimate of market value for this business?

   Solution: investment × rate = annual net income or value

   _____ × 13% = $97,500

   factor missing: divide

   $97,500   ÷ 0.13 = _____

   Answer: $750,000 market value

MULTIPLE CHOICE

Circle the letter that best answers the question. Check your responses (including solutions) using the Answer Key at the end of the chapter. Note that the questions are divided according to subject matter and applicable chapters covered in the textbook.

Commissions and Sales (Chapter 2)

1. A real estate salesperson earns $24,000 per year. If she receives 60% of the 7% commissions paid to her firm on her sales, what is her monthly dollar volume of sales?
   A. $33,333.33
   B. $45,000.00
   C. $47,619.08
   D. $90,000.00

2. A triangular lot measures 350 feet along the street and 425 feet deep on the side perpendicular to the street. If a broker sells the lot for $0.75 (75 cents) per square foot and his commission rate is 9%, what is the amount of commission earned?
   A. $5,020.31
   B. $6,693.75
   C. $10,040.63
   D. $14,875.00

3. A buyer pays $45,000 for a lot. Five years later she puts it on the market for 20% more than she originally paid. The lot eventually sells for 10% less than the asking price. At what price is the house sold?
   A. $44,100
   B. $48,600
   C. $49,500
   D. $54,000

Prorations (Chapter 7, Section 2)

4. A buyer is to assume a seller's existing loan with an outstanding balance of $20,000 as of the date of closing. The interest rate is 6% and payments are made in arrears. Closing is set for October 10. What will be the entry in the seller's closing statement?
   A. $33.30 credit
   B. $33.30 debit
   C. $22.00 debit
   D. $22.00 credit

Principal, Interest, Points (Chapter 3)

5. If the monthly interest payment due on a mortgage on December 1 is $570 and the annual interest rate is 6%, what is the outstanding mortgage balance?
   A. $61,560.00
   B. $63,333.33
   C. $114,000.00
   D. $131,158.00

Area Calculations (Chapter 6, Section 2)

6. A rectangular lot measures 40 yards deep and has a frontage of 80 feet. How many acres does the lot contain?
   A. 0.07
   B. 0.21
   C. 0.22
   D. 0.70

7. In planning the development of a tract of land, the developer allocates one-half of the total area to single-family dwellings, one-third to multifamily dwellings, and 20 acres for roads and recreation areas. What is the total number of acres in the tract?
   A. 36.67
   B. 56.67
   C. 120
   D. 320

8. The outside dimensions of a rectangular house are 35 feet by 26.5 feet. If the walls are all 9 inches thick, what is the square footage of the interior?
   A. 827.5 sq ft
   B. 837.5 sq ft
   C. 927.5 sq ft
   D. 947.7 sq ft

9. A property owner plans to fence his land, which is rectangular in shape and measures 300 feet by 150 feet. How many fence posts will be required if there is to be a post every 15 feet?

    A. 45

    B. 60

    C. 61

    D. 450

Costs, Profits, Loss, and Rates of Return (Chapter 4)

10. What is the sales price of an apartment complex having an annual rental of $80,000 with expenses of $8,000 annually if the purchaser receives an 8% return?

    A. $66,240

    B. $800,000

    C. $864,000

    D. $900,000

11. The owner of an apartment building earns a net income of $10,200 per year. The annual operating cost is $3,400. The owner is realizing a net return of 14% on the investment. What price was paid for the building?

    A. $48,572

    B. $72,857

    C. $97,143

    D. $142,800

Ad Valorem Taxes, Assessments, Tax Rates (Chapter 9)

12. If the tax value is 100% of the assessed value and the assessed value is $63,250, what are the annual taxes if the rate is $2.10 per $100?

    A. $132.83

    B. $1,328.25

    C. $3,011.90

    D. $3,320.16

13. A house has an assessed value of $142,000. The property is taxed at 80% of assessed value at a rate of $2.12 per $100. If the assessed valuation is to be increased by 18%, what is the amount of taxes to be paid on the property?

    A. $2,638.49

    B. $2,841.82

    C. $3,119.84

    D. $4,232.50

Market Value, Capitalization Rates, Depreciation (Chapter 4)

14. An office building produces a gross income of $12,600 per year. The vacancy factor is 5%, and annual expenses are $3,600. What is the market value if the capitalization rate is 12%?

    A. $15,120

    B. $69,750

    C. $99,750

    D. $105,000

15. A building now 14 years old has a total economic life of 40 years. If the original value of the building was $150,000, what is the present depreciated value?

    A. $52,500

    B. $60,000

    C. $97,500

    D. $202,500

ANSWER KEY

Commissions and Sales

1. 24,000 is 60% of total commission

   $24,000 = 60\% \times$ total commission

   factor missing: divide

   $24,000 \div 0.60 = \$40,000$

   sales price $\times$ rate of commission = total commission

   _____ $\times$ 7% = $40,000

   factor missing: divide

   $40,000 \div 0.07 = \$571,429$ per year in sales

   divide by 12 to get monthly volume of sales

   $571,429 \div 12 = \$47,619.08$, or (C)

2. area of a triangle = $0.5 \times$ base $\times$ height

   0.5×350 ft $\times 425$ ft = 74,375 sq ft

   74,375 sq ft $\times$ 0.75/sq ft = $55,781.25 sales price

   $55,781.25 \times 0.09 = \$5,020.31$, or (A)

3. $45,000 \times 1.20$ (120%) = $54,000 asking price

   $54,000 \times 0.90 = \$48,600$ sold price, or (B)

Prorations

4. loan balance $\times$ rate of interest = annual interest

   $20,000 \times 0.06 = $ _____

   product missing: multiply

   annual interest = $1,200

   $1,200 \div 12$ mos = $100/mo

   $100 \div 30 = \$3.33$/day

   $10 \times \$3.33 = \$33.30$ debit to seller, or (B)

Principal, Interest, Points

5. loan balance $\times$ rate of interest = annual interest

   _____ $\times$ 6% = ($570 $\times$ 12)

   factor missing: divide

   $6,840 \div 0.06 = \$114,000$, or (C)

Area Calculations

6. 40 yd $\times$ 3 ft/yd = 120 ft

   120 ft $\times$ 80 ft = 9,600 sq ft

   9,600 sq ft $\div$ 43,560 sq ft = 0.22 acres, or (C)

7. $\frac{1}{2} + \frac{1}{3} = $ unknown area

   $\frac{3}{6} + \frac{2}{6} = \frac{5}{6}$

   $\frac{6}{6}$ (entire area) $- \frac{5}{6} = \frac{1}{6}$

   Remainder = 20 acres

   $\frac{1}{6} = 20$ acres

   Entire tract = 20 $\times$ 6 = 120 acres, or (C)

8. 9 inches thick on each of two ends = 1.5 ft

   35 ft $-$ 1.5 ft = 33.5 ft

   26.5 ft $-$ 1.5 ft = 25 ft

   33.5 ft $\times$ 25 ft = 837.5 sq ft, or (B)

9. (2 $\times$ 300 ft) + (2 $\times$ 150 ft) = 900 feet

   900 ft $\div$ 15 ft/post = 60 posts, or (B)

Costs, Profits, Loss, Rates of Return

10. investment of value $\times$ rate of return = annual net income

    _____ $\times$ 8% = $72,000

    factor missing: divide

    $72,000 \div 0.08 = \$900,000$, or (D)

11. investment $\times$ rate = annual net income

    _____ $\times$ 14% = $10,200

    factor missing: divide

    $10,200 \div 0.14 = \$72,857$, or (B)

Ad Valorem Taxes, Assessments, Tax Rates

12. assessed value $\times$ tax rate = annual taxes

    $63,250 \times 0.0210 = $ _____

    product missing: multiply

    annual taxes: $1,328.25, or (B)

13. $142,000 \times \$1.18 = \$167,560$ increased valuation

    $167,560 \times 0.80 = \$134,048$ new tax basis

    assessed value $\times$ tax rate = annual taxes

    $134,048 \times 2.12/100 = $ _____

    product missing: multiply

    $134,048 \times 0.0212 = \$2,841.82$ (rounded), or (B)

Market Value, Capitalization Rates, Depreciation

14. market value (investment) × cap rate = annual net income

    annual net income = $12,600 − vacancy factor − expenses

    vacancy factor = $12,600 × 0.05 = $630

    $12,600 − $630 − $3,600 = $8,370 annual net income

    _____ × 12% = $8,370

    factor missing: divide

    $8,370 ÷ 0.12 = $69,750, or (B)

15. 1 ÷ 40 years = 2 $\frac{1}{2}$% per year depreciation

    14 years × 2.5%/yr. = 35% depreciation to date

    100% − 35% = 65% remaining value

    original value × % not lost = current value

    $150,000 × 0.65 = $97,500, or (C)

Appendix
Sample Broker
Licensing Exam

IN THIS APPENDIX The following New York licensing exam consists of 100 questions. The questions are weighted approximately in number according to the amount of time allotted to the subject. For review purposes, this means that the more time allotted to a topic in the 45-hour course, the more questions on that topic that will appear on your course and state exam.

I. The Broker's Office—Operation, Management, and Supervision

(10 hours) 17 questions

1. Mary Seaver, a salesperson associated with Leisure Homes Realty, advised a seller that his property would sell for at least $150,000. Relying on this, the seller listed the property at $150,000. Comparable sales and listings of competitive properties were in the range of $105,000 to $110,000. The seller refused several offers between $106,000 and $112,000 during the 120-day term of the listing. The seller eventually sold his property for $98,000 since expiration of the listing with Leisure Homes. Which of the following is TRUE?

    A. Seaver has done nothing wrong and thus is not liable for any damage

    B. because Seaver is an agent of Leisure Homes Realty, Leisure Homes is the only party that may be held liable for the seller's damages

    C. Seaver committed an act of misrepresentation and may be liable for the resulting financial loss the seller incurred

    D. because the seller did not sell the property during the listing period, Seaver is entitled to a commission

2. While a broker was listing a property, the owner told the broker that the house contains 2,400 square feet of heated living area. Relying on this information, the broker represented it to prospective buyers as containing 2,400 square feet. After purchasing the property, the buyer accurately determined that the house has only 1,850 square feet and sued for damages for the difference in value between 2,400 square feet and 1,850 square feet. Which of the following is correct?

    A. the broker is not liable because he relied on the seller's positive statement as to the square footage

    B. the seller is not liable because the broker, not the seller, represented the property to the buyer as containing 2,400 square feet

    C. the theory of caveat emptor applies; thus, neither the seller nor the broker is liable to the buyer

    D. both the broker and the seller are liable to the buyer

341

3. A real estate broker is NOT responsible for which of the following?

   A. acts of sales associates while engaged in brokerage activities

   B. appropriate handling of funds in trust or escrow accounts

   C. adhering to a commission schedule recommended by the local board of REALTORS®

   D. representing property honestly, fairly, and accurately to prospective buyers

4. Which of the following must licensed New York attorneys comply with to engage in real estate brokerage?

   A. obtain a New York broker license if they do not have salespeople working under their supervision

   B. obtain a broker license if they have salespersons working under their supervision

   C. take continuing education

   D. complete 90 hours of qualifying education

5. Real estate brokers who have been licensed continuously for 15 years require how much continuing education?

   A. 22 1/2 hours

   B. none

   C. 45 hours

   D. one state-approved course regardless of the hours

6. A broker deposited a buyer's check for earnest money in the amount of $6,000 in her escrow account. Prior to the closing and at the seller's request, the broker took $1,200 from the escrow account to pay for the cost of damage repairs caused by termites in the house. This expense was necessary so the seller could provide the required termite certificate to the buyer at the closing. Which of the following statements about this transaction is correct?

   A. because the $1,200 disbursement from the broker's escrow account was made at the seller's request and benefited both buyer and seller, the broker acted properly

   B. the broker's action constituted an act of commingling and, as such, was improper

   C. the broker's action was not proper

   D. the broker's action was proper because brokers manage escrow accounts

7. Individuals are eligible for a salesperson license when they reach the age of:

   A. 18

   B. 19

   C. 20

   D. 21

8. Which of the following is a key word used to determine whether a real estate broker is or is not legally entitled to a commission?

   A. acceptance

   B. accountability

   C. assignment

   D. assumption

9. Betsy is a salesperson and is married to a broker, Josh, who has been a broker for one year. Josh decides to open a real estate brokerage firm, incorporate, and make Betsy the vice president who will market properties. Which of the following is TRUE?

   A. Betsy can assume the title of vice president

   B. real estate firms may not be incorporated in New York

   C. Betsy cannot be a principal in the firm because she holds only a salesperson license

   D. Josh cannot open his own firm because he must have at least two years' experience as a broker

10. One of the main purposes of the Sherman Antitrust Act is to:

    A. regulate the real estate industry

    B. allow small businesses to compete effectively with larger companies

    C. protect governmental agencies from competition by private business

    D. regulate the banking industry

11. In New York, which of the following statements regarding multiple listing services is FALSE? Members:

    A. must be licensed real estate brokers

    B. must belong to a real estate board for two years in order to be admitted to multiple listing

    C. may circulate information concerning the commission that a broker has agreed upon with his client

    D. may admit members from a number of different boards of Realtors

12. All of the members of a certain real estate board decided not to do business with brokers who had offices in its territory but did not belong to the board. This activity is an example of a(n):

    A. illegal group boycott

    B. illegal market allocation agreement

    C. illegal tie-in arrangement

    D. legal activity

13. George is about to close a deal on the lease of a retail space. His client has questions about the legality of the termination clause in the lease. How should George respond to this question?

    A. if George believes the clause is legal, he should indicate this to his client and encourage him to close the deal

    B. George should not give out legal advice and should advise his client to consult an attorney

    C. George should refer this question to his broker as brokers may offer legal advice with respect to commercial deals

    D. George should advise his client to steer clear of any questionable lease arrangements and look for a more favorable deal elsewhere

14. Magda's customer is a developer who does not wish to purchase a certain subdivision before the town planning board approves the site for the construction of 12 single-family houses. Magda advises her customer that she has spoken to the board members individually and they intend to approve the site. She advises her customer to purchase the property before the approval so he can buy at a lower price. The customer purchases the property and the subdivision is not approved. Which of the following is correct?

    A. Magda committed an act of misrepresentation and may be liable to the developer for any loss the developer may have as a consequence

    B. Magda was simply doing her job as agent to obtain the best deal for her customer and bears no liability

    C. caveat emptor applies, and therefore Magda is not liable

    D. Magda is not liable simply because the information she had was accurate at the time she received it and subsequent acts of the town board were not in her control

15. Three real estate boards mutually agree to divide a certain area into geographical territories and direct their respective members to solicit listings only in the area assigned to that board. This is an example of a(n):

    A. illegal market allocation agreement

    B. illegal tie-in arrangement

    C. illegal group boycott

    D. legal arrangement between the parties

16. Rainyday Realty tells all of its customers that as a condition of purchasing a listing from their company, the customer must apply for a mortgage to Money Mortgage Company. This is an example of a(n):

    A. legal business arrangement

    B. illegal market allocation agreement

    C. illegal tie-in arrangement

    D. vicarious liability

17. The yearly IRS form that a broker must file, which indicates compensation paid to the salesperson, is a(n):

    A. W-2

    B. 1040, Schedule C

    C. 1099 misc.

    D. I-9c

II. Real Estate Agency Disclosure (Review)

(4 hours) 9 questions

18. Commission splits to sales associates are determined by:

    A. multiple listing services

    B. boards of Realtors®

    C. arrangement between broker and sales associate

    D. principals

19. An agent who accepts responsibility and vicarious liability for all agents of the principal who market the property is known as a:

    A. buyer agent

    B. seller agent

    C. broker's agent

    D. listing agent

20. Heather, a listing agent, casually suggests a price to offer on the listed property to prospective purchasers who attend her open house. What type of possible situation has arisen?

    A. unintended dual agency

    B. business as usual

    C. buyer agency

    D. intended dual agency

21. Which of the following is TRUE of dual agency relationships in the sale of one- to four-unit residential properties in New York? They:

    A. are illegal under all circumstances

    B. are allowable with disclosure and informed consent

    C. can exist only for in-house sales with disclosure and informed consent in writing

    D. are allowed only in the sale of commercial property

22. In the marketing of a one- to four-unit residential property, the disclosure regarding dual agency form need NOT be presented in which of the following situations?

    A. signing of a listing agreement

    B. at a first substantive contact with a prospective purchaser in the real estate office

    C. at a first substantive contact with a purchaser at an open house

    D. during door-to-door canvassing for listings

23. The listing arrangement in which a seller lists a property with the assistance of several brokers but owes no commission to any of the brokers if the owner sells the property is known as a(n):

    A. net listing

    B. open listing

    C. agency

    D. exclusive right to sell

24. Real estate agents must keep a copy of the signed disclosure regarding dual agency relationships form for a minimum of:

    A. two years

    B. three years

    C. four years

    D. five years

25. If a prospective purchaser refuses to sign the required disclosure form, the agent must do which of the following?

    A. refuse to show the property

    B. only make a note of the refusal and keep on file

    C. complete a declaration by real estate licensee form explaining the facts of the situation

    D. notify DOS

26. The type of listing contract that allows only one broker to list the property, but also allows the seller to forgo commission payment if the seller sells the property himself, is a(n):

    A. exclusive right to sell

    B. net

    C. open

    D. exclusive agency

III. Real Estate Finance II

(5 hours) 13 questions

27. The borrower's right to reclaim ownership of real property after foreclosure action has begun is called:

    A. right of reclamation

    B. equity of redemption

    C. subrogation

    D. estoppel

28. The real estate market is:

    A. quick to react to changes in supply and demand

    B. not subject to economic cycles

    C. subject to economic cycles

    D. not affected by supply and demand

29. If a lease specifies the rent to be 2 percent of the gross sales per annum, with a minimum annual rent of $8,000, what is the annual rent if gross sales are $1,200,000?

    A. $8,000

    B. $12,000

    C. $24,000

    D. $28,000

30. A commercial lease in which the lessee is responsible for real property taxes, property insurance, and maintenance of the leased property is a(n):
    A. net lease
    B. graduated lease
    C. gross lease
    D. index lease

31. A long-term lease for unimproved land, usually given for construction purposes, is a:
    A. sale leaseback
    B. ground lease
    C. subordinate lease
    D. net lease

32. Which of the following is NOT a requirement for a non-income verification loan?
    A. impeccable credit
    B. ownership or partnership in a business for a minimum of five years
    C. employed in the same way for at least three to five years
    D. be willing to accept a higher than normal rate of interest or pay more points for the loan

33. A lender charges a 2 percent loan origination fee and three discount points to make a 95 percent conventional insured mortgage loan in the amount of $47,500. What is the cost of these charges to the borrower?
    A. $922
    B. $1,188
    C. $1,425
    D. $2,375

34. A developer gave the seller a $385,000 purchase money first mortgage to secure payment of part of the purchase price for a tract of land. The developer was able to convey unencumbered titles to the first six lot purchasers by paying only $8,000 on the purchase money mortgage because the mortgage contained:
    A. release clauses
    B. due-on-sale clauses
    C. prepayment clauses
    D. mortgaging clauses

35. In the purchase of an office building, the buyer gave the seller a mortgage for $200,000 more than the seller's first mortgage and took title to the property subject to the first mortgage. The purchase money mortgage requires payments of interest for only the first five years, at which time the principal has to be paid and a new purchase money mortgage created. Based on the above information, which of the following statements is FALSE?
    A. the purchase money mortgage is a wrap-around term mortgage
    B. for this arrangement to work satisfactorily, the seller's first mortgage must not contain an alienation clause
    C. this arrangement must be approved by Fannie Mae
    D. the purchase money mortgage has a balloon payment

36. The clause in a mortgage enabling the lender to declare the entire balance remaining upon default of the mortgagor is the:
    A. alienation clause
    B. habendum clause
    C. acceleration clause
    D. novation clause

37. A type of loan that gives the lender the option of turning the outstanding balance of the loan into an agreed-upon percentage of ownership in the property is known as:
    A. a subordinate mortgage
    B. a convertible mortgage
    C. a bridge mortgage
    D. gap financing

38. In regard to release land subdivision financing, which of the following statements is FALSE?
    A. the security for the mortgage is the total amount of lots in the subdivision
    B. in order to transfer title to any of the lots, a portion of the mortgage lien must be satisfied
    C. the borrower usually has a monetary stake in the land before he is given a mortgage
    D. the mortgage is generally for 90 to 100 percent of the appraised value of the land

39. An alternative to a mortgage that provides 100 percent financing is a(n):

    A. interim loan

    B. sale leaseback

    C. ground lease

    D. convertible loan

IV. Real Estate Investments

(5 hours) 13 questions

40. An apartment building produces an annual net income of $10,800 after deducting $72 per month for expenses. What price for the property would provide a buyer with a net return of 12 percent?

    A. $90,000

    B. $97,200

    C. $116,641

    D. $129,600

41. The price paid for the property together with the costs incurred in acquiring the property (except for costs in arranging financing) and the costs of any capital improvements indicate the:

    A. capital gain

    B. tax basis

    C. net operating income

    D. effective gross income

42. If a rental property provides the owner with an 11 percent return on her investment of $780,000, what is the net annual income from the property?

    A. $70,512

    B. $70,909

    C. $85,800

    D. $141,025

43. In a tax-free exchange, which of the following is taxable?

    A. like-kind property

    B. boot

    C. exchange property

    D. salvage value

44. In a tax-free exchange, the property exchange must be used for which of the following?

    A. investment purposes

    B. any type of purpose

    C. home ownership without any income

    D. vacation homes only

45. Investment in land may be more risky than other types of investments because:

    A. land is always worth less than improved property

    B. the investor may have to hold the property longer than other types of investment before the full potential is realized

    C. untrustworthy investment companies seek out unsophisticated investors to buy land

    D. lenders will not loan money to purchase land

46. Before deducting operating expenses, losses from vacancies and credit losses are deducted from potential gross rental income to arrive at:

    A. net operating income

    B. effective gross income

    C. debt service

    D. gross rent roll

47. An apartment building has nine apartments that bring in a rental of $750 each per month. What is the potential gross rental income per year based on 100 percent occupancy?

    A. $6,750

    B. $67,500

    C. $75,000

    D. $81,000

48. An operating statement adjusted to reflect a potential change in income and expenses based upon an investor's knowledge of the real estate market is known as a:

    A. projection

    B. pro forma schedule

    C. feasibility study

    D. net operating statement

49. A study of how a change in one factor can affect the income to the property is known as:

    A. risk analysis

    B. sensitivity analysis

    C. feasibility analysis

    D. rate of return

50. The profit realized from the sale of real estate is known as:

    A. capital gain

    B. tax basis

    C. rate of return

    D. boot

51. Income earned through interest, annuities, and dividends are classified by the IRS as:
    A. active income
    B. passive income
    C. portfolio income
    D. nontaxable income

52. The net proceeds of an investment, after all expenses are met and that may be measured before or after taxes are considered, is known as:
    A. rate of return
    B. depreciation allowance
    C. tax shelter
    D. cash flow

V. General Business Law

(5 hours) 13 questions

53. The role of the judiciary in the federal government is to:
    A. interpret the law
    B. enact the law
    C. recommend new law
    D. write the law

54. A federal statute that defines negotiable instruments is known as the:
    A. Securities Act
    B. Real Estate Settlement Procedures Act
    C. Uniform Commercial Code
    D. blue sky laws

55. Which of the following is a type of draft?
    A. promissory note
    B. check
    C. certificate of deposit
    D. offer to purchase

56. Ronnie Lee receives a check made out to him. He then indorses the check to Tom Marsh and on the back he writes, "pay Tom Marsh" and then signs his name, Ronnie Lee. Who is the indorser and what type of indorsement is this?
    A. Tom is the indorser and this is blank indorsement
    B. Tom is the indorser and this is a special indorsement
    C. Ronnie is the indorser and this is a blank indorsement
    D. Ronnie is the indorser and this is a special indorsement

57. The advantage of a New York subchapter S corporation is that it:
    A. is the only corporate structure allowed for real estate firms
    B. does not have to register with the Division of Corporations
    C. does not have to pay the corporate franchise fee
    D. is taxed as a partnership and does not have to pay corporate double tax

58. Which of the following federal agencies regulates securities offerings?
    A. Uniform Commercial Code Commission
    B. Department of Law
    C. Securities Exchange Commission
    D. American Stock Exchange

59. Prior to a public offering, which of the following applies to the offering of condominiums and cooperatives in New York?
    A. an offering plan must be submitted to the Attorney General's office
    B. condominiums and cooperatives are not securities and do not require state registration
    C. only condominiums and cooperatives valued at over $10 million need register with the Attorney General's office
    D. only cooperatives and not condominiums need register with the Attorney General's office

60. Which of the following is true of the U.S. Supreme Court?
    A. it is a trial court
    B. it is the nation's highest court
    C. it only hears cases originating in the federal court system
    D. its decisions may be appealed to the U.S. Court of Appeals

61. Outside of New York City, which court has jurisdiction over indictable crimes committed within the county?
    A. county court
    B. supreme court
    C. city court
    D. criminal court

62. New York City's court system is divided into which of the following two courts?

    A. surrogate's court and criminal court

    B. civil court and criminal court

    C. supreme court and criminal court

    D. surrogate's court and civil court

63. In which of the following bankruptcy choices is the debtor's nonexempt property sold for cash with any proceeds distributed to creditors?

    A. Chapter 13

    B. Chapter 11

    C. Chapter 9

    D. Chapter 7

64. Exemptions to the federal gift tax include which of the following?

    A. gifts to a spouse

    B. gifts to all relatives

    C. all gifts of real property

    D. all gifts valued less than $15,000 if given to different individuals

65. The Hopefuls are one of many relatives that claim ownership to a parcel of land bordering the Hudson River. They possess a handwritten instrument deeding the property to them on March 1, 1947. Which of the following legal statutes invalidates the deed?

    A. Statute of Limitations

    B. Doctrine of Laches

    C. Statute of Frauds

    D. Estates, Powers, and Trusts Law

VI. Construction and Development

(4 hours) 9 questions

66. A purchaser usually arranges to have a professional inspection of the seller's property:

    A. prior to signing the contract for purchase and sale

    B. upon execution of the contract for purchase and sale, which contains specific wording and contingency agreements about the nature and type of inspection

    C. upon filling out a property condition disclosure form

    D. only if required by a lender

67. A roof overhang extending without permission onto an adjoining property is an example of a(n):

    A. easement appurtenant

    B. encroachment

    C. license

    D. easement in gross

68. New York Article 9-A of the Real Property Law addresses:

    A. salesperson and broker licenses

    B. residential housing sold on the installment plan

    C. vacant subdivided land sold on the installment plan

    D. commercial construction standards

69. Which of the following is an example of a material defect in a property?

    A. hardwood floors covered with carpeting

    B. lead-based paint

    C. a broken window

    D. peeling wallpaper

70. Due diligence inspections of a property might be conducted by a lender because:

    A. liability for problems with property may be passed on to the new owner

    B. they are required by New York law in the sale of vacant land

    C. the seller usually requires this type of inspection in the terms of the contract of sale

    D. they are a requirement of Fannie Mae

71. If a material defect exists in a property that is sold through a real estate agent:

    A. the agent is always responsible for nondisclosure of the defect

    B. the agent is responsible only if he knows of the defect or has reason to know and did not disclose it

    C. sellers are liable only for nondisclosure of material defects no matter what the agent knew

    D. buyers must assume full responsibility for all defects once the property transfers title

72. An example of an express dedication occurs when:

    A. a developer deeds a municipality a parcel of his land to use for a park

    B. a municipality grants a portion of land to a private individual

    C. the public has had continuous access to privately owned land without a formal acknowledgment or deed by the owner

    D. there is a special ceremony honoring the donor

73. A type of zoning that is illegal in New York is:

    A. spot zoning

    B. nonconforming use

    C. exclusionary zoning

    D. incentive zoning

74. Eminent domain:

    A. is an example of voluntary alienation

    B. is government's right to take land for public use with just compensation to the owner

    C. allows the property owner to sue the government to regain her property

    D. is another form of adverse possession

VII. Conveyance of Real Property & Title Closing & Costs (Review)

(3 hours) 7 questions

75. The statement made by a grantor to a qualified public official that the signing of a deed was done by him and was a voluntary act is called a(n):

    A. abstract

    B. acknowledgment

    C. covenant

    D. conveyance

76. The difference between a condominium and cooperative purchase is:

    A. A condominium purchase is a fee simple estate and a cooperative purchase is for corporate shares

    B. A cooperative purchase is secured by a mortgage; a condominium purchase is not

    C. The condominium association purchases all properties first and deeds them over to the seller; this is not allowable with cooperative purchases

    D. There is essentially little or no difference

77. A co-owner of real property automatically received a deceased partner's share of ownership. This is called:

    A. intestate succession

    B. inheritance by devise

    C. right of survivorship

    D. inheritance by descent

78. Four brothers received title to a large tract of land from their grandfather, who gave each brother a one-fourth undivided interest with equal rights to possession of the land with rights of survivorship to the other brothers if one dies. All four received their title on their grandfather's seventieth birthday. The brothers most likely hold title in which of the following ways?

    A. in severalty

    B. joint tenants

    C. as tenants by the entirety

    D. as remaindermen

79. A seller paid an annual hazard insurance premium of $540 for a policy effective February 12. At settlement on April 16 of the same year, the buyer purchased the policy from the seller. This transaction is correctly entered on the settlement statements as:

    A. $96 seller credit

    B. $444 buyer credit

    C. $96 buyer credit

    D. $444 seller credit

80. The recordation of a deed after transfer of title provides protection against subsequent claimants for title through which type of notice?

    A. actual

    B. chain of title

    C. formal

    D. constructive

81. A sales contract provided that the buyer was to pay $65,000 for a seller's property by giving a purchase money mortgage for $30,000 and the balance in cash at closing. The buyer made a good faith deposit of $6,500 when he made the offer. The seller's share of the real property taxes credited to the buyer was $850. The buyer's other closing costs totaled $900. What amount must the buyer pay at closing?

    A. $27,650
    B. $27,700
    C. $28,550
    D. $35,050

VIII. Real Estate Property Management

(5 hours) 13 questions

82. Which of the following is one of the basic responsibilities of a property manager?

    A. appraising the property annually
    B. evicting all minority tenants to provide for a more stable complex
    C. producing the best possible net operating income for the owner
    D. preparing the annual tax returns and attending audits with the IRS

83. A person living on the managed premises as a salaried employee engaged to manage and lease apartments is called a(n):

    A. property manager
    B. rental agent
    C. employee manager
    D. resident manager

84. The monthly accounting by the property manager is called:

    A. stabilized budget
    B. property management report
    C. management budget
    D. financial report

85. What net annual operating income must a property manager produce from a property to provide an 8 percent return to the owner, who paid $763,000 for the property?

    A. $9,538
    B. $61,040
    C. $95,375
    D. $104,849

86. Which of the following most accurately describes a property manager?

    A. fiduciary
    B. trustee
    C. escrow agent
    D. resident manager

87. A projected budget over the economic life of the improvements of the property for variable expenses such as repairs and remodeling is known as the:

    A. operating budget
    B. capital reserve budget
    C. stabilized budget
    D. maintenance budget

88. The term "risk management" in reference to the ownership of real property refers to:

    A. obtaining appropriate insurance coverage
    B. tenant selectivity
    C. stabilized budgeting
    D. competent property managers

89. A property manager may NOT ask about which of the following when reviewing tenants for residential rental apartments:

    A. past landlord references
    B. employment status
    C. ability to pay security deposit and first month's rent
    D. marital status

90. In New York, a rental agent working for one owner:

    A. must have a salesperson's license
    B. does not need a salesperson or broker license
    C. must have an apartment information vendor's license
    D. must have an apartment sharing agent's license

91. The consideration of appropriate tenant mix is most important in:

    A. farm management
    B. residential management
    C. condominium management
    D. retail management

92. Which of the following is NOT a reason for obtaining a property management designation?

    A. it enhances credibility

    B. it provides a means of education

    C. it can lead to more job opportunity

    D. at least one designation is necessary in New York to practice property management

93. Which of the following is NOT a duty of the property manager?

    A. showing and leasing property

    B. deciding owners' objectives

    C. collecting rent

    D. providing for the protection of tenants

94. The first step in creating an owner-management relationship is a:

    A. management proposal

    B. management report

    C. management agreement

    D. management fee

IX. Taxes and Assessments

(2 hours) 6 questions

95. If the market value of a property is $90,000, the tax rate is 90 mills, and the assessment is 70 percent, what is the amount of the annual tax bill?

    A. $567

    B. $5,670

    C. $7,000

    D. $8,100

96. The tax rate is determined by:

    A. whether or not an assessing unit has full value assessment

    B. the amount of revenue required to accomplish the budgetary requirements of the assessing unit

    C. the equalization rate for the local assessing unit

    D. a vote of the population at large

97. If property owners believe that an assessment is wrong, they can file a written complaint with the local board of assessment review. This complaint is known legally as a:

    A. judicial summons and complaint

    B. grievance

    C. tax protest

    D. certiorari

98. Which of the following is NOT grounds for assessment protest?

    A. unequal assessment

    B. excessive assessment

    C. inability to pay taxes based on assessment

    D. misclassification

99. For most properties, which of the following account for the difference in tax bills among properties within a municipality?

    A. assessed value

    B. market value

    C. highest and best use

    D. tax levy

100. Which of the following best describes a special assessment? It:

    A. can only be levied through an in rem legal proceeding

    B. is an unfair apportionment of the tax burden

    C. can only be levied on the taxable status date

    D. is a specific lien against the property until paid

I. The Broker's Office—Operation, Management, and Supervision

1. C
2. D
3. C
4. B
5. B
6. C
7. A
8. A
9. C
10. B
11. B
12. A
13. B
14. A
15. A
16. C
17. C

II. Real Estate Agency Disclosure (Review)

18. C
19. C
20. A
21. B
22. D
23. B
24. B
25. C
26. D

III. Real Estate Finance II

27. B
28. C
29. C
30. A
31. B
32. B
33. D
34. A

35. C
36. C
37. B
38. D
39. B

IV. Real Estate Investments

40. A
41. B
42. C
43. B
44. A
45. B
46. B
47. D
48. B
49. B
50. A
51. C
52. D

V. General Business Law

53. A
54. C
55. B
56. D
57. D
58. C
59. A
60. B
61. A
62. B
63. D
64. A
65. C

VI. Construction and Development

66. B
67. B
68. C

69. B
70. A
71. B
72. A
73. A
74. B

VII. Conveyance of Real Property & Title Closing & Costs (Review)

75. B
76. A
77. C
78. B
79. D
80. D
81. C

VIII. Real Estate Property Management

82. C
83. D
84. B
85. B
86. A
87. B
88. A
89. D
90. B
91. D
92. D
93. B
94. A

IX. Taxes and Assessments

95. B
96. B
97. B
98. C
99. A
100. D

Glossary

The following contains terminology from this textbook for the broker syllabus, required terminology from the salesperson syllabus, and general terminology that is useful to the real estate professional.

abandonment The surrender or release of a right, claim, or interest in real property.

absorption field A part of a septic system, it is a system of narrow trenches through which the discharge from the septic tank infiltrates into the surrounding soil.

abstract of title A history of a title and the current status of a title based on a title examination.

abutting Parcels of land next to each other, which share a common border.

acceleration clause A provision in a mortgage that permits the lender to declare the entire principal balance of the debt immediately due and payable if the borrower is in default.

acceptance Voluntary expression by the person receiving the offer to be bound by the exact terms of the offer; must be unequivocal and unconditional.

access The right to go onto and leave a property.

accession Property owners' rights to all the land produces or all that is added to the land, either intentionally or by mistake.

accessory apartment uses Uses that are incidental or subordinate to the main use of the building, such as a laundromat.

accord and satisfaction A new agreement by contracting parties that is satisfied by full performance, thereby terminating the prior contract as well.

accretion The gradual building up of land in a watercourse over time by deposits of silt, sand, and gravel.

accrued expenses Expenses seller owes on the day of closing but for which the buyer will take responsibility (such as property taxes).

acknowledgment A formal statement before an authorized official (e.g., notary public) by a person who executed a deed, contract, or other document, that it was (is) his free act.

acquisition The act of acquiring a property.

acquisition cost The basis used by the FHA to calculate the loan amount.

acre A land area containing 43,560 square feet.

action to quiet title A lawsuit to clear a title to real property.

act of waste Abuse or misuse of property by a life tenant.

actual age Chronological age.

actual eviction The removal of a tenant by the landlord because the tenant breached a condition of a lease or other rental contract.

actual notice The knowledge a person has of a fact.

adjoining lands Lands sharing a common boundary line.

adjustable rate mortgage (ARM) A mortgage in which the interest rate changes according to changes in a predetermined index.

adjusted basis Value of property used to determine the amount of gain or loss realized by an owner upon sale of the property; equals acquisition cost plus capital improvements minus depreciation taken.

adjusted sales price The amount realized minus fix-up expenses.

adjustments Additions or subtractions of dollar amounts to equalize comparables to subject property in the sales comparison approach to estimating value.

administrative law judge (ALJ) A judge who hears complaints and makes decisions regarding statutory violations of law.

administrative discipline A directive by the Department of State which may result in fines or the suspension or revocation of a license.

administrative law Laws which address administrative directives in the form of rules, regulations, and orders to carry out regulatory powers.

administrator A male appointed by a court to administer the estate of a person who has died intestate.

administrator's deed One executed by an administrator to convey title to estate property.

administratrix A female appointed by a court to administer the estate of a person who has died intestate.

ad valorem Latin meaning "according to value"; real property is taxed on an ad valorem basis.

adverse possession A method of acquiring title to real property by conforming to statutory requirement; a form of involuntary alienation of title.

affirmative action A policy expressed in some form of legislative act with respect to the handling of certain public or private acts of conduct.

affirmative easement A legal requirement that a servient owner permit a right of use in the servient land by the dominant owner.

agency The fiduciary relationship between a principal and an agent.

agent A person hired by another to act on his or her behalf.

agreement A contract requiring mutual assent between two or more parties.

agricultural districts Created and protected by New York statute, these areas are used for animal grazing and crop production.

air rights Rights in the air space above the surface of land.

alienage The citizenship or immigration status of any person who is not a citizen or national of the United States.

alienation Transfer of title to real property.

alienation clause A statement in a mortgage or deed of trust entitling the lender to declare the entire principal balance of the debt immediately due and payable if the borrower sells the property during the mortgage term. Also known as due-on-sale clause.

allodial system The type of land ownership existing in the United States whereby individuals may hold title to real property absolutely.

alluvion Increased soil, gravel, or sand on a stream bank resulting from flow or current of the water.

Americans with Disabilities Act A federal law protecting the rights of individuals with physical or mental impairments.

amortization schedule Designation of periodic payments of principal and interest over a specific term to satisfy a mortgage loan.

amortized mortgage One in which uniform installment payments include payment of both principal and interest.

amortizing Applying periodic payments first toward the interest and then toward the principal eventually to pay off a debt.

amperage The amount of current or electricity flowing though a wire.

anchor store A well-known commercial retail business, such as a national chain store or regional department store, placed in a shopping center to generate the most customers for all stores in the shopping center.

annexation Addition of an area into a city.

annual percentage rate (APR) The actual effective rate of interest charged on a loan expressed on a yearly basis; not the same as simple interest rate.

anticipation The principle that property value is based on expectations or hopes of the future benefits of ownership.

antitrust violations Any business activity where there is a monopoly, a contract, a conspiracy, or a combination that negatively impacts an individual's or a company's ability to do business.

apartment information vendor A licensed individual who is paid to provide information concerning the location and availability of residential real property.

apartment sharing agent A licensed individual who is paid to arrange and coordinate meetings between current owners of real property who wish to share their housing with others.

apportionment Division of property and school tax monies so that school districts, counties, towns and cities in the different municipalities all pay their fair share of the tax levy.

appraisal An estimate of value of particular property at a particular time for a specified purpose.

appraisal by capitalization Income approach to appraisal of income-producing real estate.

appraisal process An organized and systematic program for estimating real property value.

appraisal report Documentation containing an estimate of property value and the data on which the estimate is based.

appreciation An increase in property value.

approaches to value Methods of estimating real property value: sales comparison, income, and cost.

approved assessing unit A division of local government that has completed a property reevaluation and been certified by the New York State Office of Real Property Services.

appurtenances All rights or privileges that result from ownership of a specific property and move with the title.

appurtenant easement A right of use in the adjoining land of another that moves with the title to the property benefiting from the easement.

arbitration A form of resolving a dispute that includes two or more opposing parties and a neutral third party; the neutral third party makes a judgment after hearing both sides.

area variance Permission to use land in a manner not normally allowed by the dimensional or physical requirements of the zoning ordinance.

arrears Delinquency in meeting an obligation; or, paid at the end of a period (e.g., at the end of the month) for the previous period; payments in arrears include interest for using the money during the previous period.

Article 6-E A section of the New York State law addressing regulations for certified and licensed real estate appraisers.

Article 9-A A section of the New York Real Property Law addressing the purchase or lease of vacant subdivided lands sold through an installment contract in or outside of New York.

Article 12-A The section of the New York Real Property Law pertaining to real estate salespersons and brokers.

Article 78 proceeding An appeal brought forth because of a ruling by a government agency.

asbestos A fibrous mineral found in many building materials that, when improperly disturbed, can cause serious lung illnesses.

"as is" Words in a contract of sale indicating that a property is sold without warranty as to condition.

assessed value The dollar amount of worth to which a local tax rate is applied to calculate the amount of real property tax.

assessing units Local counties, cities, towns, villages, school districts, and special districts that raise money through real property taxes.

assessment A percentage of a property's market value.

assessment roll Yearly list that contains all real property in a jurisdiction, with information about each parcel including its assessed value and exempt status.

assessor An official of local government who has the responsibility for establishing the value of property for tax purposes.

assignee One to whom contractual rights are transferred.

assignment Transfer of legal rights and obligations by one party to another.

assignment of lease Transfer by a lessee of the entire remaining term of a lease without any reversion of interest to the lessee.

assignor The person transferring contractual rights to another.

associate real estate broker A licensed real estate broker who wishes to work under the name and supervision of another licensed broker.

assumable mortgage One that does not contain an alienation clause.

attorney-in-fact A person appointed to perform legal acts for another under a power of attorney.

auction A form of property sale in which people bid against one another.

automatic stay Bankruptcy court order that suspends certain actions of creditors against the debtor or the debtor's property.

availability An economic characteristic of land denoting that land is a commodity with a fixed supply base.

avulsion Sudden loss or gain of land as a result of water or shift in a bed of a river that has been used as a boundary.

balloon framing Method of construction that uses a single system of wall studs that runs from the foundation through the first and second floors to the ceiling support.

balloon mortgage One in which the scheduled payment will not fully amortize the loan over the mortgage term; therefore, to satisfy the debt fully, it requires a final payment called a balloon payment, larger than the uniform payments.

bargain-and-sale deed A form of deed with or without covenants of title.

base rent The fixed or minimum rent portion in a percentage lease.

basis The value of property for income tax purposes; consists of original cost plus capital improvements less accrued depreciation.

bearing walls Walls that support the ceiling and/or roof.

beneficiary (a) Recipient of a gift of personal property by will; (b) Lender in a deed of trust.

bequest A gift of personal property by will.

bilateral contract An agreement based on mutual promises that provide the consideration.

bill of sale An instrument transferring ownership of personal property.

binder A written document for the purchase and sale of real property that does not generally contain all of the essential elements of a valid contract.

blanket mortgage One in which two or more parcels of real property are pledged to secure payment of the note.

blind ad An ad for real property placed by a real estate broker that does not indicate that the advertiser is a broker.

blockbusting For profit, to induce or attempt to induce any person to sell or rent any dwelling by representations regarding the entry into the neighborhood of individuals of a particular race, color, religion, sex, or national origin.

blueprint A building plan that is a detailed architectural rendering of the structure.

blue sky laws Federal and state securities laws and regulations to protect investors from fraud.

board of assessment review An appointed body consisting of three to five members that hears and decides upon grievances from taxpayers.

board of directors Governing and decision-making board of a cooperative.

bona fide In good faith.

book value Dollar worth as it appears on the owner's books, usually for tax purposes; also known as historic value.

boot Cash received in a tax-free exchange.

breach of contract Failure, without legal excuse, to perform any promise that forms the whole or part of a contract.

bridge loan A loan for a short duration of time.

brokerage The business of bringing buyers and sellers together and assisting in negotiations for the terms of sale of real estate.

broker's agent One who is hired through a broker to work for that broker.

BTU Abbreviation for British thermal unit. It stands for the amount of heat required to raise the temperature of one pound of water by one degree Fahrenheit.

building codes Public controls regulating construction.

building envelope The materials of a building that enclose the interior.

building permit Permission from the appropriate local government authority to construct or renovate any type of property.

building specifications Written narratives that explain the building plan.

bundle of rights The rights of an owner of a freehold estate to possession, enjoyment, control, and disposition of real property.

buydown The voluntary paying of discount points by a borrower to reduce mortgage interest rate at the time the loan is made.

buyer agent A real estate agent who works in the best interests of a buyer.

buyer brokerage An agency relationship between a buyer and a broker.

capital gain Tax laws allowing investors to exclude a percentage of their profit on real estate investments from taxation.

capital improvement An item that adds value to the property, adapts the property to new uses, or prolongs the life of property; maintenance is not a capital improvement.

capitalization The process of converting future income into an indication of the present value of a property by applying a capitalization rate to net annual income.

capitalization formula Investment or value of real estate times the capitalization rate equals the annual net income of the real estate.

capital loss Occurs when an investment property or other type of investment is sold at a loss.

capitalization rate The rate of interest appropriate to the investment risk as a return on the investment.

capital reserve budget Projected budget over the economic life of improvements on the property for repairs, decorating, remodeling, and capital improvements.

cap rate Another name for capitalization rate.

case law Legal precedent derived through court decisions.

cash flow Income produced by an investment property after deducting operating expenses and debt service.

caveat A warning or caution such as a disclosure that a property lies in an Agricultural District that is addended to a contract of sale.

caveat emptor Latin meaning: let the buyer beware.

cease and desist list A list of homeowners compiled by DOS in a cease and desist zone who do not wish to be solicited by real estate agents.

cease and desist zone A designation given by DOS to certain geographic areas that have been subject to intense and repeated solicitation by real estate agents. *See* cease and desist list.

census tract Small geographical areas established through cooperation between the local community and the Bureau of Census.

certificate of deposit Note containing an acknowledgment by a bank that a sum of money has been received; the bank must repay the money together with interest at an agreed-upon rate when the CD expires.

certificate of occupancy A document issued by a local government agency, after a satisfactory inspection of a structure, authorizing that the structure can be occupied.

certificate of title opinion A report, based on a title examination, setting forth the examiner's opinion of the quality of a title to real property.

cession deed A deed used to relinquish real property to a municipality for a road or something of that nature.

chain In land measurement, a distance of 66 feet.

chain of title Successive conveyances of title to a specific parcel of land.

change The principle stating that change is continually affecting land use and therefore altering value.

Chapter 7 bankruptcy Liquidation form of bankruptcy in which the debtor's nonexempt property is sold for cash.

Chapter 11 bankruptcy Reorganization form of bankruptcy that provides a method for reorganizing the debtor's financial affairs under the supervision of the bankruptcy court.

Chapter 13 bankruptcy A consumer debt adjustment form of bankruptcy that permits the court to supervise the debtor's plans for the payment of unpaid debts by installments.

chattel Personal property.

check A type of draft and three-party negotiable instrument containing an order to pay.

chlordane Chemical insecticide and termiticide that was banned in the early 1980s.

chlorofluorocarbons (CFCs) Man-made chemical substances that were used in hundreds of applications, including refrigerators and air conditioners.

chronological age Actual age of an item.

circuit breaker A device that trips or switches the electrical power off for a given circuit if the current increases beyond the capacity of the system.

civil action A lawsuit between private parties.

civil law Laws which address the private rights of citizens to sue and seek remedies through the courts for a wrongful action against them.

Civil Rights Act of 1866 A federal law that prohibits all discrimination on the basis of race.

Civil Rights Act of 1968 *See* Fair Housing Act of 1988.

client The principal of the agent.

closed-end mortgage One that cannot be refinanced.

closed mortgage One that imposes a prepayment penalty.

closing costs Expenses incurred in the purchase and sale of real property paid at the time of settlement or closing.

closing statement An accounting of the funds received and disbursed in a real estate transaction.

cloud on a title A claim against a title to real property.

cluster development A type of development that provides for planned unit developments (PUDs), which create a neighborhood of cluster housing and supporting business establishments.

cluster zoning A form of zoning providing for several different types of land use within a zoned area.

Coastal Zone Management Program A program coordinated by DOS to preserve and protect New York's coastline.

Code of Ethics and Standards of Practice Guidelines for conduct required by license laws and by the National Association of REALTORS®.

codicil A supplement or appendix to a will either adding or changing a bequest.

coinsurance clause A requirement of hazard insurance policies that property be insured for a certain percent of value to obtain the full amount of loss.

collateral Property pledged as security for payment of a debt.

color of title A defective claim to a title.

commercial law Laws that are applicable to the rights and relations of persons engaged in commerce or trade carried on for profit.

commercial mortgage A mortgage usually made to a business that may include an assignment of leases, personal guarantees, and a substantial down payment.

commercial property Property producing rental income or used in business.

commercial zones Areas that are zoned for structures that house retail stores, restaurants, hotels, and service businesses.

commingling An agent's mixing money or property of others with the agent's personal or business funds or other property.

commission A fee paid for the performance of services, such as a broker's commission.

commissioner's deed A form of judicial deed executed by a commissioner.

commitment A promise, such as a promise by a lending institution to make a certain mortgage loan.

common areas Property to which co-owners hold title as a result of ownership of a condominium unit.

common law Law by judicial precedent or tradition as contrasted with a written statute.

community-based planning A form of land use control originating in the grassroots of a community.

community planning A master plan for the orderly growth of a city or county to result in the greatest social and economic benefits to the people.

community property A form of co-ownership limited to husband and wife; does not exist in New York.

comparable A property that is similar to a property being appraised by the sales comparison approach.

comparative market analysis An analysis of the competition in the marketplace that a property will face upon sale attempts.

compensatory damages The amount of money actually lost, which will be awarded by a court in case of a breached contract.

competent parties Persons and organizations legally qualified to manage their own affairs, including entering into contracts.

competition The principle stating that when the net profit a property generates is excessive, very strong competition will result.

complete performance Execution of a contract by virtue of all parties having fully performed all terms.

completion bond A guarantee by a developer that ensures a municipality that off-site improvements to a subdivision will be made upon completion of the total project; also known as a subdivision bond.

condemnation Exercise of the power of eminent domain; taking private property for public use.

condemnation value Market value of condemned property.

condition Any fact or event that, if it occurs or fails to occur, automatically creates or extinguishes a legal obligation.

condominium A form of ownership of real property, recognized in all states, consisting of individual ownership of some aspects and co-ownership in other aspects of the property.

condominium declaration The document that, when recorded, creates a condominium; also called a master deed.

conforming loans Those processed on uniform loan forms and according to FNMA/FHLMC guidelines.

conformity Homogeneous uses of land within a given area, which results in maximizing land value.

consent decree Called nolo contendere in criminal cases, it is a compromise in civil lawsuits where the accused party agrees to stop the alleged illegal activity without admitting guilt or wrongdoing.

consideration Anything of value, as recognized by law, offered as an inducement to contract.

constitutional law Laws which address the role of the Supreme Court and its authority as relates to the President, Congress and the states; also deals with the powers of Congress and the executive branch.

construction loan A short-term loan, secured by a mortgage, to obtain funds to construct an improvement on land.

construction mortgage A temporary mortgage used to borrow money to construct an improvement on land.

constructive eviction Results from some action or inaction by the landlord that renders the premises unsuitable for the use agreed to in a lease or other rental contract.

constructive notice One in which all affected parties are bound by the knowledge of a fact even though they actually have not been notified of such fact.

consumer price index (CPI) An index of the change in prices of various commodities and services, providing a measure of the rate of inflation.

contingency A condition in a contract relieving a party of liability if a specified event occurs or fails to occur.

contract An agreement between competent parties upon legal consideration to do, or abstain from doing, some legal act.

contract buyer's policy Title insurance that protects contract buyer against defects in contract seller's title.

contract for deed A contract of sale and a financing instrument wherein the seller agrees to convey title when the buyer completes the purchase price installment payments; also called installment land contract and installment plan.

contract rent The amount of rent agreed to in a lease.

contribution The principle that for any given part of a property, its value is the result of the contribution that part makes to the total value by being present, or the amount that it subtracts from total value as a result of its absence.

conventional life estate One created by intentional act of the parties.

conventional mortgage loan One in which the federal government does not insure or guarantee payment to the lender.

conversion Change in a form of ownership, such as changing rental apartments to condominium ownership.

convertible mortgage A provision in a mortgage that gives the lender the option of converting the outstanding balance into an agreed-upon percentage of ownership in the property.

convey To pass to another (as in title).

conveyance Transfer of title to real property.

cooling-off period A three-day right of rescission for certain loan transactions.

cooperating broker or agent One who participates in the sale of a property.

cooperative A form of ownership in which stockholders in a corporation occupy property owned by the corporation under a lease.

co-ownership Title to real property held by two or more persons at the same time; also called concurrent ownership.

corporation A form of organization existing as an entity.

corporation franchise tax A tax calculated on the net profit of the corporation.

corporation law Laws which address federal and state formation and operation of corporations.

corrective maintenance Repair of a nonfunctioning item.

correlation A step in the appraisal process in which the appraiser weighs the appraisal approaches to reach a rational conclusion as to the value of the subject property; also known as reconciliation.

cost The total dollar expenditure for labor, materials, and other items related to construction.

cost approach An appraisal method whereby the cost of constructing a substitute structure is calculated, depreciation is deducted, and land value is added.

cost recovery A type of income tax deduction available for real estate and personal property that allows the total cost of the property that is depreciable to be deducted over a certain timeframe.

counteroffer A new offer made by an offeror rejecting an offer.

covenant A promise in writing.

covenant against encumbrances A promise in a deed that the title causes no encumbrances except those set forth in the deed.

covenant for further assurances A promise in a deed that the grantor will execute further assurances that may be reasonable or necessary to perfect the title in the grantee.

covenant of quiet enjoyment A promise in a deed (or lease) that the grantee (or lessee) will not be disturbed in his use of the property because of a defect in the grantor's (or lessor's) title.

covenant of right to convey A promise in a deed that the grantor has the legal capacity to convey the title.

covenant of seisin A promise in a deed assuring the grantee that the grantor has the title being conveyed.

covenant of warranty A promise in a deed that the grantor will guarantee and defend the title against lawful claimants.

credit In a closing statement, money to be received or credit given for money or an obligation given.

creditor One to whom a debt is owed.

criminal law Laws that declare what conduct is criminal and prescribes the punishment to be imposed for such conduct.

cubic-foot method A means of estimating reproduction or replacement cost using the volume of the structure.

cul-de-sac A dead-end street with a circular turn-around at the dead end.

cumulative zoning A type of zoning permitting a higher-priority use even though it is different from the type of use designated for the area.

curable depreciation A condition of property that exists when correction is physically possible and the cost of correction is less than the value increase.

curtesy A husband's interest in the real property of his wife.

customer The party whom the agent brings to the principal as sellers or buyers of the property.

damages The amount of financial loss incurred as a result of another's action.

debit In a closing statement, an expense or money received against a credit.

debt service Principal and interest payments on a debt.

decedent A deceased person.

declaration Master deed containing legal description of the condominium facility, a plat of the property, plans and specifications for the building and units, a description of the common areas, and the degree of ownership in the common areas available to each owner.

declaration of restrictions The instrument used to record restrictive covenants on the public record.

decree A court order.

dedication An appropriation of land or an easement therein by the owner to the public.

dedication by deed The deeding of a parcel of land to a municipality.

deductible expenses Costs of operating property held for use in business or as an investment. These expenses are subtracted from gross income to arrive at net income.

deed A written instrument transferring an interest in real property when delivered to the grantee.

deed in lieu of foreclosure Conveyance of title to the mortgagee by a mortgagor in default to avoid a record of foreclosure; also called friendly foreclosure.

deed of correction A deed executed to correct an error in a prior deed; also called a deed of confirmation.

deed of gift A warranty or quitclaim deed conveying title as a gift to the grantee.

deed of trust A form of mortgage in which there is a third party, who is called a trustee.

deed restriction Limitation on land use appearing in deeds.

default Failure to perform an obligation.

defeasance clause A statement in a mortgage or deed of trust giving the borrower the right to redeem the title and have the mortgage lien released at any time prior to default by paying the debt in full.

defeasible Subject to being defeated by the occurrence of a certain event.

defeasible fee A title subject to being lost if certain conditions occur.

defect With regard to a property, any condition that would: have a material adverse effect on value; adversely impair the health or safety of the occupants; and/or if not repaired, removed, or replaced would significantly shorten or adversely affect the expected normal life of the premises.

deficiency judgment A court judgment obtained by a mortgagee for the amount of money a foreclosure sale proceeds were deficient in fully satisfying the mortgage debt.

delivery and acceptance The transfer of a title by deed requires the grantor to deliver and the grantee to accept a given deed.

demise To convey an estate for years; synonymous with lease or let.

demography The study of the social and economical statistics of a community.

density Number of persons or structures per acre.

Department of Housing and Urban Development (HUD) A federal agency involved with housing.

Department of Veteran Affairs Offers a 100% loan that guarantees repayment of the top portion of the loan to the lender in the event the borrower defaults.

depreciated value The original basis of a property less the amount of depreciation taken at any point in time.

depreciation (a) Loss in value from any cause; (b) Deductible allowance from net income of property when arriving at taxable income.

descent The distribution of property to legally qualified heirs of one who has died intestate.

description by monument A legal description sometimes used when describing multiple-acre tracts of land and may refer to permanent objects such as a stone wall, large trees, or boulders.

description by reference A valid legal description that may be found on a deed which references a plat of subdivision or other legal document.

devise A gift of real property by will.

devisee The recipient of a gift of real property by will.

direct cost The cost of labor and materials.

disability The impairment of any life function.

disclosure and informed consent disclosure Explanation by a real estate agent of his position in the agency relationship and the verbal and written consent of the relationship by the client or customer.

disclosure of information The prompt and total communication to the principal by the agent of any information that is material to the transaction for which the agency is created.

Disclosure Regarding Dual Agency Relationship Form Pursuant to Section 443 of the New York Real Property Law, this document must be presented by a licensee and signed by all parties at the first substantive meeting with prospective purchasers or sellers.

disclosure statement—Regulation Z An accounting of all financial aspects of a mortgage loan required of lenders to borrowers in residential mortgage loans by Regulation Z of the Federal Reserve Board.

discount points A percentage of the loan amount the lender requires for making a mortgage loan.

discriminatory advertising Any advertising that states or indicates a preference, limitation, or discrimination on the basis of race, color, religion, sex, national origin, disability, familial status, age, or marital status in offering housing or commercial property for sale or rent.

disintermediation The loss of funds available to lending institutions for making mortgage loans, caused by depositors' withdrawal of funds for making investments that provide greater yields.

distribution box A part of a septic system, distributes the flow from the septic tank evenly to the absorption field or seepage pits.

distribution panel The location of circuit breakers or fuses.

dominant tenement Land benefiting from an easement appurtenant.

dower A wife's interest in her husband's real property.

draft A three-party negotiable instrument containing an order to pay.

drawee A person ordered in a draft to make payment.

drawer A person who signs a draft and is identified as the one ordering payment.

dual agent A broker/salesperson who attempts to represent both buyer and seller in the same transaction.

due diligence Investigation and review of a property to determine any legal liability.

due-on-sale clause *See* Alienation clause.

due process Mandate that anyone involved in a legal matter is entitled to a legal proceeding according to established rules and regulations.

duress The inability of a party to exercise his free will because of fear of another party.

duty of disclosure A responsibility for revealing all information that affects the agency agreement.

earnest money A deposit a buyer makes at the time of submitting an offer, to demonstrate the true intent to purchase; also called binder, good faith deposit, or escrow deposit.

easement A nonpossessory right of use in the land of another.

easement appurtenant *See* appurtenant easement.

easement by condemnation Created by the exercise of the government's right of eminent domain.

easement by grant Created by the express written agreement of the landowners, usually in a deed.

easement by implication Arising by implication from the conduct of the parties.

easement by necessity Exists when a landowner has no access to roads and is landlocked.

easement by prescription Obtained by use of the land of another for the legally prescribed length of time.

easement in gross A right of use in the land of another without the requirement that the holder of the right own adjoining land.

eaves The lowest part of the roof, which projects beyond the walls of the structure.

economic depreciation Physical deterioration of property caused by normal use, damage caused by natural and other hazards, and failure to maintain property adequately.

economic life The period of time during which a property is financially beneficial to the owner.

economic obsolescence Loss in value caused by things such as changes in surrounding land use patterns and failure to adhere to the principle of highest and best use.

economic rent The amount of rent established by the market value of a property.

effective age The age of a property based on remaining economic life.

effective demand A desire for property accompanied by financial ability to satisfy the desire by purchasing the property.

effective gross income Total potential income less deductions for vacancy and credit losses plus other income.

effective interest rate Actual rate of interest being paid.

egress The right to leave a parcel of land entered (ingress) by law.

electromagnetic field Created when electricity flows through a wire.

Emergency Tenant Protection Act A law in effect in New York City and other municipalities that gives tenants, in most cases, entitlement to a one- or two-year lease renewal.

eminent domain The power of government to take private property for public use.

enabling acts Laws passed by state legislatures authorizing cities and counties to regulate land use within their jurisdictions.

encroachment Trespass on the land of another as a result of intrusion by some structure or other object.

encumbrance A claim, lien, charge, or liability attached to and binding upon real property.

endorsement Additional coverage on an insurance policy to include a specific risk.

enforceable A contract in which the parties may legally be required to perform.

environmental impact statement A requirement of the National Environmental Policy Act and the State Environmental Quality Review Act prior to initiating or changing a land use that may have an adverse effect on the environment.

Environmental Protection Agency (EPA) A federal agency that oversees land use.

Environment Policy Act A federal law that requires filing an environmental impact statement with the EPA prior to changing or initiating a land use or development.

Equal Credit Opportunity Act (ECOA) A federal law prohibiting discrimination in consumer loans.

equitable distribution Theory which governs the division of marital property in New York.

equitable title An interest in real estate such that a court will take notice and protect the owner's rights.

equity of redemption The borrower's right to redeem the title pledged or conveyed in a mortgage after default and prior to a foreclosure sale by paying the debt in full, accrued interest, and lender's costs.

erosion The wearing away of land by water, wind, or other processes of nature.

escheat The power of government to take title to property left by a person who has died without leaving a valid will (intestate) or qualified heirs.

escrow The deposit of funds or documents with a neutral third party, who is instructed to carry out the provisions of an agreement.

escrow account (a) An account maintained by a real estate broker in an insured bank for the deposit of other people's money; also called trust account; (b) An account maintained by the borrower with the lender in certain mortgage loans to accumulate the funds to pay an annual insurance premium, a real property tax, or a homeowners' association assessment.

estate at sufferance Continuing to occupy property after lawful authorization has expired; a form of leasehold estate.

estate at will A leasehold estate that may be terminated at the desire of either party.

estate for years A leasehold estate of definite duration.

estate from year-to-year A leasehold estate that automatically renews itself for consecutive periods until terminated by notice by either party; also called estate from period-to-period or periodic tenancy.

estate in fee An estate in fee simple absolute.

estate in real property An interest sufficient to provide the right to use, possession, and control of land; establishes the degree and duration of ownership.

estoppel certificate A document executed by a mortgagor or mortgagee setting forth the principal amount.

estovers The right of a life tenant or lessee to cut timber on the property for fuel or to use in making repairs.

evaluation A study of the usefulness or utility of a property without reference to the specific estimate of value.

eviction A landlord's action that interferes with the tenant's use or possession of the property. Eviction may be actual or constructive.

exclusive agency listing A listing given to one broker only (exclusive), who is entitled to the commission if the broker or any agent of the listing broker effects a sale but imposes no commission obligation on the owner who sells the property to a person who was not interested in the property by efforts of the listing broker or an agent of the listing broker.

exclusive right to rent This contract is between an owner or lessor and a broker or agent in the rental of residential property.

exclusive right to sell listing A listing given to one broker only, who is entitled to the commission if anyone sells the property during the term of the listing contract.

exclusive-use zoning A type of zoning in which only the designated use may be made of property within the zoned district.

executed contract An agreement that has been fully performed.

execution Signing a contract or other legal document.

execution of judgment Judicial proceeding in which property of a debtor is seized (attached) and sold to satisfy a judgment lien.

executor A male appointed in a will to see that the terms of the will are carried out.

executory contract An agreement that has not been fully performed.

executrix A female appointed in a will to see that the terms of the will are carried out.

exercise of option Purchase of optioned property by the optionee.

express agency An agency relationship created by oral or written agreement between principal and agent.

express contract One created verbally or in writing by the parties.

extended coverage An insurance term referring to the extension of a standard fire insurance policy to cover damages resulting from wind, rain, and other perils.

face amount Amount of insurance coverage shown on the declaration page.

Fair Housing Act of 1968 A federal prohibition on discrimination in the sale, rental, or financing of housing on the basis of race, color, religion, sex, or national origin.

Fair Housing Act of 1988 A federal prohibition on discrimination in sale, rental, financing, or appraisal of housing on the basis of race, color, religion, sex, national origin, handicap, or familial status.

Fair Housing Amendments Act of 1988 A law adding to the Fair Housing Act provisions to prevent discrimination based on mental or physical impairment or familial status.

fair market value A price for property agreed upon between buyer and seller in a competitive market with neither party being under undue pressure.

familial status Defined under fair housing law as an adult with children under 18, a person who is pregnant, or one who has legal custody of a child or who is in the process of obtaining custody.

family An individual, or two or more persons related by blood, marriage, or adoption, living together in one dwelling; or a group of up to three people who are not married, blood relatives, or adopted, living together as a single housekeeping unit; or one or more persons living together in a single housekeeping unit as distinguished from a hotel, club, and so on.

Fannie Mae The shortened name for the Federal National Mortgage Association (FNMA), a privately owned corporation that purchases FHA, VA, and conventional mortgages.

fascia In house construction, the area of material facing the outer edge of the soffit.

feasibility study A detailed statistical analysis that involves the investigation of all facets of a real estate investment project and the comparison of the data with other similar projects.

Federal Financial Institutions Reform, Recovery, and Enforcement Act of 1989 (FIRREA) Defines minimal requirements governing the licensure and certification of appraisers and mandates and empowers individual states to license and certify appraisers.

Federal Housing Administration (FHA) The U.S. agency that insures mortgage loans to protect lending institutions.

Federal Reserve System The U.S. agency that regulates monetary policy and, thereby, the money supply and interest rates.

Federal Trade Commission An administrative body that has the power to declare trade practices unfair, particularly with regard to antitrust legislation.

fee simple absolute An inheritable estate in land providing the greatest interest of any form of title.

fee simple on condition A defeasible fee (title), recognizable by the words "but if."

felony Any serious crime above a misdemeanor which is generally punishable by imprisonment.

FHA-insured loan A mortgage loan in which payments are insured by the Federal Housing Administration.

fiduciary A person, such as an agent, placed in a position of trust in relation to the person for whose benefit the relationship is created; essentially the same as a trustee.

filtering down Properties in neighborhoods that were once middle income or upper income decline in value.

finance charge An amount imposed on the borrower in a mortgage loan, consisting of origination fee, service charges, discount points, interest, credit report fees, and finders' fees.

fire insurance policy *See* homeowner's policy.

first mortgage One that is superior to later recorded mortgages.

first substantive meeting The first contact or meeting when some detail and information about the property is shared with parties who express some interest in the real estate transaction.

fixed expenses Expenditures such as property taxes, license fees, and property insurance; subtracted from effective gross income to determine net operating income.

fixed lease One in which the rental amount remains the same for the entire lease term; also called flat, straight, or gross lease.

fixed-rate mortgage One in which the interest does not change.

fixture Personal property that has become real property by having been permanently attached to real property.

fix-up expenses Costs incurred by the seller of a principal residence in preparing it for sale.

flashing A metallic material that is used in certain areas of the roof and walls to prevent water from seeping into the structure.

flat lease One in which the rental amount does not change during the lease term.

flexible payment mortgage A loan that allows smaller mortgage payment in the first years of purchase and then increases the amount of payment later on.

flitch beam A double top plate used to tie the walls together and provide additional support for the ceiling and roof system.

floating slab A type of foundation constructed by pouring the footing first and then pouring the slab.

footing The concrete base below the frost line that supports the foundation of a structure.

forbearance The act of refraining from taking legal action for payment of a mortgage despite the fact that it is due.

foreclosure The legal procedure of enforcing payment of a debt secured by a mortgage or any other lien.

forfeiture clause A statement in a contract for deed providing for giving up all payments by a buyer in default.

formal will A will, in writing, signed by the testator or testatrix in front of two witnesses.

foundation walls Poured concrete, masonry block, or brick sides of a structure.

framing The wooden skeleton of the structure.

framing members Lumber with a nominal dimension of two inches thick used for constructing the wooden skeleton of the home.

fraud An intentional false statement of a material fact.

Freddie Mac A nickname for Federal Home Loan Mortgage Corporation (FHLMC), a corporation owned by the Federal Home Loan Bank System, which purchases FHA, VA, and conventional mortgages.

freehold estate A right of title to land.

free market An economic condition in which buyer and seller have ample time to negotiate a beneficial purchase and sale without undue pressure or urgency.

friable A quality of some asbestos that causes it to crumble, allowing toxic particles to escape into the air that may lodge in the lungs.

friendly foreclosure An absolute conveyance of title to the lender by the mortgagor in default to avoid a record of foreclosure; also called deed in lieu of foreclosure.

frieze board A decorative and functional board that prevents wind and moisture from penetrating the junction of the soffit and sheathing.

front foot A linear foot of property frontage on a street or highway.

full covenant and warranty deed A deed containing the strongest and broadest form of guarantee of title.

fully amortizing mortgage One in which the scheduled uniform payments will pay off the loan completely over the mortgage term.

functional obsolescence Loss in value resulting from things such as faulty design, inadequacies, overadequacies, and out-of-date equipment.

fuse A device that is part of a wiring system that will melt and open the circuit when overheating occurs, causing electrical power to stop.

future interest The rights of an owner of an estate who will vest at some upcoming time.

gain realized The excess of the amount realized over the adjusted basis.

gap financing Usually a short-term loan to provide funds over and above an already existing loan until more permanent financing is in place. *See also* bridge loan.

general agent One with full authority over property of the principal, such as a property manager.

general lien One that attaches to all of the property of a person within the court's jurisdiction.

General Obligations Law *See* Statute of Frauds.

general partnership The partners are personally liable for partnership debts exceeding partnership assets.

general warranty deed A deed denoting an unlimited guarantee of title.

GIM *See* gross income multiplier.

Ginnie Mae A nickname for Government National Mortgage Association (GNMA), a U.S. government agency that purchases FHA and VA mortgages.

girder The main carrying beam of a house that spans the distance from one side of the foundation to the other.

good faith estimate Lender's estimate of borrower's settlement costs, required by RESPA to be furnished to borrower at time of loan application.

grace period In a mortgage, a specified time frame in which the payment may be made without the borrower being in default.

graduated lease One in which the rental changes from period to period over the lease term, increasing in stair-step fashion; used for new business tenants whose income increases over time.

graduated payment mortgage (GPM) One in which the payments are lower in the early years but increase on a scheduled basis until they reach an amortizing level.

grant A transfer of title to real property by deed.

grantee One who receives title to real property by deed.

granting clause The statement in a deed containing words of conveyance.

granting theory A type of mortgage lending practice in which a disinterested third party holds legal title to a property in security for the loan through a deed of trust; not used in New York.

grantor One who conveys title to real property by deed.

grievance A written complaint, filed by a property owner with the local board of assessment review, protesting the validity of an assessment.

gross income Income received without subtracting expenses.

gross income multiplier (GIM) A factor used in calculating estimated value of income property.

gross lease One in which the lessor pays all costs of operating and maintaining the property and real property taxes.

gross operating income Gross scheduled rental income minus losses from vacancies and credit losses.

gross rent multiplier (GRM) A method of estimating the value of income property.

ground lease A lease of unimproved land.

ground rent Lessee's payment under a ground lease.

ground water Water obtained from underground.

group boycott A conspiracy wherein a person or group is persuaded or coerced into not doing business with another person or group.

group home A residential facility for five or more adults who have been institutionalized and then released.

habendum clause The statement in a deed beginning with the words "to have and to hold" and describing the estate granted.

habitable Suitable for the type of occupancy intended.

headers Wooden reinforcements for the placement of doors and windows.

heirs Persons legally eligible to receive property of a decedent.

heterogeneous A variety of dissimilar uses of property; nonhomogeneous.

highest and best use The use of land that will preserve its utility and yield a net income flow in the form of rent that, when capitalized at the proper rate of interest, represents the highest present value.

holder in due course Holder of a negotiable instrument who takes an instrument for value, in good faith, and without notice that it is defective or overdue.

holding period The length of time a property is owned.

holdover tenant A tenant who remains in possession of property after a lease terminates.

holographic will One handwritten by the testator.

Home Buyer's Guide A booklet explaining aspects of loan settlement required by RESPA.

home equity loan A loan against the equity in a home.

home occupations A small business or occupation that may be conducted only by the residents of the dwelling and must be incidental and secondary to the use of the dwelling.

homeowners' association An organization of owners having the responsibility to provide for operation and maintenance of common areas of a condominium or residential subdivision; also called property owners' association.

homeowner's policy An insurance policy protecting against a variety of hazards.

homeowner's warranty (HOW) An insurance policy protecting against loss caused by structural and other defects in a dwelling.

homestead The land and dwelling of a homeowner.

homogeneous Similar and compatible, as in land uses.

HUD Form No. 1 A standard settlement form required by RESPA.

HVAC An acronym that stands for heating, ventilation, and air conditioning.

hydronic system A process in a heating system in which liquids such as water are heated or cooled.

hypothecate To pledge property as security for the payment of a debt without giving up possession.

illiquidity An investment that is not easily convertible to cash.

illusory offer One that does not obligate the offeror.

immobility Incapable of being moved, fixed in location; an important physical characteristic of land.

implied agency Agency that exists as a result of actions of the parties.

implied contract One created by deduction from the conduct of the parties rather than from the direct words of the parties; opposite of an express contract.

implied warranty One presumed by law to exist in a deed, though not expressly stated.

improved land Land on which structures or roads exist.

improvements Changes or additions made to a property, such as walls or roads, and so on. These typically increase the value of a property, except in some cases of overimprovement.

incentive zoning Offers incentives to developers and property owners to construct amenities that would provide certain types of uses and enjoyment for the residents of the municipality.

income approach The primary method for estimating the value of properties that produce rental income; also called appraisal by capitalization.

income property One that produces rental income.

income shelter Deductible allowances from net income of property to arrive at taxable income and tax losses allowed to offset passive and active income.

incompetent Describes a person who is not capable of managing his or her own affairs, under law.

incorporeal Intangible things such as rights.

increasing or diminishing returns The cost of the improvement is compared to the increase in value to the property after the improvement is completed. Under *diminishing* returns, the increase in value is less than the cost of the improvement. Under *increasing* returns, the increase in value is more than the cost of the improvement.

incurable depreciation That which is not physically correctable or not economically practical to correct.

indemnification Reimbursement or compensation paid to someone for a loss already suffered.

independent contractor Worker who holds nonemployee status under the law.

indestructibility A physical characteristic of land describing that land as a permanent commodity that cannot be destroyed.

indirect costs Costs that support a construction project such as architectural fees.

indorsee The person who is the payee on an indorser.

indorsement A signature other than a maker, drawee, or an acceptor that is placed on an instrument to negotiate (or transfer) it to another.

indorsor The person who transfers or indorses a negotiable instrument to another.

industrial zones Areas that are zoned for structures that are used for light or heavy manufacturing and warehouses.

informed consent Agreement by a buyer or seller to a type of agency relationship after considering the various alternatives.

infrastructure Services and systems that support a community, such as hospitals, schools, and roadways.

ingress The right to enter a parcel of land; usually used as "ingress and egress" (both entering and leaving).

injunction A court instruction to discontinue a specified activity.

in rem legal proceeding An action that is brought against the real property directly and not against an individual and his personal property.

installment land contract *See* contract for deed.

installment sale A transaction in which the seller receives the sale price over a specified period of time.

instrument A written legal document such as a contract, note, or mortgage.

insurable interest The degree of interest qualifying for insurance.

insured conventional loan One in which the loan payment is insured by private mortgage insurance to protect the lender.

insured value The cost of replacing a structure completely destroyed by an insured hazard.

interest (a) Money paid for the use of money; (b) an ownership or right.

interim financing A short-term or temporary loan, such as a construction loan.

interspousal deed Conveys real property from husband to wife or wife to husband.

Interstate Land Sales Full Disclosure Act A federal law regulating the sale across state lines of subdivided land under certain conditions.

intervivos trust A trust set up while the parties are living.

intestate The condition of death without leaving a valid will.

intestate succession Distribution of property by descent as provided by statute.

invalid Not legally enforceable.

investment The outlay of money for income or profit.

investment syndicate A joint venture, typically controlled by one or two persons, hoping for return to all investors.

investment value The highest price an investor would pay in light of how well he believes a given property would serve his financial goals.

involuntary alienation Transfer of title to real property as a result of a lien foreclosure sale, adverse possession, filing a petition in bankruptcy, condemnation under power of eminent domain, or, upon the death of the titleholder, to the state if no heirs exist.

involuntary lien An act wherein a creditor places a claim on real and/or personal property of another to obtain payment of a debt.

irrevocable That which cannot be changed or canceled.

joint tenancy A form of co-ownership that includes the right of survivorship.

joint venture Participation by two or more parties in a single undertaking.

joists Wooden framing members used in the construction of floors and ceilings.

judgment A court determination of the rights and obligations of parties to a lawsuit.

judgment lien A general lien resulting from a court decree.

judicial deed One executed by an official with court authorization.

judicial foreclosure A court proceeding to require that property be sold to satisfy a mortgage lien.

junior mortgage One that is subordinate to a prior mortgage.

jurisdiction The extent of authority of a court.

kickback Payment by a broker of any part of a compensation to a real estate transaction to anyone who is not licensed or who is not exempt from the license law.

laches Loss of legal rights because of failure to assert them on a timely basis.

land The surface of the earth, the area above and below the surface, and everything permanently attached thereto.

land contract *See* contract for deed.

land grant Conveyance of land as a gift for the benefit of the public.

landlease A type of lease that allows a lessee the right to use land for any purpose for a specified period of time.

landlocked Describes property with no access to a public road.

land patent Instrument conveying public land to an individual.

land trust Type of trust in which title to land is held by a trustee for the benefit of others.

land use controls Governmental restrictions on land use (e.g., zoning laws and building codes).

lead A toxic metallic element found in some homes in paint, dust, and water.

lead agency The governmental agency that oversees the environment impact process and makes final decisions.

lease A contract wherein a landlord gives a tenant the right of use and possession of property for a limited period of time in return for rent.

leased fee Lessor's interest in leased property.

leasehold estate Nonfreehold estate; of limited duration, providing the right of possession and control but not title.

leasehold mortgage One in which a leasehold (nonfreehold) estate is pledged to secure payment of the note.

legacy A gift of personal property by will.

legal capacity The ability to contract.

legal description A description of land recognized by law.

legal entity A person or organization with legal capacity.

legality of object Legal purpose.

legatee Recipient of the gift of personal property by will.

lessee A tenant under a lease.

lessor A landlord under a lease.

leverage The use of borrowed funds; the larger the percentage of borrowed money, the greater the leverage.

levy Imposition of a tax, executing a lien.

license A personal privilege to do a particular act or series of acts on the land of another.

lien A claim that one person has against the property of another for some debt or charge, entitling the lien-holder to have the claim satisfied from the property of the debtor.

lienee One whose property is subject to a lien.

lien foreclosure sale Selling property without consent of the owner who incurred the debt resulting in a lien, as ordered by a court or authorized by state law, and title conveyed to purchaser by judicial deed.

lienor The one holding a lien against another.

lien theory A type of mortgage lending practice in which a mortgage loan constitutes a lien against the real property; the theory of mortgage lending in New York.

life estate A freehold estate created for the duration of the life or lives of certain named persons; a non-inheritable estate.

life estate in remainder A form of life estate in which certain persons, called remaindermen, are designated to receive the title upon termination of the life tenancy.

life estate in reversion A form of life estate that goes back to the creator of the estate in fee simple upon termination.

life estate pur autre vie An estate in which the duration is measured by the life of someone other than the life tenant. *See also* pur autre vie.

life tenant One holding a life estate.

like-kind property Real or personal property that qualifies for tax treatment as a tax-free exchange.

limited liability corporation (LLC) Business arrangement formed by two or more persons who are not personally liable for the obligations of the LLC; the LLC is taxed as a partnership.

limited liability partnership (LLP) A business arrangement formed by professionals such as attorneys and accountants who are all limited partners and are not personally liable for the obligations of the partnership.

limited partnership An organization consisting of one or more general partners and several partners with lesser roles.

liquidated damages Money to be paid and received as compensation for a breach of contract.

liquidity The attribute of an asset's being readily convertible to cash.

lis pendens Latin, meaning "a lawsuit pending." *See* notice of lis pendens

listing contract A contract whereby a property owner employs a real estate broker to market the property described in the contract.

litigation A lawsuit.

littoral rights Rights belonging to owner of land that borders a lake, ocean, or sea.

loan commitment Obligation of a lending institution to make a certain mortgage loan.

loan origination fee Financing charge required by the lender.

loan-to-value ratio The relationship between the amount of a mortgage loan and the lender's opinion of the value of the property pledged to secure payment of the loan.

location (situs) An economic characteristic of land having the greatest effect on value in comparison to any other characteristic.

lot and block A type of legal description used in a deed in addition to a metes and bounds description.

L.S. Signifies *locus signilli*, a Latin term meaning "in place of the seal."

management agreement A contract in which an owner employs a property manager.

management plan A long-range program prepared by a property manager indicating to the owner how the property will be managed.

management proposal A program for operating a property submitted to the owner by a property manager.

margin Measure of profit.

marital property Property acquired during the marriage and distributed equitably, taking into account various factors.

marketable title One that is free from reasonable doubt and that a court would require a purchaser to accept.

market allocation agreement An agreement between competitors dividing or assigning a certain area or territory for sales.

market value A property's worth in terms of price agreed upon by a willing buyer and seller when neither is under any undue pressure and each is knowledgeable of market conditions at the time.

master deed The instrument that legally establishes a condominium; also called condominium declaration.

material fact Important information that may affect a person's judgment.

materialman's lien *See* mechanic's lien.

mechanic's lien A statutory lien available to persons supplying labor (mechanics) or material (materialmen) to the construction of an improvement on land if they are not paid.

mediation The use of a neutral third party to discuss and attempt to resolve a dispute.

meeting of the minds A condition that must exist for creation of a contract.

merger The absorption of one thing into another.

merger clause Clause in a real estate contract in which the contract is fulfilled and the conveyed deed supersedes the contract.

metes and bounds A system of land description by distances and directions.

mill One-tenth of a cent.

mineral rights A landowner's ability to take minerals from the earth or to sell or lease this right to others.

minor A person who has not attained the statutory age of majority.

misdemeanor A lesser crime than a felony which may be punished by a fine and/or imprisonment.

misrepresentation (a) A false statement or omission of a material fact; (b) In real estate, making an intentionally false statement to induce someone to contract.

monolithic slab A type of foundation where the footing and slab are poured at the same time.

monument A type of property description mainly used by surveyors; the description is drawn from permanent objects such as a stone wall, large trees, or boulders.

moratorium A delay in allowing development of property within the municipality.

mortgage A written instrument used to pledge a title to real property to secure payment of a promissory note.

mortgage assumption The transfer of mortgage obligations to purchaser of the mortgaged property.

mortgage banker A licensed individual or form of organization that makes and services mortgage loans.

mortgage broker A licensed individual who arranges a mortgage loan between a lender and a borrower for a fee.

mortgagee The lender in a mortgage loan, who receives a mortgage from the borrower (mortgagor).

mortgagee's title insurance policy A policy that insures a mortgagee against defects in a title pledged by a mortgagor to secure payment of a mortgage loan.

mortgage insurance premium (MIP) A payment for insurance to protect the lender and/or insurer against loss if default occurs.

mortgage principal The amount of money (usually the loan amount) on which interest is either paid or received.

mortgage satisfaction Full payment of a mortgage loan.

mortgage value The value sufficient to secure payment of a mortgage loan.

mortgaging clause The statement in a mortgage or deed of trust that demonstrates the mortgagor's intent to mortgage the property to the mortgagee.

mortgagor The borrower in a mortgage loan who executes and delivers a mortgage to the lender.

multiple exchange A transaction in which more than two like-kind properties are exchanged.

multiple listing service (MLS) An organized method of sharing or pooling listings by member brokers.

mutual assent The voluntary agreement of all parties to a contract as evidenced by an offer and acceptance.

mutual mistake An error of material fact by both parties.

narrative appraisal report A statement of an opinion of value containing the element of judgment as well as the data used in arriving at the value estimate.

National Association of REALTORS® (NAR) The largest and most prominent trade organization of real estate licensees.

National Electric Code National standard for electrical installation and service.

negative amortization When the loan payment amount is not sufficient to cover interest due, the shortfall is added back into the principal, causing the principal to grow larger after payment is made.

negative covenant *See* restrictive covenant.

negative easement A right in the land of another prohibiting the servient owner from doing something on the servient land because it will affect the dominant land.

negligence Legal term describing failure to use the care that a reasonable person would use in like circumstances.

negotiable instrument An unconditional promise or order to pay a fixed amount with or without interest.

net income Gross income less operating expenses; also called net operating income.

net lease One in which the lessee pays a fixed amount of rent plus the costs of operation of the property.

net listing A method that is illegal in New York of establishing the listing broker's commission as all money above a specified net amount to the seller.

net operating income Gross operating income minus operating expenses.

New York State Energy Code Regulation that sets minimum requirements for the design of energy efficiencies for new buildings and renovations to existing buildings.

New York State Human Rights Law Created to eliminate and prevent discrimination in residential and commercial real estate as well as in employment, public accommodations, places of amusement, and educational institutions.

New York State Office of Parks, Recreation, and Historic Preservation (OPRHP) Oversees public recreational areas and administers federal and state preservation programs authorized by federal and state law.

New York State Uniform Fire Prevention and Building Code Provides minimum standards for the construction and renovation of all types of buildings in New York.

nonconforming use Utilization of land that does not conform to the use permitted by a zoning ordinance for the area; may be lawful or unlawful.

nonfreehold estate Leaseholds; estates with a length determined by agreement or statute; establishes possession of land as opposed to ownership in fee.

nonhomestead Classification of real property that is not for residential purposes and includes commercial, industrial, special franchise and utility property, and some vacant land.

nonhomogeneity A physical characteristic of land describing that land as a unique commodity.

nonrecourse note A note in which the borrower has no personal liability for payment.

nonsolicitation order An order issued by the secretary of state prohibiting licensees from soliciting listings in certain areas of the state.

notary public A person authorized by a state to take oaths and acknowledgments.

notice of lis pendens A statement on the public record warning all persons that a title to real property is the subject of a lawsuit and any lien resulting from the suit will attach to the title held by a purchaser from the defendant.

novation Substitution of a new contract for a prior contract.

null and void Invalid; without legal force or effect.

obligee One to whom an obligation is owed.

obligor One who owes an obligation to another.

obsolescence Loss in property value caused by economic or functional factors.

occupancy Physical possession of property.

offer A promise made to another conditional upon acceptance by a promise or act made in return.

offer and acceptance Necessary elements for the creation of a contract.

offeree One to whom an offer is made.

offeror One making an offer.

open-ended listing contract One without a termination date.

open-end mortgage One that may be refinanced without rewriting the mortgage.

open listing A listing given to one or more brokers in which the broker procuring a sale is entitled to the commission but imposes no commission obligation on the owner in the event the owner sells the property to someone who was not interested in the property by one of the listing brokers.

open mortgage One that does not impose a prepayment penalty.

operating budget A yearly budget of income and expense for a specific property, prepared by a property manager.

operating expenses Costs of operating a property held as an investment.

operating statement A report of receipts and disbursements resulting in net income of rental property.

operation of law The manner in which rights and liabilities of parties may be changed by application of law without the act or cooperation of the parties.

opinion of title *See* certificate of title opinion.

optionee One who receives an option.

optionor One who gives an option.

option to purchase A contract whereby a property owner (optionor) sells a right to purchase his or her property to a prospective buyer (optionee).

option to renew A provision setting forth the method and terms for renewing the lease.

oral will A will usually restricted to the granting of personal property because it conflicts with the Statute of Frauds, which states that the conveyance of real property must be in writing.

ordinance A law enacted by a local government.

origination fee A service charge by a lending institution for making a mortgage loan.

outlots/out parcels Land that is outside of the main area of development.

overimprovement An improvement to land that results in the land not being able to obtain its highest and best use.

ownership The right to use, control, possess, and dispose of property.

ownership in severalty Title to real property held in the name of one person only.

owner's title insurance policy A policy insuring an owner of real property against financial loss resulting from a title defect.

package mortgage One in which personal property as well as real property is pledged to secure payment of the note.

package policy Insurance coverage for property damage and liability loss all within one premium.

parcel A specific portion of land such as a lot.

parens patriae The right of government to litigate and therefore protect in the name of the public good.

parol evidence rule A concept allowing that oral explanations can support the written words of a contract but cannot contradict them.

participation mortgage (a) One in which two or more lenders share in making the loan; (b) One in which a lender shares in the profit produced by an income property pledged to secure the loan payment in addition to receiving interest and principal payments.

partition A legal proceeding dividing property of co-owners so each will hold title in severalty.

partnership A form of business organization in which the business is owned by two or more persons, called partners.

partnership law Laws that address the form of business organization composed of two or more individuals.

party wall A common wall used by two adjoining structures.

passive activity income Any trade or business in which the taxpayer does not materially participate.

payee A recipient of money.

payment cap If the interest rate on the loan changes and therefore the monthly payments increase, the lender allows a payment cap in which the monthly payment remains the same and the money for the higher interest rate is added to the principal.

percentage lease One in which the rental amount is a combination of a fixed amount plus a percentage of the lessee's gross sales.

percolation The movement of water through soil.

percolation (perc) test A test of soil to determine if it is sufficiently porous for installation of a septic tank.

periodic lease *See* periodic tenancy.

periodic tenancy A lease that automatically renews for successive periods unless terminated by either party; also called an estate from year to year.

per se illegal Legal doctrine stating that an activity is specifically not allowable under the law.

personal property All property that is not land and is not permanently attached to land; everything that is movable; chattel.

personal property law Laws that relate to ownership of other than real property.

physical deterioration Loss in value caused by unrepaired damage or inadequate maintenance.

pitch The slope of the roof.

PITI Acronym denoting that a mortgage payment includes principal, interest, taxes, and insurance.

planned unit development (PUD) A form of cluster zoning providing for both residential and commercial land uses within a zoned area.

planning A program for the development of a city or county designed to provide for orderly growth.

plat A property map, recorded on the public record in plat books.

plat book A record of subdivision maps generally filed with the county clerk.

platform framing The most common type of framing in residential construction in which the framing of the structure rests on a subfloor platform.

pledge To provide property as security for payment of a debt or for performance of a promise.

plottage Combining two or more parcels of land into one tract that has more value than the total value of the individual parcels.

points *See* discount points.

police power The power of government to regulate the use of real property for the benefit of the public.

polychlorinated biphenyls (PCBs) A manmade, odorless, liquid organic compound and carcinogen appearing in groundwater and soil.

population density The number of people within a given land area.

positive misrepresentation A person's actual statement that is false and known to be false.

possession When one either actively or constructively occupies a property; implies constructive notice that the possessor has certain legal rights.

post-and-beam framing A type of construction in which the framing members are much larger than ordinary studs and larger posts can be placed several feet apart instead of 16 or 24 inches on center.

potential gross income The amount of rental income that would be received if all units were rented 100 percent of the time and there were no credit losses.

power of attorney An instrument appointing an attorney-in-fact; creates a universal agency.

prepaid expenses Costs the seller pays in advance but were not fully used up (such as utility payments or property taxes due), shown as a credit to the seller and a debit to the buyer.

prepaid items Funds paid at closing to start an escrow account, as required in certain mortgage loans; also called prepaids.

prepayment penalty clause A financial charge imposed on a borrower for paying a mortgage prior to expiration of the full mortgage term.

prescription A method of acquiring an easement by continuous and uninterrupted use without permission.

prescriptive easement One obtained by prescription.

preventive maintenance Program of regularly scheduled checks on equipment to ensure proper functioning.

price The amount a purchaser agrees to pay and a seller agrees to accept under the circumstances surrounding a transaction.

price fixing Competitors in a group or industry conspire to charge the same or similar price for services rendered.

prima facie case A suit that is sufficiently strong that it can be defeated only by contrary evidence.

primary financing The loan with the highest priority.

primary mortgage market The activity of lenders' making mortgage loans to individual borrowers.

prime rate The interest rate a lender charges to the most creditworthy customers.

principal (a) In the law of agency, one who appoints an agent to represent her; (b) Amount of money on which interest is paid or received.

priority liens Special liens that receive preferential treatment (such as mechanic's liens).

private land use control Regulations for land use by individuals or nongovernment organizations in the form of deed restrictions and restrictive covenants.

private mortgage insurance (PMI) A form of insurance coverage required in high loan-to-value ratio conventional loans to protect the lender in case the borrower defaults in the loan payment.

private placement exemption Allows issuers of securities to raise capital from an unlimited number of accredited investors without having to register with the Securities Exchange Commission.

private property That which is not owned by government.

privity of contract An agreement that exists only between lessor and lessee for the right to demand and receive the specific benefit.

probate The judicial determination of a will's validity.

procedural law Laws that address the rules as to how a lawsuit proceeds through the court system and also deals with the functions of administrative agencies.

procuring cause The basis for a direct action that results in successfully completing an objective.

profit The right to participate in profits of another's land.

proforma schedule An operating statement adjusted to reflect a potential change in income and expenses based upon the investor's knowledge of the real estate market.

promissory note A written promise to pay a debt as set forth in the writing.

promulgate To put in effect by public announcement.

property condition disclosure form (PCD) A comprehensive checklist pertaining to the condition of the property; seller property condition disclosure is mandatory in New York in the sale of one- to four-unit residential properties.

property description An accurate legal description of land.

property management Comprehensive, orderly, continuing program analyzing all investment aspects of a property to ensure a financially successful project.

property management report A periodic financial report prepared for the owner by a property manager.

property manager One who manages properties for an owner as the owner's agent.

property report Disclosure required under Interstate Land Sales Disclosure Act.

proprietary lease A lease in a cooperative apartment.

proration Division of certain settlement costs between buyer and seller.

prospectus A disclosure statement used as a selling tool by the issuer of securities.

public grant A grant of a power, license, or real property from the state or government to a private individual.

public land use control Regulation of land use by government organizations in the form of zoning laws, building codes, subdivision ordinances, and environmental protection laws.

public liability insurance A type of insurance that covers the risks an owner assumes when the public enters the premises.

public open space Land that is not intensely developed for residential, commercial, industrial, or institutional use.

public property That which is owned by government.

public record Constructive notice, for all to see, of real property conveyances and other matters.

punitive damages Court-ordered awards for extremely bad behavior by a party; intended to punish and indicate that the behavior will not be tolerated.

pur autre vie Translated, means for the life of another; a life estate measured by the life of someone other than the life tenant.

purchase money mortgage A mortgage given by a buyer to a seller to secure payment of all or part of the purchase price.

qualified fee simple A defeasible fee (title), recognizable by words "as long as."

quantity survey A method for estimating replacement or reproduction cost.

quasi judicial Rulings that are subject to review and change in the state and federal courts.

quiet enjoyment Use or possession of property that is undisturbed by an enforceable claim of superior title.

quiet title action A lawsuit to remove a cloud on a title.

quitclaim A deed to relinquish or release a claim to real property.

quitclaim deed A deed of release that contains no warranty of title; used to remove a cloud on a title.

radius Distance from the center of a circle to the perimeter; part of a metes and bounds description.

radon A colorless, odorless, radioactive gas present in the soil that enters a home through small spaces and openings.

rafter A wooden framing member used in the roof of a structure.

rate cap With adjustable rate mortgages, limits on interest rates during the lifetime of a loan.

rate of return Percentage of net income produced by a property or other investment.

ratification After-the-fact acceptance of an agency agreement.

ratify To reaffirm a previous action.

ready, willing, and able Describes a buyer who is ready to buy, willing to buy, and financially able to pay the asking price.

real estate Land and everything permanently attached to land.

real estate broker A person or an organization who negotiates real estate sales, exchanges, or rentals for others for compensation.

Real Estate Investment Trust (REIT) A form of business trust owned by shareholders making mortgage loans.

real estate market A local activity in which real property is sold, exchanged, leased, and rented at prices set by competing forces.

real estate salesperson A person performing any of the acts included in the definition of real estate broker but while associated with and supervised by a broker.

Real Estate Settlement Procedures Act (RESPA) A federal law regulating activities of lending institutions in making mortgage loans for housing.

reality of consent Mutual agreement between the parties to a contract; meeting of the minds; to exist and be free of duress, fraud, undue influence, and misrepresentation.

realized gain Actual profit resulting from a sale.

real property The aggregate of rights, powers, and privileges conveyed with ownership of real estate.

real property law Laws that address the acquisition, transfer, and possession of an interest in real estate and the rights attached to it.

REALTOR® A registered trademark of the National Association of REALTORS®; its use is limited to members only.

realty Land and everything permanently attached to land.

reciprocity Mutual agreement by certain states to extend licensing privileges to each other.

recognized gain The amount of profit that is taxable.

reconciliation (a) The process of checking accounting of settlement statement; (b) The adjustment process in appraising, whereby comparables are adjusted to the subject property.

recordation Written registration of an owner's title in public records to protect against subsequent claimants.

recording Registering a document on the public record.

rectangular survey system A type of land description utilizing townships and sections.

redemption *See* equity of redemption.

redlining The refusal of lending institutions to make loans for the purchase, construction, or repair of a dwelling because the area in which the dwelling is located is populated by minorities.

reentry The owner's right to regain possession of real property.

referee's deed A type of judicial deed allowing conveyance of real property through a court-appointed individual.

referral fee A percentage of a broker's commission paid to another broker for sending a buyer or seller to him or her.

refinancing Obtaining a new mortgage loan to pay and replace an existing mortgage.

registration statement A filing statement required by the Securities Exchange Commission containing pertinent information about the securities offering.

Regulation Z Requirement issued by the Federal Reserve Board in implementing the Truth-in-Lending Act, which is a part of the Federal Consumer Credit Protection Act.

regulatory taking Under its power of eminent domain, government may take and develop land for public use.

reject To refuse to accept an offer.

release clause A provision in a mortgage to release certain properties from the mortgage lien when the principal is reduced by a specified amount.

remainder interest A future interest in a life estate.

remainderman One having a future interest in a life estate.

remise To release or give up.

rent roll The number of rental units currently occupied in a building multiplied by the rental amount per unit.

replacement cost The amount of money required to replace a structure with another structure of comparable utility.

replacement reserve A fund to replace assets when they wear out.

repossession Regaining possession of property as a result of a breach of contract by another.

reproduction cost The amount of money required to build an exact duplicate of a structure.

rescission Cancellation of a contract when another party is in default.

resident manager A person employed to manage a building; may live on the premises.

residual income Income allocated to the land under the principle of highest and best use.

restrictive covenant Restriction placed on a private owner's use of land by a nongovernmental entity or individual.

reverse annuity mortgage A mortgage used by older people in which the lender makes payments to the borrower for a contracted period of time; upon the death of the homeowner or sale of the property, the money is paid back.

reversion Return of title to the holder of a future interest, such as the grantor in a life estate not in remainder.

reversionary interest A provision stating the owner's interest: that possession of property will go back to owner at end of lease.

revocation Withdrawal of an offer.

rider Addendum to cover supplemental issues of an agreement.

right of assignment Allows lender to sell mortgage at any time and obtain money invested rather than wait for completion of loan term.

right of first refusal A statement in a lease or condominium articles of association that provides for a lessee or an association to have the first opportunity to purchase the property before it is offered to anyone else.

right of inheritance The right for property to descend to the heirs of the owner as set out by will or by intestate succession.

right of redemption Real property owners are given the opportunity to satisfy liens against their property prior to foreclosure proceedings.

right of survivorship The right of an owner to receive the title to a co-owner's share upon death of the co-owner, as in the case of joint tenancy or tenancy by the entirety.

right-of-way An easement allowing someone to use the land of another.

riparian rights The rights of an owner of property adjoining a watercourse such as a river, including access to, and use of, the water.

risk factor The potential for loss.

risk management Controlling and limiting risk in property ownership.

rule of reason Legal doctrine that means if an activity is reasonable, then it is allowable under law.

running-with-the-land Rights moving from grantor to grantee along with a title.

sale leaseback A transaction wherein an owner sells a property to an investor who immediately leases back the property to the seller as agreed in the sales contract.

sales comparison approach The primary approach in estimating the value of vacant land and single-family, owner-occupied dwellings.

sales contract An agreement between buyer and seller on the price and other terms and conditions of the sale of property.

satisfaction of mortgage Legal instrument signifying a mortgage has been paid in full.

scarcity (a) An economic characteristic of real property; (b) In appraisal, supply of property in relation to effective demand.

secondary mortgage market The market in which lenders sell mortgages.

second mortgage One that is first in priority after a first mortgage.

secured creditor One who has filed a financing statement or who possesses a written security agreement as security for extending credit to a debtor.

Securities Act of 1933 Regulates securities offered by individuals, general or limited partnerships, and unincorporated associations, or individuals.

Securities Exchange Commission Federal agency that requires the registration of securities offered to the public.

security deposit A sum of money that the landlord requires of the tenant prior to lease, to be refunded at end of lease based upon condition of the premises.

seepage pit A covered pit through which the discharge from the septic tank infiltrates into the surrounding soil.

seisin (or seizin) Possession of a freehold estate in land.

seller agent A listing agent, subagent, or broker agent who works in the best interests of the seller.

sensitivity analysis A study of how a change in one factor can affect the income to the property.

septic system A household wastewater treatment system consisting of a house sewer, septic tank, distribution box, and absorption field or seepage pit.

service drop Aboveground electrical cables that come from the nearest pole connecting to the service entrance conductors of a structure.

service lateral Underground electrical wiring connecting to a structure.

servient tenement Land encumbered by an easement.

setback The distance from a front or interior property line to the point where a structure can be located.

severalty Ownership by only one person.

shared appreciation mortgage A mortgage that allows the lender to benefit from the appreciation of property value in exchange for a lower rate of interest to the borrower.

sheathing A material such as plywood or sheetrock that covers the framing members of a structure; also a type of insulation material.

Sherman and Clayton Antitrust Acts Federal legislation including imposition of civil and punitive damages for antitrust activities

sick building syndrome A chemical illness that may be caused by indoor air quality inside a commercial building.

sill plate The first wooden member of a structure used as the nailing surface for the floor system.

single agent An agent who works only for the buyer or the seller.

situs Location of land.

slab-on-grade construction A type of concrete flooring that is part of the foundation and is poured on a prepared and graded surface.

soffit A wood, vinyl, or aluminum material placed under the roof extension of a structure.

sole plate A horizontal base plate that serves as the foundation for the wall system.

sole proprietorship A business owned by one individual.

special agent Agent with limited authority to act on behalf of the principal, such as in the situation created by a listing.

special assessment A levy by a local government against real property for part of the cost of making an improvement to the property, such as street paving, installing water lines, or putting in sidewalks.

special purpose real estate The result of combining both the land and its improvements for a singular highest and best use.

special-use permit A permit for a use that is not allowed in the zone without the approval of the planning board or other legislative body.

special warranty deed A deed containing a limited warranty of title.

specific lien One that attaches to one particular property only.

specific performance A court instruction requiring a defaulting party to a contract to buy and sell real property to perform his obligations specifically under the contract.

sponsor An individual or entity who develops an offering plan for a cooperative or condominium.

spot zoning In New York, illegal rezoning of a certain property in a zoned area to permit a different type of use than that which is authorized. It is for the benefit of an individual and against the best interests of the health, safety, and welfare of the community.

square-foot method A technique used to estimate the total cost of construction, in which the total number of square feet to be constructed is multiplied by a cost-per-square-foot figure to derive total cost.

stabilized budget A forecast of income and expense as may be reasonably projected over several years; prepared by a property manager.

standard fire policy The most common fire insurance policy indemnifying the insured against loss by fire.

State Environmental Quality Review Act (SEQRA) A New York law requiring preparation of an environmental impact statement on any project that requires government approval and may have a significant effect on the environment.

State of New York Mortgage Association (SONYMA) An agency that raises money from the sale of New York tax-free bonds and uses these funds for mortgage loans.

Statute of Frauds A law in effect in all states; in New York, the General Obligations Law, requiring certain contracts to be in writing to be valid.

Statute of Limitations State laws establishing the time period within which certain lawsuits may be brought.

statutory foreclosure A foreclosure proceeding that allows a statutory time period after a foreclosure sale during which the borrower may still redeem the title.

statutory law A body of law which addresses everyday behavior.

steep slope Land with a slope that ranges from 30 percent to 45 percent or more.

steering The practice of directing prospective purchasers toward or away from certain neighborhoods to avoid altering the racial/ethnic make-up of these areas.

straight-line depreciation A type of income tax depreciation that allows investment property to be deducted in installments over a number of years.

straight-term mortgage A loan in which the borrower pays interest only for a specified term and, at the end of the term, is required to pay the principal.

strip center More than four stores located conveniently and with easy access to a main roadway.

studs Wooden framing members used for forming the wall skeleton of a structure.

subagent A person appointed by an agent with the permission of the principal to assist in performing some or all of the tasks of the agency.

subchapter S corporation Corporate formation whereby corporate income and expenses flow through to shareholders as if a partnership.

subdivider One who formats land into lots for building purposes in accordance with state and local requirements.

subdivision A tract of land divided into lots or plots and eventually used for building purposes.

subdivision regulation (ordinance) Public control of the development of residential subdivisions.

sublease The transfer of only part of a lease term with reversion to the lessee; a lesser lease estate.

subordinate Lower in priority.

subordinate lease A lease that can be canceled by a lender if the borrower defaults on a mortgage loan.

subordinate mortgage A junior mortgage that is lower in priority to another mortgage.

subrogation of rights The substitution of the title insurance company in the place of the insured for filing a legal action.

substitution The principle providing that the highest value of a property has a tendency to be established by the cost of purchasing or constructing another property of equal utility and desirability provided that the substitution can be made without unusual delay.

subsurface rights Rights to the area below the earth's surface.

supply and demand The principle stating that the greater the supply of any commodity in comparison to demand, the lower the value; conversely, the smaller the supply and the greater the demand, the higher the value.

survey Document showing measurements, boundaries, and area of a property.

survivorship The right of the surviving co-owner to receive the title automatically of a deceased co-owner immediately without probate.

swing loan A type of interim loan wherein a borrower uses the equity that he has in one property to obtain the money necessary to buy another property.

tacking A procedure used to preserve the adverse possession claim where the possession of the property is taken over from one person to another, sometimes through inheritance.

take-out loan Permanent financing arranged to replace a short-term construction loan.

taking The act of a government body obtaining a property under its power of eminent domain.

taking title subject to a mortgage Accepting a title pledged to secure a mortgage and with no personal liability for payment of the note.

taxable gain The amount of profit subject to tax (recognized gain).

taxable status date In New York, as of March 1 in towns, and January 1 in villages, real property is assessed with respect to its condition. The date may differ in other municipalities.

taxation One of the powers of government to tax, among other things, real property.

tax basis This consists of the price paid for the property, plus expenses incurred in acquiring the property (other than those incurred in arranging financing) plus the cost of any capital improvements. *See* basis.

tax certiorari proceeding A judicial review in state supreme court of a decision of the local assessment board of review.

tax credit An amount of money that may be deducted from a tax bill to arrive at the net amount of tax due.

tax-deductible expense An amount of money that may be deducted from gross income in arriving at net taxable income before depreciation, if any.

tax deed A deed conveying title to real property to a new owner that a municipality obtained as a result of the original owner's failure to pay real estate taxes.

tax depreciation A provision of tax law permitting a property to take an ordinary business deduction for the amount of annual depreciation.

tax exemption Program that allows taxpayers relief from paying certain school or property taxes in whole or in part.

tax-free exchange Trading of like-kind properties held as an investment or for use in business.

tax levy The amount that a municipality must raise by taxing real property to meet budgetary requirements.

tax lien An encumbrance against a property initiated by the taxing jurisdiction for delinquency in paying real property taxes.

tax rate The amount of dollars needed by the municipality to meet budgetary requirements divided by the taxable assessed and nonexempt value of all the real property within that jurisdiction.

tax shelter A method of tax avoidance such as protecting income from taxation by allowable depreciation.

tenancy by the entirety A form of co-ownership limited to husband and wife, with the right of survivorship.

tenancy in common A form of co-ownership that does not include the right of survivorship.

tenancy for years *See* estate for years.

tenant relocator A person who arranges, for a fee, the relocation of commercial or residential tenants from buildings that are to be demolished, rehabilitated, or remodeled.

tenements Right of ownership of real estate held by a person.

term mortgage One that requires the mortgagor to pay interest only during the mortgage term, with the principal due at the end of the term.

testamentary trust A trust set up within a person's will and effective upon the death of the person who created the trust.

testate To have died leaving a valid will.

testator A male who has died and left a valid will.

testatrix A female who has died and left a valid will.

testers Volunteers from state or private agencies who enforce fair housing by claiming to be home-seekers, thereby finding out if brokers deal fairly with all clients or customers.

tie-in arrangement Agreement between a party selling a product or service with a purchaser that as a condition of the sale, the purchaser will buy another product from the seller or the purchaser will not buy a product or use a service of another.

"time is of the essence" A closing must take place on or before the exact date stipulated in the contract.

time value of money The determination of which particular investment would bring the greatest return on dollars invested for a given period of time.

title Ownership of the rights to possess real property.

title closing The consummation of a real estate contract; a meeting in which the buyer, seller, and closing agent meet to execute documents and disburse funds.

title examination A search of the public record to determine the quality of a title to real property.

title insurance An insurance policy protecting the insured from a financial loss caused by a defect in a title to real property.

title search Examination of successive property ownership and investigation of other items which may affect clear title to property.

title theory A disinterested third party holds legal title to a property in security for the loan through a *deed of trust*; not used in New York.

title transfer tax A tax imposed on the conveyance of title to real property by deed.

topography The physical features and contours of land.

Torrens system A system of title recordation.

tort Wrongful act that is committed either intentionally or unintentionally.

tract An area of land.

trade fixtures Items that are installed by a commercial tenant and are removable upon termination of the tenancy.

trade name A sole proprietorship that does business under an assumed name.

transferability The ability to transfer property ownership from seller to buyer.

transfer of development rights A developer can buy the development rights to another property, such as a historic property, that cannot use them.

trespass Unlawful entry on the land of another.

triple net lease A lessee pays all the expenses associated with the property in addition to the rent.

trust A legal relationship under which title to property is transferred to a person known as trustee.

trustee One who holds title to property for the benefit of another called a beneficiary.

trustor One who conveys title to a trustee.

trusts and wills Laws which address the succession to the ownership of an estate by inheritance or any act of law.

Truth-in-Lending Act (TILA) *See* Regulation Z.

underground storage tanks Tanks located underground and utilized for the bulk storage of chemicals and petroleum.

underimprovement Use of land that is not its highest and best use and therefore does not generate the maximum income.

underwriting The act of reviewing loan documentation and evaluating a borrower's ability and willingness to repay the loan and sufficiency of the collateral value of the property.

undisclosed principal A principal whose identity may not be disclosed by an agent.

undivided interest Ownership of fractional parts not physically divided.

undue influence Any improper or wrongful influence by one party over another whereby the will of a person is overpowered so that he or she is induced to act or prevented from acting according to free will.

unencumbered property Property that is free of any lien.

unenforceable contract One that appears to meet the requirements for validity but would not be enforceable in court.

Uniform Commercial Code (UCC) A standardized and comprehensive set of commercial laws regulating security interests in personal property.

Uniform Irrevocable Consent and Designation Form A document that allows a summons to be served upon out-of-state residents in New York.

unilateral contract An agreement in which there is a promise in return for a specific action, which together supply the consideration.

uninsured conventional loan One in which the loan payment is not insured to protect the lender.

unintentional misrepresentation An innocent false statement of a material fact.

unities of title Time, title, interest, and possession.

unit-in-place method Technique used in appraising real estate under the cost approach, in which the cost of replacement or reproduction is grouped by stages of construction.

universal agent Agent who has complete authority over any activity of principal; for example, power of attorney.

unsecured creditor One who has not filed a financing statement or who does not possess a written security agreement as security for extending credit to a debtor.

urea formaldehyde foam insulation (UFFI) A type of foam containing formaldehyde, a gaseous compound that can cause illness, which was widely used for home insulating.

useful life The period of time that a property is expected to be economically useful.

use variance Permission to use the land for a purpose that under the current zoning restrictions is prohibited.

usury Charging a rate of interest higher than the rate allowed by law.

utility Capable of serving a useful purpose.

vacancy rate A projected rate of the percentage of rental units that will be vacant in a given year.

vacant land Unimproved land, which could include land brought back to its natural state or land that does not possess improvements necessary to serve some kind of purpose.

VA-guaranteed loan A mortgage loan in which the loan payment is guaranteed to the lender by the Department of Veteran Affairs.

valid contract An agreement that is legally binding and enforceable.

valuable consideration Anything of value agreed upon by parties to a contract.

valuation Establishes an opinion of value utilizing an objective approach based on facts related to the property, such as age, square footage, location, and cost to replace.

value in exchange The amount of money a property may command for its exchange; market value.

value in use The present worth of the future benefits of ownership; a subjective value that is not market value.

variable expense An expense that is not specifically predictable and is subject to the needs of a property at any given time.

variance A permitted deviation from specific requirements of a zoning ordinance because of the special hardship to a property owner.

vendee Purchaser.

vendor Seller.

vendor's affidavit Document signed under oath by the vendor stating that the vendor has not encumbered title to real estate without full disclosure to vendee.

vesting options Choices buyers have in how to acquire property.

vicarious liability A person is responsible for the actions of another.

voidable contract An agreement that may be voided by the parties without legal consequences.

void contract An agreement that has no legal force or effect.

voltage The electrical pressure that pushes through the wires.

voluntary alienation The transfer of title freely by the owner.

voluntary lien A type of lien in which an individual consents to placing a security against himself or his property.

watts A measurement of amperage calculated for different electrical usage; also calculated in kilowatts.

wetlands Federal- and state-protected transition areas between uplands and aquatic habitats that provide flood and storm water control, surface and ground-water protection, erosion control, and pollution treatment.

words of conveyance Wording in a deed demonstrating the definite intention to convey a specific title to real property to a named grantee.

wraparound mortgage A junior mortgage in an amount exceeding a first mortgage against the property.

writ of attachment Court order preventing any transfer of attached property during litigation.

yield The return on an investment.

zoning A public law regulating land use.

zoning board of appeals A local appointed board that has the power to review administrative rulings made by the planning board or other legislative body.

zoning map A map that divides the community into various designated districts.

zoning ordinance A statement setting forth the type of use permitted under each zoning classification and specific requirements for compliance.

Index